# BORDERLINE CONDITIONS
## and
# PATHOLOGICAL NARCISSISM

# BORDERLINE
# CONDITIONS
## and
# PATHOLOGICAL
# NARCISSISM

Otto F. Kernberg, M.D.

JASON ARONSON, INC.
NEW YORK

To Paulina, Martin, Karen, and Adine

***Classical Psychoanalysis and Its Applications:***
*A Series of Books*
*Edited by Robert Langs, M.D.*

Langs, Robert—"THE TECHNIQUE OF PSYCHOAN-ALYTIC PSYCHOTHERAPY" VOL. I AND II

Kestenberg, Judith—"CHILDREN AND PARENTS: PSYCHOANALYTIC STUDIES IN DEVELOPMENT"

Sperling, Melitta—"THE MAJOR NEUROSES AND BEHAVIOR DISORDERS IN CHILDREN"

Giovacchini, Peter—"PSYCHOANALYSIS OF CHA-RACTER DISORDERS"

Kernberg, Otto—"BORDERLINE CONDITIONS AND PATHOLOGICAL NARCISSISM"

Nagera, Humberto—"FEMALE SEXUALITY AND THE OEDIPUS COMPLEX"

Hoffer, Willie—"THE EARLY DEVELOPMENT AND EDUCATION OF THE CHILD"

Meissner, William—"THE PARANOID PROCESS"

## Series Introduction

Otto Kernberg brings to psychoanalysis and to the study of human behavior his ability as an original researcher, clinician and theoretician and his talent for synthesizing different approaches, developing an optimal integrating frame of reference for many challenging cases. His writings on such diverse subjects as Rorshach test, various neurotic syndromes, object-relations theory, countertransference, the Kleinian school, character pathology, the capacity to love, the borderline syndrome, the process outcome of psychotherapy and psychoanalysis, the nature and treatment of narcissistic personalities, and the hospital treatment of schizophrenic patients have earned him a much-deserved international reputation as a psychoanalyst of remarkable scope and vision. His work has afforded psychotherapists and psychoanalysts crucial insight into the nature of some of their most baffling and least understood patients, and has provided them with important clinical techniques. This book represents his widely heralded work with borderline and narcissistic personality organizations, and is clearly among his most brilliant contributions. Otto Kernberg stands high among those psychoanalysts who have demonstrated that the applications of classical psychoanalysis affords us the most meaningful, in-depth understanding of the full range of psychopathological syndromes, including some of our most disturbed and difficult patients.

**Robert Langs, M.D.**

# ACKNOWLEDGMENTS

This book includes studies that originated in connection with my work in the Psychotherapy Research Project of the Menninger Foundation. I owe to Dr. Robert Wallerstein, former director of that project and director of research of the Menninger Foundation, the initial stimulation and encouragement to pursue my special work regarding borderline conditions as part of the overall project design. Throughout the time of his leadership of the Project team, and also later—when, after Dr. Wallerstein's departure from Topeka, I became the director of that research project—I was privileged to have the consistent support and constructive critique of the entire staff of the Project. Among them, I am particularly indebted to Drs. Gertrude Ticho, Ernst Ticho, Ann Appelbaum, Stephen Appelbaum, Leonard Horwitz, Esther Burstein, and Lolafaye Coyne, who read and discussed with me in detail the various aspects of the work included in this book. Dr. Ernst Ticho's thinking regarding the relationship and differences between psychoanalysis and psychotherapy has greatly influenced my technical approach to borderline patients.

Other friends and colleagues who have been stimulating and helpful include the late Dr. Herman van der Waals, former director of the Topeka Institute for Psychoanalysis and of the C. F. Menninger Memorial Hospital, whose thinking was crucial in helping me to develop my formulations regarding the narcissistic personality and its treatment and Dr. Jerome D. Frank, professor emeritus of psychiatry, Johns Hopkins University

x

School of Medicine, and director of the psychotherapy research team of the Henry Phipps Clinic, who initiated me in the complex formulations and procedures of psychotherapy research.

Mrs. Virginia Eicholtz, managing editor of the *Bulletin of the Menninger Clinic*, was extremely patient with me and yet appropriately strong and persuasive in transforming my English into real English.

My wife, Dr. Paulina Kernberg, has been my most searching and creative critic. Without her constant questioning and yet encouraging review of my work, I could not have done it.

Finally, I am deeply grateful to Mrs. Mary Patton, chief secretary of the Menninger Foundation Research Project, and my secretary during the time of my directorship of the C. F. Menninger Memorial Hospital, and to Mrs. Jean Thomas, senior secretary of the General Clinical Service of the New York State Psychiatric Institute, for their dedication, precision, and extraordinary efficiency in preparing this book for publication.

# PREFACE

This book presents a systematic analysis of borderline conditions—their psychopathology, diagnosis, prognosis, and treatment. It reflects thirteen years' effort to develop a concept of this broad and vexing category of psychopathology in the light of contemporary ego psychology and psychoanalytic object relations theory.

One subgroup of borderline patients, namely, the narcissistic personalities, presented a particularly difficult challenge; these patients seemed similar to, and yet in some ways different from, the ordinary borderline patients; they seem to have a defensive organization similar to borderline conditions, and yet many of them function on a much better psychosocial level. Attempts to clarify these and other clinical issues concerning narcissistic personalities led me to a particular conception of the diagnosis and treatment of these patients—the subject matter of Part II.

The review of the literature on borderline conditions is spread over various chapters of Part I: Chapter 1 includes the earlier literature (to 1967) regarding diagnosis; Chapter 3, the literature of those years devoted to treatment; and Chapter 5 includes more recent literature (from 1968 to 1972) regarding both diagnosis and treatment. Because my later work is in part influenced by—or a reaction to—some of the more recent literature on borderline conditions, I felt it would be preferable to maintain this division.

O.K.

# CONTENTS

# BORDERLINE CONDITIONS
## and
# PATHOLOGICAL NARCISSISM

# PART I

# Borderline Personality Organization

One

# The Syndrome

I shall attempt a systematic description of the symptomatic, structural, and genetic-dynamic aspects of the so-called "borderline" personality disorders. In the literature this psychopathology is referred to by various terms: "borderline states" (35), "preschizophrenic" personality structure (43), "psychotic characters" (14), "borderline personality" (40, 44). Some authors leave it unclear whether the terms "ambulatory schizophrenia" (53) and "pseudoneurotic schizophrenia" (24) refer to borderline personality disorder or to more regressed, psychotic patients whose symptomatology resembles the borderline condition. Psychoanalytic investigations of "as if" personalities (2), schizoid personality structure (6), and patients with severe ego distortions (16) appear to deal with patients who are also related to the borderline group.

—There exists an important group of psychopathological constellations which have in common a rather specific and remarkably stable form of pathological ego structure. The ego pathology differs from that found in the neuroses and the less severe characterological illnesses on the one hand, and the psychoses on the other. These patients must be considered to occupy a borderline area between neurosis and psychosis. The term *borderline personality organization*, rather than "borderline states" or other terms, more accurately describes these patients who do have a specific, stable, pathological personality organization (29); their personality organization is not a transitory state fluctuating between neurosis and psychosis.

The presenting symptoms of these patients may be similar to the presenting symptoms of the neuroses and character disorders; therefore, without a thorough diagnostic examination the particular characterological organization of these patients may be missed, with the result of a poor prognosis for treatment. Borderline personality organization requires specific therapeutic approaches which can only derive from an accurate diagnostic study.

Transient psychotic episodes may develop in patients with borderline personality organization when they are under severe stress or under the influence of alcohol or drugs. Such psychotic episodes usually remit with relatively brief but well-structured treatment approaches. When classical analytic approaches are attempted with these patients, they may experience a loss of reality testing and even develop delusional ideas which are restricted to the transference. Thus, they develop a transference psychosis rather than a transference neurosis (50). These patients usually maintain their capacity for reality testing, except under these special circumstances—severe stress, regression induced by alcohol or drugs, and a transference psychosis (14). In clinical interviews the formal organization of the thought processes of these patients appears intact. Psychological testing, particularly with the use of nonstructured projective tests, will often reveal the tendency of such patients to use primary-process functioning (43).

While it is possible to identify the main differences between borderline personality organization and psychotic states (14), it is usually more difficult to identify the differences between borderline personality organization and the neuroses. Because of this difficulty, I have attempted in this paper to clarify the complex distinctions between borderline personality organization and the neuroses.

## REVIEW OF THE LITERATURE

This attempt to analyze the descriptive, structural, and genetic-dynamic aspects of borderline personality organization, with a special consideration of the characteristic pathology of object relationships, draws on the work of many authors with different theoretical positions and with different therapeutic approaches. The early literature consists largely of clinical descriptions of patients who would now be considered "borderline." Such are the descriptions by Zilboorg (53), Hoch and Polatin (24), and, from psychological testing, Rapaport, Gill, and Schafer (43). Zilboorg (54) later expanded his description, and Hoch and Cattell (23) elaborated on the diagnosis of "pseudoneurotic schizophrenia." Other aspects of the symptoms of some borderline patients were studied by Bychowski (1), who also described important structural characteristics of these patients, such as the persistence of dissociated primitive ego states and the cleavage of parental images into good and bad objects. It is to be noted that both Zilboorg and Hoch, who made fundamental contributions to the descriptive analysis of borderline conditions, believed that all such patients were schizophrenic. They seem to have been unaware that they were confronted with a different form of psychopathology.

Until recently, much confusion in the literature was caused by the fact that the term "borderline" was used to refer both to the transitory acute manifestations of patients who were rapidly regressing from neurotic symptomatology to an overt psychotic reaction, and also to patients who function chronically in a stable way at a level which was on a borderline between neurosis and psychosis (40, 44, 49). The term "borderline" should be reserved for those patients presenting a chronic characterological organization which is neither typically neurotic nor typically psychotic, and which is characterized (i) by typical symptomatic constellations; (ii) by a typical constellation of defensive operations of the ego; (iii) by a typical pathology of internalized object relationships; and (iv) by characteristic genetic-dynamic features. Frosch (14) has contributed to the differential diagnosis of borderline personality organization from psychosis. He stresses that although borderline patients have alterations in their relationship with reality and in their feelings of reality, their capacity to test reality is preserved, in contrast to patients with psychotic reactions.

The literature on the structural aspects of borderline personality organization can be divided into two groups: (i) considerations of the nonspecific manifestations of ego weakness and regression to primitive cognitive structures related to primary-process thinking; and (ii) considerations of the specific defensive operations that are characteristic of borderline personality organization. The first group was influenced by Rapaport, Gill, and Schafer (43), especially by their finding that there existed a group of "preschizophrenic" patients who revealed a predominance of primary-process thinking on psychological testing, which also reflected marked ego weakness in comparison with the typical neurotic patients. Knight (35, 36) synthesized both the general descriptive features of these patients and the implications from their ego weakness for treatment. He called attention to the severe regression in the transference, and to the need to modify accordingly the psychotherapeutic approach to these patients.

Important contributions to the second group, that is, to an understanding of the specific defensive operations which are a part of the structural organization of these patients, have come from a different theoretical orientation; particularly from the analysis of the processes of splitting, and its particular relevance to schizoid patients, as described by Fairbairn (6, 7) and Melanie Klein (34). The first reference to the mechanism of splitting was made by Freud (12, 13), but later the term was expanded by Fairbairn. He used the term to refer more to an active defensive mechanism rather than to a description of a certain lack of integration of the ego. Further contributions to the concept of splitting as a central defensive operation of the ego at regressed levels, and to its relationship with other related mechanisms, were made by Rosenfeld (45, 46) and Segal (47). I have reported elsewhere a somewhat different, and certainly more restricted definition of the term "splitting" than that used by authors of the Kleinian school (29).

Edith Jacobson made additional contributions to the analysis of the specific defensive operations in borderline patients (25, 26, 27). Anna Freud (10) suggested that there existed a general need for a chronological listing of defensive operations of the ego, ranging from those characteristics of very early stages of ego development in which a clear-cut separation between ego and id had not yet taken place, to those characteristics of the more mature ego. The possibility of developing a conception of mental illness as a unitary process, and a conception of the different forms of psychopathology as related to specific orders or levels of defensive organization, has been proposed by Karl Menninger et al. (39). Menninger's work has stimulated my efforts to improve our understanding of the specific "archaic" levels of defensive organization in patients with borderline personality organization.

The most important contribution to the understanding of borderline personality organization and to the treatment of these patients comes from the analysis of the pathology of their internalized object relationships. Helene Deutsch's (2) article on "as if" personalities was a first and fundamental contribution. The independent conclusions of Fairbairn (7, 8) and Melanie Klein (34) followed later.

A number of important contributions to the analysis of the pathology in internalized object relationships have come from ego psychology. These contributions point toward phenomena similar to those described with a different terminology by the British school of psychoanalysis influenced by Fairbairn and Klein; for example, Edith Jacobson's analysis of *The Self and the Object World* (28), Greenson's (17, 18) important findings, and Erik Erikson's (5) study of identity diffusion. Jacobson has contributed not only to the clarification of the pathology of the internalized object relationships of borderline patients, but also to an understanding of the relationship of that particular pathology of object relations to the vicissitudes of ego and superego formation in borderline patients. Greenson's detailed analysis of the pathology of internalized object relations of borderline patients and of its reflection on the current pathological relationships with others illustrates how a psychoanalytic understanding can be the best instrument not only for an understanding of the genetic and dynamic aspects of these patients, but also for a descriptive clarification of their chaotic behavior. Khan (30) has stressed the structural elements in regard to both specific defensive operations and the specific pathology of the object relationships of these patients.

Many of the authors referred to above also consider the genetic-dynamic aspects of borderline personality organization, and all of them stress the importance of pregenital, especially oral conflicts in these patients, and the unusual intensity of their pregenital aggression. They also stress the peculiar combination of pregenital drive derivatives and genital ones, and these issues are described in detail by Melanie Klein (33), and by Paula Heimann (22).

Because the therapeutic implications of the borderline personality organization will not be discussed in this chapter, the literature relevant to treatment will not be reviewed here. However, because of the implications for diagnostic analysis Wallerstein's (50) description of psychotic transference reaction in patients who diagnostically are not psychotic, and Main's (38) illustration of the effects of the defensive operations of these patients on the immediate hospital environment must be mentioned. The diagnostic use of the countertransference reactions that borderline patients frequently evoke in the therapist are described in Chapter 2. Two published panel discussions on borderline conditions have added to an understanding of these conditions (40, 44). Many questions that remain unanswered about the borderline personality organization are posed in an article by Gitelson (16) and the report of a panel on this subject, of which Gitelson's article was a part (49); Rosenfeld's comments during that panel discussion are pertinent. The special issues related to borderline conditions in childhood are summarized by Ekstein and J. Wallerstein (4), and by Geleerd (15).

I shall now attempt to analyze the descriptive, structural, and genetic-dynamic aspects of borderline personality organization.

## DESCRIPTIVE ANALYSIS: THE "PRESUMPTIVE" DIAGNOSTIC ELEMENTS

Patients suffering from borderline personality organization present themselves with what superficially appear to be typical neurotic symptoms. However, the neurotic symptoms and character pathology of these patients have peculiarities which point to an underlying borderline personality organization. Only a careful diagnostic examination will reveal the particular combinations of different neurotic symptoms. No symptoms are pathognomonic, but the presence of two, and especially of three, symptoms among those which will be enumerated strongly points to the possibility of an underlying borderline personality organization. All of these descriptive elements are only presumptive diagnostic signs of borderline personality organization. The definite diagnosis depends on characteristic ego pathology and not on the descriptive symptoms. The following symptomatic categories are not an exhaustive list.

## 1. Anxiety

Such patients tend to present chronic, diffuse, free-floating anxiety. This symptom becomes particularly meaningful when a variety of other symptoms or pathological character traits are present. The anxiety, therefore, exceeds the binding capacity of the other symptoms and character traits. One exception is that of chronic anxiety reaction which has secondarily acquired the specific meaning of a conversion symptom, but this probably can be detected only through analytic exploration. Also, some patients in intensive psychotherapy may use anxiety itself as a resistance, a defensive operation which can become quite chronic, and this type of anxiety is to be excluded from the type of anxiety under discussion.

## 2. Polysymptomatic Neurosis

Many patients present several neurotic symptoms, but here I am considering only those presenting two or more of the following neurotic symptoms:

a. Multiple phobias, especially those which impose severe restrictions on the patient's daily life: also important here are phobias related to one's own body or appearance (fear of blushing, fear of talking in public, fear of being looked at), in contrast to phobias not involving one's own body but external objects (typical animal phobias, fear of storms, heights, etc.), and finally phobias involving transitional elements toward obsessive neurosis (fear of dirt, fear of contamination). Multiple phobias, especially those involving severe social inhibitions and paranoid trends, are presumptive evidence of borderline personality organization.

b.   Obsessive-compulsive symptoms which have acquired secondary ego syntonicity, and therefore a quality of "over-valuated" thoughts and actions: although reality testing is maintained, and the patient wants to rid himself of his absurd thoughts or acts, he also tends to rationalize these acts. For example, a patient with compulsive hand-washing and contamination rituals had an elaborate system of "reasonable" considerations in regard to cleanliness, the dangers of dirt, etc. Also important here are patients with obsessive thoughts of a paranoid or hypochondriacal nature.

c.   Multiple, elaborate, or bizarre conversion symptoms, especially if they are chronic, or even a monosymptomatic conversion reaction of a severe kind extending over many years' duration; also, the conversion symptoms of an elaborate kind, bordering on bodily hallucinations or involving complex sensations or sequence of movements of bizarre quality.

d.   Dissociative reactions, especially hysterical "twilight states" and fugues, and amnesia accompanied by disturbances of consciousness.

e.   Hypochondriasis: this infrequent and controversial constellation is probably more related to character pathology than to symptomatic neurosis. It is relevant here only in that excessive preoccupation with health and a chronic fear of illness, when it manifests itself in the form of chronic symptoms, health rituals, and withdrawal from social life in order to concentrate on one's health and symptoms, is often found in the borderline personality organization. This is not true of patients suffering from intense anxiety with mild hypochondriacal trends secondary to the anxiety itself.

f.   Paranoid and hypochondriacal trends with any other symptomatic neurosis: this is a typical combination indicating a presumptive diagnosis of borderline personality organization. Many patients, of course, have slight paranoid traits and, as has been mentioned above, some hypochondriacal trends secondary to anxiety; but here I am talking only about patients with clear-cut, rather strong paranoid personality trends, and with clear-cut hypochondriacal trends not secondary to intense anxiety reaction.

It has to be stressed again that the presence of any of the

above-mentioned symptoms is not in itself presumptive evidence of borderline personality organization. The presence of two or more of these symptomatic categories should alert one to the possibility of the underlying borderline pathology of the personality structure.

### 3. Polymorphous Perverse Sexual Trends

I am referring here to patients who present a manifest sexual deviation within which several perverse trends coexist. For example, a male patient of this group presented heterosexual and homosexual promiscuity with sadistic elements. Another male patient, also a homosexual, exhibited himself to women. A female patient presented homosexuality and perverse masochistic heterosexual trends. Patients whose genital life centers on a stable sexual deviation, and excepially those who combine such a stable deviation with constant object relationships, are not included in this category. On the other hand, there are patients whose manifest sexual behavior is completely inhibited but whose conscious fantasies, and especially masturbatory fantasies, involve multiple perverse trends as necessary conditions for achieving sexual gratification. Such symptoms are presumptive evidence of borderline personality organization. The more chaotic and multiple the perverse fantasies and actions and the more unstable the object relationships connected with these interactions, the more strongly is the presence of borderline personality organization to be considered. Bizarre forms of perversion, especially those involving primitive aggressive manifestations or primitive replacement of genital aims by eliminatory ones (urination, defecation), are also indicative of an underlying borderline personality organization.

### 4. The "Classical" Prepsychotic Personality Structures

a. The paranoid personality (paranoid trends of such intensity that they themselves determine the main descriptive diagnosis);

b. The schizoid personality;

c. The hypomanic personality and the "cyclothymic" personality organization with strong hypomanic trends.

It has to be stressed that chronically depressed patients who present severe masochistic character traits, or what Laughlin (37) has called the "depressive personality," are *not* included here, in spite of the fact that depression as a syndrome can present itself with features which are borderline between neurotic and psychotic levels of depression. This category of patients will be included in a later discussion of masochistic character trends.

## 5. Impulse Neurosis and Addictions

I am referring here to those forms of severe character pathology in which there is chronic, repetitive eruption of an impulse which gratifies instinctual needs in a way which is ego dystonic outside of the "impulse-ridden" episodes, but which is ego syntonic and actually highly pleasurable during the episode itself. Alcoholism, drug addictions, certain forms of psychogenic obesity, and kleptomania are all typical examples. This group actually merges with those forms of sexual deviation in which the perverse symptom appears in an eruptive, episodic way, while other than during specific episodes the perverse impulse is ego dystonic and even strongly rejected. This group also merges with the "acting-out" personality disorders in general (which I shall consider below), the difference with this latter group being a quantitative one. Impulse neuroses seem to center around one preferred, temporarily ego-syntonic outlet which provides direct instinctual gratification; by contrast, the "acting-out" characters present a more generalized lack of impulse control, more chaotic combinations of impulse and defense in several areas, and less clear-cut ego syntonicity and less crude, direct gratification of a determined impulse.

## 6. "Lower Level" Character Disorders

I am referring here to severe character pathology typically represented by the chaotic and impulse-ridden character, in contrast to the classical reaction-formation types of character structure and the milder "avoidance trait" characters. I shall try to clarify this point further when dealing with the structural analysis of borderline personality organization, and shall then refer to the suggestion made elsewhere (29) that one might classify character pathology along a continuum ("high level" to "low level") according to the degree to which repressive mechanisms or splitting mechanisms predominate. From a clinical point of view, most typical hysterical personalities are not borderline structures; the same holds true for most obsessive-compulsive personalities and the "depressive personality" (37) structures or better integrated masochistic personalities. In contrast, many *infantile personalities* and most typical *narcissistic personalities* present underlying borderline organization; the *"as if" personalities* also belong to this latter group. All clear-cut *antisocial personality structures* that I haveexamined have presented a typical borderline personality organization.

I shall briefly review the differential diagnosis of hysterical personalities, infantile personalities, and narcissistic personalities, which from my point of view do represent a continuum in that the hysterical personality is a typical "high level" character neurosis; the infantile personality a "middle range" one, actually reaching into the typical borderline field; and the narcissistic personality a typical "low level" character disorder, although it reaches up into the middle range of the continuum.

a. HYSTERICAL PERSONALITY AND INFANTILE PERSONALITY.    One might group the main character constellations in hysterical personalities as related to the following headings: (i) emotional lability; (ii) "overinvolvement"; (iii) the combination of dependent and exhibitionistic traits; (iv) pseudohypersexuality and sexual inhibition; (v) selective competitiveness with men and women; and (vi) masochistic traits. Rather than giving a systematic overview of what is implied under all these headings, I would like to stress only what is relevant from the point of view of differential diagnosis with the infantile personality structure (3), with which the hysterical personality tends to become confused at times.

(i) *Emotional Lability.* In the hysterical personality, pseudohyperemotionality is used as a defensive operation reinforcing repression; it is especially marked in areas of conflict (sexual involvements) and as a typical transference resistance. But these patients may appear to be quite stable emotionally and appropriate in their emotional reactions in nonconflictual areas. A hysterical patient who gets from one emotional crisis into the next in the relationship with her husband or in the transference may be remarkably stable and appropriate at her job. In contrast, the emotional lability in the infantile personality is generalized and diffuse. There are few, if any, conflict-free areas in their life, and this reflects a higher degree of social inappropriateness as compared to the hysterical personality. Hysterical personalities manifest a lack of impulse control in specific areas and only at the height of some conflict; infantile personalities manifest a lack of impulse control in a much more general way.

(ii) "Overinvolvement." The hysterical overinvolvement in relationships with others may appear quite appropriate on the surface. Nonsophisticated observers usually consider it in women as typical feminine charm. Childlike clinging, the need of constant closeness, develops only in certain selected relationships, and is especially remarkable in heterosexual relationships in which it represents a regressive defense against genital fears. The "extroversion" of hysterical personalities, the quick but superficial intuitive resonance with others, and the overidentification with the emotional implications of fantasy, art, or literature, develops within the frame of solid, secondary-process thinking and realistic evaluation of the immediate reality. In the infantile personality, in contrast, childlike overidentification is of a more desperate, inappropriate nature; there is a gross misreading of the motives, of the inner life of others, even if on the surface there is a good adaptation to them. Long-term involvements show a regressed, childlike, oral-aggressive demandingness in the infantile personality which is not typical of hysterical patients.

(iii) Dependent and Exhibitionistic Needs. The need to be loved, to be the center of attention and of attraction, has more of a sexual implication in the hysterical personality, in which oral-dependent needs are linked with direct genital exhibitionistic trends. In the infantile character the need to be the center of interest and attraction is less sexualized and it has a more helpless, mainly orally determined, inappropriately demanding nature, and the exhibitionism has a "cold" quality, reflecting more primitive narcissistic trends.

(iv) *Pseudohypersexuality and Sexual Inhibition.* The combination of sexual provocativeness on the surface and of sexual inhibition underneath, such as is reflected in frigidity, is typical of the hysterical personality structure. In the infantile personality, sexual provocativeness tends to be more direct, more crude, more inappropriate socially, and reflects when it is present a more orally determined exhibitionism and demandingness than a really sexualized approach to the opposite sex. Sexual promiscuity in hysterical women is much less frequent than that in infantile women. The hysterical personality reveals strong oedipal aspects of sexual involvements (such as chronic involvement with older or unavailable men), and there exists the capacity for a stable relationship with the sexual partner as long as certain neurotic preconditions for the relationship are fulfilled. In the infantile personality, in contrast, promiscuity is of a more "drifting" quality, with very little stability of object relationships. Also, in contrast to the general predominance of diffuse repression of sexual fantasies in the hysterical personality, there may be conscious sexual fantasies of a primitive, polymorphous perverse quality in the infantile personality.

(v) *Competitiveness with Men and Women.* In hysterical personalities there is usually a much clearer differentiation in the pattern of competitiveness with the same sex in contrast to that with the opposite sex. Hysterical women who tend to compete with men (in order to deny their sexual inferiority) tend to develop stable characterological patterns in this regard; in their competitiveness with other women, oedipal rivalry tends to predominate over other origins of the competitiveness. In contrast, in the infantile personality there is less differentiation in the typical behavior toward men and toward women; there is less chronic competitiveness in general, and there is rapid shifting between intense positive and negative feelings, between submission and childlike imitation of others, on the one hand, and stubborn, pouting oppositionalism of short duration, on the other.

(vi)  *Masochism.* I shall refer to this aspect in the context of the general discussion of the depressive-masochistic personality structure. In brief, what I call "high level" masochism, as reflected in character traits dynamically related to a strict, punitive superego, is frequently a part of the hysterical personality structure. In contrast, "middle range" or "low level" masochistic character traits, with much less guilt and with direct interpenetration of sadistic and masochistic traits, are prevalent in the infantile personality.

The hysterical personality, in summary, gives evidence of a better integrated ego and superego, of a much broader range of conflict-free ego functions and structures, and of a predominance of oedipal conflicts over oral ones, although oral conflicts are also present. The sexual conflicts of the hysterical personality represent much more genital than pregenital conflicts (3). In the infantile personality, in contrast, pregenital and especially oral problems predominate. There is a reduced capacity for stable object relationships in comparison to the hysterical personality, and there is a breakdown of repression, with the emergence of primitive, polymorphous sexual fantasies. Infantile personalities show a childlike "dependency" of a more oral-demanding, aggressive kind than that seen in the hysterical personality. On a deeper level, patients with infantile personality structure really present an incapacity to depend on others, related to severe distortions in their internalized object relationships.

b.  NARCISSISTIC PERSONALITY.    It has been said above that typical hysterical personalities do not present an underlying borderline personality organization, which many infantile personalities do, and that the same is true for most narcissistic personalities. Let us now briefly describe this last group: I would suggest that when the term "narcissistic personality structure" is strictly reserved to the patients presenting the constellation of character traits to be mentioned, most of these patients present an underlying borderline personality organization.

"Narcissistic" as a descriptive term has been both abused and overused. There does exist, however, a group of patients in whom the main problem appears to be the disturbance of their self-regard in connection with specific disturbances in their object relationships, and whom we might consider almost a "pure culture" of pathological development of narcissism (48). It is for these patients that I would reserve the term "narcissistic personalities." On the surface, these patients do not appear to be severely regressed; some of them may function socially very well, and they usually have much better impulse control than the infantile personality.

These patients present an unusual degree of self-reference in their interactions with other people, a great need to be loved and admired by others, and a curious apparent contradiction between a very inflated concept of themselves and an inordinate need for tribute from others. Their emotional life is shallow. They experience little empathy for the feelings of others, they obtain very little enjoyment from life other than from the tributes they receive from others or from their own grandiose fantasies, and they feel restless and bored when external glitter wears off and no new sources feed their self-regard. They envy others, tend to idealize some people from whom they expect narcissistic supplies, and to depreciate and treat with contempt those from whom they do not expect anything (often their former idols). In general, their relationships with other people are clearly exploitative and sometimes parasitic. It is as if they feel they have the right to control and possess others and to exploit them without guilt feelings—and behind a surface which very often is charming and engaging, one senses coldness and ruthlessness. Very often such patients are considered to be "dependent" because they need so much tribute and adoration from others, but on a deeper level they are completely unable really to depend on anybody because of their deep distrust and depreciation of others.

Analytic exploration very often demonstrates that their haughty, grandiose, and controlling behavior is a defense against paranoid traits related to the projection of oral rage, which is central in their psychopathology. On the surface these patients appear to present a remarkable absence of object relationships; on a deeper level, their interactions reflect very intense, primitive, internalized object relationships of a frightening kind and an incapacity to depend on internalized good objects (46). The antisocial personality may be considered a subgroup of the narcissistic personality. Antisocial personality structures present the same general constellation of traits that I have just mentioned, in combination with additional severe superego pathology.

The present effort to group character pathology according to the degree to which it may reflect presumptive indicators of borderline personality organization raises two questions: (i) Is it possible to make clear-cut descriptive differential diagnoses among all these character constellations? (ii) Is not a dangerous rigidity implied in attempting to pinpoint character pathology along a continuum? The fact is that within any form of character organization there tends to be much fluctuation and, for example, there are rather typical hysterical personalities who do have borderline features. To the first of these two questions I would respond affirmatively, suggesting that descriptive differential diagnosis is possible within the usual limitations of descriptive diagnosis in clinical psychiatry. Unfortunately, the development of this point would go beyond the scope of this paper. In regard to the second question my response would again be in the affirmative, recognizing the fact that an individual patient presenting any of the particular character constellations mentioned here might be placed at any point along the entire continuum of character pathology. For example, patients with typical narcissistic character may not be "borderline" at all. Nevertheless, I have gradually come to the conclusion that when the descriptive diagnosis is well founded and any particular features of the individual case which appear to go beyond that descriptive diagnosis are carefully recorded, it is indeed possible to place the patient tentatively along a continuum of severity of character pathology. His placement on the "lower level" of the continuum is presumptive evidence of borderline character pathology.

c. DEPRESSIVE-MASOCHISTIC CHARACTER STRUCTURES. (i) *Depressive Personality*. The depressive-masochistic character structure is a very complex form of character pathology, but for this very reason it may serve to illustrate the continuum of character pathology. The "depressive personality" as described by Laughlin (37) would be a good example of the "high level" character structure, characterized mainly by reaction formations. Although pregenital pathology predominates in its genesis, structurally this form of pathology is quite close to the hysterical and obsessive-compulsive characters. A somewhat different form of masochistic personality organization is also to be considered at that same high level of our continuum. I refer here to the masochistic traits that are frequently seen in hysterical personalities, and represent dynamically an acting out of unconscious guilt over genitality (for example, a hysterical patient with a severe superego representing mainly the internalized, prohibitive oedipal mother).

(ii) *Sadomasochistic Character.* There is a lower level of masochistic personality organization which would probably occupy some point in the "middle range" of our continuum, typically represented by the "sadomasochistic" character. A good number of "help-rejecting complainers" (9) can probably be included here. Some infantile personalities also present these traits. Masochistic and sadistic character traits appear in some combination, the depressive perfectionism is absent, and sadistic instinctual derivatives find a more direct way into impulsive character traits. In this group we find some borderline patients, in contrast to the "higher level" group of patients with depressive personality features.

(iii) *Primitive Self-destructiveness.* There exists a "low level" group of masochistic characters, in which rather primitive sexualization of masochistic needs occurs, masochistic perverse trends may be present, and aggression is discharged indiscriminately toward the outside or toward one's own body. Patients with severe self-destructiveness (but without a well-integrated superego and with a remarkable absence of the capacity to experience guilt) are members of this group. Typical examples are provided by patients who obtain nonspecific relief of anxiety by cutting themselves or by some other form of self-mutilation, or by impulsive suicidal gestures carried out with great rage and practically no depression. From a dynamic point of view, preoedipal conflicts predominate in these patients, and rather primitive fusion and defusion of aggressive and sexual impulses occur. Most, if not all, of these patients present an underlying borderline personality organization.

In the three levels of character pathology related to depressive-masochistic traits, it can be noted that patients on the higher level actually experience more depression than those on the lower one. This brings us back to the question of whether depression as a symptom may be of diagnostic value in our analysis of borderline personality organization.

(iv) *Symptomatic Depression.* First of all, depression as a symptom has to be differentiated from depressive-masochistic character traits. Second, the quality of symptomatic depression is important, in that the more depression is combined with authentic guilt feelings, remorse, and concern about oneself, the more it is a reflection of superego integration. Depression which has more of the quality of impotent rage, or of helplessness-hopelessness in connection with the breakdown of an idealized self concept, has much less value as an indicator of superego integration. This is important for our discussion, because the better the integration of the superego, the higher the level of character pathology. Third, the quantity of symptomatic depression itself and the degree to which it has a disorganizing effect upon all ego functions are important. Severe depression approaching the psychotic degree of depressive reaction, which tends to produce ego disorganization in the form of "depressive depersonalization" and severe withdrawal from emotional relationships with reality, may be tentatively considered as one further presumptive indicator of borderline personality. In such instances, in spite of the fact (or rather because of the fact) of "intact" superego functioning, the ego is not able to withstand an excessively severe, sadistic superego. The combination of these three considerations (quality of the depression, quantitative factors, and level of depressive-masochistic character organization) in regard to the presence of depression makes it evident that depression as a symptom should not be used directly as an indicator of borderline personality organization. Excessive depression and its absence may both indicate "low level" character organization. The quality as well as the quantity of depression is important here.

I have detailed the analysis of the problem of depressive-masochistic character traits and of symptomatic depression in order to stress that the suggestion of a continuum of "high level" and "low level" character pathology is not meant as a simple ordering of diagnostic labels, and requires specialized descriptive, but also dynamic and structural, clinical judgments.

In summary, to focus on the descriptive aspects of psychopathology makes it possible, if present in sufficient intensity, to warrant the presumptive diagnostic conclusion of borderline personality organization. The definite conclusion in regard to this diagnosis, though, has to depend on the structural analysis of these cases, my next topic.

## STRUCTURAL ANALYSIS

From a psychoanalytic viewpoint, the term "structural analysis" may have several meanings. First, it refers to the analysis of mental processes from the point of view of the three psychic structures (ego, id, superego). This is the original sense in which Freud used the term to contrast it with the older "topographic" point of view. Second, structural analysis in a broader sense refers to Hartmann's (20) and especially Rapaport and Gill's (42) viewpoints of the ego as a combination of: (a) "structures" or configurations of a slow rate of change which determine the channeling of mental processes, (b) these mental processes or "functions" themselves, and (c) "thresholds." From a clinical point of view, this second way of using the term "structural analysis" is reflected in the focus on cognitive structures (mainly primary- versus secondary-process thinking) (41), and defensive structures (constellation of defense mechanisms and the defensive aspects of character). There is a third meaning of the term "structural analysis." The term has been used more recently to describe the analysis of the structural derivatives of internalized object relationships (8, 29). The first and second meanings of structural analysis are of course intimately related, and may be unified in Hartmann's consideration of the id, ego, and superego as three overall structures of the psychic apparatus which are defined by their respective functions, overall structures within which substructures are determined by specific functions, and then in turn the substructures determine new functions. In my attempt to analyze borderline personality organization, I shall first apply the kind of structural analysis which considers the ego as an overall structure which integrates substructures and functions, and then analyze the specific structural derivatives of internalized object relationships which are relevant to this form of psychopathology.

## 1.   Nonspecific Manifestations of Ego Weakness

The overextension and abuse of the concept "ego weakness" have made some people abandon its use altogether. If the various aspects of "ego weakness" are individualized and differentiated, this concept remains useful. There are "specific" aspects of ego weakness, namely, the predominance of primitive mechanisms of defense characteristic of the borderline personality organization. By "nonspecific" aspects of ego weakness, I refer to three characteristics (51): (a) *lack of anxiety tolerance;* (b) *lack of impulse control;* (c) *lack of developed sublimatory channels.* The presence of some degree of lack of differentiation of self and object images and the concomitant blurring of ego boundaries can be considered one other "nonspecific" aspect of ego weakness in the borderline field, but this aspect is closely linked to the pathology of internalized object relationships and will be taken up in that context. The rigidity of characterological patterns is sometimes mistakenly considered to be a sign of ego strength; neither excessive rigidity of character pathology nor its "overfluidity" in itself represent ego strength or weakness, but rather both are specific modes of organization of the character pathology.

*Lack of anxiety tolerance* is reflected in the degree to which any additional anxiety to that habitually experienced moves the patient toward further symptom formation, alloplastic behavior, or ego regression. It has to be stressed that it is not the degree of anxiety which is important here, but how the ego reacts to any additional anxiety "load." This variable may be difficult to observe in patients who present chronic and severe anxiety. Complete absence of anxiety is not in itself an indicator of the degree of anxiety tolerance. From a practical point of view, skilled diagnostic examination over a number of weeks is perhaps the only way of adequately assessing this variable.

Impulse-ridden character disorders are a typical example of a *lack of impulse control*. Nevertheless, nonspecific, generalized lack of impulse control has to be differentiated from highly individualized "lack of impulse control" as part of defensive characterological formation. I have noted elsewhere (29) that what appears on the surface to be simply a lack of impulse control connected with ego weakness, may reflect highly specific defensive operations and represent the emergence into consciousness of a dissociated identification system. In this case, the specificity of this "lack of impulse control" is manifested typically by the ego syntonicity of the impulses being expressed during the time of impulsive behavior, by the repetitive nature of the kind of lack of impulse control involved, by the lack of emotional contact between that part of the patient's personality and the rest of the self experience, and finally by the bland denial which secondarily defends this dissociated "breakthrough." In contrast, nonspecific lack of impulse control can be seen typically in the infantile personality structure. Here it appears as unpredictable, erratic impulsivity, a simple reflection of an increase of anxiety or of any particular drive derivative. It is an effort at the dispersion of intrapsychic tensions rather than the reenactment of a specific, dissociated identification system.

The *lack of developed sublimatory channels* is again difficult to evaluate; constitutional capacities such as the intelligence level and particular skills must be evaluated, and the patient's potentiality has to be compared with his achievements. The social environment of the patient also has to be considered. In a highly stimulating, culture-oriented social environment the lack of enjoyment and creativity of the borderline patient may be obscured by his surface adaptation to that optimal environment. In contrast, patients chronically submerged in a socially severely deprived environment may appear as bland, joyless, and uncreative superficially, without necessarily revealing the more severe aspects of lack of sublimatory capacity on a deeper level. Creative enjoyment and creative achievement are the main aspects of sublimatory capacity; they may be the best indicators of the extent to which a conflict-free ego sphere is available, and their absence, therefore, is an important indicator of ego weakness.

## 2.  Shift Toward Primary-Process Thinking

Rapaport's (41) analysis of the levels of cognitive structures according to the degree to which secondary-process or primary-process thinking predominates in them is relevant here. Actually, this may still be considered the most frequently relied upon clinical manifestation of borderline personality organization. Much of the thinking of Rapaport et al. (43) in regard to the structural differentiation between neurotic patients, "preschizophrenic" patients, and psychotic patients (the "preschizophrenic" corresponding broadly to the borderline personality organization) is linked with their analysis of levels of cognitive structures, as is also these authors' utilization of the battery of projective tests to evaluate the degree to which secondary-process or primary-process thinking predominates. Patients with borderline personality organization seldom give evidence in clinical mental-status examinations of formal disorder of their thought processes. However, on projective testing, and especially in response to unstructured stimuli, primary-process thinking tends to appear in the form of primitive fantasies, in a decrease in the capacity to adapt to the formal givens of the test material, and particularly in the use of peculiar verbalizations.

It is questionable whether this shift in the direction of primary-process functioning represents a "nonspecific" formal regression of the ego, as was thought in the past (35). It may well be that regression to primary-process thinking is the final outcome of several aspects of borderline personality organization: (a) the reactivation of pathological, early internalized object relationships connected with primitive drive derivatives of a pathological kind; (b) the reactivation of early defensive operations, especially generalized dissociative or splitting mechanisms affecting the integration of cognitive processes; (c) the partial refusion of primitive self and object images affecting the stability of ego boundaries; and (d) regression toward primitive cognitive structures of the ego because of nonspecific shifts in the cathexis-countercathexis equilibrium. Whatever its origin, the regression toward primary-process thinking is still the most important single structural indicator of borderline personality organization. Its detection through the use of projective tests makes sophisticated psychological testing an indispensable instrument for the diagnosis of borderline personality organization.

## 3.  Specific Defensive Operations at the Level of Borderline Personality Organization

One essential task in the development and integration of the ego is the synthesis of early and later introjections and identifications into a stable ego identity. Introjections and identifications established under the influence of libidinal drive derivatives are at first built up separately from those established under the influence of aggressive drive derivatives ("good" and "bad" internal objects, or "positive" and "negative" introjections). This division of internalized object relations into "good" and "bad" happens at first simply because of the lack of integrative capacity of the early ego. Later on, what originally was a lack of integrative capacity is used defensively by the emerging ego in order to prevent the generalization of anxiety and to protect the ego core built around positive introjections (introjections and identifications established under the influence of libidinal drive derivatives). *This defensive division of the ego, in which what was at first a simple defect in integration is then used actively for other purposes, is in essence the mechanism of splitting.* This mechanism is normally used only in an early stage of ego development during the first year of life, and rapidly is replaced by higher level defensive operations of the ego which center around repression and related mechanisms such as reaction formation, isolation, and undoing, all of which protect the ego from intrapsychic conflicts by means of the rejection of a drive derivative or its ideational representation, or both, from the conscious ego. In contrast, in pathological conditions when this mechanism (and other related mechanisms to which I shall refer below) persists, splitting protects the ego from conflicts by means of the dissociation or active maintaining apart of introjections and identifications of strongly conflictual nature, namely, those libidinally determined from those aggressively determined, without regard to the access to consciousness. The drive derivative in this case attains full emotional, ideational, and motor consciousness, but is completely separated from other segments of the conscious psychic experience. Under these pathological circumstances, contradictory ego states are alternately activated, and as long as these contradictory ego states can be kept separate from each other, anxiety is prevented. Such a state of affairs is, of course, very detrimental to the integrative processes which normally crystallize into a stable ego identity, and underlies the syndrome of identity diffusion (5).

For the internalization of object relationships, there are two essential tasks that the early ego has to accomplish in rapid succession: (i) *the differentiation of self images from object images which form part of early introjections and identifications;* (ii) *the integration of self and object images built up under the influence of libidinal drive derivatives with their corresponding self and object images built up under the influence of aggressive drive derivatives.* The first task is accomplished in part under the influence of the development of the apparatuses of primary autonomy, which are preconditions for the operation of introjection and identification processes. Perception and memory traces, as they are stored and integrated, help to sort out the origin of stimuli and the differential characteristics of perception, and gradually differentiate self from object images. Also, the gratification of instinctual needs and their moderate frustration foster the differentiation of self images from object images, because libidinal gratification draws attention cathexes to the interaction between self and objects and fosters the differentiation in that area, and because frustration brings to awareness the painful absence of the fulfilling objects and thus contributes to differentiate self from nonself. Excessive gratification of instinctual needs may retard the differentiation between self and objects. From a clinical point of view, however, excessive frustration of early instinctual needs (especially oral) is probably the main cause of the lack of differentiation between self and objects, because *excessive frustration reinforces the normal disposition to regressive refusion of self and object images,* representing early merging fantasies between self and object in an attempt to retain or regain absolute gratification (28). The second task is, as mentioned above, that *self and object images built up under the influence of libidinal drive derivatives have to be integrated with their corresponding self and object images built up under the influence of aggressive drive derivatives.* Thus, idealized "all good" object images have to be integrated with "all bad" object images, and the same holds true for good and bad self images. In this process of synthesis, partial images of the self and of the objects are integrated into total object and self representations, and thus self and object representations become further differentiated from each other, and also more realistic.

These two processes fail to a great extent in the case of psychosis, and to some extent in the case of borderline personality organization. In the psychoses, there is a severe defect of the differentiation between self and object images, and regressive refusion of self and object images occurs in the form of primitive merging fantasies, with the *concomitant blurring of the ego boundaries in the area of differentiation between self and nonself.* Such regressive refusion between self and object images may depend on: (i) lack of development of the apparatuses of primary autonomy; (ii) constitutionally determined lack of anxiety tolerance (even minor frustrations are intolerable, and induce regressive fusion or merging processes); (iii) excessive frustration in reality; and (iv) consequent excessive development of aggression (or constitutionally determined excessive intensity of aggressive drives). *Vicious circles involving projection of aggression and reintrojection of aggressively determined object and self images* are probably a major factor in the development of both psychosis and borderline personality organization. *In the psychoses their main effect is regressive refusion of self and object images; in the case of the borderline personality organization,* what predominates is not refusion between self and object images, but *an intensification and pathological fixation of splitting processes.*

In the case of the borderline personality organization, the pathogenic factors mentioned above in regard to the development of psychosis may also be present, but regressive refusion of self and object images or lack of development and differentiation between self and object images is not predominant. The major defect in development lies here in the incapacity to synthesize positive and negative introjections and identifications; there is a lack of the capacity to bring together the aggressively determined and libidinally determined self and object images. It seems probable that in the case of the borderline personality organization, constitutional defects in the development of the apparatuses of primary autonomy are relatively unimportant. Perhaps constitutionally determined lack of anxiety tolerance interfering with the phase of synthesis of introjections of opposite quality, but especially severe intensity of aggressive drive derivatives are the main pathological factors. As mentioned above, excessive aggression may stem both from a constitutionally determined intensity of aggressive drives or from severe early frustration, and *extremely severe aggressive and self-aggressive strivings connected with early self and object images are consistently related to borderline personality organization.*

When self and object images are relatively well differentiated from each other, and when regressive refusion of these images is therefore relatively absent, then the differentiation of ego boundaries develops relatively undisturbed; consequently, the typical borderline patient maintains to a major degree intact ego boundaries, and the related capacity for reality testing. But the *lack of synthesis of contradictory self and object images* has numerous pathological consequences. Splitting is maintained as an essential mechanism preventing diffusion of anxiety within the ego and protecting the positive introjections and identifications. The need to preserve the good self, and good object images, and good external objects in the presence of dangerous "all bad" self and object images leads to a number of subsidiary defensive operations. All of these subsidiary defensive operations, together with splitting itself, constitute the characteristic defense mechanisms present in the borderline personality organization. I shall describe these defensive operations, differentiating them from their later, less pathological counterparts, that is, those defense mechanisms which occur in conjunction with repression in patients with neurotic and nonborderline character pathology.

(i) _Splitting._ This is an essential defensive operation of the borderline personality organization which underlies all the others which follow. It has to be stressed that I am using the term "splitting" in a restricted and limited sense, referring only to the active process of keeping apart introjections and identifications of opposite quality. This narrow use of the term has to be differentiated from its broader use by some authors. I have suggested elsewhere (29) that the integration, or synthesis, of introjections and identification of opposite qualities possibly provides the most important source of neutralization of aggression (in that libidinal and aggressive drive derivatives are fused and organized as part of that integration), and that therefore one consequence of pathological circumstances under which splitting is excessive is that this neutralization does not take place sufficiently, and an essential energy source for ego growth fails. Splitting, then, is a fundamental cause of ego weakness, and as splitting also requires less countercathexis than repression, a weak ego falls back easily on splitting, and a vicious circle is created by which ego weakness and splitting reinforce each other. The direct clinical manifestation of splitting may be the alternative expression of complementary sides of a conflict in certain character disorders, combined with bland denial and lack of concern over the contradiction in his behavior and internal experience by the patient. One other direct manifestation of splitting may be a _selective_ "lack of impulse control" in certain areas, manifest in episodic breakthrough of primitive impulses which are ego syntonic during the time of their expression (and splitting is prevalent in impulse neurosis and addictions). Probably the best known manifestation of splitting is the division of external objects into "all good" ones and "all bad" ones, with the concomitant possibility of complete, abrupt shifts of an object from one extreme compartment to the other; that is, sudden and complete reversals of all feelings and conceptualizations about a particular person. Extreme and repetitive oscillation between contradictory self concepts may also be the result of the mechanism of splitting. Splitting appears not as an isolated mechanism but in combination with several others. The same is true, of course, in the case of repression, which is usually combined with other mechanisms of the "higher level" type. Splitting occurs in combination with any one or several of the following:

(ii) *Primitive Idealization*. This refers to the tendency to see external objects as totally good, in order to make sure that they can protect one against the "bad" objects, that they cannot be contaminated, spoiled, or destroyed by one's own aggression or by that projected onto other objects. Primitive idealization creates unrealistic, all-good and powerful object images, and this also affects negatively the development of the ego ideal and the superego. "Primitive idealization" is a term I propose to contrast later forms of idealization, such as that typically present in depressive patients who idealize objects out of guilt over their own aggression toward the object. I proposed the term "predepressive idealization" for this mechanism in a previous paper (29), but "primitive idealization" now seems preferable. Primitive idealization implies neither the conscious or unconscious acknowledgment of aggression toward the object, nor guilt over this aggression and concern for the object. Thus, it is not a reaction formation, but rather is the direct manifestation of a primitive, protective fantasy structure in which there is no real regard for the ideal object, but a simple need for it as a protection against a surrounding world of dangerous objects. One other function of such an ideal object is to serve as a recipient for omnipotent identification, for sharing in the greatness of the idealized object as a protection against aggression, and as a direct gratification of narcissistic needs. Idealization thus used reflects the underlying omnipotence, another borderline defense which I shall mention below. Primitive idealization may be considered a forerunner of later forms of idealization.

(iii) *Early Forms of Projection, and Especially Projective Identification*. Patients with borderline personality organization tend to present very strong projective trends, but it is not only the quantitative predominance of projection but also the qualitative aspect of it which is characteristic. The main purpose of projection here is to externalize the all-bad, aggressive self and object images, and the main consequence of this need is the development of dangerous, retaliatory objects against which the patient has to defend himself. This projection of aggression is rather unsuccessful. While these patients do have sufficient development of ego boundaries to be able to differentiate self and objects in most areas of their lives, the very intensity of the projective needs, plus the general ego weakness characterizing these patients, weakens ego boundaries in the particular area of the projection of aggression. This leads such patients to feel that they can still identify themselves with the object onto whom aggression has been projected, and their ongoing "empathy" with the now threatening object maintains and increases the fear of their own projected aggression. Therefore, they have to control the object in order to prevent it from attacking them under the influence of the (projected) aggressive impulses; they have to attack and control the object before (as they fear) they themselves are attacked and destroyed. In summary, projective identification is characterized by the lack of differentiation between self and object in that particular area, by continuing to experience the impulse as well as the fear of that impulse while the projection is active, and by the need to control the external object (29, 45). At higher levels of ego development, later forms of projection no longer have this characteristic. In the hysterical patient, for example, a projection of sexual impulses simply reinforces repression, and the hysterical woman who despises men or is afraid of men because of their sexual interest is completely unaware of her own sexual impulses and therefore does not "empathize" fearfully with the "enemy." All of this aggressive distortion of object images also influences pathologically the development of the superego.

(iv) *Denial*. Patients with a borderline personality organization typically present much evidence of the use of this mechanism, and especially of primitive manifestations of denial in contrast to higher level forms of it. Denial here is typically exemplified by "mutual denial" of two emotionally independent areas of consciousness (in this case, we might say, denial simply reinforces splitting). The patient is aware of the fact that at this time his perceptions, thoughts, and feelings about himself or other people are completely opposite to those he has had at other times; but this memory has no emotional relevance, it cannot influence the way he feels now. At a later time, he may revert to his previous ego state and then deny the present one, again with persisting memory, but with a complete incapacity for emotional linkage of these two ego states. Denial in the patients I am considering may also manifest itself only as simple disregard for a sector of their subjective experience or for a sector of the external world. When pressed, the patient acknowledges his intellectual awareness of the sector which has been denied, but again he cannot integrate it with the rest of his emotional experience. It has to be stressed that that which is denied now is something that in other areas of his consciousness the patient is aware of; that is, *emotions* are denied which he has experienced (and remembers having experienced) and awareness of the emotional relevance of a certain situation in reality is denied, of which the patient has been consciously aware or can again be made consciously aware. All of this is different from the higher level form of denial such as is implicit in the mechanism of negation (11). In negation, a mental content is present "with a negative sign"; the patient says that he knows what he himself, his therapist, or others *might* think about something, but that particular possibility is rejected as a purely intellectual speculation. In this case, the emotional relevance of what is denied has never been present in consciousness, and remains repressed. Negation in this regard is a higher form of denial linked with repression, and quite close to isolation. An intermediate level of denial, which is also quite prevalent in patients with borderline personality organization, is the denial of emotions contrary to those which are strongly experienced at that point, especially the manic denial of depression. It is important to stress that in the denial of depression, although we talk about the denial of an emotion alone, both the manic and the depressive disposition involve the activation of specific pathogenic object relationships. In this form of denial, an extreme, opposite affect is used to reinforce the ego's stand against a threatening part of the self experience. The fact that manic denial and depression tend to be so intimately linked clinically reveals a less pathological, less "crude" dissociation within the ego than that of the "lower level" of denial. Denial, then, is a broad group of defensive operations, and probably related at its higher level to the mechanisms of isolation and other higher level defenses against affects (detachment, denial in fantasy, denial "in word and act"), and at its lower level, to splitting.

(v)  *Omnipotence and Devaluation.* These two mechanisms are also intimately linked to splitting, and represent at the same time direct manifestations of the defensive use of primitive introjection and identification. Patients using these two mechanisms of defense may shift between the need to establish a demanding, clinging relationship to an idealized "magic" object at some times, and fantasies and behavior betraying a deep feeling of magical omnipotence of their own at other times. Both stages represent their identification with an "all good" object, idealized and powerful as a protection against bad "persecutory" objects. There is no real "dependency" in the sense of love for the ideal object and concern for it. On a deeper level the idealized person is treated ruthlessly, possessively, as an extension of the patient himself. In this regard, even during the time of apparent submission to an idealized external object, the deep underlying omnipotent fantasies of the patient can be detected. The need to *control* the idealized objects, to use them in attempts to manipulate and exploit the environment and to "destroy potential enemies," is linked with inordinate pride in the "possession" of these perfect objects totally dedicated to the patient. Underneath the feelings of insecurity, self-criticism, and inferiority that patients with borderline personality organization present, one can frequently find grandiose and omnipotent trends. These very often take the form of a strong unconscious conviction that they have the right to expect gratification and homage from others, to be treated as privileged, special persons. The devaluation of external objects is in part a corollary of the omnipotence; if an external object can provide no further gratification or protection, it is dropped and dismissed because there was no real capacity for love of this object in the first place. But there are other sources which influence this tendency to devaluate objects. One of them is the revengeful destruction of the object which frustrated the patient's needs (especially his oral greediness); one other source is the defensive devaluation of objects in order to prevent them from becoming feared and hated "persecutors." All these motives come together in this defensive operation against the need and the fear of others. The devaluation of significant objects of the patient's past has serious detrimental effects on the internalized object relations, and especially on the structures involved in superego formation and integration.

## 4.  Pathology of Internalized Object Relationships

It has been noted that the mechanism of splitting separates in these patients contradictory ego states related to early pathological object relationships. We may now add that the persistence of such early internalized object relationships in a rather "nonmetabolized" condition as part of these dissociated ego states is in itself pathological, and reflects the interference of splitting with those synthesizing operations which normally bring about depersonification, abstraction, and integration of internalized object relationships. Typically, each of these dissociated ego segments contains a certain primitive object image, connected with a complementary self image and a certain affect disposition which was active at the time when that particular internalization took place. In the case of borderline personality organization, differentiation of self from object images has occurred to a sufficient degree, in contrast to what obtains in psychoses, to permit a relatively good differentiation between self and object representations and a concomitant integrity of ego boundaries in most areas. Ego boundaries fail only in those areas in which projective identification and fusion with idealized objects take place, which is the case especially in the transference developments of these patients. This appears to be a fundamental reason why these patients develop a transference psychosis rather than a transference neurosis.

Now we have to examine further the area of specific pathology of internalized object relations in the borderline personality; namely, the incapacity for synthesizing the good and bad introjections and identifications. As has been mentioned above, the main etiological factors appear to be the excessive nature of primary aggression or aggression secondary to frustration, to which probably certain deficiencies in the development of primary ego apparatuses and lack of anxiety tolerance contribute. The consequences of the persistence of split-up "all good" and "all bad" introjections are multiple. First of all, the lack of interpenetration of libidinal and aggressive drive derivatives interferes with the normal modulation and differentiation of affect dispositions of the ego, and a chronic tendency to eruption of primitive affect states remains. Also, the specific affect disposition represented by the ego's capacity to experience depression, concern, and guilt cannot be reached when positive and negative introjections are not brought together. The capacity of the ego for depressive reaction appears to depend to a large extent on the tension between different, contradictory self images, which develops when good and bad self images are integrated, so that one's own aggression can be acknowledged, and when objects are no longer seen as either totally bad or totally good, so that a combination of both love and aggression toward integrated "total" objects can be acknowledged, motivating guilt and concern for the object (31, 32, 52). Borderline patients frequently present deficiencies in the capacity for experiencing guilt feelings and feelings of concern for objects. Their depressive reactions take primitive forms of impotent rage and feelings of defeat by external forces, rather than mourning over good, lost objects and regret over their aggression toward themselves and others.

The presence of "all good" and "all bad" object images which cannot be integrated interferes seriously with superego integration. Primitive forerunners of the superego of a sadistic kind, representing internalized bad object images related to pregenital conflicts, are too overriding to be tolerated, and are reprojected in the form of external bad objects. Overidealized object images and "all good" self images can create only fantastic ideals of power, greatness, and perfection, and not the more realistic demands and goals that would be brought about by superego integration. In other words, the components of the ego ideal in these cases also interfere with superego integration. Finally, the realistic demands of the parents cannot be brought together with either the ideal self and object images and their related ego ideal or with the threatening prohibitive, sadistic forerunners of the superego because both the sadistic nature and the overidealized nature of the superego forerunners distort the perception of the parental images, preventing integration.

Because of this interference with superego integration, there is a constant projection of the demanding and prohibitive aspects of superego components. The normal ego-integrating pressures of the superego are missing, as well as the capacity of the ego to experience guilt. The tendency to devaluate objects (see above) also interferes with superego integration, especially with the normally essential internalization of realistic demands from parental images; the devaluation of significant parental images prevents these patients from internalizing a most important source of superego formation (25, 26).

In summary, primitive, unrealistic self images persist in the ego, are extremely contradictory in their characteristics, and an integrated self concept cannot develop; object images cannot be integrated, either, and therefore they interfere with the more realistic evaluation of the external objects. Constant projection of "all bad" self and object images perpetuates a world of dangerous, threatening objects, against which the "all good" self images are used defensively, and megalomanic ideal self images are built up. Sufficient delimitation between self and objects (stability of ego boundaries) is maintained to permit a practical, immediate adaptation to the demands of reality, but deeper internalization of the demands of reality, especially social reality, is made impossible by the interference of these nonintegrated self and object images with superego integration. Those superego structures which do develop are under the influence of sadistic forerunners intimately linked to pregenital aggressive drive derivatives, and of other forerunners representing primitive fusion of ideal-self and ideal-object images which tend to reinforce omnipotence and megalomanic demands on the self rather than representing a modulating ego ideal. In general, superego functions tend to remain personified, do not develop to the point of superego abstraction, and are easily reprojected onto the external world (21, 28).

All these characteristics of internalized object relationships are reflected in typical characterological traits of the borderline personality organization. These patients have little capacity for a realistic evaluation of others and for realistic empathy with others; they experience other people as distant objects, to whom they adapt "realistically" only as long as there is no emotional involvement with them. Any situation which would normally develop into a deeper interpersonal relationship reveals the incapacity of these patients to really feel or empathize with another person, the unrealistic distortion of other people, and the protective shallowness of their emotional relationships. This protective shallowness has many sources. First, it reflects the emotional shallowness due to the lack of fusion between libidinal and aggressive drive derivatives, and the concomitant narrowness, rigidity, and primitiveness of their affect dispositions. The shallowness of the emotional reaction of the patients we are considering is also more directly connected with the incapacity to experience guilt, concern, and the related deepening of their awareness of and interest in others (52). An additional reason for their emotional shallowness is the defensive effort to withdraw from too close an emotional involvement, which would bring about the danger of activation of their primitive defensive operations, especially projective identification and the arousal of fears of attack by the object which is becoming important to them. Emotional shallowness also defends them from primitive idealization of the object and the related need to submit to and merge with such idealized objects, as well as from the potential rage over frustration of the pregenital, especially orally demanding needs that are activated in the relationship with the idealized object (46). The lack of superego development, and therefore the further lack of ego integration and maturation of feelings, aims, and interests, also keeps them in ignorance of the higher, more mature and differentiated aspects of other people's personalities.

Another characteristic of these patients is the more or less subtle or more or less crude expression of their pregenital and genital aims, which are all severely infiltrated with aggression. Direct exploitiveness, unreasonable demandingness, manipulation of others without consideration or even tact are quite noticeable. In this regard, the tendency to devaluate objects, mentioned above, is also relevant. The need to manipulate others also corresponds to the defensive need to keep control over the environment in order to prevent more primitive, paranoid fears connected with the projection of aggressive self and object images from coming to the surface. Many of these patients, when their efforts to control, manipulate, devalue objects, and direct gratification of their needs through exploitation of others fail, tend to withdraw and to re-create in their fantasies relationships with others in which they can express all these needs. Some protective withdrawal and gratification in fantasy are usually present even in those borderline patients who superficially may appear as quite "sociable."

These patients may feel superficially quite insecure, uncertain, and inferior in regard to their capacities or dealings with others. These feelings of inferiority and insecurity may be in part a reflection of the more realistic aspects of their evaluation of their relationships to significant others, work, and life in general, and often also reflect a realistic awareness of some of their shortcomings and failures. Yet, on a deeper level, feelings of inferiority often reflect defensive structures. It is striking when one finds so often underneath that level of insecurity and uncertainty, omnipotent fantasies, and a kind of blind optimism based on denial, which represent the patient's identification with primitive "all good" self and object images. In this connection, there are also deep feelings of having the right to exploit and to be gratified—in short, what has been classically referred to as the "narcissism" of these patients. Their narcissism does not represent simply a turning away from external objects, but the activation of primitive object relationships in which they re-enact a primitive fusion of idealized self and object images, defensively used against the "bad" self and object images, and the "bad" external objects. Feelings of inferiority frequently represent a secondary surface layer hiding the narcissistic character traits.

The presence of contradictory introjections and iden-tifications is what gives the "as if" quality to these patients. Although their identifications are contradictory and dissociated from each other, the superficial manifestations of these identifications persist as remnants of behavior dispositions in the ego. This permits some of these patients to "re-enact" partial identifications, which are nearly all dissociated, if this appears useful to them from the point of view of their superficial adaptation to reality. A chameleonlike quality of their adaptability may result, in which what they *pretend* to be is really the empty dressing of what at other moments they have to be in a more primitive way. This is quite confusing to the patients themselves. *All of this also represents what Erikson (5) has called identity diffusion; namely, the lack of an integrated self concept and an integrated and stable concept of total objects in relationship with the self. Actually, identity diffusion is a typical syndrome of the borderline personality organization,* which is not seen in less severe character pathology and neurotic patients, and which is a direct consequence of active splitting of those introjections and identifications of which the synthesis normally would bring about a stable ego identity.

In an attempt to differentiate psychotic, borderline, and neurotic patients, one might briefly say that psychotic patients have a severe lack of ego development, with mostly undifferentiated self and object images and concomitant lack of development of ego boundaries (19, 28); borderline patients have a better integrated ego than psychotics, with differentiation between self and object images to a major extent and with the development of firm ego boundaries in all but the areas of close interpersonal involvement; they present, typically, the syndrome of identity diffusion (5, 29); and neurotic patients present a strong ego, with complete separation between self and object images and concomitant delimitation of ego boundaries; they do not present the syndrome of identity diffusion. Neurotic patients have developed a stable ego identity, with the concomitant integration, depersonification, and individualization of the ego structures determined by object relationships, and they present an integrated superego, within which the pregenitally determined forerunners and the later, more realistic internalization of parental images have been integrated. Their superego may be excessively severe or sadistic, but it is sufficiently integrated to promote ego development and at least partially successful, conflict-free functioning.

## GENETIC-DYNAMIC ANALYSIS

We can now turn from the structural analysis to an examination of the typical instinctual content of the conflicts in the internalized object relationships in patients with borderline personality organization. Pregenital aggression, especially oral aggression, plays a crucial role as part of this psychopathological constellation. The dynamic aspects of the borderline personality organization have been clarified by Melanie Klein and her co-workers (22, 34, 48). Her description of the intimate relationship between pregenital and especially oral conflicts, on the one hand, and oedipal conflicts, on the other, such as occur under the influence of excessive pregenital aggression, is relevant to the borderline personality organization.

Unfortunately, some basic assumptions of Melanie Klein, to which she tended to adhere in a rather dogmatic way and which have rightly been questioned by most authors in this field—the lack of consideration of structural factors in her writings; her disregard for epigenetic development; and, finally, her rather peculiar language—have made her observations difficult for most people to accept. In order to prevent misunderstandings, I would like to specify first those aspects of Melanie Klein's analysis in regard to the problems relevant here with which I strongly disagree: (i) Her assumption of a rather full development of oedipal conflicts in the first year of life: I suggest that what is characteristic of the borderline personality organization, in contrast to less severe pathological conditions, is a specific condensation between pregenital and genital conflicts, and a *premature* development of oedipal conflicts from the second or third year on. (ii) Melanie Klein assumes an innate, unconscious knowledge of the genital organs of both sexes which I find unacceptable, and which she links with extremely early oedipal development. (iii) The entire concep-tualization of internalized objects in Melanie Klein's formula-tion does not consider structural developments within the ego, which Fairbairn has rightly criticized; and her disregard for the findings of modern ego psychology seriously weakens her descriptions. (iv) Melanie Klein's conceptualization of the superego again disregards structural concepts; and while I would agree with her suggestion that superego functions develop much earlier than what was classically thought, the lack of consideration in her writings of different levels and different forms of internalized object relationships tends toward a serious oversimplification of the issues.

A frequent finding in patients with borderline personality organization is the history of extreme frustrations and intense aggression (secondary or primary) during the first few years of life. Excessive pregenital and particularly oral aggression tends to be projected and causes a paranoid distortion of the early parental images, especially of the mother. Through the projection of predominantly oral-sadistic but also anal-sadistic impulses, the mother is seen as potentially dangerous, and hatred of the mother extends to hatred of both parents who are later experienced as a "united group" by the child. A "contamination" of the father image by aggression primarily projected onto the mother and lack of differentiation between mother and father under the influence of lack of realistic differentiation of different objects under the influence of excessive splitting operations tend to produce, in both sexes, a combined and dangerous father-mother image, with the result that all sexual relationships are later conceived of as dangerous and aggressively infiltrated.

At the same time, in an effort to escape from oral rage and fears, premature development of genital strivings takes place; this effort often miscarries because of the intensity of pregenital aggression, which contaminates genital strivings as well, and numerous pathological developments take place which differ in both sexes.

In the case of the boy, premature development of genital strivings in order to deny oral-dependent needs tends to fail because oedipal fears and prohibitions against sexual impulses toward mother are powerfully reinforced by pregenital fears of the mother, and a typical image of a dangerous, castrating mother develops. Also, the projection of pregenital aggression reinforces oedipal fears of the father and castration anxiety in particular, further reinforcing, in turn, pregenital aggression and fear. The positive oedipus complex is seriously interfered with under these circumstances. In contrast, a frequent solution is the reinforcement of the negative oedipus complex, and specifically what Paula Heimann (22) has described as the "feminine position" in boys, which represents an effort to submit sexually to father in order to obtain from him the oral gratifications which were denied from the dangerous, frustrating mother. This is a typical constellation found in predominantly orally determined male homosexuality. It is to be stressed that on some level both father and mother are seen as dangerous; heterosexuality is seen as dangerous; and homosexuality is used as a substitute way of gratifying oral needs. The danger of the reappearance of oral frustration and aggression as a consequence of homosexual involvements is always present. One other attempted solution may be the gratification of oral-aggressive needs in a heterosexual relationship, which on a deeper level represents the effort to "rob" mother sexually of what she denied orally. This constellation is frequently found in narcissistic, promiscuous men who unconsciously seek revenge against the oral, frustrating mother through pseudogenital relationships with women. Other solutions to the danger created by a premature condensation of pregenital and genital aims can be found in the development of any of the polymorphous perverse infantile trends, especially those which permit the expression of aggression.

Severe oral pathology of the kind mentioned tends to develop the positive oedipal strivings prematurely in the girl. Genital strivings for father are used as a substitute gratification of oral-dependent needs that have been frustrated by the dangerous mother. This effort tends to be undermined by the contamination of the father image with pregenital aggression deflected from mother and projected onto him, and also because oral rage and especially oral envy powerfully reinforce penis envy in women. The denial of aggression through heterosexual love tends to fail because pathologically strong penis envy is stirred up, and also because the image of the oedipally prohibitive mother is reinforced by that of the dangerous pregenital mother. One solution frequently attempted is a flight into promiscuity in an attempt to deny penis envy and dependency upon men, and also as an expression of especially strong unconscious guilt feelings about oedipal strivings.

General reinforcement of masochistic trends is another solution which attempts to gratify superego pressures stemming from both pregenital and genital mother images, internalized under the influence of the reintrojection of projected aggression. General renunciation of heterosexuality, with a search for the gratification of oral needs from an idealized mother image, which is completely split off from the dangerous, threatening mother image, is an important source of female homosexuality, quite frequent in the case of borderline personality organization. Attempts at a homosexual relationship, which implies not only a renunciation of men and the submission to the oedipal mother, but also an effort to obtain oral and other pregenital gratification from idealized, "partial" mother figures tend to fail because of the ever-present oral-aggressive needs and fears. Sadomasochistic homosexual involvements are one further consequence of this development. Other polymorphous sexual trends develop similarly to what has been described above in the case of the boys.

In summary, in both sexes *excessive development of pregenital, especially oral aggression tends to induce a premature development of oedipal strivings, and as a consequence a particular pathological condensation between pregenital and genital aims under the overriding influence of aggressive needs.* A common outcome is the presence of several of the pathological compromise solutions which give rise to a typical persistence of polymorphous perverse sexual trends in patients presenting borderline personality organization. What appears on the surface as a chaotic persistence of primitive drives and fears, the "pansexuality" of the borderline case, represents a combination of several of these pathological solutions. All of these pathological solutions are unsuccessful attempts to deal with the aggressiveness of genital trends and the general infiltration of all instinctual needs by aggression. On psychological testing, borderline patients demonstrate a lack of the normal predominance of heterosexual genital strivings over partial polymorphous drives. What appears as a chaotic combination of preoedipal and oedipal strivings is a reflection of the pathological condensation mentioned. The formulation often derived from psychological testing, that these patients present "a lack of sexual identity," is probably a misnomer. It is true that these patients present identity diffusion, but this identity diffusion has earlier and more complex sources than a simple lack of differentiation of any particular sexual orientation (28). Their "lack of sexual identity" does not reflect a lack of sexual definition, but a combination of several strong fixations to cope with the same conflicts.

This brings us to the conclusion of the present effort to apply psychoanalytic metapsychology to the clinical problems of the borderline personality organization.

## SUMMARY

The "borderline" personality disorders are examined from the descriptive, structural, and genetic-dynamic viewpoints. It is suggested that they have in common: (i) symptomatic constellations, such as diffuse anxiety, special forms of polysymptomatic neuroses, and "prepsychotic" and "lower level" character pathology; (ii) certain defensive constellations of the ego, namely, a combination of nonspecific manifestations of ego weakness and a shift toward primary-process thinking on the one hand, and specific primitive defense mechanisms (splitting, primitive idealization, early forms of projection, denial, omnipotence), on the other; (iii) a particular pathology of internalized object relations; and (iv) characteristic instinctual vicissitudes, namely, a particular pathological condensation of pregenital and genital aims under the overriding influence of pregenital aggressive needs. These various aspects of borderline personality organization and their mutual relationships are briefly examined.

### BIBLIOGRAPHY

1.    Bychowski, G. The problem of latent psychosis. *J. Am. Psychoanal. Assoc.* 1:484–503, 1953.
2.    Deutsch, H. Some forms of emotional disturbance and their relationship to schizophrenia. *Psychoanal. Quart.*, 11:301–321, 1942.
3.    Easser, B. R. & Lesser, S. R. Hysterical personality: a re-evaluation. *Psychoanal. Quart.*, 34:390–405, 1965.
4.    Ekstein, R. & Wallerstein, J. Observations on the psychotherapy of borderline and psychotic children. *The Psychoanalytic Study of the Child*, 11:303–311. New York: International Universities Press, 1956.
5.    Erikson, E. H. The problem of ego identity. *J. Am. Psychoanal. Assoc.* 4:56–121, 1956.

6.   Fairbairn, W. R. D. Schizoid factors in the personality (1940). *An Object-Relations Theory of the Personality*. New York: Basic Books, 1952, pp. 3–27.
7.   Fairbairn, W. R. D. Endopsychic structure considered in terms of object-relationships (1944). *An Object-Relations Theory of the Personality*. New York: Basic Books, 1952, pp. 82–136.
8.   Fairbairn, W. R. D. A synopsis of the development of the author's views regarding the structure of the personality (1951). *An Object-Relations Theory of the Personality*. New York: Basicbooks, 1952, pp. 162–179.
9.   Frank, J. D. et al. Two behavior patterns in therapeutic groups and their apparent motivation. *Hum. Rel.*, 5:289–317, 1952.
10.  Freud, A. *The Ego and the Mechanisms of Defense* (1936). New York: International Universities Press, 1946, pp. 45–57.
11.  Freud, S. Negation (1925). *Standard Edition*, 19:235–239. London: Hogarth Press, 1961.
12.  Freud, S. Fetishism (1927). *Standard Edition*, 21:149–157. London: Hogarth Press, 1961.
13.  Freud, S. Splitting of the ego in the process of defence (1938). *Standard Edition*, 23:275–278. London: Hogarth Press, 1964.
14.  Frosch, J. The psychotic character: clinical psychiatric considerations. *Psychiat. Quart.*, 38:81–96, 1964.
15.  Geleerd, E. R. Borderline states in childhood and adolescence. *The Psychoanalytic Study of the Child*, 13:279–295. New York: International Universities Press, 1958.
16.  Gitelson, M. On ego distortion. *Int. J. Psycho-Anal.*, 39:245–257, 1958.
17.  Greenson, R. R. The struggle against identification. *J. Am. Psychoanal. Assoc.*, 2:200–217, 1954.
18.  Greenson, R. R. On screen defenses, screen hunger, and screen identity. *J. Am. Psychoanal. Assoc.*, 6:242–262, 1958.
19.  Hartmann, H. Contribution to the metapsychology of schizophrenia (1953). *Essays on Ego Psychology*. New York: International Universities Press, 1964, pp. 182–206.
20.  Hartmann, H., Kris, E., & Loewenstein, R. M. Comments on the formation of psychic structure. *The Psychoanalytic Study of the Child*, 2:11–38. New York: International Universities Press, 1946.
21.  Hartmann, H. & Loewenstein, R. M. Notes on the superego. *The Psychoanalytic Study of the Child*, 17:42–81. New York: International Universities Press, 1962.
22.  Heimann, P. A contribution to the re-evaluation of the oedipus complex: the early stages. In: *New Directions in Psycho-Analysis*, ed. M. Klein, P. Heimann, & R. E. Money-Kyrle. New York: Basic Books, 1955, pp. 23–38.
23.  Hoch, P. H. & Cattell, J. P. The diagnosis of pseudoneurotic schizophrenia. *Psychiat. Quart.*, 33:17–43, 1959.
24.  Hoch, P. H. & Polatin, P. Pseudoneurotic forms of schizophrenia. *Psychiat. Quart.*, 23:248–276, 1949.
25.  Jacobson, E. Contribution to the metapsychology of cyclothymic depression. In: *Affective Disorders*, ed. P. Greenacre. New York: International Universities Press, 1953, pp. 49–83.
26.  Jacobson, E. Contribution to the metapsychology of psychotic identifications. *J. Am. Psychoanal. Assoc.*, 2:239–262, 1954.
27.  Jacobson, E. Denial and repression. *J. Am. Psychoanal. Assoc.*, 5:61–92, 1957.
28.  Jacobson, E. *The Self and the Object World*. New York: International Universities Press, 1964.
29.  Kernberg, O. Structural derivatives of object relationships. *Int. J. Psycho-Anal.*, 47:236–253, 1966.

30.   Khan, M. M. R. Clinical aspects of the schizoid personality: affects and technique. *Int. J. Psycho-Anal.*, 41:430–437, 1960.

31.   Klein, M. A contribution to the psychogenesis of manic-depressive states (1934). *Contributions to Psycho-Analysis 1921-1945.* London: Hogarth Press, 1948, pp. 282–310.

32.   Klein, M. Mourning and its relation to manic-depressive states (1940). *Contributions to Psycho-Analysis 1921-1945.* London: Hogarth Press, 1948, pp. 311–338.

33.   Klein, M. The oedipus complex in the light of early anxieties: general theoretical summary (1945). *Contributions to Psycho-Analysis 1921-1945.* London: Hogarth Press, 1948, pp. 377–390.

34.   Klein, M. Notes on some schizoid mechanisms (1946). In: *Developments in Psycho-Analysis,* ed. J. Riviere. London: Hogarth Press, 1952, pp. 292–320.

35.   Knight, R. P. Borderline states (1953). In: *Psychoanalytic Psychiatry and Psychology,* ed. R. P. Knight & C. R. Friedman. New York: International Universities Press, 1954, pp. 97–109.

36.   Knight, R. P. Management and psychotherapy of the borderline schizophrenic patient (1953). In: *Psychoanalytic Psychiatry and Psychology,* ed. R. P. Knight & C. R. Friedman. New York: International Universities Press, 1954, pp. 110–122.

37.   Laughlin, H. P. *The Neuroses in Clinical Practice.* Philadelphia: Saunders, 1956, pp. 394–406.

38.   Main, T. F. The ailment. *Brit. J. Med. Psychol.*, 30:129–145, 1957.

39.   Menninger, K. A., Mayman, M., & Pruyser, P. *The Vital Balance.* New York: Viking Press, 1963, pp. 213–249.

40.   Rangell, L. Panel report: The borderline case. *J. Am. Psychoanal. Assoc.*, 3:285–298, 1955.

41.   Rapaport, D. Cognitive structures. In: *Contemporary Approaches to Cognition.* Cambridge: Harvard University Press, 1957, pp. 157–200.

42.   Rapaport, D. & Gill, M. M. The points of view and assumptions of metapsychology, *Int. J. Psycho-Anal.*, 40:153–162, 1959.

43.   Rapaport, D., Gill, M. M., & Schafer, R. *Diagnostic Psychological Testing,* 2 Vols. Chicago: Year Book Publishers, 1945 and 1946, 1:16–28; 2:24–31, 329–366.

44.   Robbins. L. L. Panel report: The borderline case. *J. Am. Psychoanal. Assoc.*, 4:550–562, 1956.

45.   Rosenfeld, H. Notes on the psychopathology and psychoanalytic treatment of schizophrenia. In: *Psychotherapy of Schizophrenic and Manic-Depressive States,* ed. A. Hassan & B. C. Glueck, Jr. [Psychiatric Research Report #17]. Washington, D.C.: American Psychiatric Association, 1963, pp. 61–72.

46.   Rosenfeld, H. On the psychopathology of narcissism: a clinical approach. *Int. J. Psycho-Anal.*, 45:332–337, 1964.

47.   Segal, H. *Introduction to the Work of Melanie Klein.* New York: Basic Books, 1964.

48.   Van der Waals, H. G. Problems of narcissism. *Bull. Menninger Clin.*, 29:293–311, 1965.

49.   Waelder, R. et al. Ego distortion (Panel Discussion). *Int. J. Psycho-Anal.*, 39:243–275, 1958.

50.   Wallerstein, R. S. Reconstruction and mastery in the transference psychosis. *J. Am. Psychoanal. Assoc.*, pp. 551–583.

51.   Wallerstein, R. S. & Robbins, L. L. The psychotherapy research project of The Menninger Foundation (Part IV: Concepts). *Bull. Menninger Clin.*, 20:239–262, 1956.

52.   Winnicott, D. W. The depressive position in normal emotional development. *Brit. J. Med. Psychol.*, 28:89–100, 1955.

53.  Zilboorg, G. Ambulatory schizophrenias. *Psychiatry*, 4:149–155, 1941.
54.  Zilboorg, G. Further observations on ambulatory schizophrenia. *Amer. J. Orthopsychiat.*, 27:677–682, 1957.

Two

# Countertransference

## THE CONCEPT OF COUNTERTRANSFERENCE

Two contrasting approaches in regard to the concept of countertransference could be described. Let us call the first approach the "classical" one, and define its concept of countertransference as the unconscious reaction of the psychoanalyst to the patient's transference. This approach stays close to the use of the term as first proposed by Freud (8) and to his recommendation that the analyst overcome his countertransference (9). This approach also tends to view neurotic conflicts of the analyst as the main origin of the countertransference.

Let us call the second approach the "totalistic" one; here countertransference is viewed as the total emotional reaction of the psychoanalyst to the patient in the treatment situation. This school of thought believes that the analyst's conscious and unconscious reactions to the patient in the treatment situation are reactions to the patient's reality as well as to his transference, and also to the analyst's own reality needs as well as to his neurotic needs. This second approach also implies that these emotional reactions of the analyst are intimately fused, and that although countertransference should certainly be resolved, it is useful in gaining more understanding of the patient. In short, this approach uses a broader definition of countertransference and advocates a more active technical use of it. Some radical proponents of this approach discuss, under certain circumstances, the effect of the countertransference with the patients as part of the analytic work.

Reich (32, 33), Glover (15), Fliess (6), and to some extent Gitelson (14), are the main exponents of the "classical" approach. Among the main exponents of the "totalistic" approach are Cohen (2), Fromm-Reichmann (11), Heimann (16), Racker (31), Weigert (43), Winnicott (45, 46) and to some extent Thompson (41). Little's (23, 24) definition of counter-transference is closer to the "classical" approach, but her use of it is closer to the "radical" wing of the "totalistic" approach. She has been the most important proponent of the use of countertransference as material to be communicated to the patient. Menninger (26) and Orr (29) occupy an intermediate position.

The classical approach's main criticism of the totalistic approach is that the broadening of the term counter-transference to include all emotional phenomena in the therapist is confusing and makes the term countertransference lose all specific meaning. The classical approach implies that the broadening of the concept of countertransference tends to exaggerate the importance of the analyst's emotional reaction, with a detrimental shift away from the position of neutrality in which the analyst should ideally remain. Adherents of the classical approach also point out the danger of an excessive intervention of the analyst's personality when his emotional reaction is put so much in the foreground. On the other hand, Reich (33) points out that adherents of the totalistic approach tend to do the classical position injustice when stating that the analyst's neutrality implies detached coolness and lack of humanity on the part of the analyst. Freud (10) states quite clearly that neutrality does not mean loss of spontaneity and of the natural warmth of the analyst, and that "listless in-difference" on the analyst's part may in itself bring about resistences in the patient.

The totalistic orientation's main criticisms of the classical approach are the following: (i) The restricted definition of countertransference tends to obscure its importance by the implication that countertransference is something basically "wrong." Thus, this criticism continues, a phobic attitude of the analyst toward his emotional reaction is fostered, limiting his understanding of the analytic situation. (ii) The fusion of influences of the patient's transference and his reality on the one hand and of the therapist's past and present reality on the other gives much important information about the nonverbal communication between patient and analyst, which tends to get lost when the efforts center on eliminating the analyst's emotional reaction rather than focusing on it and on its sources. When the analyst feels that his emotional reaction is an important technical instrument for understanding and helping the patient, the analyst feels freer to face his positive and negative emotions evoked in the transference situation, has less need to block these reactions, and can utilize them for his analytic work. (iii) An important group of patients—those presenting severe character disorders and those with borderline and psychotic levels of organization who nonetheless seem able to benefit from analytically oriented psychotherapy—tend, by their intense, premature, and rapidly fluctuating transference, to evoke intensive countertransference reactions in the therapist which may at times give the most meaningful understanding of what is central in the patient's chaotic expression (19).

I want to develop further some of the positions of the totalistic approach. Not only the patient's transference but also his reality (both in the analytic situation and in his extra-analytic life) may elicit strong emotional reactions in the analyst which are actually quite justified. Winnicott (45) points out that there exists an "objective countertransference," that is, natural reactions of the analyst to rather extreme manifestations of the patient's behavior toward him. Also, as Fromm-Reichmann (11) mentions, there are aspects of the therapist's reaction to the patient which are determined by the therapist's special professional nature since he does not work in a vacuum but represents a professional standard, status, and group. These are reality aspects of the therapist in his work with any patient.

Racker (30) refers to what he calls "indirect counter-transference," that is, the therapist's emotional reaction to third persons somehow involved in the treatment program. Tower

(42) analyzes the influence of the analyst's own training analyst in his therapeutic dealings.

Gitelson (14) also considers all these reality aspects as part of countertransference reactions, but different in type from what he calls the "transference reactions" of the analyst. He states that transference reactions of the analyst are his "total" reactions to the patient's personality which tend to appear especially at the beginning of treatment and may even disqualify the analyst from continuing his work with that patient. Countertransference reactions, in contrast, Gitelson continues, are of a partial type, fluctuating, changing according to the nature of the material that the patient presents. Yet, as Cohen (2) points out, these "total" reactions to the patient's personality are present during the whole course of the analysis and not at all limited to the initial period, and implicitly cannot be differentiated from countertransference reactions in Gitelson's terms. Heimann (18) formulates a critique similar to Cohen's. Thompson (41) states that the boundary between the analyst's normal reaction to the patient and his reaction based on his own problems is difficult to evaluate.

A totalistic concept of countertransference does justice to the conception of the analytic situation as an interaction process in which past and present of both participants, as well as their mutual reactions to their past and present, fuse into a unique emotional position involving both of them. Sullivan (39, 40) makes this concept of interpersonal interaction process a cornerstone of his theories; Menninger (26) specifically underlines it in its connection with countertransference.

Most examples of countertransference in the literature refer to emotional reactions of the analyst which usually are conscious, with the unconscious aspects appearing as transitory "blind spots" in the therapist which he later overcomes by bringing his emotional reaction out into the open. One might say, of course, that only the initial, unconscious "blind spot" is countertransference, but this would not do justice to the fact that very often the problem for the therapist is not so much to find out one aspect of his feeling of which he might not have been aware but rather how to deal with the very strong emotions which he experiences and which influence the treatment. Menninger (26) states that "the manifestations of the countertransference may be conscious although the intrapsychic conditions resulting in its appearance may be unconscious." This has relevance for the management of countertransference, in that it implies the possibility of the analyst's understanding of the function of his countertransference reaction in the concrete analytic interaction, although the part of its origin stemming from his own past may remain concealed from him. Although the analyst may not be able to discover the past roots of a certain countertransference position, he may still become aware not only of the intensity and meaning of his emotional reaction but also to what extent this reaction is determined by the reality of both patient and analyst, and thus delimit the participation of the analyst's own past.

Reich (32, 33) separates "permanent countertransference" reactions from "acute countertransference" reactions, referring to the former as due to character disorder of the analyst, and the latter as determined by the different transference manifestations of the patient. She feels that permanent countertransference reactions are more difficult to deal with and ideally would require more analysis of the analyst. Yet, even countertransference reactions which reflect predominantly unresolved character problems of the therapist are intimately connected with the analytic interaction with the patient. Through the mechanism of emphatic regression in the analyst, certain conflicts of the patient may reactivate similar conflicts of the analyst's past; this regression may also reactivate previously abandoned, old character defenses of the analyst. Also, when strong negative countertransference reactions extend over a long period of time, whatever their origin, the analyst may revert to former neurotic patterns in his interaction with a particular patient which had been given up in his contact with other patients and in his life outside the analytic hours. The analyst, so to speak, becomes his worst in his relationship with a certain patient. Operating with a restricted concept of countertransference, it is tempting to write the whole reaction off as a character problem of the analyst and not consider sufficiently the specific way in which the patient provokes this reaction in the analyst.

One can describe a continuum of countertransference reactions ranging from that related to the symptomatic neuroses on one extreme to psychotic reactions at the other, a continuum in which the different reality and transference components of both patient and therapist vary in a significant way. As we proceed from the "neurotic pole" of the continuum toward the "psychotic pole," transference manifestations become increasingly predominant in the patient's contribution to the countertransference reaction of the therapist, displacing the importance of those countertransference aspects which arise from the therapist's past. When dealing with borderline or severely regressed patients, as contrasted to those presenting symptomatic neuroses and many character disorders, the therapist tends to experience rather soon in the treatment intensive emotional reactions having more to do with the patient's premature, intense and chaotic transference, and with the therapist's capacity to withstand psychological stress and anxiety, than with any particular, specific problem of the therapist's past. In other words, given reasonably well-adjusted therapists, all hypothetically dealing with the same severely regressed and disorganized patient, their countertransference reactions will be somewhat similar, reflecting the patient's problems much more than any specific problem of the analyst's past. Little (23) states that the more disintegrated the patient the greater is the need for the analyst to be well integrated, and that with psychotic patients, countertransference may have to do the whole of the work, with the underlying mechanism probably being identification with the patient's id. Will's (44) observations point in the same direction.

Thus, countertransference becomes an important diagnostic tool, giving information on the degree of regression in the patient and the predominant emotional attitude of the patient toward the therapist and the changes occurring in this attitude. The more intense and premature the therapist's emotional reaction to the patient, the more threatening it becomes to the therapist's neutrality, and the more it has a quickly changing, fluctuating, and chaotic nature—the more we can think the therapist is in the presence of severe regression in the patient. At the other extreme of the continuum, working with patients suffering from symptomatic neuroses and not too severe character disorders, such intensive emotional reactions of the therapist occur only temporarily, after a "build-up" over a period of time (generally past the initial period of treatment), and are of a much less threatening nature in so far as the stability and neutrality of the analyst are concerned.

## REGRESSION AND IDENTIFICATION IN THE COUNTERTRANSFERENCE

Fliess (5) states that the analyst's attitude is based on empathy, which in turn depends on a "transient trial identification" with the patient. Spitz (38) states that this process of trial identification may be considered a form of regression in the service of the ego. In a later article, Fliess (6) describes the transient trial identification when a major degree of regression in the countertransference occurs. Such regression motivates what Fliess calls "counteridentification" in the analyst, that is, an excessive and more permanent identification with the patient, involving a duplication in the analyst of some constituent identification of the patient. Counteridentification, he says, interferes permanently and severely with the analyst's work. Reich (33) elaborates on Fliess's concept, and states that countertransference is exactly what is implied in the failure of the transient trial identification and in the appearance of "counteridentification." She says that one consequence of this failure is the return of impulses following the Talion principle, the analyst now tending to return love for love and hate for hate, or to "get stuck" in an identification which gives him narcissistic gratification.

What Fliess considers a constituent identification in the therapist and a duplication of the equivalent constituent identification of the patient is related to what Erikson (3, 4) might call an early identity of the ego, that is, a precipitate of identifications involving very early object relationships. The danger of "getting stuck" in such a "constituent identification" has to do with the fact that it involves a repressed or dissociated early identity containing painful or traumatic interpersonal experiences that the ego could not integrate at the time when these early identifications occurred. This dissociated early ego identity also contains the derivatives of pregenital aggressive impulses, the identifications involved being of a very hostile nature because of the activation, projection, and reintrojection of these aggressive impulses in early interactions. Finally, this ego identity also involves archaic defensive operations of the ego, among which the mechanism of projective identification as described by Klein (20, 21), Heimann (17), and Rosenfeld (34, 35) seems to me to be of special interest.

I suggest in Chapter 1 projective identification may be considered an early form of the mechanism of projection. In terms of structural aspects of the ego, projective identification differs from projection in that the impulse projected onto an external object does not appear as something alien and distant from the ego because the connection of the self with that projected impulse still continues, and thus the self "empathizes" with the object. The anxiety which provoked the projection of the impulse onto an object in the first place now becomes fear of that object, accompanied by the need to control the object in order to prevent it from attacking the self when under the influence of that impulse. A consequence or parallel develop-ment of the operation of the mechanism of projective identification is the blurring of the limits between the self and the object (a loss of ego boundaries), since part of the projected impulse is still recognized within the ego, and thus self and object fuse in a rather chaotic way.

When very early conflictual object relationships become manifest in the transference, as frequently is the case in severe character disorders and more disorganized patients, the therapist is involved in a process of empathic regression in order to continue his emotional contact with the patient. At some point of regression, the therapist's own early identifications may become reactivated, together with the mechanism of projective identification. The therapist is now faced by several dangers from within: (i) the reappearance of anxiety connected with early impulses, especially those of an aggressive nature which now are directed toward the patient; (ii) a certain loss of his ego boundaries in the interaction with that particular patient; and (iii) the strong temptation to control his patient in consonance with an identification of him with an object of the analyst's own past.

Fliess and Reich point out the dangers of such developments in the countertransference. Yet, the emotional experience of the analyst at that point can also be useful. It may provide information of the kind of fear the patient is undergoing at that time and of the fantasies connected with it, because this process in the analyst has come about by "duplicating" a process in the patient. Also, when the therapist is able to face the awareness of his own aggressive impulses without feeling too threatened by them, this may provide the basis for a most helpful transmission of emotional security to the patient.

Fortunately, there are important compensatory mechanisms operating in the analyst. Some aspects of his ego remain intact, while others are involved in the empathic regression to the point where projective identifications occur as part of the activation of a "constituent identification" in him. What remains functioning at a mature level in the analyst is the main part of his ego, including his advanced ego identity and the adaptive and cognitive structures connected with it. Projective identification involves loss of ego boundaries in the analyst only in the sector of his interaction with the patient, and in compensation special stress is exerted on his more advanced ego functions which normally keep the ego boundaries well delimited.

Even with severely regressed patients, the therapist may have lost his "analytic objectivity" during the hour, but after leaving the sessions or a few hours later slowly regains his equilibrium. A process of working through occurs in the therapist by which the stable, adaptive and cognitive structures formed around his later and more mature ego identity act, one might say, in a supportive way toward the part of his ego in which primitive identifications, defense mechanisms, and impulses have been activated and where ego boundaries have become fluid. When this process fails, the analyst gradually loses his capacity to "snap out" of the countertransference position created by a certain patient. Over a period of days or weeks or months, the analyst finds himself more and more involved in a permanent emotional distortion in regard to that patient. Some symptoms of this "fixed" countertransference position are, other than those general symptoms of counter-transference reaction as mentioned in the literature (2, 15, 24, 26, 46), the development of suspiciousness in connection with that particular patient, even paranoid fantasies about unex-pected attacks from him and the form that these might take; a broadening of the inner reaction to that particular patient so that other people are involved in emotional reactions of the therapist which have to do with the relationship with that particular patient; and finally, the development of a kind of "microparanoid" reaction in the analyst. What has happened is that the working through within the analyst's ego has failed, mainly because the patient has successfully managed to destroy the more stable and mature ego identity of the analyst in their relationship, and the analyst is duplicating the patient's emotional position, without ego control.

We have to keep in mind that the analyst experiences a regression in the service of the ego, in order to keep in touch with the patient, and not as a reaction to the onslaught of the patient's behavior. The very tolerance and neutrality toward the patient, which is part of the analyst's efforts to keep in emotional touch with him, may reinforce the danger of the analyst's being unprotected in facing the inappropriate, especially aggressive behavior of borderline patients. In fact, some analysts especially interested in working with severely regressed patients unwillingly become the passive victims of the patient's behavior because so much of the analyst's efforts are absorbed by the struggle with his inner emotional reactions triggered off by that patient.

Ego identity depends on the continuity and confirmation of the self concept, and this holds true also for the analyst in his relationship with any patient. In the particular interaction with a patient who threatens the analyst both by inducing an important countertransference regression and by his behavior, this confirmation does not take place. The analyst's identity is continuously undermined and finally the very forces—the structures of his mature ego identity—which otherwise would compensate for his regression in the service of the ego are no longer available. From a practical point of view, this consideration underlines the importance of some external structure as part of the analytic work with severely regressed patients, a certain limit to what the patients can do and will be permitted to do, a limit to which the analyst must then firmly and unwaiveringly adhere, direct indications to the patient that certain behavior is not permitted in the hour, increased structure through hospitalization, or other adjunctive treatment devices.

Racker (31) further develops the utilization of countertransference reactions of the analyst to obtain information about the inner emotional constellation of the patient, classifying the identifications that take place in the countertransference reaction in two types: "concordant identification" and "complementary identification." "Concordant identification," according to Racker, is an identification of the analyst with the corresponding part of the patient's psychic apparatus: ego with ego, superego with superego. Under the influence of concordant identification, the analyst experiences in himself the central emotion that the patient is experiencing at the same time, and, Racker states, one might consider empathy as a direct expression of concordant identification.

"Complementary identification" (a concept first expressed by Helene Deutsch) refers to the identification of the analyst with the transference objects of the patient. In that position, the analyst experiences the emotion that the patient is putting into his transference object, while the patient himself is experiencing the emotion which he had experienced in the past in his interaction with that particular parental image. For instance, the analyst may identify with a superego function connected with a stern, prohibitive father image, feeling critical and tempted to control the patient in some particular way, while the patient may be experiencing fear, submission, or rebelliousness connected with his relationship to his father. Racker states that the analyst fluctuates between these two kinds of countertransference identifications.

It is precisely at the level of regression in which projective identification in the analyst occurs where the maximal development of complementary identification takes place. And, as stated, while the analyst is struggling with the upsurge of primitive impulses in himself and the tendency to control the patient as part of his efforts to control these impulses, he also thus reproduces the early relationship with a significant parental image of the patient. Thus a highly meaningful and specific situation is brought about which, when understood and worked through, may provide a cornerstone of the analytic work with that particular patient. Under these circumstances, the analyst may bring about fundamental changes in the ego structure of the patient through the corrective experience implied in the analytic situation. In contrast, the greatest danger confronting the analytic situation at this point is the threat of a traumatic repetition of the early frustrating childhood experience of the patient in the analytic situation. What the analyst does when he becomes unable to "snap out" of his countertransference bind is to re-establish the vicious circle of the patient's interaction with the parental image.

## SOME CHRONIC
## COUNTERTRANSFERENCE FIXATIONS

The reappearance of the previous neurotic character structure of the analyst, which had been generally abandoned but which becomes reactivated strongly in his dealings with a particular patient, has already been mentioned. Its reappearance frequently acquires a peculiar form, so that the analyst's particular pathology becomes molded in the therapeutic interaction and resembles the patient's own personality structure or complements it in such a way that the patient and therapist seem "prematched" to each other. This kind of chronic countertransference bind is, of course, very harmful to both participants. What happens in these circumstances is that the neurotic character defenses of the analyst are his safest defense against rather primitive anxieties that tend to emerge in his countertransference, and the peculiar complementary character formation that he establishes with the patient is the product of the mutual influence of projective identification in both of them.

With borderline and psychotic reactions, or at times of very deep regression in all kinds of patients in analytic treatment, conflicts around pregenital aggression have been found to occupy a central position (12, 13, 20, 22, 24, 36, 46). Throughout the literature, the examples of the most serious counter-transference disturbances and difficulties in handling it are those involving this kind of severe, archaic aggression in the patient, expressed typically by the therapist's emotional reaction to the patients who always seem to have to bite the hand that feeds them. Wherever one stands in regard to the controversy about whether there exists a death instinct or whether aggression is secondary to frustration, there is sufficient evidence that there is a strong predisposition in the psychic apparatus to turn aggression against the self. Aggression and aggression against the self are fused in the patient's efforts to destroy the analyst's capacity to help him, and both elements are also present in the analyst's emotional response to this situation.

In very simple terms, the experience of giving something good and receiving something bad in return, and the im-possibility of correcting such experience through the usual means of dealing with reality, is a dramatic part of the analyst's work. It resembles that other basic experience in which building up of what Erikson calls "basic trust" fails, or what Melanie Klein calls the "securing of the good inner object" fails. It is as if in his relationship with that particular patient, the analyst would have to lose confidence in the forces that could neutralize aggression; this in turn reactivates the analyst's masochism. Money-Kyrle (28) points out how the patient's aggression feeds into the superego functions of the analyst, provoking in him paranoid fears or depressive guilt.

In dealing with borderline personality organization, dedicated therapists of all levels of experience may live through phases of almost masochistic submission to some of the patient's aggression, disproportionate doubts in their own capacity, and exaggerated fears of criticisms by third parties. During these phases, the analyst comes to identify himself with the patient's aggression, paranoid projection, and guilt. Secondary defenses against this emotional position of the analyst, especially his characterological defenses, may obscure this basic situation.

The reappearance of the old neurotic character structure of the analyst in a peculiar complementary integration with the patient's characterological pathology is one form this chronic countertransference bind may take. One other frequent secondary defense is a narcissistic withdrawal or detachment of the therapist from the patient, so that empathy is also lost and the possibility of continuing an analytic approach with that patient is threatened. There are cases which are discontinued, emotionally speaking, quite some time before an unsuccessful termination actually occurs. One other defensive solution, perhaps more pathological than the one mentioned, is the narcissistic withdrawal of the analyst from reality, with the appearance of unrealistic certainty of being able to help this patient (one might say, the reappearance of archaic omnipotence). The therapist now tends to establish himself in a kind of island with such a particular patient, helps the patient to deflect his aggression from the analyst to external objects, and absorbs some of this aggression in masochistic submission to the patient, rationalized as "total dedication," which also provides some narcissistic gratification. After a period of time this latter defensive operation tends to break down, frequently in a rather abrupt way, after which the symptomatology of the patient reappears and simultaneously treatment often comes to an end. Such a "Messianic spirit" is quite different from authentic concern for the patient, because mature concern has to include reality.

Narcissistic withdrawal from the patient in the form of passive indifference or inner abandonment by the therapist, and narcissistic withdrawal from external reality in a complementary relationship with that patient, are potential dangers particularly in analysts whose narcissism has not been sufficiently worked through in their own analysis. Such analysts fall back more easily on their narcissistic character defenses; this happens not only because of the defensive return to old character patterns, but also because these character defenses themselves are so often directed against pregenital conflicts involving early aggression. Countertransference regression is especially threatening in these cases.

## THE IMPORTANCE OF CONCERN
## AS A GENERAL TRAIT OF THE ANALYST

One important force active in neutralizing and overcoming the effect of aggression and self-aggression in the counter-transference is the capacity of the analyst to experience concern. Concern in this context involves awareness of the serious nature of destructive and self-destructive impulses in the patient, the potential development of such impulses in the analyst, and the awareness by the analyst of the limitation necessarily inherent in his therapeutic efforts with his patient. Concern also involves the authentic wish and a need to help the patient in spite of his transitory "badness." On a more abstract level, one might say that concern involves the recognition of the seriousness of destructiveness and self-destructiveness of human beings in general and the hope, but not the certainty, that the fight against these tendencies may be successful in individual cases. In an analysis of the importance of hope as a basic human tendency, Menninger (27) describes hope as the manifestation of the life instinct against the forces of destructiveness and self-destructiveness. Money-Kyrle (28) says that concern for the patient's welfare stems from the combination of reparative drives in the analyst counteracting his early destructive tendencies, and from his parental identifications. Frank (7), in a different context, stresses the importance of the therapist's faith in himself and his technique as a prerequisite for therapeutic success. One might, in addition, describe concern also negatively, saying that it does not mean an abandonment of the analytic position, of the analyst's neutrality; concern for the patient cannot mean abandonment of reality either.

Psychoanalysts of different orientations would describe different genetic and dynamic conditions underlying the capacity for concern. Winnicott (47) suggests that concern stems from modulated and restricted guilt feelings. He suggests that the child's successful working through of repeated cycles of aggression, guilt, and reparation makes this development possible. Whatever its origin, the manifestations of the analyst's capacity for concern may be described in connection with the immediate reality of the treatment situation of any particular patient. In concrete terms, concern implies ongoing self-criticism by the analyst, unwillingness to accept impossible situations in a passive way, and a continuous search for new ways of handling a prolonged crisis. It implies active involvement of the therapist as opposed to narcissistic withdrawal, and realization of the ongoing need of consultation with and help from one's colleagues. The last point is important: willingness to review a certain case with a consultant or colleague, as contrasted with secrecy about one's work, is a good indication of concern.

There are professional pressures on the analyst tending to restrict his capacity to accept his limitations and his efforts to overcome them. During his analytic training, the candidate has to struggle with the temptation to use his patients narcissistically because their treatment may be a requisite for his graduation: the wish to keep a "good" patient and to get rid of a "bad" patient may represent a countertransference reaction strongly influenced by the candidate's wishes or fear in connection with the fulfillment of his requirements. Benedek (1) further describes some of the countertransference complications arising in the analyst within the setting of a psychoanalytic society. Pressures which act on the analyst when he is part of a complex treatment setting also influence his countertransference and may limit, realistically or in his fantasy, his inner freedom to deal with difficult treatment situations. Savage (37) mentions this point in connection with psychoanalytically oriented therapy of schizophrenic patients in a hospital setting. Main (25) conducted an illustrative research involving the study of countertransference reactions occurring in a hospital setting.

Not all difficulties or crises in treatment, however, involve countertransference binds. The therapist's lack of experience or of technical or theoretical knowledge has to be differentiated from his countertransference reaction. This is not easy because these two factors influence each other.

The analyst's insight into the meaning of his counter-transference reaction does not itself help the patient. What helps the patient is the analyst's using this information in his transference interpretations; the analyst's taking the necessary steps to protect himself and his patient from treatment situations which might realistically be impossible to handle; and the analyst's providing the patient, through their relationship, evidence of the analyst's willingness and capability to accompany the patient into his past without losing the sight of the present.

## SUMMARY

Contrasting views of countertransference and its clinical use are outlined. It is suggested that countertransference may be helpful in evaluating the degree of regression in the patient and in clarifying the transference paradigms in borderline personality organization..

Patients with the potential for severe regression in analysis or expressive psychotherapy tend to foster serious counter-transference complications, especially "counteridentification."

It is suggested that countertransference complications in the form of "counteridentification" are related to the partial reactivation of early ego identifications and early defensive mechanisms in the analyst. While these counteridentifications may be the source of important information about the analytic situation, they are also a serious threat to the analysis, and predispose the analyst to the development of "chronic countertransference fixation."

The following signs of chronic countertransference fixation are described: reappearance of abandoned neurotic character traits of the analyst in his interactions with a particular patient; "emotional discontinuation" of the analysis; unrealistic "total dedication"; "micro-paranoid" attitudes toward the patient. These countertransference complications present themselves especially in the treatment of patients with a potential for severe regression, particularly in borderline personality organization.

The importance of "concern" as a general trait of the

analyst, helpful in protecting him from the countertransference complications mentioned, is described. Some of the characteristics, preconditions, and realistic limitations of the development of concern are mentioned.

## BIBLIOGRAPHY

1. Benedek, T. Countertransference in the training analyst. *Bull. Menninger Clin.*, 18:12–16, 1954.
2. Cohen, M. B. Countertransference and anxiety. *Psychiatry*, 15:231–243, 1952.
3. Erikson, E. H., Growth and crises of the healthy personality (1950). In: *Identity and the Life Cycle* [*Psychological Issues*, 1:50–100]. New York: International Universities Press, 1959.
4. Erikson, E. H. The problem of ego identity. *J. Am. Psychoanal. Assoc.*, 4:56–121, 1956.
5. Fliess, R. The metapsychology of the analyst. *Psychoanal. Quart.*, 11:211–227, 1942.
6. Fliess, R. Countertransferences and counteridentification. *J. Am. Psychoanal. Assoc.*, 1:268–284, 1953.
7. Frank, J. D. The dynamics of the psychotherapeutic relationship. *Psychiatry*, 22:17–39, 1959.
8. Freud, S. The future prospects of psycho-analytic therapy (1910). *Standard Edition*, 11:139–151. London: Hogarth Press, 1957.
9. Freud, S. Recommendations for physicians on the psycho-analytic method of treatment (1912). *Standard Edition*, 12:109–120. London: Hogarth Press, 1958.
10. Freud, S. *Psychoanalysis and Faith: The Letters of Sigmund Freud and Oskar Pfister*, ed. H. Meng & E. L. Freud. New York: Basic Books, 1963, p. 113.
11. Fromm-Reichmann, F. *Principles of Intensive Psychotherapy*. Chicago: University of Chicago Press, 1950.
12. Fromm-Reichmann, F. Some aspects of psychoanalytic psychotherapy with schizophrenics. In: *Psychotherapy with Schizophrenics*, ed. E. B. Brody & F. C. Redlich. New York: International Universities Press, 1952.
13. Fromm-Reichmann, F. Basic problems in the psychotherapy of schizophrenia. *Psychiatry*, 21:1–6, 1958.
14. Gitelson, M. The emotional position of the analyst in the psycho-analytic situation. *Int. J. Psychoanal.*, 33:1–10, 1952.
15. Glover, E. *The Technique of Psycho-Analysis*. New York: International Universities Press, 1955.
16. Heimann, P. On counter-transference. *Int. J. Psychoanal.*, 31:81–84, 1950.
17. Heimann, P. A combination of defence mechanisms in paranoid states. In: *New Directions in Psycho-Analysis*, ed. M. Klein, P. Heimann, & R. E. Money-Kyrle. London: Tavistock Publications, 1955, pp. 240–265.
18. Heimann, P. Countertransference. *Brit. J. Med. Psychol.*, 33:9–15, 1960.
19. Kernberg, O. Manejo de la contratransferencia en la escuela analitica de Washington. Presented to the Chilean Society of Psychoanalysis, December, 1960.
20. Klein, M. Notes on some schizoid mechanisms. *Int. J. Psychoanal.*, 27:99–110, 1946.
21. Klein, M. On identification. In: *New Directions in Psycho-Analysis*, ed. M. Klein, P. Heimann, & R. E. Money-Kyrle. London: Tavistock Publications, 1955, pp. 309–345.
22. Lidz, R. W. & Lidz, T. Therapeutic considerations arising from the intense

symbiotic needs of schizophrenic patients. In: *Psychotherapy with Schizophrenics*, ed. E. B. Brody & F. C. Redlich. New York: International Universities Press, 1952.

23.   Little, M. Countertransference and the patient's response to it. *Int. J. Psychoanal.*, 32:32–40, 1951.

24.   Little, M. Countertransference. *Brit. J. Med. Psychol.*, 33:29–31, 1960.

25.   Main, T. F. The ailment. *Brit. J. Med. Psychol.*, 30:129–145, 1957.

26.   Menninger, K. A. *Theory of Psychoanalytic Technique*. New York: Basic Books, 1958.

27.   Menninger, K. A. Hope. *Amer. J. Psychiat.*, 116:481–491, 1959.

28.   Money-Kyrle, R. E. Normal countertransference and some of its deviations. *Int. J. Psychoanal.*, 37:360–366, 1956.

29.   Orr, D. W. Transference and countertransference: a historical survey. *J. Am. Psychoanal. Assoc.*, 2:621–670, 1954.

30.   Racker, H. A contribution to the problem of countertransference. *Int. J. Psychoanal.*, 34:313–324, 1953.

31.   Racker, H. The meaning and uses of countertransference. *Psychoanal. Quart.*, 26:303–357, 1957.

32.   Reich, A. On countertransference. *Int. J. Psychoanal.*, 32:25–31, 1951.

33.   Reich, A. Further remarks on countertransference. *Int. J. Psychoanal.*, 41:389–395, 1960.

34.   Rosenfeld, H. Remarks on the relation of male homosexuality to paranoia, paranoid anxiety and narcissism. *Int. J. Psychoanal.*, 30:36–47, 1949.

35.   Rosenfeld, H. Transference-phenomena and transference-analysis in an acute catatonic schizophrenic patient. *Int. J. Psychoanal.*, 33:457–464, 1952.

36.   Rosenfeld, H. Notes on the psychoanalysis of the super-ego conflict in an acute schizophrenic patient. In: *New Directions in Psycho-Analysis*, ed. M. Klein, P. Heimann, & R. E. Money-Kyrle. London: Tavistock Publications, 1955, pp. 180–219.

37.   Savage, C. Countertransference in the therapy of schizophrenics. *Psychiatry*, 24:53–60, 1961.

38.   Spitz, R. A. Countertransference: comments on its varying role in the analytic situation. *J. Am. Psychoanal. Assoc.*, 4:256–265, 1956.

39.   Sullivan, H. S. *Conceptions of Modern Psychiatry*. New York: Norton, 1953.

40.   Sullivan, H. S. *The Interpersonal Theory of Psychiatry*. New York: Norton, 1953.

41.   Thompson, C. M. Countertransference. *Samiksa*, 6:205–211, 1952.

42.   Tower, L. E. Countertransference. *J. Am. Psychoanal. Assoc.*, 4:224–255, 1956.

43.   Weigert, E. Contribution to the problem of terminating psychoanalyses. *Psychoanal. Quart.*, 21:465–480, 1952.

44.   Will, O. A. Human relatedness and the schizophrenic reaction. *Psychiatry*, 22:205–223, 1959.

45.   Winnicott, D. W. Hate in the countertransference. *Int. J. Psychoanal.*, 30:69–75, 1949.

46.   Winnicott, D. W. Countertransference. *Brit. J. Med. Psychol.*, 33:17–21, 1960.

47.   Winnicott, D. W. The development of the capacity for concern. *Bull. Menninger Clin.*, 27:167–176, 1963.

# Three

# General Principles of Treatment

## INTRODUCTION

This chapter continues the discussion of borderline personality organization. Elsewhere (15), I suggested that there exist two levels of ego organization resulting from the degree of synthesis of "identification systems." The term "identification systems" was used to include introjections, identifications, and ego identity as a progressive sequence in the process of internalization of object relationships. The organization of identification systems takes place first at a basic level of ego functioning at which primitive dissociation or "splitting" is the crucial mechanism for the defensive organization of the ego. Later, a second, more advanced level of defensive organization of the ego is reached, at which repression becomes the central mechanism replacing splitting. Splitting can be defined, in this restricted sense, as the active process of keeping apart identification systems of opposite quality.

I also suggested that patients with so-called "borderline" personality disorders present a pathological fixation at the lower level of ego organization, at which splitting and other related defensive mechanisms predominate. The persistence of the lower level of ego organization itself interferes with the normal development and integration of identification systems and, therefore, also with the normal development of the ego and superego.

In the first chapter, the term "borderline personality

organization" for these conditions instead of "borderline states," or other nomenclature, was used because it appears that these patients present a rather specific, quite stable, pathological personality organization rather than transitory states on the road from neurosis to psychosis, or from psychosis to neurosis. The clinical syndromes which reflect such borderline personality organization seem to have in common: (i) typical symptomatic constellations, (ii) typical constellations of defensive operations of the ego, (iii) typical pathology of internalized object relations, and (iv) characteristic instinctual vicissitudes. Under severe stress or under the effect of alcohol or drugs, transient psychotic episodes may develop in these patients; these psychotic episodes usually improve with relatively brief but well structured treatment approaches. When psychoanalysis is attempted, these patients may develop a particular loss of reality-testing and even delusional ideas restricted to the transference situation—they develop a transference psychosis rather than a transference neurosis.

In the first chapter the analysis of the structural characteristics of borderline personality organization was emphasized. Structural analysis referred to two issues: (i) ego strength and the characteristic defensive operations of the ego of these patients, and (ii) the pathology of their internalized object relationships. In regard to the first issue, in the borderline personality organization there are nonspecific manifestations of ego weakness, represented especially by a lack of anxiety tolerance, a lack of impulse control, and a lack of developed sublimatory channels. In addition, there are specific aspects of ego weakness: particular defenses in these patients bring about distortions in ego functioning which clinically also manifest themselves as ego weakness. The implication of this observation is that the therapeutic undoing of these particular defenses may actually strengthen the ego, rather than create further ego weakness. Splitting, primitive idealization, early forms of projection (especially projective identification), denial, and omnipotence constitute characteristic defense constellations in patients with borderline personality organization.

In regard to the second issue involved in the structural

analysis of these patients, namely the pathology of their internalized object relationships, I attempted to trace the origin of that pathology, as well as its consequences for ego and superego development, with special stress on the syndrome of identity diffusion.

Finally, I suggested that in borderline patients there is an excessive development of pregenital and, especially, oral aggression which tends to induce premature development of oedipal strivings, and as a consequence, there is a particular pathological condensation of pregenital and genital aims under the overriding influence of aggressive needs. It is this constellation of instinctual conflicts which determines the peculiar characteristics of the transference paradigms of the patients that will be discussed below.

In the present chapter I shall examine the difficulties of the treatment of these patients, and present some general propositions about psychotherapeutic strategy with them. A general outline of these propositions follows.

— Many patients with borderline personality organization do not tolerate the regression within a psychoanalytic treatment, not only because of their ego weakness and their proneness to develop transference psychosis, but also, and very predominantly, because the acting out of their instinctual conflicts within the transference gratifies their pathological needs and blocks further analytic progress. What appears on the surface as a process of repetitive "working through" is in reality a quite stable compromise formation centered in acting out of the transference within the therapeutic relationship.

Efforts to treat these patients with supportive psy-chotherapy frequently fail. Supportive psychotherapy aims at reinforcing the defensive organization of the patient, tries to prevent the emergence of primitive transference paradigms, and tries to build up a working relationship in order to help the patient achieve more adaptive patterns of living. Such an approach prevents regression within the transference; transference psychosis does not develop; and the kind of therapeutic stalemate previously mentioned is avoided. However, a supportive approach frequently fails because the characteristic defenses predominating in these patients interfere with the building up of a working relationship, the "therapeutic alliance" (38; 51). The negative transference aspects, especially the extremely severe latent negative transference dispositions, tend to mobilize even further the pathological defenses of these patients. The final outcome of such an approach is often the splitting up of the negative transference, much acting out outside the treatment hours, and emotional shallowness in the therapeutic situation. The "emptiness" of the therapeutic interaction over long periods of time may be a consequence of such a supportive approach, and this emptiness also tends in itself to produce therapeutic stalemates. In this case, instead of the turbulent, repetitive acting out of the transference within the hours, a situation develops in which the therapist attempts to provide support, which the patient seems incapable of integrating.

In most patients with borderline personality organization, a special form of modified analytic procedure or psychoanalytic psychotherapy may be indicated. This psychotherapy differs both from the classical psychoanalytic procedure, and from the more usual forms of expressive and supportive psychoanalytically oriented psychotherapies. Following Eissler (3), this psychotherapeutic procedure can be described as representing the introduction of several "parameters of technique" into the psychoanalytic situation, without expecting them to be fully resolved. The term "modification of technique" seems preferable to that of "parameter of technique," when such modification is introduced into a treatment situation that corresponds to a psychoanalytic psychotherapy rather than to a classical psychoanalysis (7).

The main characteristics of this proposed modification in the psychoanalytic procedure are: (i) systematic elaboration of the manifest and latent negative transference without attempting to achieve full genetic reconstructions on the basis of it, followed by "deflection" of the manifest negative transference away from the therapeutic interaction through systematic examination of it in the patient's relations with others; (ii) confrontation with and interpretation of those pathological defensive operations which characterize borderline patients, as they enter the negative transference; (iii) definite structuring of the therapeutic situation with as active measures as necessary in order to block the acting out of the transference within the therapy itself (for example, by establishing limits under which the treatment is carried out, and providing strict limits to nonverbal aggression permitted in the hours); (iv) utilization of environmental structuring conditions, such as hospital, day hospital. foster home, etc., if acting out outside of the treatment hours threatens to produce a chronically stable situation of pathological instinctual gratification; (v) selective focusing on all those areas within the transference and the patient's life which illustrate the expression of pathological defensive operations as they induce ego weakening and imply reduced reality testing; (vi) utilization of the positive transference manifestations for maintenance of the therapeutic alliance, and only partial confrontation of the patient with those defenses which protect the positive transference; (vii) fostering more appropriate expressions in reality for those sexual conflicts which, through the pathological condensation of pregenital aggression and genital needs, interfere with the patient's adaptation; in other terms, "freeing" the potential for more mature genital development from its entanglements with pregenital aggression.

## REVIEW OF THE PERTINENT LITERATURE

A general review of the literature on borderline conditions is included in Chapter 1. From the point of view of the treatment of borderline conditions, Knight (18, 19) and Stone (42) present the most comprehensive overview. The main question raised in the literature is whether these patients can be treated by psychoanalysis or whether they require some form of psychotherapy. Intimately linked with this question is the delimitation of what is psychoanalysis and what is not. Thus, for example, Fromm-Reichmann (6), who has contributed significantly to the treatment of borderline and psychotic patients, implies that the psychoanalytic procedure may be used for such patients, but she extends the concept of what is referred to as psychoanalysis to include what many other authors would definitely consider analytically oriented psychotherapy.

Gill (8, 9) has attempted to delimit classical psychoanalysis from analytically oriented psychotherapies, stating that psychoanalysis, in a strict sense, involves consistent adherence by the analyst to a position of neutrality (and neutrality, he rightly states, does not mean mechanical rigidity of behavior with suppression of any spontaneous responses). He believes that psychoanalysis requires the development of a full, regressive transference neurosis and that the transference must be resolved by techniques of interpretation alone. In contrast, Gill further states, analytically oriented psychotherapies imply less strict adherence to neutrality; they imply recognition of transference phenomena and of transference resistance, but they use varying degrees of interpretation of these phenomena without permitting the development of a full-fledged transference neurosis, and they do not imply resolution of the transference on the basis of interpretation alone.

This delimitation is a useful one but exception can be taken to Gill's (9) implication that in psychoanalysis the analyst "actively produces" the regressive transference neurosis. In agreement with Macalpine (25), Gill (9) states that "the analytic situation is specifically designed to enforce a regressive transference neurosis." However, the analytic situation permits the development of the regressive pull inherent in the emergence of the repressed, pathogenic childhood conflicts. Macalpine's description of what she calls the regressive, infantile setting of the analytic situation seriously neglects the progressive elements given in that situation, such as the respect of the analyst for the patient's material, for his independence, and the implicit trust and confidence the analyst has for the patient's capacity to mature, and to develop his own solutions (46).

To return to the main point, Gill's definition is very helpful in differentiating psychoanalysis proper from the psychoanalytically oriented or exploratory psychotherapies. Eissler (3) has further clarified this issue in his discussion of the "parameters of technique," which imply modifications of the analytic setting usually necessary in patients with severe ego distortions. He suggests that the treatment still remains psychoanalysis if such parameters are introduced only when indispensable, not transgressing any unavoidable minimum, and when they are used only under circumstances which permit their self-elimination, their resolution through interpretation before termination of the analysis itself. Actually, as Gill (9) points out, this involves the possibility of converting a psychotherapy into analysis. Additional clarifications of the differences between psychoanalysis and other related psychotherapies can be found in papers by Stone (41), Bibring (1), and Wallerstein and Robbins (47).

From the viewpoint of Gill's delimitation of psychoanalysis, it appears that authors dealing with the problem of the treatment of borderline conditions may be placed on a continuum ranging from those who recommend psychoanalysis, to those who believe that psychotherapy rather than psychoanalysis, and especially a supportive form of psychotherapy, is the treatment of choice. Somewhere in the middle of this continuum there are those who believe that some patients presenting borderline personality organization may still be analyzed while others would require expressive psychotherapy; and also there are those who do not sharply differentiate between psychoanalysis and psychotherapy.

The first detailed references in the literature to the therapeutic problems with borderline patients were predominantly on the side of recommending modified psychotherapy with supportive implications, in contrast to classical psychoanalysis. Stern (39, 40) recommends an expressive approach, with a constant focus on the transference rather than on historical material, and with constant efforts to reduce the clinging, childlike dependency of the patient on the analyst. He feels that these patients need a new and realistic relationship, in contrast to the traumatic ones of their childhood; he believes that such patients can only gradually develop the capacity to establish a transference neurosis similar to that of the usual analytic patient. He concludes that analysis may and should be attempted only at later phases of their treatment. Schmideberg (35) recommends an approach probably best designated as expressive psychotherapy, and is of the opinion that these patients cannot be treated by classical analysis. Knight's (18, 19) important contributions to the psychotherapeutic strategy with borderline cases lean definitely in the direction of the purely supportive approach, on one extreme of the continuum. He stresses the importance of strengthening the ego of these patients, and of respecting their neurotic defenses; he considers "deep interpretations" dangerous because of the regressive pull that such interpretations have, and because the weak ego of these patients makes it hard enough for them to keep functioning on a secondary process level. He stresses the importance of structure, both within the psychotherapeutic setting and in the utilization of the hospital and day hospital, as part of the total treatment program for such patients.

Somewhere toward the middle of the spectrum are the approaches recommended by Stone (42) and Eissler (3). Stone feels that borderline patients may need preparatory psychotherapy but that at least some of these patients may be treated with classical psychoanalysis either from the beginning of treatment or after some time to build up a working relationship with the therapist. Stone also agrees with Eissler that analysis can be attempted at later stages of treatment with such patients only if the previous psychotherapy has not created transference distortions of such magnitude that the parameters of technique involved cannot be resolved through interpretation. Eissler suggested that in some cases it might be necessary to change analysts for the second phase of the treatment. Glover (10) implies that at least some of these cases are "moderately accessible" to psychoanalysis.

At the other end of the spectrum are a number of analysts influenced to varying degrees by the so-called British school of psychoanalysis (2; 13; 21; 31; 36; 49, 50). These analysts believe that classical psychoanalytic treatment can indeed be attempted with many, if not all, borderline patients. Some of their contributions have been of crucial importance to the better understanding of the defensive organization, and the particular resistances characteristic of patients with borderline personality organization. Despite my disagreement with their general assumption about the possibility of treating most borderline patients with psychoanalysis, I believe that the findings of these analysts permit modifications of psychoanalytically oriented psychotherapies specifically adapted to the transference complications of borderline patients: I am referring here especially to the work of Little (22, 23, 24), Winnicott (49), Heimann (13), Rosenfeld (33), and Segal (36).

My suggestions for treatment outlined in the present chapter would appear in the middle zone of the continuum: in my opinion, in most patients presenting borderline personality organization a modified analytic procedure or special form of expressive psychoanalytic psychotherapy rather than classical psychoanalysis is indicated. This expressive approach should involve consistent interpretive work with those defensive operations reflecting the negative transference and contributing directly or indirectly to maintaining the patient's ego weakness. There are some patients with borderline personality organization for whom psychoanalysis is definitely indicated and I shall attempt to identify them.

## TRANSFERENCE AND COUNTERTRANSFERENCE CHARACTERISTICS

An important feature of the therapeutic problems with borderline patients is the development of transference psychosis. Several authors have described the characteristics of this transference regression, and a general summary about this issue can be found in a paper by Wallerstein (48).

Perhaps the most striking characteristic of the transference manifestations of patients with borderline personality organization is the premature activation in the transference of very early conflict-laden object relationships in the context of ego states that are dissociated from each other. It is as if each of these ego states represents a full-fledged transference paradigm, a highly developed, regressive transference reaction within which a specific internalized object relationship is activated in the transference. This is in contrast to the more gradual unfolding of internalized object relationships as regression occurs in the typical neurotic patient. Clinical experience reveals that the higher levels of depersonified and abstracted superego structures are missing to an important extent, and the same is true for many autonomous ego structures, especially neutralized, secondarily autonomous character structures. Thus the premature activation of such regressed ego states represents the pathological persistence of "nonmetabolized" internalized object relations of a primitive and conflict-laden kind.

The conflicts that typically emerge in connection with the reactivation of these early internalized object relations may be characterized as a particular pathological condensation of pregenital and genital aims under the overriding influence of pregenital aggression. Excessive pregenital, and especially oral, aggression tends to be projected and determines the paranoid distortion of the early parental images, particularly those of the mother. From a clinical point of view, whether this is a consequence of severe early frustration or actual aggression on the mother's part, whether it reflects excessive constitutional aggressive drive derivatives, whether it reflects a lack of capacity to neutralize aggression or lack of constitutionally determined anxiety tolerance, is not so important as the final result—the paranoid distortion of the early parental images. Through projection of predominantly oral-sadistic and also anal-sadistic impulses, the mother is seen as potentially dangerous, and hatred of the mother extends to a hatred of both parents when later they are experienced as a "united group" by the child. A "contamination" of the father image by aggression primarily projected onto mother and lack of differentiation between mother and father tend to produce a combined, dangerous father-mother image and a later conceptualization of all sexual relationships as dangerous and infiltrated by aggression. Concurrently, in an effort to escape from oral rage and fears, a "flight" into genital strivings occurs; this flight often miscarries because of the intensity of the pregenital aggression which contaminates the genital strivings (12).

The transference manifestations of patients with borderline personality organization may at first appear completely chaotic. Gradually, however, repetitive patterns emerge, reflecting primitive self-representations and related object-representations under the influence of the conflicts mentioned above, and appear in the treatment as predominantly negative transference paradigms. The defensive operations characteristic of borderline patients (splitting, projective identification, denial, primitive idealization, omnipotence) become the vehicle of the transference resistances. The fact that these defensive operations have, in themselves, ego-weakening effects (see 15, and Chapter 1) is suggested as a crucial factor in the severe regression that soon complicates the premature transference developments.

What is meant by "ego weakness" in borderline patients? To conceive of ego weakness as consisting of a rather frail ego barrier which, when assaulted by id derivatives, is unable to prevent them from "breaking through" or "flooding" the ego, appears insufficient. Hartmann and his colleagues' (11) and Rapaport's (28) analyses of the ego as an overall structure within which substructures determine specific functions, as well as being determined by them, convincingly imply that ego weakness should be conceptualized not simply as absence or weakness of such structures, but as replacement of higher-level by lower-level ego structures. One aspect of ego weakness in patients with borderline personality organization is evidenced by the "lower" defensive organization of the ego in which the mechanism of splitting and other related defenses are used, in contrast to the defensive organization of the ego around the "higher" mechanism of repression and other related defenses in neuroses (15). Also, the failure of normal integration of the structures derived from internalized object relationships (integrated self-concept, realistic object representations, integration of ideal-self and ideal-object representations into the ego ideal, integration of superego forerunners with more realistic introjections of parental images into the superego, etc.) interferes with the process of identity formation and individualization, and with neutralization and abstraction of both ego and superego functions. All of this is reflected in the reduction of the conflict-free ego sphere, clinically revealed in the presence of "nonspecific" aspects of ego weakness, particularly a lack of anxiety tolerance, a lack of impulse control, and a lack of developed sublimatory channels (see Chapter 1).

In addition, and most importantly from the point of view of psychotherapeutic intervention with these patients, "nonspecific" ego weakness is also evident in the relative incapacity of the patients with such a pathological ego organization tentatively to dissociate their ego into an experiencing and an observing part and in the related incapacity to establish a therapeutic alliance. The dynamics of borderline personality organization are much more complicated than what is conveyed by the metaphor of "flooding" the ego because of its "weak barriers," because underneath the "weaknesses" are extremely strong, rigid, primitive, and pathological ego structures.

Let us now return to the issue of transference regression in these patients. Once they embark upon treatment, the crucial decompensating force is the patient's increased effort to defend himself against the emergence of the threatening primitive, especially negative, transference reactions by intensified utilization of the very defensive operations which have contributed to ego weakness in the first place. One main "culprit" in this regard is probably the mechanism of projective identification, described by Melanie Klein (16) and others (13; 26; 32; 36). Projective identification is a primitive form of projection, mainly called upon to externalize aggressive self- and object-images; "empathy" is maintained with the real objects onto which the projection has occurred, and is linked with an effort to control the object now feared because of this projection (see Chapters 1 and 2).

In the transference this is typically manifest as intense distrust and fear of the therapist, who is experienced as attacking the patient, while the patient himself feels empathy with that projected intense aggression and tries to control the therapist in a sadistic, overpowering way. The patient may be partially aware of his own hostility but feel that he is simply responding to the therapist's aggression, and that he is justified in being angry and aggressive. It is as if the patient's life depended on his keeping the therapist under control. The patient's aggressive behavior, at the same time, tends to provoke from the therapist counteraggressive feelings and attitudes. It is as if the patient were pushing the aggressive part of his self onto the therapist and as if the countertransference represented the emergence of this part of the patient from within the therapist (26; 27).

It has to be stressed that what is projected in a very inefficient and self-defeating way is not "pure aggression," but a self-representation or an object-representation linked with that drive derivative. Primitive self- and primitive object-representations are actually linked together as basic units of primitive object relationships (15), and what appears characteristic of borderline patients is that there is a rapid oscillation between moments of projection of a self-representation while the patient remains identified with the corresponding object representation, and other moments in which it is the object-representation that is projected while the patient identifies with the corresponding self-representation. For example, a primitive, sadistic mother image may be projected onto the therapist while the patient experiences himself as the frightened, attacked, panic-stricken little child; moments later, the patient may experience himself as the stern, prohibitive, moralistic (and extremely sadistic) primitive mother image, while the therapist is seen as the guilty, defensive, frightened but rebellious little child. This situation is also an example of "complementary identification" (27).

The danger in this situation is that under the influence of the expression of intense aggression by the patient, the reality aspects of the transference-countertransference situation may be such that it comes dangerously close to reconstituting the originally projected interaction between internalized self- and object-images. Under these circumstances, vicious circles may be created in which the patient projects his aggression onto the therapist and reintrojects a severely distorted image of the therapist under the influence of the projected aggressive drive derivatives, thus perpetuating the pathological early object relationship. Heimann (13) has illustrated these vicious circles of projective identification and distorted reintrojection of the therapist in discussing paranoid defenses. Strachey (43) has referred to the general issue of normal and pathological introjection of the analyst as an essential aspect of the effect of interpretation, especially in regard to modifying the superego. This brings us to the problem of the influence of "mutative interpretations" (43) on the establishment and maintenance of the therapeutic alliance.

It was mentioned above that one aspect of ego weakness in patients with borderline personality organization is the relative absence of an observing ego. We may now add that this factor is compounded by the patient's distortion of the therapist resulting from excessive projective operations under the influence of the negative transference. To establish a therapeutic alliance with the therapist becomes equal to submission to him as a dangerous, powerful enemy, and this further reduces the capacity for the activation of the observing ego.

A repeated observation from the Psychotherapy Research Project at The Menninger Foundation, about the psychotherapy of borderline patients, is that a high price was paid when the therapist tried to stay away from the latent negative transference and attempted to build a therapeutic relationship with the patient in an atmosphere of denial of that negative transference. Frequently, under these conditions, the results were an emotionally shallow therapeutic relationship, and a pseudosubmission by the patient to what he experienced as the therapist's demands. Serious acting out or even interruption of the treatment followed periods in which the therapist thought that the patient was "building up an identification" with him, or "introjecting value systems" of the therapist, while the patient remained emotionally detached. The implication is that a consistent undoing of the manifest and latent negative transference is an important, probably indispensable, prerequisite for a broadening of the observing ego and for solidifying a therapeutic alliance.

The gradual broadening of the conflict-free ego sphere together with a broadening of the observing ego throughout therapy facilitates the disruption of the vicious circle of projection and reintrojection of sadistic self- and object-images in the transference. Strachey (43), in his description of mutative interpretations, identifies two phases of such interpretations: the first phase consists of a qualitative modification of the patient's superego; and the second consists of the patient's expressing his impulses more freely, so that the analyst can call attention to the discrepancy between the patient's view of him as an archaic fantasy object, and the analyst as a real external object. Strachey implies that first the patient permits himself to express his aggression in a freer way, as his superego prohibitions decrease; only then can the patient become aware of the excessive, inappropriate nature of his aggressiveness toward the external object and be able to acquire insight into the origin of his reaction; so the need to project such aggression once again onto the analyst gradually decreases. I would add to this description that, both in the phase of superego modification and in the phase of differentiation between the patient's fantasied object and the analyst as a different object, an observing ego is needed. Thus, the observing ego and interpretation of projective-introjective cycles mutually reinforce each other.

The discussion of projective identification leads to the issue of how the intensity of projection and reintrojection of aggressive drive-derivatives in the transference interferes with the observing functions of the ego; and this interference in itself contributes to the transference regression. Yet, the most important way in which projective identification contributes to the transference regression is the rapid oscillation of projection of self- and object-images; this rapid oscillation undermines the stability of the patient's ego boundaries in his interactions with the therapist.

Elsewhere (15, Chapter 1) I have commented on the differentiation between self- and object-representations which are part of early introjections and identifications. The organizing function of this differentiation of ego boundaries was stressed. In the psychosis, such differentiation between self- and object-images does not take place sufficiently and ego boundaries are therefore missing to a major extent. In contrast, in patients presenting borderline personality organization, this differentiation has taken place sufficiently, and therefore ego boundaries are more stable. The borderline patient is capable of differentiating the self from external objects, internal experience from external perception, and reality testing is also preserved to a major extent. This capacity of the borderline patient is lost within the transference regression.

Rapidly alternating projection of self-images and object-images representing early pathological internalized object relationships, produces a confusion of what is "inside" and "outside" in the patient's experience of his interactions with the therapist. It is as if the patient maintained a sense of being different from the therapist at all times, but concurrently he and the therapist were interchanging their personalities. This is a frightening experience which reflects a breakdown of ego boundaries in that interaction, and as a consequence there is a loss of reality-testing in the transference. It is this loss of reality-testing in the transference which most powerfully interferes with the patient's capacity to distinguish fantasy from reality, and past from present in the transference, and also interferes with his capacity to distinguish his projected transference objects from the therapist as a real person. Under such circumstances, the possibility that a mutative interpretation will be effective is seriously threatened. Clinically, this appears as the patient experiencing something such as, "Yes, you are right in thinking that I see you as I saw my mother, and that is because she and you are really identical." It is at this point that what has been referred to above as a transference psychosis is reached.

At this point, the therapist and the transference object become identical, the loss of reality-testing is reflected in the development of delusions, and even hallucinations may complicate the transference reaction. The therapist may be identified with a parental image: one patient felt that the therapist had become her father and would rape her. At other times the therapist may be identified with a projected dissociated self-representation: one patient became convinced that his analyst carried on an affair with the patient's mother and threatened to kill him.

"Transference psychosis" is a term which should be reserved for the loss of reality-testing and the appearance of delusional material within the transference that does not affect very noticeably the patient's functioning outside the treatment setting. There are patients who have a psychotic decompensation during treatment which is for all purposes indistinguishable from any other psychotic breakdown, and which affects their life in general as well as the therapeutic situation. It may be that regression in the transference did contribute to the breakdown, but it is questionable whether the term transference psychosis is always warranted under these conditions. In contrast, patients with a typical transference psychosis may develop delusional ideas and what amounts to psychotic behavior within the treatment hours, over a period of days and months, without showing these manifestations outside the hours. Hospitalization may sometimes be necessary for such patients, and at times it is quite difficult to separate a transference-limited psychotic reaction from a broader one. Nevertheless, in many borderline patients this delimitation is quite easy, and it is often possible to resolve the transference psychosis within the psychotherapy (14; 22; 29; 30; 48). Control of transference acting out within the therapeutic relationship becomes of central importance.

Transference acting out within the therapeutic relationship refers to the acting out of the transference reaction in the hours, within the treatment setting itself. As part of the transference regression, any patient may tend to act toward the therapist rather than reflect on his feelings about him. For example, rather than verbally expressing strong feelings of anger and reflecting on the implications and sources of this anger, a patient may yell at the therapist, insult him, and express his emotions in what amounts to direct actions rather than verbally, over a period of weeks and months. This, of course, is not exclusive to borderline patients, but in the typical analytic treatment of neurotic patients such acting out during the hours only occurs at points of severe regression after many months of build-up, and can usually be resolved by interpretation alone. This is not so in the case of patients with borderline personality organization, and the therapist's efforts to deal with acting out within the therapeutic relationship by interpretation alone, especially when it is linked with a transference psychosis, frequently appears to fail. This is partly so because of the loss of the observing ego by virtue of the projective-introjective cycles mentioned and because of the loss of ego boundaries and of the reality testing that goes with it. To a major degree, however, such unrelenting transference acting out is highly resistant to interpretation because it also gratifies the instinctual needs of these patients, especially those linked with the severe, preoedipal aggressive drive-derivatives so characteristic of them. It is this gratification of instinctual needs which represents the major transference resistance. Two clinical examples will illustrate this point.

A hospitalized borderline patient literally yelled at her hospital physician during their early half-hour interviews, and her voice carried to all the offices in the building. After approximately two weeks of such behavior, which the hospital physician felt unable to influence by any psychotherapeutic means, he saw her by chance shortly after leaving his office. He was still virtually trembling, and was struck by the fact that the patient seemed completely relaxed, and smiled in a friendly way while talking to some other patients with whom she was acquainted. Before entering the hospital, the patient had engaged in bitter fights with her parents for many years. In the hospital, all this fighting centered on her physician, while the hospital staff was surprised by the relaxation she showed with other personnel. It gradually became clear that her angry outbursts toward her physician reflected a gratification of her aggressive needs far beyond any available to her before she entered the hospital, and that this gratification in itself was functioning as the major transference resistance. When this was conveyed to her, and the hospital physician limited the amount of yelling and insulting that would be permitted in the hours, the patient's anxiety increased noticeably outside the hours, her conflictual patterns became more apparent within the hospital, and shifting attitudes in the transference became apparent, indicating movement in the therapy.

Another patient who was seen in expressive psychotherapy demanded an increase of his hours in an extremely angry, defiant way. Over a period of time it was interpreted to him that it was hard for him to tolerate the guilty feelings over his own greediness, and that he was projecting that guilt onto the therapist in the form of fantasies of being hated and depreciated by him. It was also interpreted that his demands to see the therapist more often represented an effort to reassure himself of the therapist's love and interest in order to neutralize his distrust and suspiciousness of the therapist's fantasied hatred of him. The patient seemed to understand all this but was unable to change his behavior. The therapist concluded that the patient's oral aggression was being gratified in a direct way through these angry outbursts, and that this development might contribute to a fixation of the transference. The therapist told the patient of his decision not to increase the hours and at the same time presented as a condition for continuing the treatment that the patient exercise some degree of control over the form and appropriateness of the expression of his feelings in the hours. With this modification of technique in effect, a noticeable change occurred over the next few days. The patient became more reflective, and finally was even able to admit that he had obtained a great satisfaction from being allowed to express intense anger at the therapist in such a direct way.

The acting out of the transference within the therapeutic relationship becomes the main resistance to further change in these patients, and parameters of technique required to control the acting out should be introduced in the treatment situation. There is a danger of entering the vicious circle of projection and reintrojection of sadistic self- and object-images of the patient as the therapist introduces parameters of technique. He may appear to the patient as prohibitive and sadistic. This danger can be counteracted if the therapist begins by interpreting the transference situation, then introduces structuring parameters of techniques as needed, and finally interprets the transference situation again without abandoning the parameters. Some aspects of this technique have been illustrated in a different context by Sharpe (37), who demonstrates how to deal with acute episodes of anxiety.

In many cases, the consistent blocking of the transference acting out within the therapeutic relationship is sufficient in itself to reduce and delimit the transference psychosis to such an extent that further interpretive work may suffice to dissolve it. The very fact that the therapist takes a firm stand and creates a structure within the therapeutic situation which he will not abandon tends to enable the patient to differentiate the therapist from himself, and thus to undo the confusion caused by frequent "exchange" of self- and object-representation projections by the patient. Also, such a structure may effectively prevent the therapist's acting out his counter-transference, especially the very damaging chronic counter-transference reactions which tend to develop in intensive psychotherapy with borderline patients (44).

Chronic countertransference fixations are to an important degree a consequence of the patient's success in destroying the analyst's stable and mature ego identity in their relationship (Chapter 2). In order to keep in emotional contact with the patient, analysts working with patients presenting borderline personality organization have to be able to tolerate a regression within themselves, which on occasions may reactivate the remnants of early, conflict-laden relationships in the therapist. Aggressive impulses tend to emerge in the analyst, which he has to control and utilize in gaining a better understanding of the patient. The extra effort needed for this work with the countertransference and the very tolerance and neutrality toward the patient which is part of the analyst's effort to keep in emotional touch with him, increase the stress within the therapist. At the same time, the aggressive behavior of patients with severe transference regression continuously undermines the analyst's self-esteem and self-concept in their interaction, and thus also the integrating ego function of the analyst's ego identity. Thus, the analyst may be struggling at the same time with the upsurge of primitive impulses in himself, with the tendency to control the patient as part of his efforts to control these impulses, and with the temptation to submit in a masochistic way to the patient's active efforts of control (26). Under these circumstances, pathological, previously abandoned defensive operations and especially neurotic character traits of the analyst may become reactivated, and the patient's and the analyst's personality structures come to appear as if they were "prematched" to each other, interlocked in a stable, insoluble transference-countertransference bind. The establishment and maintenance of structuring parameters or modifications of technique is, then, a fundamental, protective technical require- ment at that point and often has to be maintained throughout a great part of the course of the psychotherapy with borderline patients.

The issue of the indications for hospitalization, in order to provide this structure when it is not possible to provide it otherwise, is examined in Chapter 6. I would only stress that for some patients hospitalization is indispensable to creating and maintaining an environmental structure which effectively controls transference acting out.

Does the transference psychosis also represent the reproduction of unconscious, pathogenic object relationships of the past, and thus provide further information about the patient's conflicts? Sometimes it appears difficult to find evidence in the patient's past of interactions with the parental figures characterized by the violence and primitiveness of the transference reaction at the level of a regressive transference psychosis. At other times, the transference indeed appears to reflect actual, very traumatic experiences that these patients have undergone in their infancy and early childhood (7; 14). It is probable that the transference in all of these patients originates, to a large extent, in the fantasy distortions which accompanied the early pathogenic object relationships, as well as in the relationships themselves, and in the pathological defensive operations mobilized by the small child to extricate himself from the threatening interpersonal relationships. The transference psychosis represents a condensation of actual experiences, a gross elaboration of them in fantasy, and efforts to modify or turn away from them (17). This brings us to the technical problems of dealing with the pathological defensive operations characteristic of borderline patients which were mentioned above. Interpretive work attempting to undo these pathological operations as they enter the transference may further serve to resolve the transference psychosis and to increase ego strength.

Because the acting out of the transference within the therapeutic relationship itself appears to be such a meaningful reproduction of past conflicts, fantasies, defensive operations, and internalized object relationships of the patients, one is tempted to interpret the repetitive acting out as evidence for a working through of these conflicts. The repetition compulsion expressed through transference acting out cannot be considered working through as long as the transference relationship provides these patients with instinctual gratification of their pathological, especially their aggressive needs. Some of these patients obtain much more gratification of their pathological instinctual needs in the transference than would ever be possible in extratherapeutic interactions. The patient's acting out at the regressed level overruns the therapist's effort to maintain a climate of "abstinence." At the other extreme, to maintain such a rigid and controlled treatment structure that the transference development is blocked altogether, and especially the negative transference remains hidden, appears also to induce a stalemate of the therapeutic process, which is as negative in its effect as unchecked transference acting out. A "purely supportive" relationship, understood as a careful avoidance of focusing on the transference, often brings about a chronic shallowness of the therapeutic relationship, acting out outside the treatment hours which is rigidly split off from the transference itself, pseudosubmission to the therapist, and a lack of change despite years of treatment. There are patients who in spite of all efforts cannot tolerate transference regression, nor the establishment of any meaningful relationship, without breaking it off; nevertheless, the overall psychotherapeutic chances are much better when attempts are made to undo emotional shallowness and bring about a real emotional involvement within the therapy. The price is high, the danger of excessive transference regression unavoidable, but with a careful and consistent structuring of the therapeutic relationship it should be possible in most cases to prevent the development of insoluble transference-countertransference binds.

How much of a "real person" does the therapist need to appear to be in the patient's eyes? Several authors have stressed the importance of the therapist appearing as a "real person," permitting the patient to use him as an object for identification and superego introjection. Gill (9) has stated that " . . . we have failed to carry over into our psychotherapy enough of the nondirective spirit of our analysis." If what is meant by "real person" refers to the therapist's direct and open interventions, his providing structure and limits, and his active refusal to be forced into regressive countertransference fixations, then the therapist should indeed be a real person. However, if what is meant by "real person" is that the regressive transference reactions of borderline patients, their inordinate demands for love, attention, protection, and gifts should be responded to by "giving" beyond what an objective, professional psychotherapist-patient relationship would warrant, objection must be made to the therapist being such a "real person." What has been called the excessive "dependency needs" of these patients actually reflects their incapacity really to depend upon anyone, because of the severe distrust and hatred of themselves and of their past internalized object images that are reactivated in the transference. The working through of the negative transference, the confrontation of the patients with their distrust and hatred, and with the ways in which that distrust and hatred destroys their capacity to depend on what the psychotherapist can realistically provide, better fulfills their needs. Clinical experience has repeatedly demonstrated that the intervention of the psychotherapist as a particular individual, opening his own life, values, interests, and emotions to the patient, is of very little, if any, help.

The supposition that the patient may be able to identify himself with the therapist while severe, latent, negative transference dispositions are in the way, o are being acted out outside the treatment setting, appears highly questionable. The development of an observing ego appears to depend not on the therapist's offering himself as an unconditional friend, but as a consequence of a combined focus on the pathological cycles of projective and introjective processes, on transference distortion and acting out, and on the observing part of the ego itself. In this connection, what Ekstein and Wallerstein (4) have observed in regard to borderline children, holds true for adults also:

> This maintenance of the therapeutic relationship, often made possible by interpreting within the regression, thus lays the foundation for the new development of identificatory processes rather than the superimposition of an imitative facade . . .

A systematic focus on and analysis of the manifest and latent negative transference is essential to undo the vicious cycle of projection and reintrojection of pathological, early self- and object-representations under the influence of aggressive drive derivatives. This systematic analysis, together with the blocking of transference acting out and a direct focusing on the observing function of the ego, represent basic conditions for change and growth in the therapy. In addition, the interpretation of the negative transference should stop at the level of the "here and now," and should only partially be referred back to its genetic origins, to the original unconscious conflicts of the past. At the same time, the ventilation and interpretation of the negative transference should be completed by a systematic examination and analysis of the manifestations of these negative transference aspects outside the therapeutic relationship, in the patient's immediate life in all areas of interpersonal interactions.

The rationale for this suggestion is that the regressive nature of the transference reaction makes it hard enough for the patient to differentiate the therapist as a real person from the projected transference objects, and that genetic reconstructions, by further opening up regressive channels, may further reduce the reality-testing of the patient. This does not mean that the patient's past should not be drawn into the transference interpretation when that past is a conscious memory for the patient rather than a genetic reconstruction, and when it reflects realistic aspects of his past and preconscious fantasy distortions of it. Sometimes a reference to an experience from the past relating to what the patient erroneously perceives in the therapist now, may actually help the patient to separate reality from transference. The secondary "deflection" of the negative transference by incorporating its interpretation into the broader area of the patient's interactions outside the treatment and his conscious past tends to foster the patient's reality-testing and to provide considerable support within an essentially expressive psychotherapeutic approach.

The question of "insight" in borderline patients deserves discussion. Unfortunately, one frequently finds that what at first looks like insight into "deep" layers of the mind and into unconscious dynamics on the part of some borderline patients is actually an expression of the ready availability of primary process functioning as part of the general regression of ego structures. Insight which comes without any effort, is not accompanied by any change in the patient's intrapsychic equilibrium, and, above all, is not accompanied by any concern on the patient's part for the pathological aspects of his behavior or experience, is questionable "insight." Findings from the Psychotherapy Research Project at The Menninger Foundation encourage a restriction of the concept of insight, especially in applying it to the description of borderline patients. "Authentic" insight is a combination of the intellectual and emotional understanding of deeper sources of one's psychic experience, accompanied by concern for and an urge to change the pathological aspects of that experience.

The differentiation of "positive" and "negative" transference requires further scrutiny. To classify a transference as positive or negative is certainly a rather crude oversimplification. Transference is usually ambivalent and has multiple aspects within which it is often hard to say what is positive and what is negative, what is libidinally derived and what is aggressively derived. Patients with borderline personality organization are especially prone to dissociate the positive from the negative aspects of the transference, and often tend to produce an apparent "pure" positive or "pure" negative transference. It is important to undo this artificial separation, which is one more example of the operation of the mechanism of splitting in these cases. It would be misleading to understand the emphasis on a consistent working through of the negative transference as implying a neglect of the positive aspects of the transference reactions. On the contrary, emphasis on the positive as well as on the negative transference is essential for decreasing the patient's distorted self- and object-images under the influence of aggressive drive-derivatives, and for reducing his fears of his own "absolute" badness. The positive aspects of the transference have to be highlighted, therefore, in combination with the ventilation of the negative aspects of the transference. It is important to deal with the here-and-now of the positive as well as the negative aspects of the transference of borderline patients, without interpreting the genetic implications of their aggressive and libidinal drives (46). At the same time, a good part of the positive transference disposition available to the patient may be left in its moderate, controlled expression, as a further basis for the development of a therapeutic alliance and for the ultimate growth of the observing ego (34).

## PSYCHOTHERAPEUTIC APPROACHES
## TO THE SPECIFIC DEFENSIVE OPERATIONS

I referred earlier (15; Chapter 1) to the mechanism of splitting and other related ones (primitive idealization, projective identification, denial, omnipotence), all of which are characteristic of borderline patients. Here I will limit myself to stating how these defensive operations appear from a clinical point of view, and to suggest overall psychotherapeutic approaches in dealing with them.

### 1. Splitting

It needs to be stressed once more that the term "splitting" is used here in a restricted, limited sense, referring only to the process of active keeping apart of introjections and identifications of opposite quality; and this use of the term should be differentiated from its broader use by other authors. The manifestations of splitting can be illustrated with a clinical example.

The patient was a single woman in her late thirties, hospitalized because of alcoholism and drug addiction. She appeared to make remarkably steady progress in the hospital after an initial period of rebelliousness. She started psychotherapy several months before her discharge from the hospital, and then continued in outpatient psychotherapy. In contrast to her previously disorganized life and work, she seemed to adjust well to work and social relations outside the hospital, but established several relationships, each of a few months duration, with men who appeared to exploit her and with whom she adopted quite masochistic attitudes. The therapeutic relationship was shallow; the patient was conventionally friendly. A general feeling of "emptiness" appeared to hide a strong suspiciousness, which she emphatically denied and only later admitted to her former hospital physician but not to her psychotherapist. After a period of several months of complete abstinence, she got drunk, became quite depressed, had suicidal thoughts, and had to be rehospitalized. At no point did she let the therapist know what was going on and he only learned about this development after she was back in the hospital. Once out of the hospital again, she denied all transference implications and indeed all emotional implications of the alcoholic episode. It must be stressed that she had the memory of strong emotions of anger and depression during the days in which she was intoxicated, but she no longer felt connected with that part of herself and repeatedly expressed her feelings that this was simply not her, and she could not see how such an episode could possibly occur again.

This marked the beginning of a long effort on the therapist's part, over a period of several months, to bring the usual "empty," "friendly" but detached attitude of the patient together with her emotional upheaval during the alcoholic crisis, and especially with her efforts to hide that crisis from the therapist. Only after two more episodes of this kind, separated from each other by periods of apparently more adaptive behavior and good functioning over several months, did it become evident that she was experiencing the therapist as the cold, distant, hostile father who had refused to rescue her from an even more rejecting, aggressive mother. The patient, at one point, told the therapist with deep emotion how on one occasion, in her childhood, she had been left abandoned in her home, suffering from what later turned out to be a severe and dangerous illness, by her mother who did not wish her own active social life to be interfered with. The patient felt that if she really expressed to the psychotherapist-father how much she needed him and loved him, she would destroy him with the intensity of her anger over having been frustrated so much for so long. The solution was to keep what she felt was the best possible relationship of detached friendliness with the therapist, while splitting off her search for love, her submission to sadistic father representatives in her masochistic submission to unloving men, and her protest against father in alcoholic episodes during which rage and depression were completely dissociated emotionally from both the therapist and her boyfriends.

Efforts to bring all this material into the transference greatly increased the patient's anxiety; she became more distrustful and angry with the psychotherapist, the drinking reverted to her old pattern of chaotic involvements with men associated with excessive intake of alcohol, and all efforts to deal with this acting out through psychotherapeutic means alone failed. The decision was made to rehospitalize her. It should be stressed that from a superficial point of view the patient appeared to have done quite well earlier in the psychotherapy but now appeared to be much worse. Nevertheless, it was the psychotherapist's conviction that for the first time he was dealing with a "real" person. He hoped that a continuation of psychotherapy combined with hospitalization for as long as necessary might help her to finally overcome the stable, basic transference paradigm outlined above.

This case illustrates a strong predominance of the mechanism of splitting, its defensive function against the emergence of a rather primitive, predominantly negative transference, and its consequences evident in the shallowness and artificiality of the therapeutic interaction. A therapeutic alliance could not be established with this patient before the mechanism of splitting had been sufficiently overcome. Only consistent interpretation of the patient's active participation in maintaining herself "compartmentalized" finally could change the stable, pathological equilibrium. Consistent efforts had to be made to bridge the independently expressed, conflicting ego states, and the secondary defenses protecting this dissociation had to be sought out and ventilated in the treatment. With these patients it is not a matter of searching for unconscious, repressed material, but bridging and integrating what appears on the surface to be two or more emotionally independent, but alternately active ego states.

## 2. Primitive Idealization

Primitive idealization (Chapter 1) manifests itself in the therapy as an extremely unrealistic, archaic form of idealization. This idealization appears to have as its main function the protection of the therapist from the patient's projection onto him of the negative transference disposition. There is a projection onto the therapist of a primitive, "all good" self- and object-representation, with a concomitant effort to prevent this "good" image from being contaminated by the patient's "bad" self- and object-representations.

One patient felt that he was extremely lucky to have a psychotherapist who represented, according to the patient, the best synthesis of the "intellectual superiority" of one country where the therapist was born, and the "emotional freedom" of another country where the patient thought he had lived for many years. On the surface, the patient appeared to be reassured by a clinging relationship with such an "ideal" therapist, and protected against what he experienced as a cold, rejecting, hostile environment by a magical union with the therapist. It soon developed that the patient felt that only by a strenuous, ongoing effort of self-deception, and deception to the therapist about himself, could he keep his good relationship with the therapist. If the therapist really knew how the patient was feeling about himself, the therapist would never be able to accept him, and would hate and depreciate him. This, by the way, illustrates the damaging effects of overidealization for the possibility of utilizing the therapist as a good superego introjection, in contrast to an overidealized, demanding one. It later turned out that this idealization was developed as a defense against the devaluation and depreciation of the therapist, seen as an empty, pompous and hypocritically conventional parental image.

It is hard to convey in a few words the unrealistic quality of the idealization given the therapist by these patients, which gives quite a different quality to the transference from the other, less regressive idealization that may be seen in the usual neurotic patients. This peculiar form of idealization has been described as an important defense in narcissistic personality structures (20; 33). Psychotherapists who themselves present strong narcissistic traits in their character structure may at times be quite easily drawn into a kind of magical, mutual admiration with the patient, and may have to learn through bitter disappointment how this defensive operation may effectively undermine the establishment of any realistic therapeutic alliance. To firmly undo the idealization, to confront the patient again and again with the unrealistic aspects of his transference distortion, while still acknowledging the positive feelings that are also part of this idealization, is a very difficult task because underneath that idealization are often paranoid fears and quite direct, primitive aggressive feelings toward the transference object.

## 3. Early Forms of Projection, and Especially Projective Identification

Projective identification is central in the manifestations of the transference of patients presenting borderline personality organization. Heimann (13) and Rosenfeld (32) describe how this defensive operation manifests itself clinically.

One patient, who had already interrupted psychotherapy with two therapists in the middle of massive, almost delusional projections of her hostility, was finally able to settle down with a third therapist, but managed to keep him in a position of almost total immobility over a period of many months. The therapist had to be extremely careful even in asking questions; the patient would indicate by simply raising her eyebrow that a question was unwelcome and that therefore the therapist should change the subject. The patient felt that she had the right to be completely secretive and uncommunicative in regard to most issues of her life. She used the therapy situation on the surface as a kind of magical ritual and, apparently on a deeper level, as an acting out of her needs to exert sadistic control over a transference object onto which she had projected her aggression.

The acting out within the therapy hours of this patient's need to exert total, sadistic control over her transference object could not be modified. The therapist thought that any attempts to put limits on the patient's acting out, or to confront her with the implications of her behavior, would only result in angry outbursts on the patient's part and in interruption of the treatment.

This raises the question of how to cope with patients who begin psychotherapy with this kind of acting out, and who attempt to distort the therapeutic situation to such a gross extent that either their unrealistic demands are met by the therapist or the continuation of the treatment is threatened. Some therapists believe that it may be an advantage to permit the patient to start out in therapy without challenging his unrealistic demands, hoping that later on, as the therapeutic relationship is more established, the patient's acting out can be gradually brought under control. From the vantage point of long-term observation of a series of cases of this kind, it seems preferable not to attempt psychotherapy under conditions which are unrealistic. If the therapist fears that an attempt to control premature acting out would bring psychotherapy to an interruption, the necessity of hospitalization should be considered and this should be discussed with the patient. One indication for hospitalization is precisely that of protecting the beginning psychotherapeutic relationship with patients in whom regressive transference acting out cannot be handled by psychotherapeutic means alone, and where the confrontation of the patient with his pathological defensive operations threatens to induce excessive regression. Hospitalization under these circumstances may serve diagnostic as well as protective functions, and should be considered even with patients who, even without psychotherapy, would most likely continue to be able to function outside a hospital. If psychotherapy is indicated, and if the psychotherapy is unrealistically limited by premature acting out, hospitalization, even though stressful for the patient, is preferable to undertaking a psychotherapy within which the necessary structuring is interfered with by the same pathology for which definite structuring is indicated.

Projective identification is a main culprit in creating unrealistic patient-therapist relationships from the very beginning of the treatment. The direct consequences of the patient's hostile onslaught in the transference, his unrelenting efforts to push the therapist into a position in which he finally reacts with counteraggression and the patient's sadistic efforts to control the therapist, can produce a paralyzing effect on the therapy. It has already been suggested that these developments require a firm structure within the therapeutic setting, consistent blocking of the transference acting out, and in the most simple terms, a protection of the therapist from chronic and insoluble situations. To combine this firm structure with consistent clarifications and interpretations aimed at reducing projective mechanisms is an arduous task.

## 4. Denial

In the patients we are considering, denial may manifest itself as simple disregard for a sector of the patient's subjective experience or a sector of his external world. When pressed, the patient can acknowledge his awareness of the sector which has been denied, but cannot integrate it with the rest of his emotional experience. It is relatively easy to diagnose the operation of denial because of the glaring loss of reality-testing that it brings about. The patient acts as if he were completely unaware of a quite urgent, pressing aspect of his reality.

One patient, who had to meet a deadline for a thesis upon which his graduation and the possibility of a job depended, simply dropped the subject of the thesis in the psychotherapy sessions during the last two weeks before the deadline. He had discussed with his psychotherapist his fear of and anger toward the members of the committee in charge of examining his paper, and his denial here served the purpose, primarily, of protecting him against his paranoid fears of being discriminated against, and from those teachers whom he supposed wished to humiliate him in public. The therapist repeatedly confronted the patient with his lack of concern about finishing the paper and with his lack of effort to complete it. While interpreting the unconscious implications of this neglect, the therapist explored and confronted the patient with the many ways in which he was preventing himself from completing the paper in reality.

Denial can take quite complex forms in the transference, such as the defensive denial of reality aspects of the therapeutic situation in order to gratify transference needs.

One patient, in an attempt to overcome her anger about the analyst's unwillingness to respond to her seductive efforts, developed fantasies about the analyst's hidden intentions to seduce her as soon as she expressed her wishes for sexual intimacy with him in a submissive, defenseless way. At one point this fantasy changed to the fantasy that she was actually enjoying being raped by her father and by the analyst, and at one time intense anxiety developed in her, with a strong conviction that the analyst was actually her father, that he would sadistically rape her, and that this would bring about disaster. Out of the several implications of this transference development, the need to deny the reality of the analyst's lack of response to her sexual overtures, and her anger about this, seemed to predominate. The analyst pointed out to her that in one part of her she knew very well that the analyst was not her father, that he was not going to rape her, and that as frightening as these fantasies were, they still permitted her to deny her anger at the analyst for not responding to her sexual demands. The oedipal implications were excluded, for the time being, from his comment. The patient relaxed almost immediately and at this point the analyst commented on her reluctance to enter into an intimate relationship with her fiancé because of the fear that her unrealistic angry demands on him would stand in the way of her sexual enjoyment, and because her projection onto her fiancé of her own anger would turn the actual intimacy into a threat of sadistic rape for her. This opened the road to further insight about her denial of aggressive impulses as well as of reality.

This last example illustrates what the consistent working through of the pathological defenses which predominate in borderline patients attempts to accomplish. The working through of these defenses increases reality-testing and brings about ego strengthening, rather than inducing further regression. This example also illustrates the partial nature of the transference interpretation and the deflection of the transference outside the therapeutic relationship.

At times the patient especially needs to deny the positive aspects of the transference, because of his fear that the expression of positive feelings will bring him dangerously close to the therapist. The patient fears that such excessive closeness will free his aggression in the transference as well as the (projected) aggression of the therapist toward him. Schlesinger (34), in illustrating this particular use of denial, has suggested that denial in the area of positive transference reaction should be respected because it may actually permit the patient to keep himself at an optimal distance from the therapist.

## 5. Omnipotence and Devaluation

These two, intimately linked defensive operations of

omnipotence and devaluation refer to the patient's identification with an overidealized self- and object-representation, with
the primitive form of ego-ideal, as a protection against
threatening needs and involvement with others. Such "self-
idealization" usually implies magical fantasies of omnipotence,
the conviction that he, the patient, will eventually receive all the
gratification that he is entitled to, and that he cannot be touched
by frustrations, illness, death, or the passage of time. A
corollary of this fantasy is the devaluation of other people, the
patient's conviction of his superiority over them, including the
therapist. The projection of that magical omnipotence onto the
therapist, and the patient's feeling magically united with or
submissive to that omnipotent therapist, are other forms which
this defensive operation can take.

This defensive operation is actually related to the primitive
idealization mentioned above. The fractionating of the defensive operations which are characteristic of borderline patients
into completely separate forms may clarify their functioning
but it does necessarily oversimplify the issue. There are
complex intertwinings of all these defensive operations, and
they present themselves in various combinations.

A patient with severe obesity and feelings of intense
insecurity in social interactions eventually became aware of her
deep conviction that she had the right to eat whatever she
wanted and to expect that whatever her external form, she
would still be admired, pampered, and loved. She paid only lip
service to the acknowledgement that her obesity might reduce
her capability to attract men, and became very angry with the
therapist when the reality of this consideration was stressed.
The patient began psychotherapy with the assumption that she
could come for her appointment with the therapist at any time,
take home the magazines in his waiting room, and need not care
at all about leaving cigarette ashes all over the furniture. When
the implication of all this behavior was first pointed out to her,
she smiled approvingly of the therapist's "perceptiveness," but
no change occurred. It was only after the therapist made very
clear to her that there were definite limits to what he would
tolerate, that she became quite angry, expressing more openly
the derogatory thoughts about the therapist that com-

plemented her own feelings of greatness. The conscious experience of this patient was that of social insecurity and feelings of inferiority. Her underlying feelings of omnipotence remained unconscious for a long time.

## INSTINCTUAL VICISSITUDES AND PSYCHOTHERAPEUTIC STRATEGY

A predominant characteristic of the instinctual development of patients with borderline personality organization is the excessive development of pregenital drives, especially oral aggression, and of a particular pathological condensation of pregenital and genital aims under the overriding influence of aggressive needs. This instinctual development has direct relevance for the therapeutic approach to these patients. The therapist should remember that in the midst of the destructive and self-destructive instinctual manifestations are hidden potentials for growth and development, and especially that what appears on the surface to be destructive and self-destructive sexual behavior may contain the roots of further libidinal development and deepening interpersonal relationships.

There was a time when a typical misunderstanding of the implications of psychoanalytic theory and practice was the assumption that sexual activity in itself was a therapeutic factor. We have advanced a long way from such misunderstandings, and have learned that often what appears on the surface to be genital activity is actually in the service of aggressive, pregenital aims. With patients presenting borderline personality organization the opposite danger of seeing only their pregenital, destructive aims, to the neglect of acknowledging their efforts to overcome their inhibited sexual orientation, appears to be a frequent clinical problem.

A promiscuous, divorced, young woman, hospitalized after a psychotic regression which followed years of disorganized behavior, was restricted in the hospital from male patients. On several occasions a few minutes of unobserved time had been enough for her to have intercourse in an impulsive way with other patients, practically strangers. Over many months this patient was regularly controlled and in the sessions with her hospital physician the implications of her behavior were discussed only in terms of her "lack of impulse control" and her "inappropriate behavior." When a new hospital physician tried to evaluate further the implications of her sexual behavior, it evolved that her sexual activity had deep masochistic implications, and represented the acting out of her fantasy of being a prostitute. The hospital physician took the position that not all sexual freedom implied prostitution, and in discussing these issues with her, the patient became very angry with him stating that he was "immoral," and she became very anxious and very angry with him when he eliminated the restrictions. She then became involved sexually with several other patients in a provocative manner, all of which the hospital physician used further to confront her with the masochistic fantasies and the pattern of becoming a prostitute, and the implication of her submission to a primitive, sadistic superego which represented a prohibitive, combined father-mother image. She was finally able to establish a good relationship with one patient, with whom she fell in love, went steady for a two-year period, and whom she eventually planned to marry. During the latter part of these two years they had sexual intercourse, characterized by her being able for the first time in her life to have tender as well as sexual feelings toward just one man and by her taking precautions not to get pregnant, which was in contrast to her previous behavior.

To dissociate the normal, progressive trends within the pathological sexual behavior from its pregenital aims is easier said than done. This must be a continuous concern of the psychotherapist working with such patients.

## FURTHER COMMENTS ON THE MODALITY OF TREATMENT

This particular form of expressive, psychoanalytically oriented psychotherapy is a treatment approach which differs from classical psychoanalysis in that a complete transference neurosis is not permitted to develop, nor is transference resolved through interpretation alone. It is an expressive psychotherapeutic approach in that unconscious factors are considered and focused upon, especially in regard to the negative transference and to the consistent work with the pathological defenses of these patients. Parameters of technique or modifications of technique are used when necessary to control transference acting out, and although some of these parameters may be resolved during the course of the treatment itself, this is not necessarily possible nor desirable with all of them. There are also clearly supportive elements implicit in this approach. First, in the manipulation of the treatment situation, which the therapist has to undertake as part of the need to structure it. The frequency of the hours, the permissiveness or restriction in regard to out-of-hour contacts, the limits to which the patient may express himself, all may be considered as examples of factors which may be changed as the treatment demands. Second, clarifications of reality take up an important segment of the therapist's communications, and direct suggestions and implicit advice-giving are difficult to avoid under these circumstances.

The therapist should try to remain as neutral as possible, but neutrality here does not mean inactivity, and beyond certain degrees of activity on his part, the issue of whether the therapist is still neutral or not becomes academic. In general, it appears preferable to keep this kind of therapy in a face-to-face situation in order to stress the reality aspects of it, but there is nothing magical in itself about either lying on the couch or sitting in front of the therapist. There are treatments carried out on the couch which in effect are psychoanalytic psychotherapy rather than psychoanalysis.

The goal of ego strengthening is ever present in this expressive, psychoanalytically oriented treatment. The working through of the pathological defenses characteristic of the borderline personality organization permits repression and other related defenses of a higher level of ego organization to replace the ego-weakening, pathological defenses of the lower level: this in itself strengthens the ego. Conflict resolution is necessarily partial, but at times a great deal can be achieved with this kind of treatment approach.

One final and very important question remains. Are some

of these patients analyzable either from the beginning of the treatment, or after a period of preparatory psychotherapy of the type suggested? The differences of opinion in this regard were referred to above in the review of the literature. There are specific patients within the large group presenting borderline personality organization who appear to benefit very little from the expressive, psychoanalytically oriented treatment approach I propose, and where nonmodified psychoanalysis is the treatment of choice from the beginning. This is particularly true for patients presenting the most typical forms of narcissistic personality organization.

Such patients present an unusual degree of self-reference in their interactions with other people, a great need to be loved and especially to be admired by others, and present an apparent contradiction between a very inflated concept of themselves and an inordinate need for tributes from others. Superficially, these patients do not appear to be severely regressed and some of them may function very well socially; they usually have much better impulse control than the average patient presenting borderline personality organization. They may be quite successful and efficient. It is only their emotional life which, on sharper focus, appears to be shallow and reflects an absence of normal empathy for others, a relative absence of enjoyment from life other than from the tributes they receive, and a combination of grandiose fantasies, envy, and the tendency to depreciate and manipulate others in an exploitative way.

These patients usually have such solidified, functioning pathological character structures that it is very difficult to mobilize their conflicts in the transference using the therapeutic approach proposed in this paper. Many of these patients appear to tolerate classical psychoanalysis without undue regression. Some of them unfortunately not only tolerate the analytic situation but are extremely resistant to any effort to mobilize their rigid characterological defenses in the transference. Ernst Ticho (45) has suggested that there exists one group of indications for psychoanalysis which may be called "heroic indications." This indication is for patients in whom, although it seems more or less doubtful whether psychoanalysis would be of help, it seems reasonably beyond doubt that any treatment other than psychoanalysis would not be of help. Narcissistic personalities are part of this group. There are other authors who also feel that psychoanalysis is the treatment of choice for these patients, and who have contributed decisively to our understanding of the dynamics of these patients and the technical difficulties in their analyses (20; 33). In every patient presenting a borderline personality organization, at one point during the diagnostic examination the question of analyzability should be considered and psychoanalysis should be rejected only after all the contraindications have been carefully evaluated.

This chapter attempts to outline a general psychotherapeutic strategy with patients presenting borderline personality organization. The danger of such an outline is that it may be misinterpreted as a set of fixed rules, or that because of its necessarily comprehensive nature, it may appear too general. It is hoped that this outline may contribute to the overall frame of reference for therapists who are working with these patients and who are, therefore, well acquainted with the complex tactical therapeutic issues that each patient presents.

### BIBLIOGRAPHY

1.    Bibring, E. (1954). "Psychoanalysis and the dynamic psychotherapies." *J. Amer. Psychoanal. Assoc.*, 2.
2.    Bion, W. R. (1957). "Differentition of the psychotic from the non-psychotic personalities." *Int. J. Psycho-Anal.*, 38.
3.    Eissler, K. R. (1953). "The effect of the structure of the ego on psychoanalytic technique." *J. Amer. Psychoanal. Assoc.*, 1.
4.    Ekstein, R. and Wallerstein, J. (1956). "Observations on the psychotherapy of borderline and psychotic children." *Psychoanal. Study Child*, 11.
5.    Erikson, E. H. (1956). "The problem of ego identity." *J. Amer. Psychoanal. Assoc.*, 4.
6.    Fromm-Reichmann, F. (1950). *Principles of Intensive Psychotherapy* (Chicago: Univ. of Chicago Press).
7.    Frosch, J. Personal Communication.
8.    Gill, M. M. (1951). "Ego psychology and psychotherapy." *Psychoanal. Quart.*, 20.
9.    ———(1954). "Psychoanalysis and exploratory psychotherapy." *J. Amer. Psychoanal. Assoc.*, 2.
10.   Glover, E. (1955). "The analyst's case-list (2)." In: *The Technique of Psycho-Analysis*. (London: Bailliere; New York: Int. Univ. Press.)
11.   Hartmann, H., Kris, E. and Loewenstein, R. M. (1946). "Comments on the formation of psychic structure." *Psychoanal. Study Child*, 2.
12.   Heimann, P. (1955a). "A contribution to the reevaluation of the Oedipus complex: the early stages." In: *New Directions in Psycho-Analysis*, ed. Klein *et al.* (London: Tavistock: New York: Basic Books.)

13.    ———(1955b). "A combination of defence mechanisms in paranoid states." *ibid.*
14.    Holzman, P. S. and Ekstein, R. (1959). "Repetition-Functions of Transitory Regressive Thinking." *Psychoanal. Quart.,* 28.
15.    Kernberg, O. (1966). "Structural derivatives of object relationships." *Int. J. Psycho-Anal.,* 47.
16.    Klein, M. (1946). "Notes on some schizoid mechanisms." In: *Developments in Psycho-Analysis,* ed. Riviere. (London: Hogarth, 1952.)
17.    ———(1952). "The origins of transference." *Int. J. Psycho-Anal.,* 33.
18.    Knight, R. P. (1953a). "Borderline states." In: *Psychoanalytic Psychiatry and Psychology,* ed. Knight and Friedman. (New York: Int. Univ. Press, 1954.)
19.    ———(1953b). "Management and psychotherapy of the borderline schizophrenic patient." *ibid.*
20.    Kohut, H. (1968). "The psychoanalytic treatment of narcissistic personality disorder." *Psychoanal. Study Child* 23, 86-113.
21.    Little, M. (1951). "Countertransference and the patient's response to it." *Int. J. Psycho-Anal.,* 32.
22.    ———(1958). "On delusional transference (transference psychosis)." *Int. J. Psycho-Anal.,* 39.
23.    ———(1960a). "Countertransference." *Brit. J. Med. Psychol.,* 33.
24.    ———(1960b). "On basic unity." *Int. J. Psycho-Anal.,* 41.
25.    MacAlpine, I. (1950). "The development of the transference." *Psychoanal. Quart.,* 19.
26.    Money-Kyrle, R. E. (1956). "Normal countertransference and some of its deviations." *Int. J. Psycho-Anal.,* 37.
27.    Racker, H. (1957). "The meanings and uses of countertransference." *Psychoanal. Quart.,* 26.
28.    Rapaport, D. (1957). "Cognitive structures." In: *Contemporary Approaches to Cognition,* by Bruner *et al.* (Cambridge: Harvard Univ. Press, 1957.)
29.    Reider, N. (1957). "Transference psychosis." *J. Hillside Hosp.,* 6.
30.    Romm, M. E. (1957). "Transient psychotic episodes during psychoanalysis." *J. Amer. Psychoanal. Assoc.,* 5.
31.    Rosenfeld, H. (1958). Contribution to the Discussion on "Variations in classical technique." *Int. J. Psycho-Anal.,* 39.
32.    ———(1963). "Notes on the psychopathology and psychoanalytic treatment of Schizophrenia." In: *Psychotherapy of Schizophrenic and Manic-Depressive States,* ed. Azima and Glueck, Jr. (Washington: Amer. Psychiat. Assoc.)
33.    ———(1964). "On the psychopathology of narcissism: a clinical approach." *Int. J. Psycho-Anal.,* 45.
34.    Schlesinger, H. (1966). "In defence of denial." Presented to the Topeka Psychoanalytic Society, June 1966. (Unpublished.)
35.    Schmideberg, M. (1947). "The treatment of psychopaths and borderline patients." *Amer. J. Psychother.,* 1.
36.    Segal, H. (1964). *Introduction to the Work of Melanie Klein.* (London: Heinemann; New York: Basic Books.)
37.    Sharpe, E. F. (1931). "Anxiety, outbreak and resolution." In: *Collected Papers on Psycho-Analysis.* (London: Hogarth, 1950.)
38.    Sterba, R. (1934). "The fate of the ego in analytic therapy." *Int. J. Psycho-Anal.,* 15.
39.    Stern, A. (1938). "Psychoanalytic investigation of and therapy in the borderline group of neuroses." *Psychoanal. Quart.,* 7.

40.   ——(1945). "Psychoanalytic therapy in the borderline neuroses." *Psychoanal. Quart.*, 14.
41.   Stone, L. (1951). "Psychoanalysis and brief psychotherapy." *Psychoanal. Quart.*, 20.
42.   ——(1954). "The widening scope of indications for psychoanalysis." *J. Amer. Psychoanal. Assoc.*, 2.
43.   Strachey, J. (1934). "The nature of the therapeutic action of psycho-analysis." *Int. J. Psycho-Anal.*, 15.
44.   Sutherland, J. D. Personal Communication.
45.   Ticho, E. Selection of Patients for Psychoanalysis or Psychotherapy. Presented at the 20th Anniversary Meeting of the Menninger School of Psychiatry Alumni Association. Topeka, Kansas, May 1966a. (Unpublished.)
46.   Ticho, G. Personal Communication.
47.   Wallerstein, R. S. and Robbins, L. L. (1956). "The psychotherapy research project of The Menninger Foundation: IV. Concepts." *Bull. Menn. Clin.*, 20.
48.   Wallerstein, R. S. (1967). "Reconstruction and mastery in the transference psychosis." *J. Amer. Psychoanal. Assoc.*, 15.
49.   Winnicott, D. W. (1949). "Hate in the countertransference." *Int. J. Psycho-Anal.*, 30.
50.   ——(1960). "Countertransference." *Brit. J. Med. Psychol.*, 33.
51.   Zetzel, E. R. (1966). "The analytic situation." In: *Psychoanalysis in the Americas*, ed. Litman. (New York: Int. Univ. Press, 1966.)

# Four

# Prognosis

This chapter deals with the prognosis for intensive, long-term psychotherapeutic treatment of patients with borderline personality organization. In Chapter 3, I outlined a type of modified analytic procedure or psychoanalytic psychotherapy as the treatment of choice for patients with these conditions and pointed out that some of these patients are analyzable either from the beginning of the treatment or after a period of preparatory psychotherapy of the type suggested. The prognostic considerations outlined here may help in making decisions about long-term psychoanalytic psychotherapy and analyzability of patients with borderline personality organization.

This contribution incorporates the author's analyses of clinical data from the Psychotherapy Research Project of The Menninger Foundation (25, 19) and findings from the overall quantitative outcome studies of that Project (12, 2). I intend to examine the following elements relevant to prognosis: 1) the descriptive characterological diagnosis, 2) the degree and quality of ego weakness, 3) the degree and quality of superego pathology, 4) the quality of object relationships, and 5) the skill and personality of the therapist. I shall spell out which aspects of these elements are prognostically important and which are not relevant for the prognosis of these patients.

## THE DESCRIPTIVE CHARACTEROLOGICAL DIAGNOSIS

The descriptive diagnosis is a crucial prognostic factor for patients with borderline personality organization. This, however, is true mainly for the diagnosis of the patient's character pathology, and not for the diagnosis of his neurotic symptomatology; for neurotic symptoms appear at all levels of psychopathology, and some patients with severe character pathology present very few neurotic symptoms. Therefore, neurotic symptoms are not useful indicators of the severity of illness. Indications are that the prognosis is worse for borderline patients without neurotic symptoms. Especially in cases of severe character pathology, when the patient does not suffer from any neurotic inhibition or symptom, his motivation to seek help and persist in the treatment effort is less than in similar cases with some neurotic suffering.

We have found that the presence of anxiety is a good predictor for improvement in psychotherapy (2, 15), probably operating as a reinforcer of the patient's motivation for psychotherapeutic work. Clinically, however, the degree of anxiety or neurotic suffering in general, seems much less important than the degree of ego syntonicity or ego dystonicity of the character pathology. One might say that anxiety and suffering in general may bring the patient to treatment, and may help him stay in treatment; but the degree of ego syntonicity of his character pathology (partly a process variable, eventually depending on the patient-therapist relationship) will determine whether the patient will continue to want to get rid of his symptoms, or will prefer to get rid of the "threat" of treatment. In other words, the presence of anxiety is an initially favorable prognostic element for establishing a therapeutic relationship, but a more accurate prognosis requires that it be gradually replaced by the prognostic indicators derived from the patient's character pathology.

It has to be stressed, however, that while the intensity or type of neurotic symptomatology does not seem to have crucial *prognostic* value for patients with borderline personality organization, symptoms do have an important *diagnostic* value. In Chapter 1, I described the characteristics of neurotic symptoms which point to an underlying borderline personality organization, and included such symptoms with the "presumptive" diagnostic elements of borderline personality organization.

Returning to the diagnosis of the patient's character structure as an important prognostic element in borderline conditions, it is the *type* of character pathology which is prognostically important, in addition to the general importance of ego syntonicity or ego dystonicity of the character traits. It is certainly not enough to diagnose a patient as presenting "borderline personality organization." The predominant constellation of character pathology should always be included in the descriptive diagnosis, together with the predominant neurotic symptomatology.

## 1. Predominant Type of Character Constellation

It is important to diagnose as precisely as possible the type of character pathology that the patient presents. For example, a good descriptive diagnosis of a patient may read: "(1) depressive reaction with some anxiety symptoms; (2) infantile personality, with paranoid trends, in a borderline personality organization." A diagnosis formulated in this way has the advantage of providing immediate information about the structural and dynamic-genetic aspects of the diagnosis, in addition to the purely descriptive ones. The diagnosis of "borderline personality organization" involves such structural and genetic-dynamic considerations (Chapter 1). The specification of the type of character pathology also adds to the structural and genetic-dynamic analysis of the patient's pathology because different types of character pathology involve different levels of instinctual development, superego development, defensive operations of the ego, and vicissitudes of internalized object relationships (11).

When the pathological character constellation is diagnosed in terms of both the level of character pathology (11) and the predominant constellation of pathological character traits, the diagnosis has direct, intimate relevance to the prognosis and treatment. If the diagnosis involves the conclusion that one is dealing with a borderline personality organization, this immediately reflects the psychotherapeutic strategy indicated in that case (Chapter 3). What, then, are the prognostic implications for different types of character pathology found in patients with borderline personality organization?

a. Patients with *hysterical personality* functioning on a borderline level usually have a good prognosis for psychoanalytic psychotherapy; these patients frequently present a predominance of orally determined conflicts, generalized or partial areas of ego weakness, and a "double-layer of defensive operations" (11) which may be reflected in intensive shifts in the regressive levels during therapy hours, but which is eminently treatable in long-term, intensive psychotherapy. Some of these patients can be treated with unmodified psychoanalysis.

b. *Infantile personalities* also have a good prognosis for psychoanalytic psychotherapy (Chapter 3); classical psychoanalysis is usually contraindicated in these patients.

c. For *narcissistic personalities*, the prognosis depends on whether or not the borderline functioning is overt. Narcissistic personalities with overt borderline functioning do not have a good prognosis for such an expressive, analytically oriented approach; they may need a long preparatory period of a mostly supportive approach (for which I have found very little use in most other borderline conditions). In contrast, narcissistic personalities who do not function on an overt borderline level in spite of presenting structurally a typical borderline personality organization should be treated with psychoanalysis or, if not feasible, perhaps not at all (beyond whatever circumscribed, crisis oriented, short-term treatment may be indicated). These patients have a remarkable capacity for keeping emotional distance and avoiding involvement in the treatment process when their pathological defenses are not examined systematically as they enter the transference.

In a later chapter (see Chapter 8), I examine the treatment of narcissistic personalities and the differential diagnosis between such personalities and other types of narcissistic character defenses, and I propose a classification into three types of narcissistic character constellations: (a) Narcissistic implications of pathological character traits in general, insofar as they protect and maintain self-esteem: the more rigid the pathological character traits, the more one finds narcissistic implications in such traits, in addition to their specific functions of maintaining repression of structuralized intrapsychic conflicts. (b) Narcissistic character traits representing fixation on the level of infantile narcissism and reflecting defenses linked with all kinds of genital or pregenital conflicts; the infantile-narcissistic aspects of many hysterical and obsessive character traits are typical examples. (c) Pathological narcissism proper—a specific character constellation which reflects a particular pathology of internalized object relationships, and particular distortions of ego and superego structures. I propose that the diagnosis of narcissistic personality should be reserved exclusively to the third category of narcissism mentioned, and I emphasize the particular difficulties for treatment that these patients present. Although practically all borderline patients present severe character pathology and, therefore, narcissistic character traits in the broader sense [types (a) and (b)], it is important to carefully differentiate "narcissism" used in that broad sense from the specific pathological structures of the narcissistic personality in a strict sense. In general, the more the pathological narcissistic structures of the narcissistic personality are present, the more serious is the prognosis.

    d. *Antisocial personalities* have a very poor prognosis for the entire range of psychological treatments. (I am referring here to antisocial personalities in a strict sense, and not to patients who simply present antisocial behaviors as such.) This differential diagnosis frequently arises in the case of adolescents who enter into difficulties with the law. An effective differential diagnosis of the character constellations which may be involved in antisocial behavior requires several diagnostic considerations:

    (i) Does the antisocial behavior really reflect personal psychopathology, or is it "antisocial" from the viewpoint of some conventional, social prejudice?

    (ii) Does the antisocial behavior reflect a "normal" adaptation to a pathological social environment? An affirmative answer to this question has a rather benign implication; however, in so diagnosing adolescent antisocial behavior, caution has to be exerted, because it is questionable to what extent a relatively normal psychological development would permit, say, an adolescent to identify himself only with the antisocial subculture of his immediate social environment. Even under circumstances of most severe social deprivation there exists an undercurrent of awareness of more normal social values which should permit the relatively healthy individual not to identify himself completely with an anti-social subgroup.

(iii) Does the antisocial behavior reflect an "adjustment reaction of adolescence," that is, is the antisocial behavior really the by-product of an acute emotional crisis, or of an acute interpersonal conflict that the adolescent faces? When this is the case, there are usually other neurotic symptoms present, such as anxiety and/or depression, and general conflicts around rebelliousness and dependency. When the antisocial behavior is clearly limited in time and confined to an episode of extreme emotional turmoil, a diagnosis of "adjustment reaction of adolescence" may be justified. Unfortunately, however, this diagnosis has been grossly overused, and frequently one finds all kinds of severe psychopathology and especially severe character pathology underestimated or simply ignored in making this diagnosis. Masterson (16) and Robins (20) have provided impressive evidence regarding the severity of psychopathology frequently missed by the diagnosis of "adjustment reaction of adolescence." In my opinion, this diagnosis should be made only after excluding the following much more frequent and much more severe forms of psychopathology.

(iv) Does the antisocial behavior reflect some form of severe character pathology other than an antisocial personality structure proper? Probably the most frequent category into which antisocial behavior falls, this category involves antisocial behavior as one aspect of an infantile personality, or a narcissistic personality, etc. Although the prognosis is naturally more serious for this category than for categories (b) and (c), if the other prognostic elements presented later in this paper are favorable, antisocial behavior as part of character pathology other than antisocial personality proper does not imply untreatability. The considerations regarding the analysis of superego pathology are of particular prognostic importance in these cases.

(v) Does the antisocial behavior reflect an antisocial personality proper? If the answer is yes, the prognosis is very poor. This diagnosis can only be established by careful evaluation of the patient's history rather than by means of a short-term diagnostic examination, and often only after prolonged observation of the patient, in the course of which the quality of his object relationships and the type and degree of superego pathology can be more accurately evaluated. The treatment of such patients within specialized structured environments (combining the characteristics of both a high-security prison and a psychiatric hospital) has been reported to be of help in some cases, at least in bringing about more or less lasting behavioral changes in the direction of a better social adjustment.

e. The prognosis for patients suffering from *sexual deviations* and who function on a borderline level varies according to the underlying personality structure. Sexual deviations associated with underlying narcissistic personality structure generally have poor prognosis because of the particular difficulties for an analytic therapeutic approach in the case of narcissistic personalities; the prognosis is better in the case of other forms of character pathology. The treatment of sexual difficulties in patients with overt borderline functioning may take a long time because of the need to approach the dynamic aspects of such sexual deviations very cautiously and gradually in patients with the regressive potential of borderline personality organization. The quality of object relationships is a crucial prognostic factor in all conditions of sexual deviation. The better the capacity for maintaining nonexploitative object relationships, the better the prognosis; the more unstable the patient's object relationships, the worse the prognosis. Patients with borderline personality organization who have lived in virtual isolation for many years, and whose entire sexual life has taken masturbatory forms with exclusively or predominantly perverse fantasies, have a guarded prognosis with regard to their sexual difficulties.

f. The prognosis for patients suffering from *alcoholism and drug addiction*—frequent syndromes present with borderline personality organization—also depends on the underlying personality structures. Once again, narcissistic personality structures underlying such symptoms make the prognosis more serious. In addition, the effectiveness of impulse control and the possibility of replacing the patient's incapacity to suppress the addictive symptom with some temporary external structure during the treatment become crucial issues. If the patient has sufficient impulse control to prevent the symptom from interfering with the treatment, or if a protective environment is available in the form of hospitalization, day hospital, or some other treatment arrangement, the prognosis improves.

h.  For patients with the "classical" *prepsychotic personality structures* (the paranoid personality, the schizoid personality, and the hypomanic personality) the prognosis varies.

(i)  *Paranoid personalities* functioning on a borderline level have a better prognosis if the treatment is structured so that their need for omnipotent control does not distort the therapeutic relationship. Some paranoid patients attempt to start the treatment under conditions of secrecy, or to exert an unrealistic control of the therapist which distorts the therapeutic relationship and often ends up in therapeutic stalemate (9). Ideally, if the patient cannot accept the realistic demands and limitations involved in entering a psychotherapeutic relationship, there is an advantage in keeping the patient hospitalized while the initial stages of the psychotherapeutic relationship are established. In this way, the cloak of secrecy that paranoid patients establish regarding many areas of their lives, and their efforts to omnipotently control the therapist can be compensated for by the observations provided by the hospital staff and by the mutual support of the treatment team.

(ii)  For the *schizoid personality*, the prognosis is more guarded. Patients with strong, overt schizoid features may present such a pervasive distance and withdrawal from the therapeutic interaction that the therapist's ability and even his willingness to engage the patient in a meaningful relationship may become seriously taxed. Schizoid patients utilize splitting mechanisms to such an extent that all emotional, one might even say, human elements of the patient-therapist relationship may appear to be completely destroyed or dispersed, thus producing an atmosphere of emotional shallowness and emptiness which is very hard for the therapist to tolerate over a long period of time. Guntrip (8) convincingly outlined these typical, dynamic characteristics of schizoid patients which create a maximum stress on the therapist; I agree with his observation that the personality of the therapist becomes very important under these conditions. It may well be that the prognosis for schizoid patients depends especially on the personal qualities of the therapist as reflected in his technique. That is, the therapist cannot help the patient by "offering" him his own personality; only by using his natural warmth, emotional wealth, and his capacity for empathy to systematically and persistently analyze the patient's defensive withdrawal can he help the patient.

(iii) *Hypomanic personalities* have a bad prognosis; the issue here is really the patient's degree of tolerance of depression; the more the patient tolerates depression without severe decompensation, the better the prognosis. In their preferred defensive operations, hypomanic personalities are related to narcissistic personalities, and much that applies technically to the latter, applies to the former (see Chapter 8). All in all, however, the prognosis is poorer for hypomanic personalities than for narcissistic personalities.

i. The prognosis of the so-called *"chaotic," or impulse-ridden character disorders* is fair but varies individually according to the presence of nonspecific manifestations of ego weakness, which will be considered later. Patients with multiple sexual perversions, with heterosexual and/or homosexual promiscuity, and patients with polymorphous perverse sexual trends (so characteristic of borderline conditions in general) also belong to this group. In general, the more chaotic and multiple the perverse fantasies and actions, and the more unstable the object relationships connected with these sexual interactions, the more strongly the diagnosis of borderline personality organization is warranted, but, at the same time, the better the prognosis (in contrast to patients with a stable sexual deviation and underlying narcissistic personalities). The implication is that a chaotic sexual life, reflecting general borderline functioning but without an underlying narcissistic personality structure, has a much better prognosis than what the instability and broad variety of pathological sexual behavior at first would seem to indicate. When, however, the multiple perverse fantasies and/or activities reflect a more general inability to establish stable object relationships, the prognosis becomes worse for that very reason.

j. Patients with predominantly *obsessive-compulsive personalities* have a good prognosis even if they function on a borderline level; it is important to differentiate, however, obsessive-compulsive personality structures proper from narcissistic personalities and from schizoid personalities, who also present a surface coldness, intellectualization, and distance.

k. *Depressive-masochistic personalities* functioning on a borderline level also have a relatively good prognosis, with some reservations. First, the more sadistically infiltrated character structures, the so-called sadomasochistic personalities, have a poorer prognosis than depressive personalities in a strict sense (Chapter 1). Second, patients who present generalized self-destructiveness reflected in interpersonal behavior in which the main intention seems to be self-harm (such as the propensity for chronic suicidal acts, or, even more so, a tendency for a repetitive major "self-mutilation") also have a poorer prognosis. The implication is that the more primitive the forms of self-directed aggression and the more diffuse the aggressive discharge in the sense of not differentiating self from non-self (in contrast to self-directed aggression integrated mainly into superego structures) the more unfavorable the prognosis. Long-term hospitalization (up to several years), concomitant with intensive, psychoanalytically-oriented psychotherapy, may be quite successful in improving chronic self-mutilators, if the treatment setting is able to contain the patient's efforts to omnipotently control his environment by means of actual or threatened self-mutilations (17).

The prognostic importance of the predominant type of character pathology is an important reason for a careful diagnostic evaluation of the patient. Thus, the more carefully one attempts to establish the descriptive diagnosis of patients, the more certain one is to include structural and genetic-dynamic considerations in addition to purely descriptive ones.

Structural and genetic-dynamic analyses refer here not to an effort to reconstruct the individual's pathogenic conflicts and his life history, but to the determination, from multiple viewpoints, of the more permanent alterations that those conflicts and past life experiences may have caused and that now are part of the individual's character structure. In more general terms, one might say that a good diagnosis requires a metapsychological analysis in the "here and now."

## 2. Ego and Superego Distortions Reflected in Individual Character Traits

Up to this point, I have examined the predominant characterological constellation as an important prognostic element regarding the treatment of borderline personality organization. Let us now focus more sharply on some particular, individualized pathological character traits as potential prognostic indicators. The more some primitive pathological superego identifications are enacted by a certain character trait, and the more such primitive identifications embedded in pathological character traits are tolerated by the patient's ego, and especially the more that self-destructive intentions (what we might call self-destructiveness as an ego-ideal) are expressed by certain character traits, the more serious becomes the prognosis.

Although the character structure mediates pressure impinging on the ego from the id, the superego, and the external world, usually id pressures are stressed in the literature. However, I want to stress the function of the character structure as a compromise formation between ego and superego pressures. Example 1: A female patient with hysterical character structure and prohibitive, punitive superego formations representing the introjection of a threatening mother image derived from oedipal conflicts, presents fantasied prohibitions against all expression of heterosexual sexuality and against competitive strivings with other women. With such a superego formation, the patient typically presents inhibition of her competitiveness with other women, submission to mother-like dominant women, and sexual inhibition. Thus, the presence of masochistic character traits may reflect the structuralization within the ego of the submissive, guilt-ridden self of the oedipal little girl toward the threatening oedipal mother. Such masochistic traits, however, may be used "adaptively" by the ego in the form of masochistic behavior toward men, especially when, as long as a heavy price is being paid for sexual gratification in the form of mental or physical suffering, sexual gratification is permitted. The masochistic character trends reflect, in such a case, structuralization of a self-image, an ego function, in relating to the superego mother introject, and some effort on the ego's part to express the id-derived impulses in a modified, masochistic but ego-syntonic way. The pathological character constellation of masochism also becomes one aspect of the self-concept, one component of the patient's ego identity. In summary, a superego introjection (the oedipal, prohibitive mother) has brought about an identification process within the ego, the identification being with the submissive, guilt-ridden little girl representing a complementary ego structure to the superego mother introject.

Example 2: A female patient with hysterical character structure and a harsh superego representing predominantly the internalization of a prohibitive, antisexual mother image, may present submissive, masochistic behavior toward dominant women, and yet a quite controlling, dominant behavior toward weak men. It is this latter behavior toward men that I wish to focus upon as an expression of a pathological character constellation which serves several functions: 1) an "identification with the aggressor" (4), that is, with the dominant oedipal mother image by means of a characterological identification with the sadistic superego; 2) a reaction formation against the submissive-masochistic ego trends; and 3) a rationalized outlet for part of the underlying aggression which represents the oedipal rebellion against mother. In this case the harsh superego may not be fully observable at first, because the identification within the character structure with such a superego reduces certain superego restraints on the ego and permits a deflection outward of aggression stemming from both superego and id pressures.

Example 3: A more severe form of this kind of development can be observed in a patient who is quite inhibited, shy, submissive in a structured environment, but shows a surprising degree of aggressiveness, arrogance, and gives an appearance of stupidity in unstructured social situations which put him into a position of dominance or power. Again, in these cases, one may find a strict, harsh superego which usually predominates in its inhibiting effect on ego functions, while under certain socially facilitating circumstances an identification with the aggressor takes place, and superego functions now emerge integrated into sadistic character traits. Under these circumstances, the ego acquires a pathological freedom from the superego by identifying with it, and freedom from unbearable aggressive impulses by permitting their rationalized expression in sadistic character traits. The arrogance represents the characterological identification with an omnipotent sadistic superego figure; the appearance of stupidity expresses the denial of external reality, an equivalent of the superego's suppression of the ego's reality testing. Bion (1), in a different context, has described arrogance and stupidity as defenses against paranoid trends; in my view, projection of superego nuclei and manifest paranoid trends may or may not coexist with these character formations, according to the degree to which superego integration is present.

In the third example mentioned, in which the identification with the superego implies an identification with a more primitive superego introject than in the first two examples, the aggression expressed in such a characterological identification becomes rather crude and potentially quite inappropriate from a social viewpoint. This is because the ego has partly abdicated its function of testing reality in social settings in order to "accommodate" the pathological foreign body represented by the characterological identification with the primitive superego. Abdication of reality testing on the ego's part is a serious complication of the consolidation of primitive identifications in the character structure. Such consolidation reflects an important distortion in the patient's identity formation, and may also reflect a faulty superego expressed in pathological aggressive behavior directed toward others and justified with "moral indignation." Reality testing (in the more general sense of testing social reality rather than in the strictly technical one of differentiating self from non-self and the related differentiation of intrapsychic from interpersonal experiences) and the capacity for introspection are both reduced under these circumstances.

In summary, the more the character structure reflects pathological primitive superego identifications integrated into the ego with a loss of higher ego and superego functions, the more serious is the prognosis.

Another important prognostic element is the extent to which contradictory character traits reflecting conflicting identifications integrated into the character structure are tolerated by the ego (or rather the self) and superego. The degree to which mutually incompatible character traits may alternate in the individual is an indication of the extent to which ego splitting is present. The predominance of splitting and other related primitive defenses in the ego is a landmark of borderline personality organization. Within this context, however, the extent to which rationalization of the individual's contradictory behavior are absent, and the extent to which such behavior reflects tolerance of contradictory identification systems by the ego and superego, are of negative prognostic value for psychological treatment.

As an illustration, a patient with serious masochistic trends and rationalization of failure as being always the fault of another's aggression or of fate, and who, at the same time, presents rather sadistic behavior with a teasing quality under certain circumstances, is not disturbed at all when confronted with the contradiction between such teasing behavior and his tendency to complain about how he is being mistreated by others; the tolerance of such contradictions within established behavior patterns is a severe prognostic sign.

The overscrupulous, obsessive patient who can be quite dishonest under certain circumstances without experiencing any conflict is another example, although in this case it is particularly the superego pathology which predominates.

### 3. Self-destructiveness as a Character Formation and Negative Therapeutic Reaction

The extent to which pathological character traits reflect the enactment of a self-destructive ideology, or what might be called self-destruction as an ego ideal, is another ominous prognostic sign for treatment. This issue transcends the descriptive classification of self-destructive character pathology and is related to the general question of the negative therapeutic reaction. Severe forms of structuralized, self-directed aggression manifest themselves as proneness for negative therapeutic reaction. This is really a crucial "process" or "transactional" variable: the extent to which a negative therapeutic reaction develops within the psychotherapeutic relationship provides prognostic information as the treatment process goes on. The reaction is not exclusive to the borderline personality organization, but it appears frequently in these patients. The more significant the history of behavior which may be interpreted predominantly as a search for social, psychological, or physical self-destructiveness, the poorer the prognosis.

It has to be stressed, however, that the self-destructive effects of certain behavior have to be distinguished from self-destruction as a major intention. A patient who loses jobs, for example, or disrupts his studies whenever he is threatened with confrontation regarding his shortcomings, may rationalize such disruptions as "self-destructive." On the surface, he is right: however, the underlying intention may be to protect a primitive grandiose self-concept. Perhaps only in cases of chronic tendency toward physical self-mutilation does one have sufficient certainty for considering this symptom as a serious prognostic sign involving primitive self-destructive needs and, implicitly, a severe potential for negative therapeutic reaction.

For example, in some patients with tendencies toward self-mutilation, who tend to relieve tension of any origin by inducing pain in themselves (by cutting themselves, burning their skin, etc.), one may observe a real pleasure or pride in the power of self-destruction—a sense of omnipotence or pride in the independence from external gratification symbolically reaffirmed by pleasurable self-destructiveness. Patients who, when they damage themselves physically or psychologically, triumphantly enjoy the suffering or defeat of those who are close to them, including the therapist, are typical examples of such pathological development. In a better functioning masochistic personality structure (depressive-masochistic personalities) such self-destructive ideology, pleasure and triumph in self-defeat, may be rationalized in the form of a submission to a particular harsh value system or religious or political group. Unconscious self-defeat as an expression of submission to a sadistic superego needs to be distinguished from conscious affirmation of self-destruction as an ego ideal which demands sacrifice of one's happiness, of good relationships with others, of success and satisfaction.

The need to defeat oneself as a necessary price to pay in order to defeat an unconsciously hated and envied helping figure is another related type of self-destructive motivation. Self-destruction here serves the purpose of "triumphing" over the envied object. The more serious cases of "negative therapeutic reaction" (3, 5, 21, 22) are often part of this group of patients. Severe forms of negative therapeutic reaction are linked with such "triumph" over others, in this case, the therapist and his life-affirmative tendencies. Guntrip (8) pointed out that identifications on the part of the patient's ego with primitive bad objects (Fairbairn's and Guntrip's "anti-libidinal ego") is an unfavorable prognostic factor in the treatment of schizoid personalities.

The term "negative therapeutic reaction" is not used to refer to general failure of treatment or to periods of heightened resistance or intense negative transference. I am referring here exclusively to those cases in which the need to destroy the helpful aspects of the psychotherapy or psychoanalysis clearly predominate in the patient's impulse-defense configuration. Freud's (5) classical description of this reaction referred to cases with a strong unconscious masochism and severe superego pathology manifested in overriding, unconscious guilt feelings. Many patients with depressive-masochistic character structures do present this type of resistance.

There are, however, patients with more serious psychopathology who present negative therapeutic reactions as part of a different constellation, namely, narcissistic personality structures whose unconscious need to defeat the therapist is related to oral envy and revengeful destruction of potential external sources of love and gratification (Chapter 8; 21).

There exists, in addition, an even more regressed level of psychopathology in which the negative therapeutic reaction becomes very predominant—patients, for example, who function either at a borderline or an openly psychotic level, and who have in common a predominance of strong pregenital aggression and some degree of blurring of self-nonself limits, so that aggression is expressed indiscriminately against others or the self. Many self-mutilating patients who obtain nonspecific relief from anxiety by inducing pain in themselves are in this category. Other patients within the borderline and psychotic field appear to place a peculiar emphasis on the need to specifically destroy other people's efforts to help them, even though they themselves succumb in the process.

One patient, a single man in his early twenties, with chronic schizophrenic reaction, was able to function quite well within the narrow range of his hospital ward. He consistently presented a derogatory smile to anybody who approached him with a helpful attitude. He wrote long letters to his parents complaining about the treatment in the hospital, while openly admitting to hospital staff that his charges against them were false and his letters were motivated by his wish to discontinue treatment by forcing his parents to take him out of the hospital. His father was a callous, distant disciplinarian; his over-solicitous, suspicious mother suffered from alcoholism and drug addiction and had undergone several psychotic episodes. Various approaches by different hospital physicians and psychotherapists led nowhere. He received one of his hospital physicians every day smiling, saying, "You will see—you cannot do anything for me." He spoke in a superficially friendly way, but there was an unshakable determination in him not to improve. In the past he had assaulted his mother, had attempted to cut off his penis, and had carefully hidden a lesion which proved to be a malignant tumor.

The interpretation finally arrived at was that the patient identified himself unconsciously with an extremely destructive mother image, and his refusal to improve reflected his fear that improvement meant separation from mother and destroying her. At the same time, he deflected his rage against his mother onto himself and all those who tried to help him. The self-destructiveness was seen as a combination of his need for self-destruction, an expression of diffuse aggression, identification with a sadistic mother image, envious hatred of all those who were not in such a slave's position, fear of mother's punishment if he tried to free himself from her, and fear for her life if any change occurred. Several members of the team referred to the patient as presenting a "cancer of the personality." This patient was not "manipulating" staff in the sense of forcing the environment into a hostile stance against him; he was, rather, very open in his almost enjoyable devaluation, destruction, and depreciation of his psychotherapist, his hospital physician, and helpers in general. At the same time, the degree of ego integration that he had achieved needs to be stressed. He conveyed the impression that he had pulled himself together at a level in which he had sufficient reality testing and impulse control to protect his attitude against all efforts to bring about further change.

The descriptive characterological aspects and their prognostic implications can usually be assessed during a careful diagnostic examination of the patient. Such examination must include, in addition to a detailed evaluation of the patient's character structure, the extent to which pathological character traits are ego syntonic or ego dystonic; the extent to which contradictory character traits, or contradictions between the patient's value system and character traits are tolerated without conflict; the extent to which the patient's ego "abdicates" its functions of reality testing, its concern and self-preservation under the influence of pathological character traits; and, above all, the extent to which self-destruction as an ego ideal is ego sytonic, or self-destructiveness is used as a weapon to defeat others.

The prognostic implications of all these findings may, however, be modified as changes take place in them as part of the developments occurring during the treatment itself. Thus, the extent to which prognostically unfavorable pathological character traits become ego dystonic as a product of the therapeutic work, the extent to which awareness of and concern about such pathological forces in himself develops in the patient, the extent to which he develops the capacity to dissociate himself from the rationalization of self-destructive needs, are important process or transactional variables which will modify the overall prognosis as treatment goes on.

There is, however, a certain temptation for therapists to rely exclusively on the prognostic indications given by the patient's response to long-term treatment itself. Since intensive treatment of patients with borderline personality organization geared to producing fundamental changes in their personality structure will take many months or years, and as any particular therapist will only be able to treat a few of the many patients with this psychopathology that he examines, a careful selection for intensive psychotherapeutic treatment of those patients with most favorable prognostic elements in their character pathology is necessary.

## THE DEGREE AND QUALITY
## OF EGO WEAKNESS

In Chapter 1, I proposed that the concept of "ego weakness" remains clinically useful if, in contrast to its overextension and abuse as a general concept, the various aspects of ego weakness are individualized and differentiated. I referred to specific aspects of ego weakness, namely, 1) the *predominance of primitive defensive operations of the ego* characteristic of the borderline personality organization, and to nonspecific aspects of ego weakness, namely to its 2) *lack of impulse control;* 3) *lack of anxiety tolerance;* 4) *lack of developed sublimatory channels.* I also mentioned two additional aspects of ego weakness: 5) the *tendency toward primary process thinking,* and (6) the *weakening of reality testing.* All these aspects reflect both a general outcome of pathological ego development and the specific results of the pathology of internalized object relationships of patients with borderline personality organization. The overall quantitative analyses of the Psychotherapy Research Project of The Menninger Foundation provide strong supportive evidence for the prognostic importance of ego strength (12, 2). The prognostic significance of each aspect of ego weakness merits examination.

1. *Predominance of primitive defensive operations of the ego.* The extent to which certain defensive constellations of the ego, that is, primitive defense mechanisms (splitting; primitive idealization; early forms of projection, and especially projective identification; denial; omnipotence; and devaluation)

predominate in contrast to higher level defensive operations (repression and related defenses), the more the diagnosis of borderline personality organization is warranted (Chapter 1). In other words, the diagnostic value of the predominant defensive constellation of the ego is extremely important. Prognostically it does not seem important which kind of defenses predominate within the general range of those characteristics of borderline conditions. However, the degree to which repression and other "higher level" defensive mechanisms and character traits (11) are present is important to the treatment recommendation (analyzability).

2. *Lack of impulse control.* This is, indeed, an important prognostic indicator. Clearly restricted loss of impulse control in limited areas of the patient's personality with simultaneous preservation of impulse control in all other areas of the patient's psychological functioning usually has defensive purposes which can be diagnosed and resolved through a combination of interpretation and the establishment of temporary parameters of technique. Generalized lack of impulse control, however, in addition to being an important indicator of ego weakness, determines the potential for acting out of the transference (within as well as outside the treatment hours).

In Chapter 3 I mentioned that transference acting out within the therapeutic relationship, i.e., in the treatment setting itself, may be highly resistant to interpretation in patients with borderline personality organization because it gratifies the instinctual needs, especially those linked with severe preoedipal aggressive drive derivatives so characteristic of these patients. This gratification of instinctual needs within the treatment is a major transference resistance; some patients obtain much more gratification of their pathological instinctual needs in the transference than would ever be possible in extratherapeutic interactions.

The lack of impulse control is a serious prognostic sign indicating that transference acting out may become a major complication of the treatment. The lack of impulse control will determine to what extent setting controls within the treatment process and/or structuralization of the patient's life (hospitalization, day hospital, foster home, etc.), outside the treatment hours will be required to permit the treatment to be carried out. Lack of impulse control, therefore, is prognostically serious because it tends to shift the treatment process into a supportive direction, essentially interfering with the need to resolve the pathological defensive structure of the patient by analytically oriented means. In other words, the less impulse control of the patient, the more the therapist is pushed in the direction of "taking over," with a concomitant erosion of the therapist's position of neutrality; the more neutrality is lost, the less an analytic approach can be maintained. A good many patients with severe loss of impulse control really need hospitalization concomitant with psychotherapy.

3. *Lack of anxiety tolerance.* Anxiety tolerance is not the degree of anxiety experienced by the patient, but the extent to which any anxiety additional to that he habitually experiences induces further symptom formation, pathological behavior, or regression. Because lack of anxiety tolerance may bring about loss of impulse control at points in treatment where increase of anxiety in the patient is unavoidable, much of what has been said regarding impulse control is true also for this variable. Thus, limited anxiety tolerance is a prognostically unfavorable indicator.

The question may be raised, however, as to what extent the use of tranquilizing medication may compensate for the loss of anxiety tolerance. In general, I would suggest tranquilizing medication as part of psychological treatment when the degree of anxiety is such that it interferes with the establishment and preservation of a meaningful patient-therapist communication. This circumstance applies, however, chiefly to the psychoses; in the majority of patients with borderline personality organization that I have examined, or whose treatment I have conducted or supervised, it was not necessary to use tranquilizing medication for that purpose.

When, however, a patient with borderline personality organization presents anxiety of a psychotic-like intensity in combination with severe lack of anxiety tolerance, tranquilizing medication is indicated. In this case, the patient should receive medication according to the following principles: 1) Tranquilizing medication should be given in a sufficient amount to produce a pharmacological, rather than a placebo effect. 2) It should be given over a sufficiently long period of time to be able to establish a new "base line" for the level of anxiety at which the patient is functioning. (When medication is given on a temporary basis, or its dosage varied frequently as part of a psychotherapeutic treatment, the level of anxiety tends to fluctuate to such an extent that it becomes very difficult to evaluate its transference implications. In other words, because of introduction of tranquilizing medication, anxiety as a fundamental process or transactional variable regulating psychotherapeutic interventions may become lost because of the irregularity of the fluctuation of its level.) 3) The unconscious meanings of taking medication as part of the psychotherapeutic relationship have to be focused upon and consistently brought into the psychotherapeutic process because the primitive defensive operations of patients with borderline personality organization may be masked by a symbolic utilization of medication. The consistent examination of defenses in the transference then becomes extremely difficult. Thus, for example, the need for omnipotent control of an object may be expressed in the patient's unconscious feeling that when he possesses medication, he has control over the therapist. Or his greedy oral demandingness may be sufficiently gratified by receiving medication so that the aggressive elements in that demandingness are partially decreased and partially masked by the absence of the very increase of anxiety that unfulfilled demandingness regarding medication would otherwise have brought up.

What has been said regarding medication could be misinterpreted as a general implicit opposition to the use of tranquilizing medication. I am referring here, however, to the use of medication as part of an intensive, long-term psychotherapy geared basically to modifying personality structure as well as the symptomatology of patients with borderline personality organization. Acute crisis interventions and short-term psychotherapy geared to the resolution of symptoms may require the use of tranquilizing and other medication as a crucial part of the total psychotherapeutic effort, but this is not the case here.

4. *Lack of developed sublimatory channels.* This crucial prognostic factor is as important as it is difficult to evaluate. Enjoyment of work and life and the capacity for creative achievement are the main indicators of sublimatory capacity; they have to be distinguished from efficiency, which may reflect the patient's particular defenses, capacities, or natural talents rather than sublimatory development.

For instance, we might compare two cases of borderline personality organization, both of them physicians, both having managed, therefore, to complete their professional studies and requirements in spite of their psychological handicaps. One of them, however, used his profession predominantly as a source of prestige and high income, with little concern for his patients and for the ongoing development of his technical skills and knowledge. This man, with a very high intelligence quotient, was able to fulfill his professional requirements and graduate in spite of long periods of disorganization and neglect of his professional functions. In short, he was largely unaware of the very values involved in his professional work beyond the narcissistic gratifications derived from it, and he was also completely uninterested in any scientific developments within his profession. The second physician had great difficulties in interpersonal relationships and utilized his scientific work and interests as an escape from too intensive relationships with people; he also used them as an attempt to escape from his own confused internal world into a "professional world" which he experienced as good and solid. His sublimatory potential was much higher.

In general, the extent to which a patient is able to invest himself in a certain activity or profession beyond strictly narcissistic needs, the degree of gratification from such activity or profession, and the extent to which the patient is concerned about the intrinsic values of that activity or profession represent his sublimatory potential. Therefore, one has to evaluate very carefully both the general quality of the patient's activities and work, and the function that the dedication to them has for him. In patients from a high socioeconomic environment who have had all the opportunities for developing skills and professions, or in patients with very high intelligence or other natural talents, such a background may provide a surface picture of accomplishment which masks the underlying lack of sublimatory potential.

The practical prognostic importance of this variable is enormous, and, in this connection, the general origin of sublimatory potential should be examined, if only briefly. I have mentioned that an individual's sublimatory potential involves an authentic dedication to something which transcends his self-interest. In more general terms, it involves concern for what is good and valuable in other people and in one's own self, the awareness of and appreciation for values or realities invested with love and from which love is received in turn in symbolic ways. Melanie Klein (13) stressed the relationship between sublimation and the general capacity for developing guilt and reparatory trends on the patient's part. Winnicott (26, 28) further examined the relationship between working through of the "depressive position" and the development of the capacity for concern.

The implication of all these observations is that, in contrast to traditional psychoanalytic thinking, sublimation does not reflect simply an economic change in the direction and utilization of instinctual drive derivatives under the influence of ego and superego functions, but a direct outcome of the vicissitudes of internalized object relationships. The capacity for developing a total object relationship, for integrating loving and hateful aspects of the relationship with others and with one's own self is a prerequisite for full development of sublimation. When borderline patients in some area of their life basically trust something good and valuable in their relationships with others (or with work, leisure, art, science, or religion) this is of important, positive prognostic value. The capacity to establish and maintain values transcending the self—abstract as it may sound, and difficult at times as it is to evaluate—is an eminently practical link between the vicissitudes of internalized object relationships on the one hand, and the capacity to benefit from a psychotherapeutic relationship, on the other.

5. *Tendency toward primary process thinking.* Patients with borderline personality organization usually do not give

evidence in clinical mental status examinations of formal disorder of their thought processes; on projective testing, however, and especially in response to unstructured stimuli, primary process thinking does appear in the form of primitive fantasies, in a definite decrease in the capacity to adapt to the formal givens of the test material, and particularly in the use of peculiar verbalizations (18). When, as part of an initial evaluation of the patient, there are clear-cut findings of formal thought disorder on a mental status examination, the presumptive diagnosis is that of a psychotic reaction. However, primary process thinking may make its appearance clinically at certain periods of intense psychotherapy in patients with borderline personality organization. Bion (1) points out how temporary disorganization of thought processes may be used for defensive purposes. The initial manifestations of primary process thinking have diagnostic and therapeutic implications; the patient's potential for primary process thinking is one more consideration in evaluating whether he might be able to benefit from nonmodified psychoanalytic treatment. The temporary appearance of primary process thinking throughout the process of treatment is not of prognostic value, but it requires focusing upon the defensive functions of communication distortion within the treatment situation.

6. *Weakening of reality testing.* Reality testing in the strict sense of the capacity to differentiate intrapsychic from externally perceived events is an ego function present in patients with borderline personality organization. Reality testing may be transitorily lost in these patients, however, under the influence of severe emotional turmoil, alcohol, drugs, and in the context of a transference psychosis. The persistence of reality testing under ordinary conditions, however, is actually a crucial point in the differential diagnosis between borderline conditions and the psychoses (7). A fundamental requirement for the diagnosis of a psychotic reaction, schizophrenia, for example, is the persistent loss of reality testing in any area of psychological functioning, and/or the presence of "productive" psychotic elements, such as hallucinations or delusions. Whenever the differential diagnosis between a borderline condition and a psychosis is being

considered, and the patient does not present loss of reality testing with regard to his behavior, his thinking, or his emotional reactions, and he does not have productive signs of psychosis, he is simply not a psychotic patient. The overextension of the diagnosis of schizophrenia on the basis of dynamic considerations, in contrast to a strictly descriptive diagnosis of this condition, has contributed to the confusion one finds in this field.

A patient who presents bizarre behavior, or bizarre judgments regarding his intrapsychic life or external reality, or a bizarre emotional reaction, needs to be confronted, as part of his psychological examination, with the abnormality the examining physician perceives in the patient in any or all of these areas. If the patient is able to spontaneously acknowledge his awareness that his behavior, judgment, or feelings are abnormal, or is able after consistent confrontation to arrive at such a conclusion, reality testing (in the strict sense defined above) is still present. By definition, then, the persistence of reality testing is characteristic of borderline patients, with the exception of its transitory loss under the conditions mentioned above.

The frequency and intensity of temporary loss of reality testing are not, in themselves, important prognostic indicators. A borderline patient who undergoes regression under psychotherapeutic treatment and develops a transference psychosis usually responds favorably to a change, permanent or temporary, in the psychotherapeutic technique. This change may consist of increased structuralization within the treatment hours or increased structuralization in the patient's life outside the treatment hours. If the patient-therapist relationship has been well established and the therapist is able to deal with the psychotic regression realistically, without excessive countertransference reactions on his part, temporary losses of reality testing are not a major difficulty in the treatment. In other words, reality testing is not a prognostic indicator, although its characteristics are part of the constellation on which the diagnosis of borderline personality organization is based. Reality testing is, however, an important diagnostic variable regarding the treatment indications for borderline personality organization, because the intensity and frequency of loss of reality testing is one of the general criteria for deciding on the possibility of psychoanalytic treatment proper in any particular case. Frequent loss of reality testing, even though temporary and easily reversed by structuralization in the treatment, is one of the elements deciding against the advisability of classical psychoanalysis, at least to start out with. Most patients with borderline personality organization require a modification of technique which includes special structuralization and/or parameters of technique (Chapter 3).

There is another sense in which the term reality testing may be used; a more general, less precise, and yet more subtle reference to the extent to which the patient is aware of his interpersonal or social reality, and especially of the moral values of others. Subtle alterations in the behavior of borderline patients within their ordinary social context (such as their frequent lack of perception of subtle "messages" from other persons, their unawareness of inappropriate appearance, of the emotional reality of others, of the influence of value judgments on the behavior of other persons, of how they themselves are perceived by others, and tactlessness), all reflect loss of the more subtle discriminatory aspects of reality testing determined by ego and superego pathology. Reality testing in this broad sense does have some prognostic value, but we are entering here an area of complex interpersonal functioning which really refers to the quality of object relationships as a prognostic indicator, which will be taken up at a later point. In summary, then, reality testing in a strict sense is not an important prognostic factor.

In summary, some factors of ego strength or weakness have definite prognostic importance, especially the nonspecific manifestations of ego strength: impulse control, anxiety tolerance, and the patient's sublimatory potential. Factors such as reality testing, predominance of primary process thinking, and type of predominant defensive operations are important for the diagnosis but not for the prognosis of patients with borderline personality organization.

## THE DEGREE AND QUALITY
## OF SUPEREGO PATHOLOGY

The degree and quality of superego pathology is a fundamental prognostic indicator of patients with borderline personality organization. Although a close correspondence exists between the level of structural organization of the ego and of the superego, derived from the fact that related vicissitudes of internalized object relationships determine ego and superego pathology (11), in patients with borderline personality organization one finds frequent irregularities in the development of the superego. Ticho (24) has stressed the importance of diagnosing the level of development of a patient's superego and the direct clinical relevance of the degree to which the superego is nonintegrated or integrated, heteronomous or autonomous. One may find a higher level of integration of superego functions in borderline patients than one would usually expect at that level of personality organization. Why, is still an open question. It may be that unusually good environmental influences in later childhood years influence positively the later superego introjections and identifications in cases where severe pregenital conflicts had determined severe ego pathology.

In spite of the usual predominance of splitting operations in the superego, reprojection of superego nuclei in the form of paranoid trends, tolerance on the superego's part of contradictory value systems, of contradictory ego states and of identifications embedded in pathological character traits that are in striking contrast to superego values, quite a variation exists in borderline patients regarding the degree to which abstracted, depersonified, integrated superego values are present. Some patients with borderline personality organization, i.e., patients with narcissistic personality structures (Chapter 8), have much more serious superego pathology than their ego functioning would indicate.

The more awareness borderline patients have of values other than their own satisfactions, the more of an abstracted, depersonified superego structure is presumably present and the better the prognosis. In contrast, the more antisocial trends are present, ego syntonic and integrated in the patient's characterological make-up, the less of an integrated, abstracted, depersonified superego is presumably present and the more unfavorable the prognosis. Some antisocial behavior in the broadest sense is seen quite frequently in patients with borderline personality organization. For example, antisocial activities, such as stealing, habitual lying, parasitism, exploitiveness, are frequent in borderline narcissistic characters, especially in the antisocial personality structure proper. Antisocial personalities in a strict sense have the worst prognosis for any kind of psychological treatment. Lesser degrees of antisocial trends may be present in other types of borderline patients: pathological lying is frequent in infantile personalities and "as-if" characters ("pseudologia fantastica" used to be considered a hysterical character feature, but actually is present in infantile personalities). What is important is not the antisocial behavior as such, but its superego implications. I referred earlier to the differential diagnosis of antisocial behavior, and it needs to be emphasized that such behavior has to be analyzed in terms of the underlying character pathology *and* superego structure.

Example 1: Mr. A. consistently lied about his finances because of an intense fear that the therapist would exploit him and mercilessly take away all his earnings. This behavior induced chronic guilt feelings toward the therapist, and Mr. A. expressed anxiety and rejection whenever he experienced a friendly attitude in the therapist. Careful exploration of the disdainful rejection of the therapist gradually led to the patient's realistic guilt feelings and to subsequent defenses against such guilt feelings. Thus, the patient utilized whatever indication he saw of inconsistency on the therapist's part as justification for angry outbursts for not being treated as "special." He reassured himself again and again that with such a therapist he was justified in not being completely truthful. In contrast, Mr. A. was quite honest in his usual dealings with other people and in his handling of money matters. There was, however, a history of "teasing" on the part of his father, who exploited the patient's financial needs in order to compensate for his own insecurity, by forcing the patient to implore him for money. The patient had learned how to extract money from his father in a manipulative way, and had become selectively dishonest, seeing this behavior as a revenge against father which calmed his guilt feelings. The ventilation of this transference paradigm became possible after the patient's mounting guilt over his behavior toward the therapist, and culminated in a "confession," the upsurge of manifest guilt and depression. In short, lying as a form of antisocial behavior did not reflect a more serious kind of superego pathology in the sense of lack of availability of internalized moral values. The patient presented a limited area of dishonesty expressing a particular transference paradigm and, yet, a strong potential for authentic guilt feelings, and a definite commitment to moral values.

Example 2: Mr. B., who had received training in an institution in which he later applied for a staff position, appealed to a former supervisor who had been very friendly, for help with his application. In order to obtain the position, it was important that the patient have a clear record. The patient knew his record was not clear. He also knew that his former supervisor was completely ignorant of his difficulties with the law. The supervisor, however, was a member of the Board who had to make the decision, and as the Board had access to that particular information about the patient's past, the patient did not get the job. After learning about the Board's decision, Mr. B. went to talk with the supervisor again, knowing that the suppressed information had come out, to ask him for further help in reversing that decision. When informed of the surprise and pain the situation had produced for the supervisor, the patient was not embarrassed at all. He did not feel guilty about the situation, but (what is even more important) experienced the supervisor's sadness and disappointment simply as an indication that the supervisor had been "brainwashed" by the Board and could no longer be counted on. I emphasize here the patient's unawareness of human concern and ethical values in other persons. In spite of his high intelligence and ordinarily good reality testing, the patient could not perceive that the supervisor did not resent the fact that the patient had a history of difficulties with the law, but rather was concerned because the patient had been untruthful, bland, and indifferent about the supervisor's feelings.

Example 3:  Mr. C., with strong urges to steal, did not do so out of fear of being caught. He had great difficulty in understanding that other people might not steal for ethical reasons.

In summary, the absence of internalized value systems, lack of awareness of such value systems in others, and lack of awareness of the interpersonal implications of such value systems are important indicators of absence of advanced superego structures and functions, a bad prognostic sign.

Superego pathology of the kind described above also implies a reduction in the more subtle aspects of reality testing in the realm of interpersonal relationships, and a reduction in the capacity for meaningful insight. Meaningful insight, in contrast to the simple availability of primary process material in the conscious and preconscious mental life of borderline patients, refers to the combination of intellectual and emotional understanding of deeper sources of one's psychic experience, accompanied by concern for and an urge to change the pathological aspects of that experience (Chapter 3). What is especially missing in patients with severe superego pathology is concern for oneself, for one's relations to others, and for what one is doing to others in terms of moral values. In other words, moral self-evaluation is one more aspect of superego functioning which, if missing, has an unfortunate prognostic implication. The capacity for experiencing guilt and depression is intimately related to the capacity for experiencing concern (28). I have stressed the evaluation of the patient's capacity for depression and guilt as a fundamental prognostic factor in the treatment of patients with narcissistic personality (Chapter 8), and this applies to patients with borderline personality organization in general.

The aggressive, impulsive behavior which is part of the serious emotional turmoil of borderline patients, and the aggressive elements of particular pathological object relationships have to be differentiated from more generalized ruthless behavior that some patients present in all their relationships with others. The implications of such ruthless behavior for superego pathology have to be evaluated very carefully in all cases. This may, at times, put the examiner or psychotherapist under a strain; it is not easy to examine the patient's internal world and his relationships with others from the viewpoint of his commitment to moral values without becoming moralistic.

One striking feature of severe superego pathology may be seen in patients who are strongly committed to a certain ethical system, and at the same time present striking behavioral contradictions to that commitment. It is very important to carefully evaluate such contradictions and the extent to which the patient tolerates them without concern or guilt. One patient, for example, a catholic priest, presented chronic heterosexual promiscuity. Another patient, a plastic surgeon suffering from chronic alcoholism, operated while intoxicated, concerned only about whether his assistants would notice anything.

During the treatment process itself, chronic lying to the therapist and lack of concern on the patient's part about such behavior also illustrates the kind of superego pathology mentioned and has ominous prognostic implications. Whenever a psychotherapist becomes aware that a patient is lying to him, confrontation, followed by full exploration of this behavior, and consistent working through until resolution take precedence over any other kind of material. Psychological treatment cannot be conducted when the basic instrument of the patient-therapist relationship, namely that of verbal communication, is seriously distorted. In a more general sense, unconscious resistances cannot be fully examined, let alone resolved, before conscious resistances have been cleared.

In summary, then, absence of integrated, abstracted, depersonified superego structures as represented by the patient's awareness of and commitment to ethical and other values is an important prognostic indicator in patients with borderline personality organization. This prognostic indicator is at the same time one of the criteria indicating or contraindicating psychoanalysis proper for selected borderline cases.

I would like to add one more normal, protective superego function which is usually missing when serious pathological developments or arrest takes place in superego formation. I am referring to the anticipatory function of the normal superego, which under circumstances of uncertainty may trigger off what Ticho (24) has called "signal guilt." Such signal guilt may induce fantasies of failure, of mistakes made, of responsibilities unfulfilled, and even mild fantasies of a "paranoid" kind; all may in turn activate the self-observing and integrating functions of the ego and produce an optimal preparation for meeting the conditions of uncertainty. For example, in a normal person, an unexpected call from "the boss" may trigger concern and mildly guilt-ridden fantasies which may then, in turn, foster self-awareness, and minor corrections of a given course of action.

This function is missing to a major extent in individuals with severe superego pathology. It is remarkable to observe how some borderline patients with a harsh superego who are quite paranoid and unrealistically oversensitive to reactions of others often show a complete lack of sensitivity and of self-criticism where uncertainty about their functioning would be appropriate; for example, when a failure in work is pointed out to them in a friendly way. It is as if minor, subtle stimuli from the environment which would trigger off "signal guilt" in normal persons were not sufficient to influence those patients; only strong environmental pressures—such as a serious criticism—may trigger an intense, paranoid distortion of that pressure. These patients respond with an "all or nothing" superego reaction instead of the normal, flexible one. In the example of an unexpected call from the boss, such patients would not pay any attention to their superior's friendly suggestions. They react only if stronger criticism of them is expressed, but then with the experience of being cruelly attacked or persecuted.

The anticipatory function of the normal superego, that is, the induction of signal guilt, concern, and mild "persecutory" fantasies under conditions of uncertainty, may normally in turn be compensated not only by the ego's move into some preventive or reparatory action, but also by the ego's (or rather the self's) basic trust in its internal goodness and in its capacity to re-establish predominantly good relationships with others. This normal ego function of compensating superego pressures contrasts sharply with the pathological need of borderline patients (whose ego identity is diffuse and whose superego is a nonintegrated, heteronomous one) to reactivate primitive dissociative mechanisms, projection, omnipotence, and denial.

Ticho (24) has suggested that the establishment of selective identifications within the superego requires the presence of an integrated self-concept in the ego. I agree that some degree of stability of the self-concept is a prerequisite for the development of higher level superego functioning, especially the internalization of the more realistically perceived demanding and prohibitive aspects of the parents. An integrated, relatively autonomous superego, in turn, strongly fosters the development of a stable sense of ego identity. It is only a pathological superego that tolerates the contradictions between mutually dissociated or split-off ego states. Thus, excessive splitting operations of the ego preventing the integration of the self-concept, and lack of integration within the superego reinforce each other.

## THE QUALITY OF
## OBJECT RELATIONSHIPS

The quality of the present relationships with significant others can be observed in the patient's interpersonal behavior and in his internal relationships with significant others, in contrast to the structural consequences of his past internalized object relationships. These latter have crucial consequences for the development of all psychic structures (10). The presence of generalized splitting of internalized self- and object images into "good" and "bad" ones, the persistent primitivization and aggressive infiltration of interpersonal relationships, the emotional turmoil, the characteristic overinvolvement as well as withdrawal and protective shallowness, all reflect the generally serious pathology of internalized object relationships of patients with borderline personality organization (Chapter 1).

There are important variations, however, regarding the quality and degree to which borderline patients actually interact with and invest themselves in other people. The stability of relationships, neurotic as such relationships may be, is one prognostically positive indicator of capacity for investment. The capacity for individualization in object relations, in the sense of some realistic discrimination between different people with whom the same kind of neurotic conflicts may be expressed, also indicates some prognostically favorable potential for object relationships. Borderline patients who have the capacity of becoming aware of what is "different" in the therapist in comparison to their other transference objects reveal such capacity for individualized relationships.

Characteristically, object constancy, or the capacity for establishing "total" object relationships is defective in borderline patients, and they express this by their lack of capacity for tolerating ambivalent reactions toward objects. The degree to which borderline patients tolerate simultaneously loving and hateful feelings toward the same person without simply shifting from one extreme set of emotional reactions to an opposite one, is a prognostically favorable indicator of better quality of object relationships. From this viewpoint, conflictual pathological dependency toward the same person over a long period of time is of better prognostic value than total withdrawal and distance from all people.

An exception, however, has to be made regarding "dependency" which really reflects chronic pathological submission to an external object representing a primitive sadistic superego image. Identification with a primitive superego figure which demands self-destructiveness as an ego ideal integrated in the patient's character structure (to which I have referred before) may be expressed in the form of a chronic submission to a very hostile damaging person. At times, one or both of the real parents may represent such a function in the patient's life. Such a submission to a realistically destructive person needs to be evaluated from the viewpoint of both the capacity for lasting object relationships and the capacity to escape from such intense self-directed aggression.

Narcissistic personalities have particularly poor object relationships, in spite of their surprisingly good surface functioning in social groups: these patients remind us that the examination of the quality of object relationships must include the internal relationships to others, in contrast to a simple observation of the patient's interpersonal behavior. Among the patients described by Freud (6) as conveying an impression "not of having worked in clay, but of having written on water," narcissistic personalities are probably predominant. The surface adaptation of narcissistic patients masks both the absence of deep object relationships in the present, and severe pathology of their internalized object relationships as expressed in pathological ego and superego structures.

In short, the analysis of the patient's actual behavior and of his internal relationships to significant others provides important prognostic considerations for patients with borderline personality organization. The more stable, the more differentiated, the more emotionally deep the internal relationships of the patient with significant others, the better the prognosis for treatment.

The quality of a person's object relationships is actualized in the prognostically most meaningful way in the quality of the relationship he establishes with the therapist. This makes the quality of object relationships a process or transactional variable of crucial prognostic value. The quality of the relationship that the patient establishes with the therapist also reveals the quality of the patient's superego, as reflected by his capacity for awareness and concern for the therapist as a person, and in the extent to which the patient is able to free himself from the chronic submission to internal sadistic primitive superego demands.

This completes the examination of the prognostic elements reflected by the patient's presenting illness and personality. I will now examine the prognostic implications of one further and crucial process variable which does not depend on the patient: the therapist's skill and personality.

## THE SKILL AND THE PERSONALITY
## OF THE THERAPIST

The quantitative study of the outcome of the Psychotherapy Research Project of The Menninger Foundation (2) stressed the importance of psychotherapeutic technique in the treatment of patients with serious ego weakness, and clarified its relationship to the skill and personality of the therapist. What follows are pertinent quotations from the final conclusions of that work: "Treatments conducted within the framework of psychoanalytic theory require a 'fit' between therapist and patient for a successful outcome. This fit is particularly crucial when the patient has low ego strength. The skill of the therapist, which includes his capacity to integrate creatively his personality traits and countertransference reactions into the technique, is the most crucial factor in the outcome of the treatment of patients with low level of psychic functioning, that is, ego weakness.

"Less skilled therapists can contribute more to the treatment if their skill and personality features are less likely to influence the outcome. Patients with high ego strength and expressive modalities of treatment (that is, modalities which 'force' the therapist into a position of rather strict neutrality) are less likely to be influenced by less skill in the therapist. Patients with high ego strength can work hard on their problems even if the treatment and the therapist are less than ideal.

"Patients with low ego strength require a highly skilled therapist whether in supportive or expressive treatment. The findings suggest that the treatment of choice for patients with low ego strength may be a form of expressive psychotherapy, conducted by a highly skilled therapist, which emphasizes the work with the transference manifestations in the therapeutic relationship."

These findings lend further strength to clinical observations partly derived from the same Psychotherapy Research Project and partly stemming from my own experience, which determined my proposal in an earlier paper (Chapter 3) of a modified psychoanalytic procedure or psychoanalytic psychotherapy as the treatment of choice for patients with borderline personality organization. Such modified analytic procedure requires a high level of psychoanalytically oriented training and experience in psychotherapy, and great skill in working through systematically the predominantly negative transference of these patients. The psychotherapist dealing with these patients has to be aware of the need for introducing parameters of technique, for introducing structuralization of the treatment in the broadest sense, and of maintaining at the same time a position of essential neutrality. The stronger the acting-out potential of the patient, the more skillfully the therapist has to introduce additional structure while still maintaining an atmosphere of respect for the patient's personality and independence. The more the therapist yields to the temptation to provide "support" in the form of premature giving of advice, and the more the therapist attempts to establish control over the patient's life, the greater the danger of blurring the transference situation, and the higher the price that will have to be paid in sacrificing the long-term goals of the treatment for a temporary decrease of the patient's anxiety. In contrast, an artificially maintained "analytic situation," in which the therapist attempts to interpret the material as it presents itself in the hours while disregarding the reality situation of the patient, and in which the therapist submits to the transference acting-out in the hours, also leads to therapeutic stalemate. The therapist's creating just the necessary structuralization—and not more—in the hours and/or in the patient's life while preserving an essentially neutral position vis-a-vis the patient requires much skill and experience: every patient tests this skill in new ways, thus determining a unique "fit" which constitutes a prognostic process variable.

How important is the personality of the therapist in determining the prognosis of treatment for patients with borderline personality organization? It is very difficult to separate the influence of the psychotherapist's personality characteristics from countertransference factors and from his technique; clinically, one finds intimate, mutual relationships among the therapist's personality, his level of technique, and his countertransference reactions (14, 27). Ticho (23) stated that personality aspects and countertransference can indeed be separated, and he stressed the importance of the personality of the psychotherapist and the analyst, especially in treating borderline patients.

"For instance, what are the personality characteristics desirable in a therapist who would treat borderline cases? The therapist of a borderline case should have a capacity for a true object relationship. The treatment of borderline cases requires a great deal of security in the analyst; and there is no question that on a continuum from the treatment of neurotics to borderline cases to psychotics, there is an increased requirement that the therapist be in control of his hostility. The analyst's attitude toward the unavoidable acting out of the patient makes a great deal of difference. If the analyst is unconcerned, the acting out gets worse; if he is overconcerned, he also encourages acting out. There is also need for a clear sense of the analyst's moral values, and any lack of conviction in the analyst about his moral values can lead to difficulties in the treatment, while a moralistic attitude is detrimental."

Ticho (23) also referred to a group of generally successful analysts and therapists who presented "unobtrusive, unpretentious, non-self-centered, self-accepting personalities." His observation points to the importance of the therapist overcoming *his* own narcissism which will influence his relationships and his effectiveness in working with patients. This is perhaps the most crucial aspect of the therapist's personality in influencing the treatment process of patients with borderline personality organization.

Narcissistic problems of the psychotherapist are a major unfavorable prognostic element in the long-term treatment of patients with borderline personality organization. The serious regressive potential of these patients, their intense, predominantly negative transference reactions, and the particular transference-countertransference complications which develop in their treatment process put a maximum of stress on the psychotherapist. The lowered capacity for sustaining object-relationships under frustrating conditions, so typical for narcissistic personalities, is a major liability for therapists with important unresolved narcissistic tendencies who attempt to treat borderline patients.

## SUMMARY

The prognosis for intensive, long-term psychotherapeutic treatment of patients with borderline personality organization has been dealt with. The prognostic elements reflected by the patient's presenting illness and personality have been outlined.

Summarizing these prognostic elements briefly, the prognosis of patients with borderline personality organization depends on: 1) the descriptive diagnosis of the predominant type of character pathology, and the extent of ego and superego pathology revealed by pathological character traits; 2) the. nonspecific manifestations of ego weakness present, especially the degree of impulse control, anxiety tolerance, and sublimatory potential; 3) the degree to which integrated, abstracted, depersonified superego structures are present, as reflected in patients' capacity for concern, guilt, depression, insight, and the extent and structural implications of antisocial trends; 4) the quality of object relationships.

I have stressed that the prognotic indicators available in the initial examinations facilitate the selection of those patients for intensive psychotherapeutic treatment who can better use the limited therapeutic resources presently available. These initial prognostic indicators also highlight areas of prognostic uncertainty which may then be clarified during the treatment process.

I have also stressed that the prognosis further depends on several process or transactional variables. These variables refer to developments and changes that occur as part of the psychotherapeutic relationship, and include the extent to which previously ego-syntonic pathological character traits may become ego dystonic, the extent to which capacities for self-awareness, introspection, and concern develop under the influence of the treatment process, the extent to which patients are able to develop authentic object relationships with their therapists, and the extent to which patients' potential for negative therapeutic reaction can be resolved.

Finally, I have examined the prognostic implications of one further, and crucial process variable which does not depend on the patient: the therapist's skill and personality. I have stressed that patients with low ego strength require a highly skilled therapist whether in supportive or expressive treatment. Creating just the necessary structuralization—and not more—in the hours and/or in the patient's life, while preserving an essentially neutral position vis-a-vis the patient requires much skill and experience on the therapist's part. Every patient tests the skill of the therapist in new ways, thus determining a unique "fit" which constitutes a prognostic process variable. It is very difficult to separate the influence of personality characteristics of the psychotherapist from countertransference factors and from his technique. Clinically, the personality of the psychotherapist or the analyst is a crucial prognostic variable in treating borderline patients.

## BIBLIOGRAPHY

1.  Bion, W. (1967), *Second Thoughts: Selected Papers on Psychoanalysis.* London: Heinemann, pp. 86–109.
2.  Burstein, E., Coyne, L., Kernberg, O. & Voth, H. (1969), The quantitative study: psychotherapy outcome. In "Psychotherapy and psychoanalysis: Final report of The Menninger Foundation's Psychotherapy Research Project," by O. Kernberg, E. Burstein, L. Coyne, A. Appelbaum, L. Horwitz, and H. Voth. *Bull. Menninger Clinic,* 1972, pp. 1-85.
3.  Cooperman, M. (1970), Defeating processes in psychotherapy. Reported in Transactions of the Topeka Psychoanalytic Society, *Bull. Menninger Clinic,* 34, 36–38.
4.  Freud, A. (1936), *The Ego and the Mechanisms of Defense.* New York: International Universities Press, 1966, pp. 117-131.
5.  Freud, S. (1923), The ego and the id. *Standard Edition,* 19:13–66. London: The Hogarth Press, 1961.
6.  ——— (1937), Analysis terminable and interminable. *Standard Edition,* 23:216–253. London: The Hogarth Press, 1961.
7.  Frosch, J. (1964), The psychotic character: clinical psychiatric considerations. *Psychiatric Quart.,* 38:81–96.
8.  Guntrip, H. (1968), *Schizoid Phenomena, Object Relations and the Self.* New York: International Universities Press, pp. 275-309.
9.  Heimann, P. (1955), A combination of defence mechanisms in paranoid states. *New Directions in Psycho-Analysis.* London: Tavistock Publications, pp. 240-265.
10. Kernberg, O. (1966), Structural derivatives of object relationships. *Internat. J. Psycho-Anal.,* 47:236–253.
11. ——— (1970), A psychoanalytic classification of character pathology. *J. Am. Psychoanal. Assoc.* 18:800–822.
12. ——— Coyne, L., Horwitz, L., Appelbaum, A. & Burstein, E. (1968), The application of facet theory and the technique of multidimensional scalogram analysis to the quantitative data. In "Psychotherapy and psychoanalysis: Final report of The Menninger Foundation's Psychotherapy Research Project," by O. Kernberg, E. Burstein, L. Coyne, A. Appelbaum, L. Horwitz, and H. Voth. *Bull. Menninger Clinic,* 1972, pp. 87-178.
13. Klein, M. (1940), Mourning and its relation to manic-depressive states. *Contributions to Psycho-Analysis 1921-1945.* London: The Hogarth Press, 1948, pp. 311-338.
14. Little, M. (1960), On basic unity. *Internat. J. Psycho-Anal.,* 41:377–384; 637.
15. Luborsky, L. (1962), The patient's personality and psychotherapeutic change. In: *Research in Psychotherapy, vol. II.* H. H. Strupp & L. Luborsky, eds. Washington, D.C., Amer. Psycholog. Assn., pp. 115-133.

16.   Masterson, J. F., Jr. (1967), *The Psychiatric Dilemma of Adolescence*. Boston: Little, Brown, pp. 119–134.
17.   Pao, P. N. (1970), Personal communication.
18.   Rapaport, D., Gill, M. M. & Schafer, R. (1945-1946), *Diagnostic Psychological Testing*, 2 vols. Chicago: Year Book Publishers, 1:16–28; 2:24–31, 329–366.
19.   Robbins, L. L. & Wallerstein, R. S. (1959), The research strategy and tactics of the psychotherapy research project of The Menninger Foundation and the problem of controls. In: *Research in Psychotherapy*, ed. E. A. Rubinstein & M. B. Parloff. Washington, D.C.: Amer. Psycholog. Assn., pp. 27–43.
20.   Robins. L. N. (1966), *Deviant Children Grown Up*. Baltimore: Williams & Wilkins, pp. 287–309.
21.   Rosenfeld, H. (1964), On the psychopathology of narcissism: a clinical approach. *Internat. J. Psycho-Anal.*, 45:332–337.
22.   ——— (1970), Negative therapeutic reaction. Reported in Transactions of the Topeka Psychoanalytic Society, *Bulletin of the Menninger Clinic*, 34:189–192.
23.   Ticho, E. (1972), The effects of the psychoanalyst's personality on the treatment. Vol. 4, in press. *Psychoanalytic Forum*. New York: International Universities Press.
24.   ——— (in press), The development of superego autonomy. *Psychoanal. Rev.*
25.   Wallerstein, R. S., Luborsky, L., Robbins, L. L. & Sargent, H. D. (1956), The psychotherapy research project of The Menninger Foundation: rationale, method and sample use: First Report. *Bull. Menninger Clinic*, 20:221–278.
26.   Winnicott, D. W. (1955), The depressive position in normal emotional development. *Brit. J. Med. Psychol.*, 28:89–100.
27.   ——— (1960), Countertransference. *Brit. J. Med. Psychol.*, 33:17–21.
28.   ——— (1963), The development of the capacity for concern. *Bull. Menninger Clinic*, 27:167–176.

# Five

# Differential Diagnosis and Treatment

## A CRITICAL REVIEW OF RECENT LITERATURE

### 1. Diagnosis

A review of the literature on the diagnosis and treatment of borderline conditions is to be found elsewhere (Chapters 1 and 3). I will limit myself here to reviewing more recent contributions to these issues.

Regarding the diagnosis of borderline conditions, Grinker et al.'s book, *The Borderline Syndrome* (15), constitutes a major contribution to the delimitation of this clinical entity. Grinker et al. define the overall characteristics of the borderline syndrome as including "anger as the main or only affect, defect in affectional relationships, absence of indication of self-identity, and depressive loneliness" (page 176). They define four subgroups within this clinical constellation: Group I—"The psychotic border," characterized by inappropriate and negativistic behavior and affects toward other patients and hospital staff; Group II—"The core borderline syndrome," characterized by negativistic and chaotic feelings and behavior, contradictory behavior and a strong acting out potential; Group III—"The adaptive, affectless defended, 'as if' person," characterized by bland adaptiveness with an "as if" quality, with superficially adaptive but affectively deficient interactions; and Group IV—"The border with the neuroses," which presents childlike clinging depression.

Grinker et al. conclude that, in general, and in contrast to schizophrenia, the borderline syndrome does not present disturbances in intellectual associational processes, nor autistic or regressive thinking, nor a characteristic family structure with "pseudo-mutuality" or "skewing," nor delusions or hallucinations, nor any deficit in the connotative aspects of language (page 93). In comparing the borderline syndrome to the neuroses, Grinker et al. state that "although depression as an affect is found in several of the borderline categories, it does not correspond with that seen in the depressive syndrome. The borderline depression is a feeling of loneliness and isolation" (page 95).

Grinker et al.'s efforts to differentiate the borderline syndrome from other personality or character disorders seems less satisfactory. They point (accurately, it seems to me) to the tendency on the part of some authors to use various characterological labels for what are essentially borderline patients, and imply that a better definition of the borderline syndrome will help clarify the vague field of diagnosis of character pathology. It may well be that because the research design of Grinker and his co-workers focused particularly on overt behavior and interaction of borderline patients within a hospital setting, the underlying structural characteristics of these patients which differentiate borderline personality organization from less severe types of character pathology were not fully explored in this study. In spite of this limitation, I think that Grinker et al.'s study is a most important research contribution to the delimitation of the borderline syndrome. Werble (28) reported a follow-up study of the patients of Grinker et al.'s experimental population. He concluded that over a five-year period after the completion of the original study, there had been little individual change in the social functioning of these patients; they were able to adapt themselves within narrowly constricted limits, with very few human object relations in their lives, and (very importantly) these former patients did not present evidence of schizophrenia at the follow-up time.

Several authors have contributed to the clinical analysis of borderline conditions. Collum (9), combining the viewpoints of Grinker et al. and those suggested in my papers on this subject, focuses upon the central nature of identity diffusion as characteristic of borderline patients. Cary (7) develops further the structural-dynamic analysis of borderline conditions, stressing the following characteristics: "Depression" within the borderline syndrome is characterized by a sense of futility and pervasive feelings of loneliness and isolation—a feeling of isolation and angry demandingness rather than neurotic and psychotic depression which would be characterized by feelings of guilt and self-derogation. He also stresses schizoid detachment as a major defense of borderline patients. I think that both Grinker et al. and Cary's analysis point to the predominantly early ego organization of borderline patients within which self and object images have not become integrated (and, therefore, where a state of "total" object relationships has not been reached). This primitive ego organization explains the primitive nature of depressive reactions of borderline patients, their lack of capacity for fully experiencing concern and their pervasive experience of emptiness (Chapter 7).

Bergeret (3, 4) has examined the structural and dynamic characteristics of borderline states from a psychoanalytic viewpoint. After reviewing both the Anglo-Saxon and recent French psychoanalytic literature, and examining clinical case material, he concludes that borderline conditions are characterized by a predominance of pregenital conflicts and a predominance of primitive structural and defensive characteristics of the ego and superego. He stresses that borderline conditions are characterized by the ego's immaturity of object relations and constitute a psychopathological category different from both neurotic structures and psychotic structures. Duvocelle (10) integrates Bergeret's and my viewpoints into an overall clinical and theoretical overview of borderline personality organization.

Mahler (23) has recently proposed that, during the rapprochement subphase of the separation-individuation process, children whose normal resolution of the rapprochement crisis fails may develop a "bad" introject, which becomes infiltrated with the derivatives of aggressive drive and may evolve into a more or less permanent split of the object world into "good" and "bad" objects. She states (p. 413), "These mechanisms, coercion and splitting of the object world, are characteristic in most cases of borderline transference." This pathological development is in contrast to the normal consequences of the resolution of the rapprochement subphase in the form of normal identity formation in the third year of life.

While all of the authors mentioned for the most part agree on the overall descriptive and perhaps even dynamic-structural characteristics of borderline conditions, the differential diagnosis of borderline conditions from other types of character pathology on the one hand, and from psychotic, particularly schizophrenic reactions on the other, has not been explored extensively in the recent literature. One paper (27) reviews the literature on the differential diagnosis of borderline conditions and concludes that "those authors who classified these patients as psychotic presented the most cogent conceptualizations and data, and it appears that these patients should best be considered as psychotic" (page 34). This paper represents a thoughtful review of the literature, but, on the basis of the evidence reviewed, I cannot agree with the conclusion.

Kohut (22) has commented on the differentiation of borderline structures from narcissistic personalities, and I deal with the complex interrelationships between borderline condition and narcissistic personalities in Chapter 9. In more general terms, I attempted an overall classification of character pathology which includes borderline conditions as the most severely regressed level of character disorders (18).

Bellak and Hurvich (2) and Hurvich (16) have recently explored the assessment of ego functions as a major dimension in the differential diagnosis of schizophrenic from non-schizophrenic conditions. The function of reality testing—a crucial variable in the differential diagnosis of borderline from psychotic conditions, (11 and Chapter 1)—has been comprehensively reviewed by Hurvich (16). Later in this chapter I will explore the utilization of reality testing in the differential diagnosis of borderline from psychotic conditions.

In addition to the English and French reviews of the borderline constellation, some Spanish reviews have also been published (26, and 25). A good overall review of the literature on borderline conditions can be found in Arlene R. Wolberg's recent book (29).

## 2. Treatment

There has been an increase of papers in the psychiatric and particularly psychoanalytic literature of recent years dealing with treatment of borderline conditions. As before, opinions are divided on whether borderline patients should be treated supportively, or with an expressive, psychoanalytic approach, or with non-modified psychoanalysis. There has been a gradual shift away from the recommendation that these patients should be treated with supportive psychotherapy, and only Zetzel (30) has recommended "regular but limited contact (very seldom more than once a week)" in order to decrease the intensity of transference and countertransference manifestations, and a stress on reality issues and structuralization of the treatment hours, all of which constitute jointly an essentially supportive approach. Zetzel acknowledged that (with her approach) "for many borderline patients, however, it may be necessary for the therapist to remain at least potentially available over an indefinitely extended period." The implication is that this supportive approach, while effective in permitting the patient to adjust better to reality, may contribute to an interminable psychotherapeutic relationship.

Various authors have recommended a modified psychoanalytic procedure or expressive psychotherapeutic approach commensurate with what I proposed in Chapter 3. Frosch (12) has spelled out the clinical approach to borderline patients within a modified psychoanalytic procedure, and, more recently (13) summarized his overall strategy of treatment with these patients. Greenson (14) proposes a similar approach, illustrating his modified psychoanalytic technique with clinical cases. Both Frosch and Greenson stress the importance of clarifying the patient's perceptions in the hours, and his attitude toward the therapist's interventions. Their approach (with which I basically agree) implies a basically neutral technical position of the therapist, and only a minimum deviation from such a position of neutrality as might be necessary. In contrast, other psychoanalytically derived psychotherapeutic approaches to borderline conditions involve more modifications of technique.

Thus, Masterson (24) suggests that "the borderline syndrome is a result of the feelings of abandonment which are in turn created by the mother's withdrawal of supplies when the patient attempts to separate and individuate. The patient's need to defend himself against his feelings of abandonment produces the developmental arrest and the clinical picture" (page 35). On this basis, he designs a special psychotherapy as specifically geared to "the resolution of the acute symptomatic crisis (the abandonment depression) and the correction and repair of the ego defects that accompany the narcissistic oral fixation by encouraging growth through the stages of separation-individuation to autonomy." It seems to me that his approach does not consider sufficiently the differences between conflicts around and defenses against symbiotic fusion (related to pathological refusion of self and object images) and conflicts related to structural conditions centering around splitting (related to the incapacity to integrate aggressively determined and libidinally determined self and object images). His approach also neglects the importance of conflicts around pregenital aggression in the etiology of borderline personality organization. In addition, one finds various characterological structures at the level of borderline personality organization, and the individual treatment technique should take into account these and other more individually determined genetic-dynamic characteristics.

Arlene R. Wolberg (29) suggests that early interpretation of the hostile transference may gratify the masochism of borderline patients rather than be helpful in the working through of the transference. She proposes that conflicts around hostility be interpreted indirectly "by projective therapeutic techniques" which focus on the expression of these conflicts onto other objects. She states that "a projective therapeutic technique allows the relation with the here and now to be handled through the use of the 'other person' emphasizing the defensive aspects of the transference behavior of the 'other' and letting the patient avoid the personal confrontation with the analyst until he is able to tolerate the anxiety he feels in the interpersonal relationship, without resorting to massive defense. The aim of treatment is to help the patient let up on the creation of defenses rather than to force him by premature confrontation to increase his defenses." I disagree with this approach, and would stress instead that the direct but noncritical focus upon both positive and negative transference aspects is most effective in helping the patient reduce his own fears over his aggression. However, many other aspects of Wolberg's technical approach to the treatment of borderline conditions are related to the approach taken by other authors who apply a modified psychoanalytic procedure. The same is true, it seems to me, with the psychotherapeutic approach for borderline conditions recommended by Chessick (8).

Masterson (24) has pointed out the need for hospitalization of some borderline adolescent patients, and suggests specific designs of the milieu to deal with their defenses and conflicts (pp. 105-109). Adler (1) has succinctly described the basic structure required for borderline patients hospitalized in short-term treatment units. He stresses the danger of permitting unchallenged regression to occur to such an extent that the acting out of conflicts within the hospital setting perpetuates the patient's gratification of pathological needs, and the danger of excessive limit setting that obscures the patient's psychopathology. The area of long-term inpatient treatment for some borderline patients who cannot be treated on an outpatient or short inpatient basis seems to me still largely unexplored in the literature.

Boyer and Giovacchini (6) recommend a nonmodified psychoanalytic approach to schizophrenic and characterological disorders. They state that the broadening of technical understanding and technique in recent years has made it possible to deal analytically with those severely regressed patients who are able to enter a regular, purely outpatient treatment setting. Although Giovacchini, in chapters dedicated to character disorders, does not refer specifically to borderline conditions (in contrast to severe character pathology in general), his observations focus upon the technical problems posed by what I would consider patients with borderline personality organization. He acknowledges that some patients "may act out with such violence that the analytic decorum is disrupted and analysis cannot proceed" (page 258). In practice, Giovacchini would set limits to the patient's acting out in the hours, and utilize parameters of technique which he would attempt to resolve through interpretation later. He recommends, for some cases, temporary discontinuation of treatment (page 261). He acknowledges "that there are some patients who need someone to manage some facet of their chaotic situation to effect sufficient stabilization so therapy can proceed. Whether this can be done by the analyst while preserving the necessary conditions for therapy . . . is still an unsettled question" (page 286).

Boyer (5) stresses the importance of interpreting early in the analytic treatment of patients with severe characterological and schizophrenic illness the aggressive drive derivatives, and reiterates his earlier thinking that an essentially nonmodified psychoanalytic technique can be maintained with these patients. Paz (26) also stresses the possibility of maintaining an essentially unmodified psychoanalytic approach with borderline conditions, and a similar approach is implied in Khan's (20,21) papers on specific defensive operations in borderline schizoid patients.

On the basis of the final outcome study of the quantitative data of the Psychotherapy Research Project of The Menninger Foundation (19), I feel strengthened in my conviction that the majority of borderline patients require a modified analytic approach while a minority may be suitable for a standard psychoanalytic procedure. In what follows, I will first briefly summarize my earlier work on the psychopathology, diagnosis, and treatment of borderline personality organization, and then present some further clinical contributions regarding the vicissitudes of the transference in these cases, the long-range treatment strategy, and the differential diagnosis with schizophrenia.

## SUMMARY OF PREVIOUS WORK

The two terms most frequently used to designate structural alterations of a patient's ego which raise the question of limits of effectiveness of psychoanalysis are "ego distortion" and "ego weakness." For all practical purposes, these two terms are applied to the same type of patients; ego distortion focuses on the highly pathological, rigid character patterns these patients present, while the term ego weakness focuses upon these patients' inadequacy or lack of certain normal ego functions. From a research viewpoint, the term ego weakness is preferable because of its quantitative implications; indeed, this term was utilized in the Psychotherapy Research Project of The Menninger Foundation to evaluate the relationship between structural alterations and inadequacy of ego functions on the one hand, and the effectiveness of psychoanalysis and psychoanalytic psychotherapy on the other (19). My work on diagnosis, prognosis and treatment of borderline conditions stems from that project.

In this chapter, I use the term ego weakness to refer to structural alterations of the ego derived from early ego disturbances, and will examine briefly, 1) the clinical manifestations of ego weakness which is typical for borderline personality organization, 2) some hypotheses regarding the origin of ego weakness, 3) complications arising from efforts to analyze patients with ego weakness and some technical implications for the treatment of these patients and, 4) some conditions improving or worsening analyzability in these cases. I will introduce at several points new material to the respective analyses developed in earlier chapters, emphasizing the diagnostic and therapeutic features of borderline personality organization. Finally, I will summarize some clinical and theoretical implications of transference psychosis and clarify further the differential diagnosis with schizophrenia.

## 1. The Clinical Manifestations of Borderline Personality Organization

Clinically, when we speak of patients with borderline personality organization, we refer to patients who present serious difficulties in their interpersonal relationships and some alteration of their experience of reality but with essential preservation of reality testing (Chapter 1). Such patients also present contradictory character traits, chaotic coexistence of defenses against and direct expression of primitive "id contents" in consciousness, a kind of pseudo-insight into their personality without real concern for nor awareness of the conflictual nature of this material, and a lack of clear identity and lack of understanding in depth of other people. These patients present primitive defensive operations rather than repression and

related defenses, and above all, mutual dissociation of contradictory ego states reflecting what might be called a
"nonmetabolized" persistence of early, pathological internalized object relationships. They also show "nonspecific"
manifestations of ego weakness. The term "nonspecific" refers
to lack of impulse control, lack of anxiety tolerance, lack of
sublimatory capacity, and presence of primary process thinking,
and indicates that these manifestations of ego weakness
represent a general inadequacy of normal ego functions. In
contrast, the primitive defensive constellation of these patients
and their contradictory, pathological character traits are
"specific" manifestations of ego weakness. In short, they
represent highly individualized, active compromise formations
of impulse and defense.

## 2.   Hypotheses Regarding the Origin of Ego Weakness

Two essential tasks that the early ego has to accomplish in
rapid succession are: 1) the differentiation of self-images from
object-images, and 2) integrating libidinally determined and
aggressively determined self- and object-images.

The first task is accomplished in part under the influence of
the development of the apparatuses of primary autonomy:
perception and memory traces help to sort out the origin of
stimuli and gradually differentiate self- from object-images.
This first task fails to a major extent in the psychoses, in which a
pathological fusion between self- and object-images determines
a failure in the differentiation of ego boundaries and, therefore,
in the differentiation of self from nonself. In contrast, in the
case of borderline personality organization, differentiation of
self- from object-images has occurred to a sufficient degree to
permit the establishment of integrated ego boundaries and a
concomitant differentiation between self and others.

The second task, however, of integrating self- and object-
images built up under the influence of libidinal drive derivatives
and their related affects with their corresponding self- and
object-images built up under the influence of aggressive drive
derivatives and related affects, fails to a great extent in
borderline patients, mainly because of the pathological

predominance of pregenital aggression. The resulting lack of synthesis of contradictory self- and object-images interferes with the integration of the self-concept and with the establishment of object-constancy or "total" object relationships. I will now examine these hypotheses in more detail.

Good enough mothering implies that mother evokes, stimulates and complements ego functions which are not yet available to the infant. For example, mother's intuitive handling of the baby permits the early detection of sources of pain, fear, and frustration, in addition to providing an optimum of gratifying, pleasurable experiences while satisfying the baby's basic needs. Intrapsychically, this means that a core experience of satisfaction and pleasure is set up in the baby, powerfully reinforced by the pleasurable affects thus released and gradually also by the propioceptive and exteroceptive perceptions linked with such experiences. Out of this core will come the basic, fused self-mother image which in turn determines basic trust. Basic trust involves recognition, and, later, anticipation of a pleasurable mother-child relationship. The basic ego disturbance is the failure to build up a sufficiently strong fused "all good" self-object image or "good internal object."

The libidinally determined good self-object image permits some attentuation or neutralization of the anxiety producing and disorganizing effects of excessive frustration, with which "bad," fused self-object images are set up. The normal relationship with mother reinforces, as well as depends upon, the buildup of this good internal fused self-object image.

Severe frustrations and the consequent predominance of aggressively-determined, "all bad" fused self-object images may interfere with the next stage of development, namely, the gradual sorting out of self from object components in the realm of the good self-object image. As Jacobson (17) points out, defensive refusion of primitive, all good self- and object-images as a protection against excessive frustration and rage is the prototype of what constitutes, if prolonged beyond the early infantile stages of development, a psychotic identification.

If and when self-images have been differentiated from object-images in the area of libidinally determined ego nuclei and, later, in the area of aggressively-determined ego nuclei, a crucial step has been taken which differentiates future psychotic from nonpsychotic ego structures. The next step is the gradual integration of contradictory (that is, libidinally-determined and aggressively-determined) self-images, with the crystallization of a central self surrounded, we might say, by object-images which in turn become integrated (in the sense that good and bad object representations related to the same external objects are integrated). This is also the point where tolerance of ambivalence begins to develop. When such integration is achieved, an integrated self-image or self-concept relates to integrated object-images and there is also a continuous reshaping and reconfirmation of both self-concept and object-images by means of mechanisms of projection and introjection linked with actual interpersonal relationships with mother and other human beings surrounding the child.

The integrated self-concept and the related integrated representation of objects constitutes ego identity in its broadest sense. A stable ego identity, in turn, becomes a crucial determinant of stability, integration, and flexibility of the ego, and also influences the full development of higher level superego functions (abstraction, depersonification, and individualization of the superego).

Failure to integrate the libidinally determined and the aggressively determined self- and object-images is the major cause for nonpsychotic ego disturbances which, in turn, determine limits in analyzability. Such lack of integration derives from pathological predominance of aggressively-determined self- and object-images and a related lack of establishment of a sufficiently strong ego core around the originally fused good self-object image. However, in contrast to conditions in which self-images have not been differentiated from object-images (the psychoses), there has been at least sufficient differentiation between self- and object-images for the establishment of firm ego boundaries in cases of ego distortion which are generally designated as borderline conditions. The problem at this point is that the intensity of aggressively-determined self- and object-images, and of defensively-idealized all good self- and object-images makes integration impossible. Bringing together extremely opposite loving and hateful images of the self and of significant others would trigger unbearable anxiety and guilt because of the implicit danger to the good internal and external object relations; therefore, there is an active defensive separation of such contradictory self- and object-images; in other words, primitive dissociation or splitting becomes a major defensive operation.

Lack of integration of self- and object-representations is at first a normal characteristic of early development; but, later, such lack of integration is used actively to separate contradictory ego states. Splitting refers to the active, defensive separation of contradictory ego states. Primitive defensive operations linked to splitting (denial, primitive idealization, omnipotence, projection and projective identification) powerfully reinforce splitting, and protect the ego from unbearable conflicts between love and hatred by sacrificing its growing integration. Clinically, the child who is going to become a borderline patient, lives from moment to moment, actively cutting off the emotional links between what would otherwise become chaotic, contradictory, highly frustrating and frightening emotional experiences with significant others in his immediate environment.

There are several significant structural consequences of these primitive defensive operations set up to protect the ego against unbearable conflict and the related pathology of internalized object relationships. First, an integrated self-concept cannot develop, and chronic overdependence on external objects occurs in an effort to achieve some continuity in action, thought, and feeling in relating to them. Lack of integration of the self-concept determines the syndrome of identity-diffusion. Second, contradictory character traits develop, representing the contradictory self- and object-images, further creating chaos in the interpersonal relationship of the future borderline patient. Third, superego integration suffers because the guiding function of an integrated ego identity is missing; contradictions between exaggerated, all good ideal object-images and extremely sadistic, all bad superego forerunners interfere with superego integration. Therefore, the superego functions which would further facilitate ego integration also are missing and this reinforces the pathological consequences of excessive reprojection of superego nuclei in the form of paranoid trends. Fourth, a lack of integrated object-representations interferes with deepening of empathy with others as individuals in their own right; lack of integration of the self-concept further interferes with full emotional understanding of other human beings; the end result is defective object-constancy or incapacity to establish total object relationships. Fifth, nonspecific aspects of ego strength (anxiety tolerance, impulse control, sublimatory potential) suffer because of the weakness of ego and superego integration. Ego strength depends on the neutralization of instinctual energy; such neutralization takes place essentially in the integration of libidinally and aggressively derived self- and object-images.

## 3. Complications in Analyzing Patients with Borderline Personality Organization, and Technical Implications for Their Treatment

In patients with ego weakness, primitive, early conflicts are not repressed; conscious mutual dissociation among contradictory primitive contents replaces repression and the normal "resistance versus content" organization of defenses and impulses. Consciousness of primitive material does not reflect insight but the predominance of splitting mechanisms—a different set of defensive constellations from those centering around repression seen in neurotic patients.

Also, deficit in nonspecific manifestations of ego strength interferes with the necessary tolerance of increased conflict awareness during treatment, and provokes excessive acting-out tendencies.

In addition, lack of differentiation of the self-concept and the lack of differentiation and individualization of objects interfere with the differentiation of present from past object relationships. Transference and reality are confused; also, the analyst is not differentiated from the transference object because of the prevalence of primitive projection. Furthermore, the lack of capacity for seeing the analyst as an integrated object in his own right, and the pathologically increased, alternating projection of self- and object-images (so that reciprocal roles are easily interchanged in the transference) weakens ego boundaries in the transference and promotes transference psychosis.

Finally, the therapeutic relationship easily replaces ordinary life, because its gratifying and sheltered nature further intensifies the temptation to gratify primitive pathological needs in the transference and acting out.

This summary reflects the typical structure of borderline personality organization and the typical treatment difficulties these patients present. Although some authors believe that a standard psychoanalysis can and should be carried out under these conditions, others, including myself, question this. However, the treatment I suggest as ideally suited for these patients is a psychoanalytically derived procedure which strongly emphasizes the interpretation of resistances and of the transference and the adherence to an essentially neutral position of the analyst.

I have suggested the following technical requirements for the psychoanalytic psychotherapy of borderline patients (Chapter 3): 1) systematic elaboration of the negative transference in the "here and now" only, without attempting to achieve full genetic reconstructions; 2) interpretation of the defensive constellations of these patients as they enter the negative transference; 3) limit-setting in order to block acting out of the transference, with as much structuring of the patient's life outside the hours as necessary to protect the neutrality of the analyst; 4) noninterpretation of the less primitively determined, modulated aspects of the positive transference to foster the gradual development of the therapeutic alliance.

## 4. Some Conditions Under Which Analyzability Improves or Worsens

Improvement or worsening of the prognosis for psychoanalysis within the context of serious ego distortions of borderline personality organization depends on structural developments which complicate borderline personality organization and which, in turn, largely depend upon further vicissitudes of internalized object relationships (Chapters 4, 8, 9).

If the borderline patient has achieved some higher level of superego integration, abstraction, and depersonification, the superego may still be sufficiently strong to carry out functions fostering ego integration at large, thus compensating for the lack of integration of the self-concept (identity diffusion). Some infantile personalities have developed surprisingly good internalized value systems; the capacity to identify with ethical, professional, and/or artistic values beyond satisfaction of their own needs; and a personal integrity in dealing with these values, professions, or arts. Although a high intelligence and particular talents may be helpful elements, most important for such a development to occur seems to be the availability of object relations at the height of the development of advanced superego structures (around ages 4 to 6 and/or throughout adolescence) which were not completely controlled by their primitive conflicts and which permitted more harmonious integration of some realistic superego demands and prohibitions. Honesty and integrity in the ordinary sense of these words are also valuable prognostic factors which may permit some infantile personalities and other borderline personality structures to undergo a nonmodified psychoanalytic procedure.

A prognostically negative development complicating borderline personality organization is a pathological fusion of "all good" self-images with early ideal self-images and early ideal object-images. Such a pathological fusion of all the "good" aspects of internalized object relationships crystalizes into an idealized, highly unrealistic self-concept which, if fostered by some realistic circumstances (such as an unusual talent, physical beauty, or intelligence), may be reinforced by reality and, paradoxically, foster better reality adaptation to "specialness." This development characterizes the narcissistic personality (Chapters 8, 9). Social functioning may improve greatly under these circumstances, but at the cost of the loss of the normal differentiation between self on the one hand, and ego ideal on the other (at the cost, therefore, of a most important superego structure). Serious superego defects are typical of narcissistic personalities and compromise their analyzability.

It hardly needs to be stressed that the idealized self-concept requires even stronger activation of primitive defensive operations to deny and project the devaluated, bad aspects of the self; therefore, these defenses perpetuate a lack of realistic integration of the self-concept. However, the very improvement in surface functioning may obscure the severity of the underlying psychopathology, and narcissistic personalities may undergo years of psychoanalysis without change. Elsewhere, I refer to the fact that these patients should, however, be treated with psychoanalysis, and I also stress the special technical requirements of their analysis (Chapter 8).

A particularly ominous development worsening the prognosis for both psychoanalysis and psychoanalytic psychotherapy is the development, within the character structure of borderline patients, of identification with primitive superego forerunners of a highly sadistic kind. Under these circumstances, primitive destructiveness and self-destructiveness are built into the ego structure, are sanctioned by the superego, and permit direct expression of aggressive impulses under conditions which can seriously threaten the physical as well as the psychic life of these patients. Self-destruction, originally expressing primitive, pregenital aggression, may become an ego ideal and gratify the patient's sense of omnipotence in that he no longer needs to fear frustration and suffering (suffering is now an enjoyment in itself). Such aggression is expressed not only by random destructiveness, but by selective destructiveness toward those on whom the patient depends for his gratification (and his improvement). Therefore, he particularly envies those on whom he depends because these objects have an internal sense of love and they even want to provide goodness for others, including the patient. These patients represent prognostically the most ominous type of identification with the aggressor (Chapter 4).

## FURTHER CONSIDERATIONS ABOUT TREATMENT

### 1.  Transference Interpretation, Regression and Reconstruction

I would now like to stress the following aspects of the

treatment of these patients: first, one has to keep in mind that ego weakness does not reflect absence of a solid defensive organization of the ego, but represents the very active presence of a rigid constellation of primitive defenses; these defenses by their effects contribute to producing and maintaining such ego weakness. Second, rather than attempting to reinforce higher level defenses or to support the patient's adaptation directly, it is helpful to consistently interpret these primitive defensive operations, especially as they enter the transference, because the interpretation of these defenses permits ego growth to resume and higher level defensive operations to take over. Third, interpretations have to be formulated so that the patient's distortions of the analyst's intervention can be simultaneously and systematically examined, and the patient's distortion of present reality and especially of his perceptions in the hour can be systematically clarified. This clarification does not mean suggestion, advice giving, or revelation regarding personal matters of the analyst to the patient, but a clear explanation of how the analyst sees the "here and now" interaction with the patient in contrast to how the analyst assumes the patient is interpretating this "here and now" interaction. Clarification of perceptions and of the patient's relationship to the interpretation is, therefore, an important component of an essentially interpretive approach which attempts to systematically analyze the primitive defensive constellation as it enters the transference.

Often, in advanced stages of treatment of borderline patients, it turns out that while the traumatic circumstances patients reported earlier were unreal, there were other, very real, chronically traumatizing parent-child interactions which they had never been consciously aware of before. It turns out that the most damaging influences were those which the patient had taken as a matter of course, and the absence of these influences are often experienced by the patient as an astonishing opening of new perspectives on life. The following case illustrates the relationship between distortion of present reality and distortion of the past in the transference of a borderline patient, and the need to clarify the patient's perceptions in the hours.

A patient reminisced about having intimate physical contact with both parents which in her mind amounted to a family shared orgy. Gradually she became aware of the fantastic nature of these memories but later she recalled experiences she had not reported because they seemed such a matter of course. The patient reacted angrily whenever the analyst stated he did not understand some verbal or nonverbal communication of hers. She did not believe him; she thought he really could read her mind and that he only pretended he could not because he wanted to make her angry. After she consistently explored her assumption that the analyst could read her mind, she remembered that her mother had told her that she could indeed read the patient's mind. The patient's rejection of interpretations that seemed false to her was experienced by her as rebelliousness against mother. The implicit omnipotence of mother, her sadistic intrusion, the patient's passive acceptance of such a style of communication during childhood and adolescence, and her secondary omnipotent utilization of this pattern, turned out to reflect the real, highly traumatic aspects of her childhood. After working through in the transference the fantastic experiences with the parents—and the defenses against them—the patient was able to perceive the more realistic aspects of the therapeutic relationship. She became aware of the real, pathological interactions with her parents, which previously had seemed natural to her.

The implications of this observation that I wish to stress are that the disturbance in reality testing of this patient was related to a double layer of transference phenomena: a) the highly distorted transference (at times of an almost psychotic nature) reflecting fantastic internal object-relationships related to early ego disturbances, and b) the more "realistic" transference related to real experiences—the highly inappropriate parentchild interactions.

Interpretation of primitive defensive operations as they are activated in the therapeutic relationship may bring about immediate, impressive improvement in the patient's psychological functioning to such an extent that such a method in itself may be used in the diagnostic process when trying to differentiate borderline from psychotic patients. Systematic

probing of primitive defensive operations, such as interpretation of splitting mechanisms in the hour, will tend to improve
immediately the functioning of the borderline patient, but will
bring about further regression into manifest psychotic symptomatology in the psychotic patient. The following cases
illustrate such improvement or regression in the diagnostic
process:

In the hospital, I examined a college student, a single girl in
her early twenties, with awkward and almost bizarre behavior,
childlike theatrical gestures, emotional outbursts, suicidal
ideation, and breakdown in her social relations and scholastic
achievements. Her initial diagnosis was hysterical personality.
She was very concerned about social and political matters, cried
over the fact that she needed to be in the hospital, but
simultaneously acted completely indifferent while talking about
her suicidal fantasies, acted as if she were drowsy or drugged,
gave clear indication of boredom with the interviews, and
complained about her inability to make up her mind about
herself. I pointed out to her the displacement of her concern
over herself to the social and political situation, the expression
of depreciation of the interviewer, the effective avoidance of
taking responsibility for herself by dissociating her concern for
herself from the chaotic, easy-go-lucky behavior geared to force
others to take over for her.

In technical terms, I interpreted primitive defensive
operations (splitting, denial, omnipotence and devaluation) as
they were apparent in the "here and now" interaction with me.
In the course of the interviews, the patient changed from an
almost psychotic appearance to that of a rather thoughtful,
perceptive although highly anxious neurotic patient. The final
diagnosis was: infantile personality, with borderline features.

In contrast to this case, I examined another college student
in her early twenties, also single, whose initial diagnosis was
that of an obsessive-compulsive neurosis, probably functioning
on a borderline level. The entire interaction was filled with
highly theoretical, philosophical considerations, and efforts to
examine more personal, emotional material only intensified the
abstract nature of the comments that followed. I attempted to
interpret to the patient the avoidance function of her

theorizing, and explored some of the emotional experiences which she expressed in theoretical, philosophical terms. I also wondered with her whether the direct, personal impact of those experiences was too much for her, her theorizing providing her with some safety by distance. For example, when exploring the unhappy nature of a relationship with a boyfriend, she discussed the theological theories about guilt; and I wondered whether it was hard for her to explore guilt feelings she might have had in connection with that relationship. As I confronted the patient with her defensive maneuvers, she became more disturbed, openly distrustful, and even more abstract. Toward the end of the interviews, there was direct evidence of formal thought disorder and the diagnosis of schizophrenic reaction was eventually confirmed.

The implications of these observations that I wish to stress are: 1) interpretation of the predominant defensive operations in borderline patients may strengthen ego functioning, while the same approach to psychotic patients may bring about further regression; 2) the intimate relationship between reality testing, the effectiveness of defensive operations, and the immediate interpersonal interaction.

The fact that interpretation of these defensive operations may increase regression in psychotic patients does not imply that interpretive approaches should not be attempted with them; but such approaches do require particular modifications of the analytic technique which contraindicate both psychoanalysis as such, and the modified approach recommended for borderline patients. The psychotic patient, with his blurring of limits between self and object-images and the subsequent loss of ego boundaries, also utilizes splitting and other related primitive defensive operations; but he uses them to keep a surface adaptation in the face of threatening primitive dangers of complete engulfment or ego-dissolution. His problem is not only to separate hatred and love completely from each other but to avoid any intensification of awareness of affects, because the very intensity of any emotional relationship in itself may trigger off the refusion of self- and object-images. Therefore, interpretation of the psychotic patient's primitive defensive operations may bring about further loss of reality testing and psychotic regression.

Primitive defensive operations, and especially pathological forms of splitting and projection which bring about total dispersal of emotional awareness, protect the tenuous social adaptation of the psychotic patient: the underlying lack of self-object differentiation is thus obscured. Intensive psychotherapy with psychotic patients highlights this self-object fusion and requires a therapeutic approach which is different from that required with borderline conditions.

The intensive, psychoanalytic psychotherapy of psychotic, particularly schizophrenic, patients requires a tolerance, on the therapist's part, of the powerful countertransference reactions triggered off by the patient's fusion experiences in the transference. The therapist has to make maximal use of his countertransference experiences to understand the patient's experience, to convey to the patient his understanding in verbal communications, and to map out gradually in these communications the implicit differences existing between the patient's experiences and the therapist's reality, and between the patient's past and the present in the transference. In contrast, the therapist working with borderline patients, needs to interpret the primitive projective mechanisms, particularly projective identification, which contribute powerfully to the alternating projection of self- and object-images, and therefore, to blurring the boundary between what is "inside" and "outside" in the patient's experience of his interactions with the therapist. Acting out of the transference and excessive gratification of primitive emotional needs in the transference of borderline conditions need to be controlled while preserving an essentially neutral attitude of the therapist.

The following, concluding comments refer specifically to borderline patients. Working through of the primitive level of internalized object relationships activated in the transference gradually permits a shift in the transference into a predominance of the higher level, more realistic type of internalized object relations related to real childhood experiences. In order to achieve improvement in distorted ego functions, the patient must come to terms at some point with very real, serious limitations of what life has given him in his early years. Here the issue of coming to terms with physical and psychological defects converge. It is probably as difficult for borderline patients eventually to come to terms with the fact of failure in their early life as it is for patients with inborn or early determined physical defects to acknowledge, mourn, and come to terms with their defects. Borderline patients gradually have to become aware of how their parents failed them—not in the distorted, monstrous ways which existed in their fantasies when beginning treatment, but failed them in simple human ways of giving and receiving love, and providing consolation and understanding, and intuitively lending a helping hand when the baby, or the child, was in trouble. Borderline patients also have to learn to give up the highly idealized, unrealistically protective fantasies about perfect past relationships with their parents; for them to really separate from their parents is a much more difficult and frightening prospect than for the neurotic patient. These patients also have to work through the corresponding idealizations and magical expectations in the transference, and learn to accept the analyst realistically as a limited human being. This painful learning process is achieved by means of eventual analysis of parameters of technique, or by means of realistically examining in the treatment situation modifications of technique and why the analyst used them. Coming to terms with severe defects in one's past requires the capacity to mourn and to work through such mourning; to accept aloneness; and to realistically accept that others may have what the patient himself may never be able to fully compensate for. Hopefully, such capacity will develop throughout the treatment, but it is hard to foretell to what extent this development will take place.

## 2. Transference Psychosis

I mentioned earlier that the lack of differentiation of the self-concept and the lack of differentiation and individualization of objects interfere with the differentiation of present from past object-relationships, and contribute to the development of transference psychosis. Transference psychosis is a characteristic complication in the treatment of patients with borderline personality organization. There are similarities and differences between the transference psychosis that borderline patients develop and the psychotic transference characteristic of psychotic patients in intensive treatment.

The similarities of transference psychosis in borderline and psychotic patients are: 1) In both, there is a loss of reality testing in the transference situation, and the development of delusional thoughts involving the therapist; hallucinatory or pseudo-hallucinatory experiences may develop in the hours. 2) In both, primitive object relationships of a fantastic nature predominate in the transference; these relationships are characterized by multiple self-images and multiple object-images, that is, fantasy structures reflecting the earliest layers of internalized object relationships which represent a deeper layer of the mind than the dyadic and oedipal-triangular relationships characteristic of transference neurosis. This is in contrast to the predominance in the transference neurosis of less severely ill patients, of later, more realistic, internalized self- and object-representations in the context of an integrated ego and superego, reflecting more realistic, past interactions with the parents. 3) In borderline and psychotic patients, there develops an activation of primitive, overwhelming affective reactions in the transference, and a loss of sense of having a separate identity from the therapist.

The differences between the transference psychosis of borderline patients and the psychotic transference of psychotic, particularly schizophrenic, patients who undergo intensive psychotherapy are:

1) In borderline patients, the loss of reality testing does not strikingly affect the patient's functioning outside the treatment setting; these patients may develop delusional ideas and psychotic behavior within the treatment hours over a period of days and months without showing these manifestations outside the hours. Also, the transference psychosis of patients with borderline personality organization responds dramatically to the treatment previously outlined. In contrast, the psychotic transference of schizophrenic patients reflects their general loss of reality testing, and the psychotic thinking, behavior, and affect expression of their life outside the treatment hours. The initial detachment of the schizophrenic patient is usually reflected in psychotic behavior in the hours which is not markedly different from his psychotic behavior outside the treatment hours. It may take a long time

for psychotic patients to develop a particular, intensive emotional relationship to the therapist, differentiated from all other interactions: when this finally does happen, the psychotic transference becomes particularly different from that of borderline patients, our next point.

2) Psychotic patients, particularly at more advanced states of development of their psychotic transference, have fusion experiences with the therapist by which they feel a common identity with him. In contrast to borderline patients, this identity confusion in the transference is not due to rapid oscillation of projection of self-and object-images (so that object relationships are activated with rapidly alternating, reciprocal role enactment on the part of patient and therapist), but is a consequence of refusion of self- and object-images, so that separateness between self and nonself no longer obtains: this reflects their regression to a more primitive stage of symbiotic self-object fusion. Borderline patients, even in the course of a transference psychosis, do experience a boundary of a sort between themselves and the therapist: it is as if the patient maintains a sense of being different from the therapist at all times, but concurrently he and the therapist are interchanging aspects of their personalities. In contrast, psychotic patients experience themselves as one with the therapist at all times; however, the nature of this oneness changes from a frightening, dangerous experience of raw aggression and confused engulfment (without differentiating who engulfs and who is the engulfed) to that of an exalted, mystical experience of oneness, goodness, and love. In short, the underlying mechanisms determining loss of ego boundaries, loss of reality testing, and delusion formation are different in the psychotic transferences of borderline and psychotic patients.

## DIFFERENTIAL DIAGNOSIS OF SCHIZOPHRENIA AND BORDERLINE CONDITIONS

We often face the task, in the early stages of the evaluation of patients, of making a careful differential diagnosis between borderline conditions and schizophrenia. It is important to make such a differential diagnosis because of the differences in the prognosis and treatment of the two conditions: I have become optimistic about the prognosis of borderline patients in a specially designed treatment program that combines intensive, psychoanalytically-oriented psychotherapy with a highly structured hospital milieu program—during the initial phase of treatment for many cases, and during more extended periods of time for some. In contrast, the prognosis for chronic schizophrenic patients is, of course, always serious.

The two major considerations in differentiating schizophrenia from borderline conditions are the issues of reality testing and transference psychosis. Having already considered transference psychosis, I will limit myself to the discussion of reality testing.

When a patient comes into the hospital with a typical history of chronic manifestations of formal thought disorder, hallucinations and delusions, bizarre behavior and affect, and disintegration of the connection between thought content, affect, and behavior, the diagnosis is usually that of a schizophrenic reaction. However, n.any borderline patients who present severe, chronic disturbances in their interpersonal relationships and a chaotic social life, and who have undergone psychoanalysis or intensive psychoanalytic psychotherapy on an outpatient basis, may have developed transitory psychotic reactions which raise the question of schizophrenia. Also, both borderline and schizophrenic patients who have received intensive drug treatment over a long period of time, or have socially stabilized in the form of chronic withdrawal from interpersonal interactions (while still functioning relatively appropriately in some isolated, mechanical work situation), require this differential diagnosis.

I have pointed out earlier, that, while both borderline and psychotic patients present a predominance of pathological, internalized object relations and primitive defensive operations (which distinguish these two categories of patients from less disturbed neurotic and characterological conditions), the functions of these primitive defensive operations in borderline conditions are different from those in schizophrenia. In patients with borderline personality organization, such primitive operations (particularly splitting, projective identification, primitive idealization, omnipotence, denial, and devaluation) protect the patients from intensive ambivalence and a feared contamination and deterioration of all love relationships by hatred. In contrast, in schizophrenic patients, these defensive operations, and particularly the pathological development of splitting mechanisms (leading to generalized fragmentation of their intrapsychic experiences and interpersonal relations), protect the patients from total loss of ego boundaries and dreaded fusion experiences with others which reflect their lack of differentiation of self and object images.

Clinically, the implications of these formulations are that while interpretation of the predominant primitive defensive operations in borderline patients tends to strengthen ego functioning and increase reality testing, the same approach may bring about further regression (uncovering the underlying lack of differentiation between self and nonself) in psychotic patients. As I have stated earlier, while interpretation of these primitive defensive operations may increase the psychotic regression in schizophrenic patients, this does not imply that a psychoanalytic or expressive approach should not be attempted. The regressive effect of interpretation of primitive defenses in the transference is only a short-term one; in the long run, intensive psychoanalytic psychotherapy with psychotic patients may develop their capacity to differentiate self from nonself, and strengthen their ego boundaries.

The temporary increase in disorganization that occurs in schizophrenic patients when primitive defensive operations are interpreted in the transference enables the clinician to differentiate these cases from borderline conditions, whose immediate functioning, particularly their reality testing, tends to improve when primitive defensive operations are interpreted in the transference. In practice, this approach means that diagnostic interviews with patients who require the differential diagnosis of borderline conditions versus a schizophrenic reaction should be structured so that this testing of defensive operations can be carried out.

It is, of course, useful to explore first whether, in the diagnostic interviews, there is any formal thought disorder, hallucinations and/or delusions; if present, these would confirm that the patient is psychotic. If the interviews reveal no formal thought disorder, no clear-cut hallucinations or delusions, I would then focus upon the more subtle aspects of the patient's thinking, affect, and behavior which would indicate some inappropriate or bizarre quality within the context of the interpersonal situation of the interviews. Confronting the patient with such subtly inappropriate or bizarre aspects of his behavior, affect, or thought content is usually anxiety provoking for him. However, when done tactfully and respectfully, and with an effort to clarify the confusing, disruptive or distorting influence of this aspect of his behavior upon the relationship with the interviewer in the "here and now," this confrontation may provide an opportunity for meaningful support of the patient.

The interviewer, following such an approach, actually carries out a boundary function between the patient's intra-psychic life which the interviewer tries to reach empathically, and the external reality represented by the social relationship between the patient and the therapist. This approach is in contrast to: 1) the classical, descriptive search for isolated symptoms in order to establish the diagnosis of schizophrenia; and 2) the psychoanalytic effort to empathize with the intrapsychic experience of the patient regardless of whether the patient can maintain reality testing of this experience.

For example, if the patient presents a strange lack of affect in the face of an emotionally meaningful subject matter, this discrepancy may be pointed out to the patient and its implications explored. A borderline patient will be able to recognize this discrepancy, while identifying with the reality implications of the interviewer's question, and will become more realistic in this regard. In contrast, the schizophrenic patient confronted with the same discrepancy, may be unable to grasp the therapist's point, or may interpret it as an attack, or may react by further increasing the discrepancy between affect and thought content. In other words, reality testing increases in borderline patients with such an approach, and decreases in schizophrenic patients.

This same approach may be applied in focusing upon an inappropriate gesturing (a behavior manifestation which may reflect a psychogenic tic or a stereotype), or upon any specific content which appears to be in serious contrast with other related thought contents, affects, or behavior. Often, multiple discrepancies among affect, thought content, and behavior are present, and the total emotional situation of the interpersonal relationship between patient and therapist will determine which of these elements represent highest priorities for investigation in terms of their urgency or their predominance in distorting the "here and now" relationship.

If this confronting approach indicates that reality testing is, indeed, maintained in all areas, a second line of exploration would be to focus directly upon primitive defensive operations and their interpretation in the transference. For example, if the patient seems highly concerned about philosophical or political matters on the one hand, and completely unconcerned about a serious immediate problem in his daily life on the other, the denial (the dissociation of concern from his immediate life situation) may be interpreted; or, if the patient indicates massive projection of aggression plus tendencies to exert sadistic control of the interviewer, a tentative interpretation of projective identification in the transference may be formulated. Again, borderline patients usually react to such interpretations with an improvement in reality testing and in their general ego functioning in the hour; schizophrenic patients tend to regress, and to experience such interpretation as frightening intrusions which threaten or blur their self-boundaries.

Often the interviewer intuitively senses that such regression may occur as a response to his interpretive efforts; thus it needs to be stressed that this approach is indicated only for diagnostic purposes. If excessive anxiety is aroused in the patient with such an approach, the psychotherapist, after reaching his diagnostic conclusion, should decrease the patient's anxiety by clarifying the relationship between the psychotic distortions and the therapist's interventions. The psychotherapist acting as a diagnostician has to balance the need to remain objective enough to arrive at a diagnosis, with the need to remain sufficiently empathic with the patient to protect him from excessive anxiety.

In summary, using the total interpersonal relationship in

order to explore discrepancies among thought content, affect, and behavior leads to clarifying the presence or absence of reality testing. Also, the interpretation of primitive defensive operations, particularly as they enter the transference situation, further intensifies the exploration of the presence or absence of reality testing.

Loss of reality testing in any one area indicates psychotic functioning. It should be stressed that this conceptualization of reality testing is a restricted, delimited one, referring exclusively to the presence or absence of the patient's capacity to identify himself fully with the external reality represented by the patient-therapist relationship. This formulation implies that there is no continuum, no gradual shift from presence to absence of reality testing, and that there are qualitative as well as quantitative differences between the structural organization of borderline and psychotic conditions. As mentioned before, this essential qualitative difference derives from the particular vicissitudes of self- and object-images in borderline and psychotic conditions, and the related capacity to differentiate self from nonself, which, in turn, determines the capacity to differentiate perception from fantasies and intrapsychic perceptions from those of external origin and the capacity to empathize with social criteria of reality.

## BIBLIOGRAPHY

1.  Adler, G. (1973) Hospital Treatment of Borderline Patients. *American Journal of Psychiatry*, 130:32-35.
2.  Bellak, L. and Hurvich, M. (1969) A Systematic Study of Ego Functions. *Journal of Nervous and Mental Disease*, 148:569-585.
3.  Bergeret, J. (1970). Les Etats Limites. *Revue Francaise de Psychoanalyse*, 34: 605-633.
4.  ———, (1972) *Abrege De Psychologie Pathologique*. Masson & Cie, Paris.
5.  Boyer, L. (1971) Psychoanalytic Technique in the Treatment of Certain Characterological and Schizophrenic Disorders. *International Journal of Psycho-Analysis*, 52:67-85.
6.  ———and Giovacchini, P. (1967) *Psychoanalytic Treatment of Characterological and Schizophrenic Disorders*. Science House, Inc., New York.
7.  Cary, G. (1972) The Borderline Condition: A Structural-Dynamic Viewpoint. *The Psychoanalytic Review*, 59:33-54.
8.  Chessick, R. (1971) Use of the Couch in the Psychotherapy of Borderline Patients. *Archives of General Psychiatry*, 25:306-313.
9.  Collum, J. (1972) Identity Diffusion and the Borderline Maneuver. *Comprehensive Psychiatry*, 13:179-184.

10. Duvocelle, A. (1971) *L'Etat Limite ou Borderline Personality Organization*. These Pour Le Doctorat En Medecine, Lille.

11. Frosch, J. (1964) The Psychotic Character: Clinical Psychiatric Considerations. *Psychiatric Quarterly*, 38:81-96.

12. ———,(1970) Psychoanalytic Considerations of the Psychotic Character. *Journal of the American Psychoanalytic Association*, 18:24-50.

13. ———(1971) Technique in Regard to Some Specific Ego Defects in the Treatment of Borderline Patients. *Psychoanalytic Quarterly*, 45:216-220.

14. Greenson, R. (1970) The Unique Patient-Therapist Relationship In Borderline Patients. Presented at the Annual Meeting of the American Psychiatric Association. (Unpublished)

15. Grinker, R., Sr., Werble, B. and Drye, R. (1968) *The Borderline Syndrome*. Basic Books, Inc., New York.

16. Hurvich, M. (1970) On the Concept of Reality Testing. *International Journal of Psycho-Analysis*, 51:299-312.

17. Jacobson, E. (1954) Psychotic Identifications. In *Depression*. New York: International Universities Press, 1971, pp. 242-263.

18. Kernberg, O. (1970). A Psychoanalytic Classification of Character Pathology. *Journal of the American Psychoanalytic Association*, 18, 800-802.

19. ———;Burstein, E.; Coyne, L.; Appelbaum, A.; Horwitz,L., and Voth, H. (1972) Psychotherapy and Psychoanalysis: Final Report of the Menninger Foundation's Psychotherapy Research Project (Bulletin of the Menninger Clinic, Vol. 36:1/2, January-March 1972).

20. Khan, M. Masud R. (1964) Ego Distortion, Cumulative Trauma, and the Role of Reconstruction in the Analytic Situation. *International Journal of Psycho-Analysis*, 45:272-279.

21. ——— (1969) On Symbiotic Omnipotence. In *The Psychoanalytic Forum*. John A. Lindon (ed.). Science House, New York.

22. Kohut, H. (1971) *The Analysis of the Self*. New York: International Universities Press.

23. Mahler, M. (1971). A Study of the Separation-Individuation Process and Its Possible Application to Borderline Phenomena in the Psychoanalytic Situation. *Psychoanalytic Study of the Child*, 26:403-424. New York/Chicago: Quadrangle Books.

24. Masterson, J. (1972) *Treatment of the Borderline Adolescent: A Developmental Approach*. Wiley-Interscience, New York.

25. Meza, C. (1970) *El colerico (borderline)*. Editorial Joaquin Mortiz, Mexico.

26. Paz, C. (1969) Reflexiones tecnicas sobre el proceso analitico en los psicoticos fronterizos. *Revista de Psicoanalisis*, 26:571-630.

27. Weisfogel, J., Dickes, R. and Simons, R. (1969) Diagnostic Concepts Concerning Patients Demonstrating Both Psychotic and Neurotic Symptoms. *The Psychiatric Quarterly*, 43:85-122.

28. Werble, B. (1970) Second Follow-up Study of Borderline Patients. *Archives of General Psychiatry*, 23:3-7.

29. Wolberg, A. (1973) *The Borderline Patient*. Intercontinental Medical Book Corporation, New York.

30. Zetzel, E. (1971) A Developmental Approach to the Borderline Patient. *American Journal of Psychiatry*, 127:867-871.

Six

# Overall Structuring and Beginning Phase of Treatment

Elsewhere (Chapters 3 and 5) I propose the following overall treatment strategy for the psychoanalytic psychotherapy of borderline patients: 1) systematic elaboration of the negative transference only in the "here and now," without attempting to achieve full genetic reconstructions; 2) interpretation of the defensive constellations of these patients as they enter the negative transference; 3) limit-setting in order to block acting-out of the transference, with as much structuring of the patient's life outside the hours as necessary to protect the neutrality of the analyst; 4) noninterpretation of the less primitively-determined, modulated aspects of the positive transference to foster the gradual development of the therapeutic alliance; 5) formulation of interpretations so that the patient's distortions of the analyst's interventions and of present reality (especially of his perceptions in the hour) can be systematically clarified; 6) working through first the highly distorted transference (at times of an almost psychotic nature) reflecting fantastic internal object relationships related to early ego disturbances, in order to reach later the transference related to real childhood experiences of these patients. A general assumption underlying this treatment strategy is that the interpretation of the predominant, primitive defensive operations characteristic of borderline personality organization and of the related primitive internalized object relations strengthens the patient's ego and brings about structural intrapsychic change which resolves borderline personality organization.

What follows are technical considerations regarding the early phase of treatment of patients with borderline personality organization, tactical approaches which stem from the general treatment strategy outlined. Borderline personality organization is an overall diagnosis which includes various types of character pathology functioning on a borderline level. It is important to diagnose as accurately as possible the predominant characterological constellations of borderline patients; the particular type of character constellation has prognostic and therapeutic implications (Chapter 4). Some of these therapeutic implications, namely, variations in technique in the early stages of treatment for different types of character constellations, will be mentioned below.

## THE OVERALL TREATMENT ARRANGEMENTS

Some borderline patients may be treated successfully with a nonmodified, standard psychoanalytic technique. However, I have found that for the majority of borderline patients, for whom the modified, psychoanalytically oriented psychotherapy outlined before is indicated, the following treatment arrangements have been helpful.

I would consider a minimum of two hours a week as indispensible for carrying out the general treatment strategy mentioned before; three hours a week would be preferable, and the frequency could go up to four or five hours a week. Fears expressed in the early literature on the treatment of borderline conditions implying that excessive frequency of appointments fosters regression seem unfounded in the light of more recent experience. What is potentially regressive in the psychoanalytic psychotherapy of borderline patients is the lack of sufficient structuring of the treatment situation, and the related acting-out of primitive, pathological needs in the transference to such an extent that the transference neurosis (or transference psychosis) replaces ordinary life. Under these circumstances, the patient obtains gratification of pathological, primitive needs in the treatment hours beyond what he could expect in any other life circumstance. In addition, premature efforts at full genetic reconstruction (before the patient has a sufficient availability of an observing ego and before he has been able to consistently correct distorted perceptions in the treatment hours) may foster a confusion in the patient's mind of the psychotherapist with the transference objects, and present and past reality may in turn be confused by the patient with his fantastic intrapsychic reality. This, of course, characterizes the development of transference psychosis.

If these dangers are avoided by an appropriate technical approach, I do not think that a high frequency of treatment hours is in itself regressive. There is an advantage in starting out with less than four or five hours weekly; this permits the therapist to observe better how the patient deals in between the treatment hours with the work done during them. Focussing on how the patient utilizes the psychotherapeutic work in between the hours is of utmost importance in assessing the development of an observing ego and of the therapeutic alliance, and also, of the more subtle types of negative therapeutic reaction (unconscious tendencies to destroy or neutralize the emotional meaning and the learning that has gone on in the hours).

A "supportive" approach which gratifies excessive, pathological dependency needs of the patient rather than interpreting the unconscious needs which interfere with his capacity to depend realistically on the therapist (for example, unconscious needs to destroy emotional supplies), also fosters regression. In other words, systematic interpretation of the primitive defensive operations characteristic of borderline conditions, control of acting-out in the hours, and firm adherence to a technically neutral position protect the patient from excessive regression regardless of the frequency of the hours.

When a borderline patient is seen once a week or less frequently, it is hard to avoid predominance of a focus on external reality to the detriment of interpretive work, or else the focus on the transference becomes so unrealistically dissociated from external reality (because of an insufficient knowledge of such reality available to the therapist) that a supportive approach becomes unavoidable in the long run. A purely supportive approach (in contrast to an interpretive focus on the transference), in turn, usually fosters splitting between the patient's external reality and the treatment situation; drives the main primitive defensive operations underground; brings about a fixation of the transference at a point of maximally unconscious, latent negative transference; and, finally, brings about the development of "lifers." "Lifers" are patients who need to remain in treatment over many years because they cannot relinquish external support nor increase sufficiently their capacity for autonomous functioning, and this syndrome is sometimes iatrogenic.

A major question in the early stages of treatment is to what extent an external structure is necessary to protect the patient and the treatment situation from premature, violent acting-out that may threaten the patient's life or other people's lives or threaten the continuation of the treatment. When the treatment starts out right after a recent or still active psychotic episode (which borderline patients may experience under excessive emotional turmoil—under the effect of drugs, alcohol, or in the course of a transference psychosis), there may be indication for a few days to a few weeks of hospital treatment, with a well-structured hospital milieu program and clarification of the immediate reality· and a combination of an understanding and clarifying and yet limit-setting milieu approach. A generally chaotic life situation, particularly when complicated by the patient's difficulty in providing meaningful information about his life to the psychotherapist, may represent another indication for short-term hospitalization. Severe suicidal threats or attempts, a deteriorating social situation, or severe acting-out with involvements with the law, are all typical examples of situations which threaten the patient's life or the continuation of treatment. Under such circumstances, short-term hospitalization may be necessary, simultaneously with the beginning or continuation of intensive psychotherapeutic treatment along the lines mentioned before.

The most important objective regarding the degree of structuring required is to set up an overall treatment arrangement which permits the psychotherapist to remain in a position of technical neutrality, that is, equidistant from external reality, the patient's superego, his instinctual needs, and his acting (in contrast to observing) ego (6). This objective can sometimes be achieved with less than full hospitalization, by means of the utilization of part-hospitalization arrangements, foster home placement, the intervention of a social worker within the patient's environment, etc. There are borderline patients who do not have a sufficient degree of observing ego for intensive, outpatient psychoanalytic psychotherapy; for example, many borderline patients with extremely low motivation for treatment, severe lack of anxiety tolerance and of impulse control, and very poor object relationships may require a long-term environmental structuring of their lives in order to make an expressive psychotherapeutic approach possible. Such long-term structuralization of their life may be provided by many months of hospitalization or a part-hospitalization environment, or by other extra-mural social services which provide the necessary limit-setting in the patient's life or support his family for this purpose. Severe, chronic acting-out, suicidal or general self-destructive trends which the patient cannot control, and some types of negative therapeutic reaction, may require such a long-term external structuralization.

Many borderline patients are able, without external structuring of their lives, to participate actively in setting limits to certain types of acting out which threaten their treatment or their safety. At times the psychotherapist has to spell out certain conditions which the patient must meet in order for outpatient psychoanalytic psychotherapy to proceed. The setting up of such conditions for treatment represents, of course, an abandonment of the position of neutrality on the part of the psychotherapist, and the setting up of parameters of technique. Such parameters of technique need to be kept at a minimum, as Eissler (3) has stressed, and the psychotherapist has to keep in mind that these parameters of technique and their impact on the transference situation eventually must be interpreted. In practice, parameters of technique which represent an excessive deviation from the position of technical neutrality may be considered modifications of technique: sometimes their eventual reduction through interpretation is not possible. Emphatic orders, prohibitions, suggestive and manipulative maneuvers of major dimensions are typical examples of potential modifications of technique. In the long run, a heavy price is paid for such modifications of technique. Pathological idealizations of the psychotherapist may turn out to be resistant to interpretations, and the transferential implication of the patient's submission to the psychotherapist may interfere with the patient's eventually freeing himself from the regressive links with his transference objects. This does not mean, however, that all prohibitions constitute a dangerous abandonment of the therapist's neutrality; on the contrary, some prohibitions which have been formulated in terms of crucial requirements of reality may represent a definite identification of the psychotherapist with the patient's observing ego. For example, prohibiting patients from yelling in the hours rather than expressing their anger in ordinary verbal communication, prohibiting patients from damaging or destroying objects in the psychotherapist's office, and prohibiting patients from actively trying to control the psychotherapist's life outside the treatment hours all represent, it seems to me, occasionally necessary efforts on the part of the psychotherapist to protect a technically neutral treatment atmosphere, and constitute eminently reducible parameters of technique.

The patient's efforts to control the psychotherapist's life may take such forms as frequent phone calls at night, actually spying upon the psychotherapist or members of his family, or even subtly trying to influence the psychotherapist's personal and professional life by means of manipulative behavior involving third parties. All these expressions of the transference need to be interpreted first, and, if they cannot be reduced through interpretation alone, dealt with by prohibition if that is necessary to protect the boundaries of the psychotherapist's life and the normal boundaries of a psychotherapeutic relationship.

If a patient has a history of frequent suicidal attempts, or of utilizing threats of suicide to control his environment (including the psychotherapist), this situation needs to be discussed fully with him. The patient must either be able to assume full control over any active expression of his suicidal tendencies (in contrast to the freedom of verbally expressing his wishes and impulses in the treatment hours), or he must be willing to ask for external protection (in the form of hospitalization or part-hospitalization) if he feels he cannot control such suicidal impulses. In other words, several brief hospitalizations arranged by the patient himself, by his family or a social worker may provide an additional, external structure needed to maintain the treatment situation; this is preferable to the therapist changing his technique in the direction of relin-́ quishing a primarily interpretive approach in the context of technical neutrality.

A similar situation exists when the patient is prone to resort to drugs or self-medication. In general, I think that any medication influencing the central nervous system is contraindicated in the course of long-term, intensive, psychoanalytic psychotherapy with borderline patients along the lines proposed, and the patient himself must take the responsibility for not influencing his level of anxiety or depression and his general psychological alertness and responsiveness by means of uncontrolled ingestion of drugs. This applies particularly to patients suffering from alcoholism or drug addiction; in these cases, if they cannot control the symptoms on their own, psychotherapeutic treatment may best start out with a period of prolonged hospitalization. Antisocial behavior, particularly if it leads to difficulties with the law, represents another situation that may have to be controlled at the beginning of treatment: because of the generally unfavorable prognostic implications of antisocial trends in borderline conditions, this is a fundamental issue to be brought under control in the early stages of treatment.

Physical illness which requires ongoing, responsible participation on the part of the patient to keep him healthy or alive, is a difficult complication in the treatment of borderline patients. For example, patients with diabetes, who need to be on a strict dietary regimen and medication, have an implicit control over their life (or death) by means of their diet and medication. Such patients may express aggression toward the therapist by neglecting themselves, thus attempting to force the therapist into a "supportive" stance, into taking the responsibility for their health and safety. Over an extended period of time, such a development may block the possibility of transference analysis and bring about a therapeutic stalemate. In general, when the patient has the power to bring about his death by simply stopping a life-preserving medication, primitive mechanisms of omnipotence and severe types of negative therapeutic reaction are powerfully reinforced. In all these cases, a decision must be made as early as possible whether the patient can commit himself to carry out full responsibility for himself, or whether some external structuring or control is needed to preserve the neutrality of the treatment setting.

In contrast, many other potentially self-destructive symptoms may be left untouched for a long period of time, if they do not threaten the patient's life or treatment. For example, it may take years before a borderline patient with severe obesity may be able to control his obesity effectively; general failure in school or at work and interpersonal difficulties of all kinds may express the patient's psychopathology and a long time may elapse before they can be brought into the focus of the treatment. At times, some prolonged observation is necessary to differentiate those symptoms which require immediate structuring of the treatment setting from others that do not. For example, mild problems of anorexia have to be differentiated from anorexia nervosa; sexual promiscuity (which usually does not threaten the treatment situation) may at times evolve into unconscious efforts to bring about a pregnancy or other social complications which would threaten the continuation of the treatment.

Sometimes the structure setting constitutes a preventive approach to what otherwise might become uncontrollable acting-out in the future; in this case, setting limits ahead of time for situations which may develop in the future constitutes a parameter of technique which needs to be formulated early, before the more intense transference distortions develop which may complicate such a prohibition in the future. For example, patients with a history of cutting themselves may require a careful discussion at the beginning of treatment of the probability that the urges to cut themselves may recur and become very intense at some stage in the treatment. The therapist may have to express firmly his expectation that the patient will candidly discuss such wishes to cut himself in the hours and assume the responsibility for not acting on them; or, if he feels he cannot control such impulses, request hospitalization at that time. Throughout such discussions, the psychotherapist makes it clear that he expects the patient to express himself verbally rather than in action. Thus, the psychotherapist institutes a parameter of technique which eventually will require resolution through interpretation.

## THE BASIC THERAPEUTIC SETTING

Insofar as the general technical approach I have outlined constitutes a modified psychoanalytic procedure, with a maximum stress on the therapist's remaining in a position of technical neutrality and on systematic interpretation of the transference in the "here and now" (with restricted interpretation of the genetic implications of the transference), such a treatment might be carried out within a standard psychoanalytic setting, with instructions to the patient to free associate and the use of the couch. This is, in effect, what is preferred by Boyer (2), Frosch (5), and Giovacchini (7). The main advantages of maintaining a standard psychoanalytic setting are that neutrality is maximally preserved under these circumstances, and that the analyst's anonymity is protected (in contrast to face-to-face interviews). The psychoanalytic setting helps to protect him from countertransference acting out, a significant danger in the psychoanalytic psychotherapy of severely regressed patients. However, in the majority of cases where a standard psychoanalytic procedure is not indicated, I prefer to carry out the treatment with face-to-face interviews. The main reason for this is that the more regressed the patient, and, therefore, the more marked the predominance of primitive character defenses, the more the nonverbal aspects of the patient's behavior will become predominant, and face-to-face interviews tend to make the nonverbal, behavioral aspects of the patient's communication more accessible to the therapist's observation. Because patients with borderline personality organization always suffer from severe character pathology represented by primitive character defenses; because their constellation of primitive defensive operations such as splitting, projective identification, omnipotence and devaluation are usually expressed in nonverbal behavior in the hours (in addition to their appearance in the verbal content); and because premature transference regression characteristic of these patients is expressed in the total interaction with the therapist, the focus on the patient's behavior is crucial from the first session on. In other words, the more we proceed from the neurotic to the borderline level of character pathology, the more the patient's nonverbal behavior becomes an increasing aspect of the total material, and face-to-face interviews permit a fuller observation of this material in the context of the overall analysis of the patient-therapist interactions.

The main dangers of face-to-face interviews are a weakened control on the part of the therapist over the expression of his countertransference reactions, and increased efforts on the patient's part to exert control over the therapist. Face-to-face sessions reduce the protection that sitting behind the couch gives both the therapist and the patient from an excessive impact of transference and countertransference material, and facilitate the patient's becoming aware of realistic characteristics of the therapist, which may play into certain defensive operations, particularly projective identification, primitive idealization and devaluation. However, there are also advantages in the patient's having available to him a more realistic perception of the therapist; such availability combined with the therapist's technique, may facilitate a gradual differentiation of self from object in the transference.

My initial instructions to patients regarding our work in the treatment hours are limited to encouraging them to speak as freely and openly as possible about what goes on in their minds in the sessions, and what is of concern to them in their daily life. Rather than stressing free association in a strict sense, I emphasize full, open communication about what the patient himself thinks is important. The understanding is that I need to know as much as possible about the patient from himself, so I can help him explore those aspects of himself in which his own understanding is limited. After my initial explanations, clarifications, and encouragements to the patient, I then deal with emerging resistances in a standard, interpretive way.

To listen with "evenly suspended" attention becomes difficult in the case of borderline patients, whose verbal communications may be contradictory and confused, and who also may provide abundant nonverbal communication which, in turn, comes in contradictory bits and is not easily integrated with the verbal material. I have found Bion's concept of the analyst as a "container" (1) to be helpful in formulating the basic task of the psychotherapist in organizing for himself the patient's material. The psychotherapist needs to evaluate what, at any point, in the contradictory bits of verbal and behavioral communication, in the confusing thoughts and feelings and expressions of the patient, is of predominant emotional relevance, and how this predominant material can be understood in the context of the patient's total communications. This material, and the integration of it in the context of the total emotional situation of the patient at that point is the subject matter of the therapist's interpretive efforts.

There is a danger of premature interpretation of genetic material in a dissociated way from other present material, a danger fostered by the availability of conscious primary process thinking and primitive emotional material that is expressed split-off from other material related to it dynamically and structurally. "Why is this patient telling me this now" is a question the psychotherapist needs to answer before he deals with primitive material, and the answer often has to be found in the psychotherapist's internal assimilation of bizarre, contradictory communications until the entire material can be reduced to an understandable human interaction between the patient and him. This approach helps to avoid the pitfalls of intellectualized genetic reconstructions, and of engagement on the patient's part in gratifying, primitive fantasies without facing the present conflicts related to those fantasies.

Often contradictory and bizarre constellations of communication defy the introspective efforts of the psychotherapist, and, at that point, the therapist should share with the patient his observations about him and his puzzlement about the meaning of what is going on. This approach is in contrast to direct, authoritative interpretation of the material without sharing the basis for the understanding—and nonunderstanding—the psychotherapist has reached so far, which fosters the patient's primitive idealization and magical expectations from treatment. Psychotherapy is work to be engaged in jointly by both patient and therapist, and frustrating as this may be for the infantile transference expectations of borderline patients, eventually fosters ego growth by helping to develop their observing ego and the therapeutic alliance.

Consistent clarification by the therapist of his perceptions of the patient, particularly of significant and puzzling confusion or contradictions in him, and stimulation of the patient to explore the implications of such confusion or contradictions may lead to an increase in his anxiety. Under the impact of primitive defensive operations and paranoid or depressive fears, the patient may experience the psychotherapist's exploration as an attack or a rejection; therefore, the patient's perceptions of the therapist's intervention need to be interpreted in the process of this clarification. In general, as has been pointed out by Frosch (4, 5) and Greenson (9), clarification of the patient's perceptions in the hours refers particularly to the interpretation of the potential distortion in the patient's mind of the meaning of the therapist's comments.

Often the therapist's comments are understood by the patient as "magical gestures" which gratify primitive transference wishes, and it is important for the therapist to interpret consistently the patient's efforts to use the therapist's comments as direct transference gratification rather than as hypotheses for further exploration by the patient of what goes on in himself. Interpretation of the patient's conscious and unconscious attitudes about the therapist's comments need to go hand in hand with all interpretive work regarding any specific conflict or transference development. Although such consistent clarification of the patient's perception of the therapist's interventions often increases the patient's anxiety, such interpretations also convey that the psychotherapist's main function is to activate the patient's observing ego, and that the therapist is confident that the patient has at least some capacity to gain understanding of himself and of his interactions, and to learn how to influence his feelings, thinking and behavior through self-understanding.

Clarification of the patient's perceptions of the therapist's interventions also permits an increase in the degree of freedom with which the therapist may express himself and explore new, anxiety-producing areas, and also permits the therapist to express more freely his uncertainty and confusion when this is the most helpful communication to make.

A major consequence of this general technical approach is the gradual integration of mutually dissociated, or generally fragmented aspects of the patient's conflicts into significant units of primitive internalized object relations. Each unit is constituted of a certain self-image, a certain object-image, and a major affect disposition linking these. These units of internalized object relations become activated in the transference, and, when they can be interpreted and integrated with other related or contradictory units—particularly when libidinally invested and aggressively invested units can be integrated—the processes of working through of the transference and of resolution of the primitive constellation of defensive operations characteristic of borderline conditions have begun. The following vignette illustrates the process of integration of the patient's material from contradictory verbal and nonverbal expression into a significant human interaction, the first step in the understanding of a significant internalized object relationship.

After prolonged silences and occasional desultory remarks which I could not put together, the patient, a woman in her middle twenties, suddenly—and for the first time—started to talk about sexual fantasies she had about being a man, about having a penis, and about becoming like me under these circumstances. At the same time, she started to make gestures as if she were bored, gave evidence of some restlessness, and looked repeatedly at her watch. The overall impact of these manifestations was confusing to me. What appeared as important content was presented as if it had no relevance to her at all, and as if other thoughts, probably related to the time of this hour, were preoccupying her. I told her how I was perceiving these various expressions, and asked her how she understood all this.

Her attitude changed immediately: With a tone of mild disapproval, she asked me if I was interested in what she had been saying; she felt that my pointing to her behavior and her glances at the watch indicated that I was distracted and not paying full attention to what she was saying. I pointed out to her that she was attributing to me a reaction which, as part of her own behavior, she had displayed only moments earlier. She replied that since she had had the fantasy all along that I was not really interested, she had been searching in her own fantasies for what would be of real interest to me, and had decided to talk about her sexual fantasies. If I was not interested in that material, she felt it was hopeless for her to try to convey anything during the hour that would raise my interest—she might as well concentrate on how much time there was left before she could leave my office. It also emerged that she was expressing behaviorally boredom and irritation which reflected her internal devaluation of the hour, and that this was a defensive operation against the fearful experience of me as indifferent and distant. Her painfully experiencing me as distant constituted the immediate, predominant transference manifestation; and her sexual fantasies could eventually be understood both as a wish to become me by having my penis as a defense against deeper wishes to be loved and cared for by me, and as a wish to submit to me sexually as a price to pay for my love and protection (a basic masochistic pattern of this patient). This example also illustrates the prevalence of splitting mechanisms (dissociation of thoughts, behavior, and feelings), of projective mechanisms, and, by implication, the utilization of my total emotional reaction as part of my efforts to "contain" the patient's material.

Once a predominant transference constellation has been understood by the therapist in terms of an immediate, emotionally significant development in the hour, the self-image, object-image, and affect involved can be clarified and interpreted. This constitutes a further step in the diagnosis of significant units of internalized object relations. It is important to clarify all these components because of the long-range therapeutic need to diagnose the mutually split-off aspects of the patient's self-concept, and the mutually split-off aspects of significant representations of others. Integration of self and objects, and thus of the entire world of internalized object relationships, is a major strategic aim in the treatment of patients with borderline personality organization.

The integration of affects with their related, fantasied or real human relations involving the patient and a significant object is another aspect of this work. The patient's affect dispositions reflect the libidinal or aggressive investment of a certain internalized object relationship, and the integration of split-off, fragmented affect states is a corollary of integration of split-off, fragmented internalized object relations. The following example illustrates the activation of a specific, primitive internalized object relationship in the transference.

The patient, an 18-year-old girl, at one point in the hour, spoke in a monotonous and halting way about matters which had earlier appeared emotionally very important to her and to me. All of a sudden, I found myself dealing with what impressed me as the patient's indifference and blandness, so much so that I had to struggle against distracting myself from listening to her. Repeated efforts on my part to clarify and explore this issue with the patient led nowhere, and finally, after a period of mounting frustration and dissatisfaction, I gave up, feeling that I was momentarily at a loss to understand the material. As I leaned back, figuratively speaking, the situation suddenly changed, and the patient began to ask me insistently for help with an immediate reality situation, a visit from her mother. The patient asked for help with various aspects of this visit. I felt that the questions raised by the patient involved mostly trivial, unimportant issues, and I gradually began to feel impatient and distant from the patient while she was increasing her verbal demands for advice. It was only then that I realized that an inversion of roles had occurred and that a specific relationship had been enacted in the transference.

The patient at first enacted an image of her own mother as a distant, aloof, indifferent person who had to be forced by the patient's plea for love and understanding to become interested; I represented the self-image of the patient as a frustrated, demanding child who was looking for a meaningful relationship. In the second part of the interaction, I had been put in the position of the indifferent and rejecting mother, while the patient was enacting her self-image of the frustrated, demanding, insistent child. Interpretation of this total situation led immediately to a sharper focus on the patient's conflicts with her mother, and, eventually, to her understanding her own participation in these conflicts by acting at times like a demanding, angry, greedy child (her self-image from the past), and at other times, like a disdainful, arrogant, rejecting mother (the reciprocal object image).

There are some further implications of these two examples (which both stem from early stages of treatment). First, transference becomes immediately a major resistance in the treatment of borderline patients and needs to be interpreted, particularly the manifest and latent negative transference manifestations which threaten to block the very establishment of a therapeutic alliance. The "therapeutic alliance" (10) or "working alliance" (8) can be strengthened, in the case of borderline patients, by ventilating the negative aspects of the transference in the "here and now" only. Working with the transference in such a restricted way in the early stages of treatment fosters the patient's observing ego and the therapeutic alliance at the same time. This approach is in contrast to permitting unconscious negative transference aspects to remain unchallenged and thus go underground, and to expect to strengthen the working relationship with the patient by nonanalytic, supportive means. Another implication is that while the psychotherapist needs to be very active in dealing with transference material in the early stages of treatment, this activity does not mean an abandonment of the position of neutrality, and it requires constant focus on the various effects of the therapist's interventions on the patient. In addition, my approach also implies an ongoing request for collaboration on the patient's part with the psychotherapeutic work, and interpretation of the transference implications of the patient's not carrying out such work. The focus on the patient's responsibilities in the hour contributes to the assessment of the long-range effects of the psychotherapeutic work, particularly the effects on the work that the patient continues to carry out in between the treatment hours.

## SPECIAL PROBLEMS IN THE EARLY STAGES OF TREATMENT

### 1. Conscious Withholding of Material

When the patient consciously withholds information, or when he lies, the psychotherapist's first priority has to be to interpret fully and reduce this suppression of information by interpretive—in contrast to educational—means. This may take weeks or months, particularly in cases with antisocial features. However long it may take, full resolution of the reality and transferential implications of the patient's lying takes precedence over all other material, except life-threatening acting out. However, because lying interferes with the psychotherapeutic approach toward all other problems including acting out, it may be preferable, if the patient who habitually lies also shows evidence of life-threatening or other treatment-threatening acting out, to start his treatment with sufficient structuring of his life such as long-term hospitalization. Patients who lie habitually, and, therefore, give evidence of serious superego deterioration, tend to project their own attitude regarding moral values onto the psychotherapist as well, and to conceive him as being dishonest and corrupt. The interpretive approach to the transference functions of lying includes, therefore, focussing on the patient's projection of his own dishonesty onto the therapist, and on the transferential implications in the "here and now" of this development.

Interpretation of lying should also include the exploration of the potential consequences of the patient's lying for the immediate and long-range future of the psychotherapeutic relationship. In the immediate context, for example, the patient may lie because he wishes to assert his superiority over the therapist and defeat his efforts, exert control over him, protect himself from dangerous retaliation that he fears from the therapist should the therapist know about matters the patient wishes to hide, or consciously exploit the psychotherapeutic relationship for ends other than receiving help. From a longer-range perspective, lying implies a basic distortion of the human nature of the patient-therapist relationship, and an indication that the patient has at least temporarily abandoned any hope or conviction of the possibility that honest discussion of his problems might be of any help. Lying also implies that, in the patient's mind, the psychotherapist is either incompetent, a fool, or dishonest in lending himself to such a parody of treatment: again, this indicates a basic hopelessness in or unavailability for any authentic human relationship. Full exploration of both the immediate and long-range implications of lying may provide, if successful, a crucial basis for changing a treatment geared to failure into a meaningful therapeutic relationship.

2. **Consistent Devaluation of All Human Help Received**

This problem may coexist with the tendency to lying, but there are many patients whose conscious and unconscious depreciation of all those who try to help them coexists with ordinary honesty in providing full information about themselves. Devaluation, a predominant defensive operation in narcissistic personalities, usually coexists with omnipotence, and it may be part of the severe kind of negative therapeutic reaction (related to unconscious envy of sources of help) which is typical of narcissistic personalities.

There are patients whose immediate devaluation of all help received stems from other reasons such as deep, unconscious distrust of the sources of help (such sources represent ultimately primitive, feared and hated parental images activated in the transference). Patients with infantile personality and chronic demandingness for more help are part of this group. In general, "excessive dependency" usually turns out to reflect an internal incapacity to really depend upon others and on what is received from them. This unconscious devaluation of help received is the counterpart of the unconscious idealization of what is received in terms of primitive, magic expectations of dependency from idealized parental images; in both cases, realistic incorporation of what the patient has received from the psychotherapist may fail, and the direct effect will be a sense of dissatisfaction, frustration, emptiness and lack of work on the part of the patient between hours. Devaluation by narcissistic personalities of the psychotherapist and of all learning occurring in the psychotherapeutic situation may be the first indication of severe, chronic negative therapeutic reaction. This is an extremely difficult issue to deal with, and, in some cases, reflects an inability on the patient's part to benefit from a psychoanalytical psychotherapy.

I point out in Chapters 8 and 9 that narcissistic personalities have varying treatment indications according to their general level of ego functioning, the extent to which there is direct expression of primitive rage from the beginning of treatment on, and the degree of negative therapeutic reaction. Narcissistic personalities functioning on a nonborderline level should ideally be treated with a nonmodified psychoanalytic procedure; these cases, in my opinion, do not require any parameters of technique, but require consistent interpretation of the narcissistic defenses in the transference as the exclusive means for resolving the narcissistic personality structure.

Patients with narcissistic personality who function on an overtly borderline level may respond to the modified, psychoanalytic psychotherapy recommended for borderline patients in general, if their mechanisms of omnipotence and devaluation and the related lack of "build-up" of the psychotherapeutic experience can be worked through within a reasonable period of time. The problem is that, given the very lengthy treatment that these patients require, there is a risk that several years of psychotherapy with two or three sessions a week will not bring about any basic change. Therefore, I now prefer a limited, trial psychotherapy of not more than a year with these cases. After such a trial period, if no basic change in the defensive structure can be achieved, a shift to a more supportive approach may be indicated. Gratifying results have been obtained by a purely supportive approach with these patients (Chapter 9).

Finally, narcissistic personalities functioning on a borderline level who present intense rage reactions from the beginning of treatment (and intensification of the devaluation of treatment as part of these rage reactions) may also require a more supportive approach after a period of structured treatment (sometimes by means of hospitalization) has been attempted. In short, I would first attempt an expressive psychotherapeutic approach with all overtly borderline narcissistic patients, but reevaluate the situation on an ongoing basis.

A consistently sharp focus on the borderline patient's behavior in the early minutes of each treatment hour provides important information regarding the work the patient has done in between hours; eventually, one would expect that patients start the hours immediately using the time in a meaningful way. Patients' tendencies to lose valuable time by long initial silences, and their unconscious and conscious efforts to have the psychotherapist take responsibility for using the hour well, or a general passivity and chronic efforts to make the therapist talk, may indicate, in addition to other meanings, an active devaluation of the treatment process by the patient. Consistent interpretation of such passivity at the beginning of the hours may lead to crucial, previously hidden aspects of the negative transference; this is particularly true in patients with narcissistic personalities.

### 3. Chronic Development of "Meaninglessness" in the Therapeutic Interaction

I am referring here to a variety of situations corresponding to various causes, all of which situations are reflected in a generally empty, meaningless, or chronically confused treatment situation. One group of patients who present this problem are the so-called inadequate personalities—patients functioning on a borderline level who have great difficulties in relating themselves to others by means of symbolic verbal communication; these patients should be treated with supportive psychotherapy, and often require life-long support, although the frequency of meetings can gradually be reduced. Schizoid personalities may also induce a chronically "empty" quality in the treatment hours over a long period of time; for these patients, systematic interpretation of the defensive functions of emotional dispersal and of latent, negative, often frankly paranoid transference dispositions is crucial. Briefer periods of lack of emotional meaning in the hours develop in most cases of borderline personality organization, and require the general technical approach outlined earlier, which is geared to reduce the split-off, fragmented content, behavior, and affect into integrated units of human interaction with the psychotherapist.

When the therapist cannot sort out, over a period of time, what appears as a completely confusing combination of material, it is important for him to evaluate whether this confusion is due to 1) particular defensive operations in the patient, to 2) countertransference reactions, or to 3) unconscious efforts on the patient's part to confuse the therapist. Open exploration with the patient of this treatment situation may provide important clues to its resolution.

## 4. Paranoid Control and Withholding

In some borderline paranoid patients conscious withholding of material is acknowledged by the patient as part of the expression of paranoid fantasies about the therapist; for example, one patient refused to give his real name over a period of several weeks. Whenever manifest paranoid ideation becomes predominant in the early hours of treatment, it is important for the therapist to evaluate carefully whether the patient is, indeed, a borderline patient, or whether the patient suffers from a paranoid psychosis. Since a psychotic paranoid patient might present serious aggressive acting out when transference psychosis develops, it is extremely important for the therapist to carry out an early, careful differential diagnosis, and not to initiate an intensive psychotherapeutic treatment without a clear understanding of all the implications of treating a psychotic patient. At times, when this diagnostic question cannot be clarified in the early treatment hours of a borderline paranoid patient, it may be preferable to start the psychotherapy with a concomitant period of brief hospitalization geared to evaluate the situation further. The long-range benefits of an early, brief hospitalization compensate for the increase of anxiety and transference distortions and other complications in these patients' daily life related to an early, brief hospitalization. In any case, it is important that the psychotherapist not permit the patient to control the treatment situation in a pathological way, as this would affect not only the psychotherapist's neutrality, but his very availability, on a simple human level, to the patient. Sometimes it is preferable not to treat a patient at all rather than to treat him under impossible conditions. Projective identification is a predominant defensive operation of paranoid patients; and one can interpret the implicit sadistic control only when, objectively, the therapist is free from being under the control of the patient.

### 5.  Early, Severe Acting Out

Quite frequently, the acting out potential of a borderline patient can be assessed fully only after psychotherapy has started. The problem then is how to provide sufficient structuring of the treatment situation; this may be difficult if the therapist is not fully aware of the extent of acting out, which may be hinted at only slightly, if at all, through the patient's behavior in the hours. In practice, minor indications inside the hours of serious emotional turmoil outside the treatment situation have to be taken very seriously, and the therapist has to explore fully with the patient what may appear to be, at first sight, a rather trivial problem in his daily life. The therapist's intuition, his experience in carrying out treatment of other patients with similar characterological problems, and his open expression of his puzzlement and concern regarding what happens outside the treatment hours, may help to bring back into the transference material that has been dissociated from the content of the hours. A particularly important clue are certain characterological defenses which appear again and again in the early minutes of the treatment hours, and remain unmodifiable in spite of consistent work with them.

For example, one patient started all her hours with a brief period of silence. She would then ask the therapist questions which had an indirect relevance to issues that were important to her, but were formulated in such a way that the therapist had to "guess" what was on her mind and would be rewarded if he "guessed right." Although it was subtle, this pattern of behavior persisted over many months in spite of the therapist's repeated efforts to interpret it. Eventually, this behavior turned out to reflect generalized, previously undetected acting out. It turned out to be a sample of an habitual behavior pattern which the patient had not mentioned as a problem within the range of the therapy. This pattern occurred in social situations, where she would ostentatiously withdraw in stubborn silence. From this vantage point, she would draw to herself the exclusive attention of important people by posing intriguing questions to them, conveying that they alone, with their intuition, were able to help her. The net effect of this behavior was that the patient had surrounded herself with a number of well-intentioned relatives and friends who would solicitously respond to her questions and provide her with extensive information about all kind of issues, while the patient, often with a mysterious smile, would "extract" from them what she felt was helpful to keep her "in control," without changing her general aloofness otherwise. The worsening of this behavior during the treatment reflected its function as a transference resistance. The interpretation of this acting out of omnipotent control outside the treatment hours channeled this character defense into the hours, where it could now be worked through more fully.

Such problems, of course, are not related only to the early treatment hours; however, the therapist may find it easier to diagnose subtle characterological defenses in the early stages of treatment, before he has become so used to them that he does not notice them. Also, because he knows the patient insufficiently, the therapist's consistent focus on all external interactions of the patient in the early stages of treatment may predict or prevent disruptive, uncontrollable acting out later on.

## 6. Misuse of Previous Information Regarding Treatment, and of "Psychotherapeutic Language"

Because borderline patients require complicated, long-term treatment arrangements, and because treatment disruptions or changes of psychotherapists due to transference acting out are frequent, therapists often see patients who have had previous treatment experience. Careful exploration in the early stages of treatment of previous experiences with other therapists always helps to prevent a repetition of the situation which led to premature interruption earlier. In the case of borderline patients, however, primitive distorted identification with partial aspects of the previous psychotherapist may be reflected in material which strikes the therapist as unauthentic or artificial. This may be particularly true of the patient's description of his emotional experiences: often borderline patients are not aware of the exact nature of their affects, and tend to label them in accordance with what they have heard psychotherapists express to them earlier; the question of genuineness of what the patient feels and how he talks about it become very important under these circumstances.

## 7. The Predominant Quality of Separation Reactions

The patient's reactions to separation from the therapist have important diagnostic, prognostic and therapeutic implications. Separations in connection with weekends, holidays, illness, vacations, etc., all tend to activate the patient's predominant level of reaction to such separations. One might place the different type of separation reactions into a continuum, from the most severe distortions of internalized object relationships to the least. The most ominous reaction is that of patients who are really unable to experience any emotional reaction at all to separations from the therapist, but who have learned to imitate such reactions from other patients, using them as rationalization for various acting out. These are usually narcissistic patients with strong antisocial features. Next on this continuum would be open acknowledgement of not having any reaction to separation from the therapist, characteristic of most patients with narcissistic personality structure. A particular type of intense, devaluating rage evidenced by some narcissistic patients functioning on a borderline level may have ominous immediate implications but, if worked through over a period of time, may actually indicate a beginning of the capacity for an intense emotional relationship with the therapist.

Of less serious implications is the intense, at times disorganizing separation anxiety that many borderline patients experience with prolonged separations from the therapist, a reaction typical of patients with infantile personality. In this case, fear of separation from the therapist usually reflects not only pathological dependency needs but fear of the destruction of the internalized image of the therapist because of the rage brought about by the frustration of separation from him. Interpretation of the unconscious implications of such separation anxiety is an important part of the treatment from early stages on. Next along the continuum would be the presence of pathologically intense mourning reactions, characteristic of borderline patients with a better integration of internalized object relations, and a generally better prognosis.

Finally, tolerance of normal mourning reactions to separations from the therapist is characteristic of advanced stages of treatment of borderline patients, and of patients with less severe types of character pathology in general. Because of the danger of premature disruption of the treatment when the patient cannot tolerate an extended separation, and because of the important information about the transference and the general quality of object relationships implied in separation reactions, careful exploration of patients' separation reactions is of crucial importance.

## 8. The Psychotherapist's Relationship with the Hospital Team

In the case of borderline patients whose treatment is carried out, either initially or during later phases of the treatment, in combination with hospitalization, it is important for the psychotherapist to keep in close relationship with the leader of the hospital management team. This raises such issues as confidentiality, danger of splitting of the transference, and general coordination of hospital treatment and psychotherapeutic work.

In my experience, I have found it helpful for the psychotherapist to receive routinely full information regarding the patient's interactions in the hospital, and for the patient to be told about this. Thus, the psychotherapist can share significant information regarding the patient's interactions in the hospital with the patient himself and integrate it into his analysis of the transference. At the same time, the psychotherapist should inform the patient that he will keep confidential all information given him by the patient, except for specific issues which the therapist might wish to explore with the hospital team. But, before doing so, he would ask the patient specifically for authorization. In other words, general confidentiality should be maintained unless specific authorization is given by the patient for the psychotherapist to share certain information with the hospital team. Finally, I explicitly inform patients that I would not feel bound by confidentiality under circumstances which would involve threats to the patient's or other people's lives; again, under these circumstances, I would first share with the patient the nature of the information I feel needs to be talked over with the hospital treatment team.

The general implication of this approach is that if hospitalization is needed and carried out during psychotherapeutic treatment, the total treatment should be integrated; in practice, this should help reduce or prevent splitting operations by which part of the transference is expressed to the hospital treatment team. In the case of outpatients where social complications, for example, pressures from the family, are expressed in the form of efforts of relatives or other persons related to the patient to establish direct contact with the psychotherapist, a social agency, or a psychometric social worker might be asked to provide a structure which keeps the psychotherapist separate from the patient's external social environment, while still containing the overall treatment situation that has evolved. Again, under these circumstances, the psychotherapist should maintain an open communication with the social worker who is seeing the family, but any information that the psychotherapist is planning to share with the social worker must be discussed with the patient.

My point is that the dangers of nonmonitored acting out and splitting of the treatment situation outweighs the dangers and complications of sharing certain information with other members of the treatment team. At times, such multiple treatment arrangements may interfere with the therapist's neutrality to such an extent that the treatment is shifted into a supportive approach; at other times, such multiple arrangements may relieve the therapist from decision-making about the patient's life, dilute otherwise unbearable counter-transference reactions, and, in short, protect the therapist's neutrality. So many variables enter into the individualized decision-making regarding this issue, that it is really difficult to generalize in this area.

In conclusion, crucial aspects of the treatment strategy and tactics with borderline patients are expressed in the requirements and arrangements of the early treatment stages. The overall objective of the early treatment phase is to create conditions which will permit a long-term psychotherapeutic engagement under favorable circumstances. Such circumstances include measures to protect the patient from potentially destructive and self-destructive consequences of his illness, and to protect the neutrality of the therapist and the psychotherapeutic strategy from being forced into a supportive model, away from the interpretive focus required by these patients. Within this overall framework, the psychotherapist should attempt to integrate the interpretation of the patient's behavior, his subjective experience, and the transferential implications of his present difficulties in the light of a developing, deepening, authentic human experience between patient and therapist.

## BIBLIOGRAPHY

1.  Bion, W. (1967) *Second Thoughts: Selected Papers on Psychoanalysis*. London: Heinemann.
2.  Boyer, L. B. (1971) Psychoanalytic Technique in the Treatment of Certain Characterologcal and Schizophrenic Disorders. *Int. J. Psycho-anal.*, 52:67-85.
3.  Eissler, K. R. (1953) The Effect of the Structure of the Ego on Psychoanalytic Technique. *J. Amer. Psychoanal. Assoc.*, 1:104-143.
4.  Frosch, J. (1970) Psychoanalytic Considerations of the Psychotic Character. *J. Amer. Psychoanal. Assoc.*, 18:24-50.
5.  ────── (1971) Technique in Regard to Some Specific Ego Defects in the Treatment of Borderline Patients. *Psychoanal. Quart.*, 45:216-220.
6.  Freud, A. (1936) *The Ego and the Mechanisms of Defense*. New York: Int. Univ. Press, 1946.
7.  Giovacchini, P. L. (ed.) (1972) *Tactics and Techniques in Psychoanalytic Therapy*. Science House, Inc.
8.  Greenson, R. R. (1967) *The Technique and Practice of Psychoanalysis*. New York: Int. Univ. Press.
9.  Greenson, R. R. (1970) The Unique Patient-Therapist Relationship in Borderline Patients. Presented at the Annual Meeting of the American Psychiatric Association. (Unpublished)
10. Zetzel, E. R. (1956) Current Concepts of Transference. *Int. J. Psycho-anal.*, 37:369-376.

## Seven

# The Subjective Experience
# of Emptiness

The normal integrated self and its related integrated conceptions of others (integrated object representations) guarantee a sense of continuity throughout time and under varying circumstances. They also guarantee a sense of belonging to a network of human relations that makes life meaningful, and they guarantee the ordinary "self-feeling" (1) we take for granted and which is normally only threatened by the most extreme and unusual psychosocial traumata or life-threatening situations. Jacobson has pointed out that this self-feeling derived from the individual's awareness of an integrated self has to be distinguished from "self-esteem" or "self-regard" which depends upon the libidinal investment of such an integrated self (1).

When, for various reasons, the normal relation between the self and the internal world of objects (the integrated object representations) is threatened, and what might be called an internal abandonment of the self on the part of internal objects or a loss of them occurs, pathological subjective experiences of a painful and disturbing nature develop. Among these experiences predominate a sense of emptiness and futility of life, chronic restlessness and boredom, and a loss of the normal capacity for experiencing and overcoming loneliness.

There are patients who describe a painful and disturbing subjective experience which they frequently refer to as a feeling of emptiness. In typical cases, it is as if this emptiness were their basic modality of subjective experience from which they attempt to escape by engagement in many activities or in frantic social interactions, by the ingestion of drugs or alcohol, or by attempts to obtain instinctual gratifications through sex, aggression, food, or compulsive activities that reduce their focusing on their inner experience. Other patients, in contrast, seem to succumb to this experience of emptiness and to acquire what might be described as a mechanical style of life—going through the motions of daily activities with a deadening sense of unreality or a blurring of any subjective experience, so that they seem to merge, so to speak, with whatever immediate inanimate or human environment surrounds them.

The subjective experience of emptiness may take various forms. Some patients with chronic neurotic depressions or depressive personality structures present this subjective experience only intermittently, and describe it as in sharp contrast to other types of subjective experience. For them, periods in which they feel empty are characterized by a sense of loss of contact with other people, who now appear distant, unavailable, or mechanical, while they themselves feel similarly. Life no longer seems to make sense, there is no hope for any future gratification or happiness, there is nothing to search for, long for, or aspire to. These patients may feel that they can no longer love anybody nor is there any reason why anybody should love them; the human world has become emptied of meaningful relationships among people, or at least of meaningful, loving relationships involving these patients. Their world of inanimate objects seems sharply delimited, as if such objects were protruding from their usual surrounding background and assuming a quality of impenetrability, lack of meaning, or unavailability. The usually appreciated and loved inanimate objects of their daily surroundings become strange and painfully meaningless.

These depressed patients' feelings of emptiness come close to the feeling of loneliness, except that loneliness implies elements of longing and the sense that there are others who are needed, and whose love is needed, who seem unavailable now. Psychoanalytic exploration regularly reveals that these patients suffer from an unconscious sense of guilt and that the "emptying" of their subjective experience reflects their superego's attack, as it were, on the self. The harsh internal punishment inflicted by the superego consists in the implicit dictum that they do not deserve to be loved and appreciated, and that they are condemned to be alone. On a deeper level, and in severe cases, internal fantasies determined by superego pressures are that because of their badness they have destroyed their inner objects and are therefore left alone in a world now devoid of love.

Other patients, that is, many patients with schizoid personality structure, may experience emptiness as an innate quality that makes them different from other people; in contrast to others, they cannot feel anything, and they may feel guilty because they do not have available feelings of love, hatred, tenderness, longing, mourning, which they observe and understand in other people but feel unavailable to experience themselves. For such schizoid patients, the experience of emptiness may be less painful than for depressed patients because there is less of a contrast between periods in which they feel empty and other times in which they would have emotional relationships with others. An internal sense of drifting, of subjective unreality, and of a soothing quality derived from this very unreality, makes the experience of emptiness more tolerable to schizoid patients and permits them to adopt passive dependent reactions toward others and thus fill time with an awareness of external reality in contrast to their subjective experience.

The subjective experience of the therapist who relates to depressed in contrast to schizoid patients with experiences of emptiness is remarkably different. In the relation with a patient presenting a depressive personality structure or chronic neurotic depression, the therapist may have a sense of intense human contact, a subjective experience of empathy, and at the same time, be aware that the patient cannot accept emotionally the very availability of the therapist in spite of his awareness of the therapist as a real person. The unconscious sense of guilt that prevents the depressed patient's accepting love or concern as it is offered, is reflected in the transference and in the therapist's emotional reaction to it. In contrast, the therapist in contact with schizoid patients describing a subjective sense of emptiness, of lack of emotional meaning of their relationship with all other people and of life in general, may experience a similar estrangement and distance and unavailability in his interactions with these patients.

One patient with strong schizoid features said in one session, after many months of therapy, that she was unable to have any feelings, and that my interpretations of feelings that she had toward me reflected my lack of awareness of how unable she was to feel anything. She described a visit to the house of a cousin whose husband other people considered a very attractive man. The way the patient described the interactions among her cousin, her cousin's husband, and other people surrounding them gave me the vague feeling that there were some sexualized tensions among them. But I was unable to really differentiate who had any sexual attraction for whom, and what all these people had to do with the patient herself.

When I raised these questions with the patient, her answers made me feel that the entire subject matter of that visit to her cousin was really irrelevant, but I could not detect anything else that would seem more relevant at the moment. I found myself growing more and more distracted, and I felt I was losing all connections among the various aspects of the material. The only thought that remained clearly in my mind was that the patient was defending herself against sexual feelings toward me, but I had no direct evidence for this, and I had the painful feeling that this was an intellectual speculation of a mechanical kind on my part on which I could not rely as the basis for an interpretation.

The patient then started to talk about how tiring it was to have to attend that social event with her cousin and to make an effort to appear involved, engaged, interested, when in fact she felt miles away and would have loved to simply be at work, carrying out mechanical tasks without any effort to respond internally. She also mentioned that she had read somewhere about a case of rape or something else involving a painful sexual experience. Again, I discovered that I had become distracted and had lost the connections of what she was saying. At the same time, I was aware of the sun shining into the office, the lines and shadows of the furniture, and realized with a shock that the patient sitting in front of me seemed an almost inanimate object, or, rather, that for me she had at that moment become impersonal, strange, and mechanical. In other words, she had just induced in me the sense of emptiness and irrelevance that she had described in her interactions with her cousin and the other people.

At that point, I told the patient that I thought that something in her was trying to make all her human contacts become dispersed and fragmented, so that any meaning of a human relationship was lost and nothing made sense anymore. I also said that I thought that, because she was frightened of her sexual fantasies, this dispersal or fragmentation might serve the purpose of protecting her from very real sexual feelings that she had had toward her cousin's husband, and that this same process might be going on with me at this moment. The patient immediately revealed that she had experienced a fantasy of embracing me and of becoming sexually excited with my holding her in a fatherly fashion.

This example illustrates a stage of resolution of what often can be a chronically resistant and frustrating situation in the therapeutic relation with schizoid personalities, namely the dispersal and fragmentation of emotions in all human relations, inducing a chronic sense of emptiness in the patient and in the therapist's response to such patients. The schizoid experience of emptiness is not close to a sense of loneliness; loneliness implies an intense, full awareness of the possibility of significant relations with others, which these patients do not have available to them for a long time in their treatment.

There are still other patients whose experience of emptiness is a major aspect of their psychopathology: patients with narcissistic personality structures—that is, those who present the development of pathological narcissism character- ized by the establishment of a pathological, grandiose self and a serious deterioration of all their internalized object relations. In contrast to the depressive and schizoid patients mentioned before, these narcissistic patients' experience of emptiness is characterized by the addition of strong feelings of boredom and restlessness. They do not have available certain aspects of the capacity for human relationships which are preserved—in their own way—by schizoid, and (even more so) by depressive patients. Patients with depressive personality, and even schizoid patients, are able to empathize deeply with human feelings and experiences involving other people, and may feel painfully excluded from and yet able to empathize with love and emotion involving others.

For example, a patient with depressive personality responded intensively to the emotional implications of novels and plays and to music, and was able to identify himself in depth with literary characters. The schizoid patient mentioned before was very interested in certain philosophical and religious ideas and, in her detached and "free floating" way, was acutely aware of and preoccupied with the life of her friends and family. She felt as if she were an observer from another planet of the "life and doings" of the people on this planet.

Patients with narcissistic personality, in contrast, do not have that capacity for empathizing with human experience in depth. Their social life, which gives them opportunities to obtain confirmation in reality or fantasy of their needs to be admired, and offers them direct instinctual gratifications, may provide them with an immediate sense of meaningfulness, but this is temporary. When such gratifications are not forthcoming, their sense of emptiness, restlessness, and boredom take over. Now their world becomes a prison from which only new excitement, admiration, or experiences implying control, triumph or incorporation of supplies are an escape. Emotional reactions in depth to art, the investment in value systems or in creativity beyond gratification of their narcissistic aims is often unavailable and indeed strange to them.

In the therapeutic relationship, narcissistic personalities tend to induce two opposite and extreme emotional reactions in the therapist. At times, when these patients project their own grandiosity onto the therapist, he may experience himself as the center of the patient's life, as the source of endless potential gratifications and wisdom which makes the patient feel fully gratified and alive. At other times, however (and this may be an unexpected shock for the beginning therapist), he may feel emptied out, helpless, lost in the presence of the completely self-sufficient, self-satisfied, and omnipotent patient, a process that may come about so abruptly and yet in such a subtle and long-lasting way that the therapist may not become aware of what is happening to him for quite some time. Under these cir-cumstances, the therapist may experience a chronic sense of emptiness when working with a narcissistic patient, of unreality and boredom, and intense guilt over such boredom; and he may realize only after some period of time that the boredom is an expression of his awareness of a pseudopresence of the other person in the room, an expression of a sham relationship in which the therapist is really being treated as a worthless appendix to the omniscient and omnipotent patient. The therapist's boredom reflects the absence of any significant object relation in the hours and alerts him to the much more generalized and chronic boredom and restlessness of the patient which reflect his general lack of object relations.

Temporary experiences of emptiness are present in many borderline cases, but not with the pervasiveness found in narcissistic patients (borderline or not) and in patients with strong schizoid personality features. There are some patients with combined narcissistic and paranoid features who alternate between periods in which they experience intense subjective, emotional involvement with potential enemies whom they have to fight off, while obtaining in the process, a sense of aliveness, and other periods of painful experience of emptiness and lack of meaning of life, when the narcissistic features predominate and no immediate enemy is available. There are narcissistic patients whose pathological narcissism constitutes an important defense against primitive paranoid tendencies, and paranoid patients in whom the involvement with potential enemies is a protection against the painful experience of emptiness. In all cases with a predominance of pathological narcissism, the experience of emptiness represents an opposite pole from that of the feeling of loneliness. Narcissistic patients often do not have available the sense of longing for or of awareness of the possibility of a significant relation with others and of missing such a relation.

I think that all I have said so far about the symptom of emptiness lends itself to the following generalizations. The subjective experience of emptiness represents a temporary or permanent loss of the normal relationship of the self with object representations, that is, with the world of inner objects that fixates intrapsychically the significant experiences with others and constitutes a basic ingredient of ego identity. Patients with a normally constituted ego identity and, therefore, a stable integrated self and a stable integrated world of internal objects, such as depressive personality structures, illustrate this process during periods when severe superego pressures threaten them with abandonment by their internal objects because of their internal sense of not deserving to be loved. However, under these circumstances, the capacity for normal object-relations always remains and may be actualized in the transference and in other interpersonal experiences.

In contrast, when there exists a lack of an integrated self and of normal relations of the self with integrated internal objects, a more deep-seated, chronic sense of emptiness and meaninglessness of the ordinary life experience ensues. Therefore, all patients with the syndrome of identity diffusion (but not with identity crises) present the potential for developing experiences of emptiness. This experience becomes particularly strong when active mechanisms of primitive dissociation or splitting constitute a predominant defense against intrapsychic conflict. Schizoid personalities, in whom splitting processes are particularly strong and may lead to a defensive dispersal and fragmentation of affects as well as of internal and external relationships involving the self and significant objects, present strong feelings of emptiness. In narcissistic personalities, where the normal relations between an integrated self and integrated internal objects are replaced by a pathological grandiose self and a deterioration of internal objects, the experience of emptiness is most intense and almost constant. In these cases, emptiness, restlessness, and boredom constitute a constellation of what might be considered a baseline of pathological narcissistic experience. Emptiness, in short, represents a complex affect state, which reflects the rupture of the normal polarity of self and objects (the basic units of all internalized object relations). Emptiness stands midway between the longing, sadness, and loneliness that represents the hope for the re-establishment of significant object relations, on the one hand, and the regressive psychotic fusion of "all good" self and object images (when the loss of the good relationship with an object cannot be tolerated), on the other.

In the transference, the patient's subjective experience of emptiness is reflected in the vicissitudes of the patient-therapist relation; the therapist may identify, by means of his analysis of the transference and countertransference situation, the nature of the pathology of internalized object relations that underlies the experience of emptiness. Such an analysis has important diagnostic and therapeutic implications; it permits the clarification of the nature of the predominant structural intrapsychic pathology and the defensive operations involved. Insofar as patients with borderline personality organization and with narcissistic pathology all present severe pathology of the self and of object representations, they require a specific over-all therapeutic strategy in dealing with their transference.

What follows is an outline of that strategy. As a first step, the therapist has to be alert to the possibility of the development of meaninglessness or futility as a basic experience for both the patient and the therapist in the treatment hours; this dehumanization of the therapeutic relation has to be diagnosed in terms of the mechanisms involved (the predominance of splitting operations, or of primitive omnipotence, or of unconscious guilt, or of unconscious envy of the therapist, etc.) and these defenses against a significant object relation in the transference, as well as their motives, have to be interpreted.

As a second step, the therapist must evaluate the ensuing primitive object relation, when these defenses are worked through, in terms of the self image and the corresponding object image involved; the therapist may represent one aspect of the patient's dissociated self and/or one aspect of a primitive object representation; and patient and therapist may interchange their enactment of respectively self or object image. These aspects of the self and of object representations then need to be interpreted and the respective human relationship clarified in the transference.

As a third step, this particular "part-object" relation activated in the transference has to be integrated with other "part-object" relations until the patient's real self and his internal conception of objects can be both integrated and

Borderline Conditions and Pathological Narcissism

consolidated. These various steps represent in essence, the sequence involved in the working through of primitive transference developments in patients with borderline personality organization and narcissistic personalities.

The psychoanalytic study of patients who attempt to escape their sense of emptiness by means of alcohol or drugs provides additional illustration of the intrapsychic structural characteristics involved. The effects of drugs and alcohol vary, I think, according to the underlying intrapsychic structures of the individuals involved.

A patient with depressive personality structure may experience, under the influence of alcohol, a subjective sense of well-being and elation which he interprets unconsciously as a reunion with a lost, prohibiting, and now forgiving parental image which had caused the unconscious sense of guilt and depression. The combination of elation and depression, of expansiveness and mourning in depressive personalities under the influence of alcohol may illustrate the working through in fantasy of the sense of guilt, the need to repair the relation with the object, and the celebration of the re-encounter with it. In contrast, for many borderline patients, drug intake activates a sense of well-being and goodness that activates the split-off "all good" self and object images and permits the denial of "all bad" internalized object relations, thus permitting an escape from intolerable guilt or sense of internal persecution. In the case of narcissistic personalities, alcohol or drug intake may constitute a predominant mechanism to "refuel" the pathological grandiose self and assure its omnipotence and protection against a potentially frustrating and hostile environment in which gratification and admiration are not forthcoming.

The addictive potential is maximum, I think, for narcissistic personality structures, and the prognosis for treatment of addictive conditions of narcissistic personalities is much worse than is the case of addictive borderline patients without narcissistic features, and of less regressed personality structures such as the depressive personality. In general terms, the implication is that the psychological functions of alcohol or drugs are strongly influenced by the predominant nature of intrapsychic structuralized object relations.

An important question has been raised in recent years regarding the relation between the subjective experience of futility and emptiness, on the one hand, and the rapid breakdown or shifts in social stability and cultural values, on the other. The question has been posed of whether contemporary social and cultural changes have affected the patterns of object relations. On the basis of the analysis underlying what I have said so far, I do not think that changes in contemporary culture have effects on patterns of object relations, if we define object relations not simply in terms of actual interactions between a person and others, but in terms of the intrapsychic structures that govern such interactions, and in terms of the internal capacity to relate in depth to others. Many authors have talked about what has been called this "age of alienation," and it has been implied that social and cultural alienation may foster disintegration of the capacity of involvement in depth with others.

Keniston (2, 3), comparing youth in protest with alienated youth, has provided important sociological evidence indicating that generalized withdrawal from relations with others and the incapacity to establish deep, lasting relations are not a direct reflection of youth culture, but stem from very early childhood conflicts and family pathology. By the same token, I do not think that changes in contemporary morality have changed the need and the capacity for intimacy in various forms. This is not to say that such changes in the patterns of intimacy could not occur over a period of several generations, if and when changes in cultural patterns affect family structure to such an extent that the earliest development in childhood would be influenced. It seems to me that one has to make a distinction between the effects of social disorganization, of severe disruption of the family structure and of earliest child development (all of which have a definite impact on the development of the personality), and the effects of rapid cultural change reflected in changing social and sexual mores: these latter do not, I think, bring about chronic experiences of emptiness and futility, unless there exists severe pathology of internalized object relations which stems from infancy and early childhood.

## BIBLIOGRAPHY

1.   Jacobson, Edith, *The Self and the Object World*. New York: International Universities Press. 1964.
2.   Keniston, K., *Young Radicals*. New York: Harcourt, Brace and World, Inc., 1968.
3.   ———, Student Activism, Moral Development, and Morality. *Amer. J. Orthopsychiat.*, 40:577-592, 1970.

PART II

# Narcissistic Personality

# Eight
# The Treatment of
# the Narcissistic Personality

In this chapter I shall discuss the etiology, diagnosis, prognosis, and some factors in the treatment of patients with narcissistic personality structure. I do not expect to treat the subject exhaustively, but I hope to shed new light on certain areas. This paper deals mainly with the clinical problem of narcissism, and such metapsychological considerations as will be presented shortly have to do only with the etiology of pathological narcissism. The broader issue of the theory of narcissism in psychoanalysis is examined in Chapter 10.

I suggested in Chapter 1 that narcissistic as a descriptive term has been both abused and overused, but that there does exist a group of patients in whom the main problem appears to be the disturbance of their self-regard in connection with specific disturbances in their object relationships, and whom we might consider almost a pure culture of pathological development of narcissism. It is for these patients that I would reserve the term narcissistic personalities. On the surface, these patients may not present seriously disturbed behavior; some of them may function socially very well, and they usually have much better impulse control than the infantile personality.

These patients present an unusual degree of self-reference in their interactions with other people, a great need to be loved and admired by others, and a curious apparent contradiction between a very inflated concept of themselves and an inordinate need for tribute from others. Their emotional life is shallow. They experience little empathy for the feelings of others, they obtain very little enjoyment from life other than from the tributes they receive from others or from their own grandiose fantasies, and they feel restless and bored when external glitter wears off and no new sources feed their self-regard. They envy others, tend to idealize some people from whom they expect narcissistic supplies and to depreciate and treat with contempt those from whom they do not expect anything (often their former idols). In general, their relationships with other people are clearly exploitative and sometimes parasitic. It is as if they feel they have the right to control and possess others and to exploit them without guilt feelings—and, behind a surface which very often is charming and engaging, one senses coldness and ruthlessness. Very often such patients are considered to be dependent because they need so much tribute and adoration from others, but on a deeper level they are completely unable really to depend on anybody because of their deep distrust and depreciation of others.

Analytic exploration very often demonstrates that their haughty, grandiose, and controlling behavior is a defense against paranoid traits related to the projection of oral rage, which is central in their psychopathology. On the surface these patients appear to present a remarkable lack of object relationships; on a deeper level, their interactions reflect very intense, primitive, internalized object relationships of a frightening kind and an incapacity to depend on internalized good objects. The antisocial personality may be considered a subgroup of the narcissistic personality. Antisocial personality structures present the same general constellation of traits that I have just mentioned, in combination with additional severe superego pathology.

The main characteristics of these narcissistic personalities are grandiosity, extreme self-centeredness, and a remarkable absence of interest in and empathy for others in spite of the fact that they are so very eager to obtain admiration and approval from other people. These patients experience a remarkably intense envy of other people who seem to have things they do not have or who simply seem to enjoy their lives. These patients not only lack emotional depth and fail to understand complex emotions in other people, but their own feelings lack differentiation, with quick flare-ups and subsequent dispersal of emotion. They are especially deficient in genuine feelings of sadness and mournful longing; their incapacity for experiencing depressive reactions is a basic feature of their personalities. When abandoned or disappointed by other people they may show what on the surface looks like depression, but which on further examination emerges as anger and resentment, loaded with revengeful wishes, rather than real sadness for the loss of a person whom they appreciated.

Some patients with narcissistic personalities present strong conscious feelings of insecurity and inferiority. At times, such feelings of inferiority and insecurity may alternate with feelings of greatness and omnipotent fantasies (10). At other times, and only after some period of analysis, do unconscious fantasies of omnipotence and narcissistic grandiosity come to the surface. The presence of extreme contradictions in their self concept is often the first clinical evidence of the severe pathology in the ego and superego of these patients, hidden underneath a surface of smooth and effective social functioning.

The defensive organization of these patients is quite similar to that of the borderline personality organization in general. They present a predominance of primitive defensive mechanisms such as splitting, denial, projective identification, omnipotence, and primitive idealization. They also show the intense, primitive quality of oral-aggressive conflicts characteristic of borderline patients. What distinguishes many of the patients with narcissistic personalities from the usual borderline patient is their relatively good social functioning, their better impulse control, and what may be described as a "pseudosublimatory" potential, namely, the capacity for active, consistent work in some areas which permits them partially to fulfill their ambitions of greatness and of obtaining admiration from others. Highly intelligent patients with this personality structure may appear as quite creative in their fields: narcissistic personalities can often be found as leaders in industrial organizations or academic institutions; they may also be outstanding performers in some artistic domain. Careful observation, however, of their productivity over a long period of time will give evidence of superficiality and flightiness in their work, of a lack of depth which eventually reveals the emptiness behind the glitter. Quite frequently these are the "promising" geniuses who then surprise other people by the banality of their development. They also are able to exert self-control in anxiety-producing situations, which may at first appear as good anxiety tolerance; however, analytic exploration shows that their anxiety tolerance is obtained at the cost of increasing their narcissistic fantasies and of withdrawing into "splendid isolation." This tolerance of anxiety does not reflect an authentic capacity for coming to terms with a disturbing reality.

In short, the surface functioning of the narcissistic personality is much better than that of the average borderline patient: therefore, their capacity for regression—even to the level of psychotic functioning when undergoing psychoanalysis—may come as a real surprise to the analyst.

## ETIOLOGICAL AND DYNAMIC FEATURES

An early effort to classify the narcissistic character as one form of libidinal type (5) did not become generally accepted, for reasons mentioned by Fenichel (3). Van der Waals (19) has clarified the issue of "pathological narcissism" by pointing out that severe narcissism does not reflect simply a fixation in early narcissistic stages of development and a simple lack of the normal course of development toward object love, but that it is characterized by the simultaneous development of pathological forms of self-love and of pathological forms of object love. According to van der Waals, normal narcissism develops simultaneously with normal object relationships, and pathological narcissism with pathological object relationships. He has also pointed out that progress in the understanding of pathological narcissism has been hampered by the fact that in psychoanalytic literature the clinical problems of narcissism are intermingled with the issue of narcissism as a meta-psychological problem.

Jacobson (6) has clarified the relationship between psychotic regression on the one hand and defensive refusion of

early self and object representations on the other. According to
Jacobson, in the earliest stages of an individual's development,
when self and object images are differentiated from each other
and thus contribute to the development of reality testing and of
ego boundaries, extremely severe frustrations in relationships
with significant early objects may bring about a dangerous
refusion of self and object images, a mechanism which allows
the individual to escape the conflict between the need for the
external object and the dread of it. Under these circumstances, a
blurring of ego boundaries, the loss of reality testing, in short,
psychotic regression, may occur. Such a development does not
take place in the case of narcissistic personalities, whose ego
boundaries are stable and whose reality testing is preserved. A.
Reich (10) has suggested that in narcissistic personalities a
regressive fusion takes place between a primitive ego ideal and
the self.

I propose that a process of refusion of the internalized self
and object images does occur in the narcissistic personality at a
level of development at which ego boundaries have already
become stable. At this point, there is a fusion of ideal self, ideal
object, and actual self images as a defense against an intolerable
reality in the interpersonal realm, with a concomitant devaluation and destruction of object images as well as of external
objects. In their fantasies, these patients identify themselves
with their own ideal self images in order to deny normal
dependency on external objects and on the internalized
representations of the external objects. It is as if they were
saying, "I do not need to fear that I will be rejected for not living
up to the ideal of myself which alone makes it possible for me to
be loved by the ideal person I imagine would love me. That ideal
person and my ideal image of that person and my real self are all
one, and better than the ideal person whom I wanted to love me,
so that I do not need anybody else any more." In other words,
the normal tension between actual self on the one hand, and
ideal self and ideal object on the other, is eliminated by the
building up of an inflated self concept within which the actual
self and the ideal self and ideal object are confused. At the same
time, the remnants of the unacceptable self images are
repressed and projected onto external objects, which are

devaluated. This process is in marked contrast to the normal differentiation between ideal self images on the one hand and ideal object images on the other, both of which represent the internalized demands of objects as well as gratification from these objects if the demands are met. The normal superego integrates ideal self images and ideal object images; the tension between actual self images and such integrated ideal ones becomes tension between the ego and superego. In patients presenting pathological narcissism, however, the pathological fusion between ideal self, ideal object, and actual self images prevents such integration of the superego, because the process of idealization is highly unrealistic, preventing the condensation of such idealized images with actual parental demands and with the aggressively determined superego forerunners. Also, actual self images, a part of the ego structure, are now pathologically condensed with forerunners of the superego, and, therefore, they interfere with the normal differentiation of the superego and ego. Although some superego components are internalized, such as prohibitive parental demands, they preserve a distorted, primitive, aggressive quality because they are not integrated with the loving aspects of the superego which are normally drawn from the ideal self and object images and are missing in these patients (15). Because there is so little integration with other superego forerunners, the generally aggressive and primitive kind of superego is easily reprojected in the form of paranoid projections. I want to stress that the primitive and aggressive nature of their superego ultimately derives from the intense oral-aggressive quality of their fixations. Narcissistic patients characteristically adapt themselves to the moral demands of their environment because they are afraid of the attacks to which they would be subjected if they do not conform, and because this submission seems to be the price they have to pay for glory and admiration; however, one frequently finds that patients of this kind, who have never shown evidence of antisocial activity, think of themselves as "crooks" and as capable of antisocial behavior "if they could get away with it." Needless to say, they also experience other people as basically dishonest and unreliable, or only reliable because of external pressures. This concept of themselves and others, of course, becomes very important in the transference.

One result of the defensive fusion of ideal self, ideal object, and actual self images is the devaluation and destruction not only of external objects but also of internalized object images. Actually, this process never goes so far that there are no internal representations of external objects: it would probably be impossible to live under such conditions. To want to be admired and loved by others requires that others should appear at least somewhat "alive," internally as well as externally. The remnants of the internalized object representations acquire the characteristics of real, but rather lifeless, shadowy people. This experience of other people, especially those who are not idealized, as lifeless shadows or marionettes, is quite prevalent in the patients I am considering. Idealized people, on whom these patients seem to "depend," regularly turn out to be projections of their own aggrandized self concepts. Idealized representatives of the self, the "shadows" of others, and—as we shall see—dreaded enemies, are all that seem to exist in the inner world of these patients. A narcissistic patient experiences his relationships with other people as being purely exploitative, as if he were "squeezing a lemon and then dropping the remains." People may appear to him either to have some potential food inside, which the patient has to extract, or to be already emptied and therefore valueless. In addition, these shadowy external objects sometimes suddenly seem to be invested with high and dangerous powers, as the patient projects onto others the primitive characteristics of his own superego and of his own exploitative nature. His attitude towards others is either deprecatory—he has extracted all he needs and tosses them aside—or fearful—others may attack, exploit, and force him to submit to them. At the very bottom of this dichotomy lies a still deeper image of the relationship with external objects, precisely the one against which the patient has erected all these other pathological structures. It is the image of a hungry, enraged, empty self, full of impotent anger at being frustrated, and fearful of a world which seems as hateful and revengeful as the patient himself.

This, the deepest level of the self concept of narcissistic patients, can be perceived only late in the course of their psychoanalytic treatment, except in the case of narcissistic patients with overt borderline features who show it quite early. British psychoanalysts who have analyzed patients with this character structure have reported the central importance of such basic dread of attack and destruction. In less disorganized patients, that is, narcissistic personalities with relatively stronger egos, one eventually encounters in the transference paranoid developments, with feelings of emptiness, rage, and fear of being attacked. On an even less regressed level, the available remnants of such self images reveal a picture of a worthless, poverty-stricken, empty person who feels always left "outside," devoured by envy of those who have food, happiness, and fame. Often the surface remnant of this line of primitive self images is undistinguishable from the shadowy remnants of devaluated object images. This devaluated concept of the self can be seen especially in narcissistic patients who divide the world into famous, rich, and great people on the one hand, and the despicable, worthless, "mediocrity" on the other. Such patients are afraid of not belonging to the company of the great, rich, and powerful, and of belonging instead to the "mediocre," by which they mean worthless and despicable rather than "average" in the ordinary sense of the term. One patient, after years of analytic treatment, began to yearn to become "average," meaning he wanted to be able to enjoy being an ordinary person, without an overriding necessity to feel great and important in order to cancel feelings of worthlessness and devaluation.

What brings about the crucial pathological fusion of ideal self, ideal object, and actual self images? These patients present a pathologically augmented development of oral aggression and it is hard to evaluate to what extent this development represents a constitutionally determined strong aggressive drive, a constitutionally determined lack of anxiety tolerance in regard to aggressive impulses, or severe frustration in their first years of life.

Chronically cold parental figures with covert but intense aggression are a very frequent feature of the background of these patients. A composite picture of a number of cases that I have been able to examine or to treat shows consistently a parental figure, usually the mother or a mother surrogate, who functions well on the surface in a superficially well-organized home, but with a degree of callousness, indifference, and nonverbalized, spiteful aggression. When intense oral frustration, resentment, and aggression have developed in the child within such an environment, the first condition is laid for his need to defend against extreme envy and hatred. In addition, these patients present some quite specific features which distinguish them from other borderline patients. Their histories reveal that each patient possessed some inherent quality which could have objectively aroused the envy or admiration of others. For example, unusual physical attractiveness or some special talent became a refuge against the basic feelings of being unloved and of being the objects of revengeful hatred. Sometimes it was rather the cold hostile mother's narcissistic use of the child which made him "special," set him off on the road in a search for compensatory admiration and greatness, and fostered the characterological defense of spiteful devaluation of others. For example, two patients were used by their mothers as a kind of "object of art," being dressed up and exposed to public admiration in an almost grotesque way, so that fantasies of power and greatness linked with exhibitionistic trends became central in their compensatory efforts against oral rage and envy. These patients often occupy a pivotal point in their family structure, such as being the only child, or the only "brilliant" child, or the one who is supposed to fulfill the family aspirations; a good number of them have a history of having played the role of "genius" in their family during childhood.

I am not sure whether these observations explain the entire story. Once, however, the kind of mechanism mentioned— defensive fusion of ideal self, ideal object, and self images— comes into operation, it is extremely effective in perpetuating a vicious circle of self-admiration, depreciation of others, and elimination of all actual dependency. The greatest fear of these patients is to be dependent on anybody else, because to depend means to hate, envy, and expose themselves to the danger of being exploited, mistreated, and frustrated. In the course of treatment, their main defenses are erected against the possibility of depending on the analyst, and the development of a situation in which they do feel dependent immediately brings back the basic threatening situation of early childhood (12).

This kind of person's incapacity to depend on another person is a very crucial characteristic. These patients often admire some hero or outstanding individual and establish with such a person what on the surface looks like a dependent relationship, yet they really experience themselves as part of that outstanding person; it regularly emerges in treatment that the admired individual is merely an extension of themselves. If the person rejects them, they experience immediate hatred and fear, and react by devaluating the former idol. If their admired person disappears or is "dethroned," they immediately drop him. In short, there is no real involvement with the admired person and a simple narcissistic use is made of him. When narcissistic personalities are themselves in a position of objective importance—for example, heading a political institution or a social group—they love to surround themselves with admirers in whom they are interested as long as the admiration is new. Once they feel they have extracted all the admiration they need, they perceive their admirers as "shadows" once more and mercilessly exploit and mistreat them. At the same time, these patients are extremely offended when one of their "slaves" wants to free himself. In the analytic situation this relationship is constantly re-enacted. These patients at times idealize the analyst and are convinced that he is the greatest analyst on earth. At the same time, on a deeper level, they experience themselves as the only patient of the analyst; I have found the literal fantasy in several patients that, when they are not in session, their analyst disappears or dies or is no longer "brilliant." Typically, over weekends and during vacations, these patients completely forget the analyst and do not permit themselves the mourning reactions that separations from the analyst induce in the usual psychoneurotic case. In short, the idealized analyst is only an extension of themselves, or they are extensions of the idealized analyst; it is the same situation in either case. There exists the danger of looking upon these patients as very dependent because of the satisfaction they obtain from such "closeness." It comes as a surprise to some therapists that patients who seemed happy to come to their sessions over many years with unending expressions of praise and admiration for their therapist are all of a sudden willing and able to drop the relationship for the slightest reason or frustration.

These patients' feelings of emptiness and boredom are intimately related to their stunted ego development, which in turn is connected with their inability to experience depression. Many authors have pointed out that the capacity for tolerating depression, linked to the capacity for mourning over a lost good object or a lost ideal image of oneself, is an important prerequisite for emotional development and especially for the broadening and deepening of feelings. In addition, the devaluation of objects and object images on the part of patients with pathological narcissism creates a constant emptiness in their social life and reinforces their internal experience of emptiness. They need to devaluate whatever they receive in order to prevent themselves from experiencing envy. This is the tragedy of these patients: that they need so much from others while being unable to acknowledge what they are receiving because it would stir up envy; in consequence, they always wind up empty. One patient fell in love with a woman whom he considered very beautiful, gifted, warm, in short, completely satisfying. He had a brief period of awareness of how much he hated her for being so perfect, just before she responded to him and decided to marry him. After their marriage he felt bored with her and became completely indifferent toward her. During his psychoanalysis he came to understand how he treated his analyst in a similar way: he depreciated everything he was receiving from his analyst in order to prevent his envy and hatred from coming to the surface. After that, the patient gradually developed strong suspiciousness and hatred toward his wife for having all that he felt he did not have, and he was also afraid that she would abandon him and leave him with even less. At the same time, however, he was able for the first time to become aware of and to be moved by her expressions of love and tenderness. His awareness of his aggressive disqualification of her and his analyst, and his increasing ability to tolerate his hatred without having to defend against it by destroying his awareness of other people made both his wife and his analyst "come alive" as real people with independent existences, and eventually permitted him to experience not only hatred but also love toward them.

## DIFFERENTIAL DIAGNOSIS

The descriptive features of narcissistic personalities usually permit their differentiation from other forms of character pathology in which narcissistic character defenses are present. All character defenses have, among other functions, a narcissistic one: they protect self-esteem. In addition, there are patients with all kinds of character pathology who present marked character defenses especially erected to protect or enhance self-esteem. These latter cases have "narcissistic character defenses" in an essentially non-narcissistic personality structure, which has to be differentiated, therefore, from the narcissistic personality in the narrow sense used in this paper. Thus, for example, the stubbornness or oppositionalism of obsessive personalities often has a strong narcissistic quality; however, there is much more stability and depth in the interpersonal relationships of obsessive personalities than in those of narcissistic personalities, in spite of the fact that both may appear superficially as quite "cold." Also, the value systems of narcissistic personalities are generally corruptible, in contrast to the rigid morality of the obsessive personality.

The differential diagnosis in distinction to hysterical character structure is also not too difficult. An exaggeration of narcissistic traits, especially those linked with exhibitionistic trends, is quite prevalent in hysterical personalities; however, the need to be admired, to be the center of attention of the hysterical personality—usually a narcissistic reaction formation against penis envy—goes together with a capacity for deep and lasting relationships with others. Women with narcissistic personalities may appear as quite "hysterical" on the surface, with their extreme coquettishness and exhibitionism, but the cold, shrewdly calculating quality of their seductiveness is in marked contrast to the much warmer, emotionally involved quality of hysterical pseudo-hypersexuality.

A. Reich (9), further analyzing narcissistic types of object choice made by women as presented in Freud's classical paper on narcissism (4), described two types of object choice in women which, broadly speaking, correspond to the differentiation between narcissistic defenses in hysterical women on the one hand and the narcissistic personality as described in this paper on the other. A. Reich's first type is the woman who develops extreme submissiveness toward men who represent her own, infantile, grandiose ego ideal; such a woman appears to wish to fuse with idealized men, overcoming in this way her experience of herself as a castrated being. These women are able to establish meaningful object relationships with men, and their fusion with and idealization of men are based on at least some realistic and discriminating evaluation of the objects. The second type of woman which A. Reich describes corresponds to the "as if" type of personality; such a woman establishes transitory pseudoinfatuations with men, infatuations which represent a more primitive, narcissistic fusion with easily devaluated and poorly differentiated objects. This latter form of object choice reflects, A. Reich says, a more severe degree of pathology and lack of differentiation of the ego ideal, which goes hand in hand with an insufficiently developed superego and with a "predominance of aggression against the objects on whom the ego ideal is built" (9).

From a diagnostic and prognostic viewpoint, it is very important for the analyst to observe what kind of new transference developments appear when narcissistic transference resistances are interpreted. A good diagnostic study involving structural considerations should make it possible to differentiate between narcissistic personalities and other character structures with narcissistic features. The effects of consistent interpretation of narcissistic transference resistances should clarify the diagnosis in cases in which doubts about the character structure still remain. For example, an obsessive patient may start out in analysis with strong narcissistic defenses against oedipal fears or against sadomasochistic dispositions; a hysterical woman may develop initially strong narcissistic defenses against oedipal involvement and especially against penis envy. In all these cases the analysis of such narcissistic character defenses soon opens the road to the underlying transference dispositions, with intense and highly differentiated transference involvements, in contrast to the process in the case of patients with narcissistic personalities. In the latter, narcissistic defenses do not change into other transference paradigms, but remain stubbornly linked to primitive, oral-aggressive drive derivatives and related primitive defense operations. Here the characteristics of the transference involvement oscillate between narcissistic grandiosity and aloofness on the one hand, and primitive, predominantly paranoid trends on the other. The patient's complete incapacity, maintained over many months and years of analytic work, to experience the analyst as an independent object is characteristic of narcissistic personalities, and is in sharp contrast to the transference involvements in other forms of character pathology where the transference may shift to reveal different, highly specific conflicts of varying psychosexual stages of development and with a highly differentiated awareness by the patient of the analyst as an independent object.

From a structural viewpoint, the main difference between narcissistic personalities and other forms of character pathology is the different nature and functioning of the ego ideal. Normally, idealized images of the parental figures and idealized self images are first condensed into the ego ideal (6), which then is further modified by the integration and incorporation of more realistically perceived parental demands, of the sadistic forerunners of the superego, and of the more advanced aspects of the prohibitive superego. Such a "toned down," less grandiose, and more attainable ego ideal permits one the normal narcissistic gratification of living up to the internalized ideal parental images, and this gratification in turn reinforces self-esteem, one's confidence in one's own goodness and one's trust in gratifying object relationships. In character pathology other than the narcissistic personality, the excessive development of narcissistic character defenses results from an exacerbation of the early infantile ego ideal as a defense against fear and guilt over multiple conflicts. Thus, for example, in the case of many female patients with hysterical personality, the need to live up to internal fantasies of being beautiful and powerful may be a protection against feelings of inferiority which in turn stem from penis envy and castration anxiety. Again, in obsessive personalities, living up to primitive ideals of perfection and cleanliness may be a most effective protection against anal-sadistic guilt and conflicts. In all these cases, the exacerbation of or fixation at the infantile ego ideal is not accompanied by a primitive fusion of the self concept with such an ego ideal, nor by a concomitant devaluation of object representations and external objects. But in narcissistic personalities, such a primitive fusion of the self with the ego ideal, and concomitant processes of devaluation of external objects and object images, do take place in order to protect the self against primitive oral conflicts and frustration. The fixations at the level of normal infantile narcissism, which are pathological in any case, have to be differentiated from the more severe, particular distortion of all internalized object relations that take place in the narcissistic personality.

The following two cases illustrate the presence of narcissistic character defenses in nonnarcissistic personalities. The first, a female patient with hysterical personality structure, had a strong, although deeply repressed, conviction that underneath what she considered her ugly, distasteful body and genitals, there was the body and the genitals of a unique, extremely beautiful woman toward whom men would feel impelled to pay homage. At that deeper level, she fantasied herself as the most attractive woman on earth, a "mother-queen-goddess" who would achieve a perfect relationship with an ideal, great "father-husband-son." In the transference, she was willing to give her love to the analyst-father if he in return would comply with that perfect image which she had of herself by admiring her and never questioning her perfection and integrity. The patient experienced the analyst's interpretations as threatening to that image of herself, a severe attack on her self-esteem, and a shattering criticism which induced quite intense depression. When her haughty, derogatory attitude toward the analyst, a part of her narcissistic self-aggrandizement, was pointed out to her, she became angry and depressed, and at that point experienced the analyst as a narcissistic, self-involved, grandiose father image. Her reaction represented part of the way she had actually experienced her father in her childhood at the height of her oedipal development. Disappointed at what she perceived as the analyst-father's "attacks" on her, she then felt lost and rejected by this idealized father, and defeated in her fantasies by other, idealized women-mothers in the competition for the father. Thus, she developed a full-fledged oedipal transference. This transference emerged after the undoing of her narcissistic character defenses, which in turn had stemmed from penis envy. At no point did she completely devaluate the transference object, or oscillate between primitive, orally determined paranoid transference distortions on the one hand, and narcissistic withdrawal into a more primitive self-idealization on the other. Since these latter elements were lacking, we may conclude that her narcissistic transference resistances did not reflect a narcissistic personality structure.

The second illustration of a narcissistic character defense was provided by a male patient with an obsessive personality structure. He was quite derogatory toward the analyst, reveled in his own interpretations of his material, and saw the analyst mainly as a background figure whose function was to applaud and admire these interpretations and insights. When this attitude was systematically examined, however, and the patient was consistently confronted with this defensive pattern, a new, deeper transference pattern evolved. In this new facet of the transference, the patient saw the analyst as a cold, indifferent, unloving mother image, and experienced feelings of sadness and loneliness, representing an early longing for his idealized mother. In this second illustration, too, when the narcissistic character defenses broke down, other transference patterns emerged in which the patient maintained a differentiated object relationship, neither devaluating the object nor taking flight into an idealized self image. In summary, both of these cases developed new, differentiated transference relationships after the narcissistic character defenses had been dissolved, whereas the narcissistic patient cannot acknowledge the analyst as an independent object and continuously and stubbornly regards him as a simple extension of the patient's own self concept, although the regression within this same transference paradigm may fluctuate.

## CONSIDERATIONS IN REGARD TO TECHNIQUE

Many experienced clinicians consider these narcissistic personalities as unlikely candidates for analysis, but at the same time as hopeless candidates for any method of treatment other than psychoanalysis. Against this extremely guarded prognosis, Stone (16) expresses a somewhat more optimistic viewpoint about the analyzability of these patients. E. Ticho (18), recognizing both the problems and the challenges of these cases, has proposed that narcissistic personalities constitute a "heroic indication for psychoanalysis." In my opinion, the fact that some of these patients not only improve with psychoanalytic treatment, but improve dramatically, shows that efforts to study the technical and prognostic features of these cases more thoroughly are well warranted.

Jones (7) published a paper on pathological narcissistic character traits as early as 1913. In 1919, Abraham (1) wrote the first paper on the transference resistances of these patients, in which he warned the therapist about the dangerous effects of narcissistic character defenses on the psychoanalytic process. He pointed to the necessity for consistent interpretation of these patients' tendencies to look down on the analyst and to use him as an audience for their own independent "analytic" work. Riviere (11), in her classic paper on the negative therapeutic reaction, describes patients who have to defeat the psychoanalytic process: they cannot tolerate the notion of improvement, because improvement would mean acknowledgment of help received from somebody else. She states that these patients cannot tolerate receiving something good from the analyst because of the intolerable guilt over their own basic aggression. Rosenfeld (12) has stressed how basic the intolerance of dependency is on the part of patients with narcissistic personality structure. Kohut (8) has illustrated how a patient with this personality structure could not tolerate the analyst's being a different, independent person. These papers all emphasize the severity of the transference resistances of narcissistic patients.

I should like to illustrate this problem of transference resistance with a case history. A patient with narcissistic character structure spent hour after hour over many months of treatment telling me how monotonous and boring analysis had become, that in his associations the same contents kept coming up again and again, and that treatment was definitely a hopeless enterprise. At the same time, he felt rather good in his life outside the analytic hours, with some relief from his feelings of insufficiency and insecurity, but he was unable to understand why this had happened. I pointed out to him that, implicit in his description of his psychoanalysis, was a description of me as the provider of useless and silly treatment. The patient denied this at first, stressing that it was only his problem, not mine, that analysis could not work. I then pointed out to him that, at the beginning of his treatment, he had considerably envied my other patients, who had already received so much more from me than he had, and that it was strange now that he should feel no envy at all of the other patients, especially in view of his statement that it was his problem only that he could not benefit from analysis. I also pointed out to him that his previous, strong envy of me had completely disappeared, for reasons which had remained obscure to him. At this point the patient became aware that he really thought that it was entirely my fault that his analysis was, according to him, a failure. He now felt surprised that he was so satisfied to continue his treatment while considering me so inefficient. I pointed out to him how much satisfaction it gave him for me to be a failure while he was a success in his life. I also pointed out that it was as if I had become the worthless self of him, while he had taken over the admired self of me. At that point he became very anxious and developed the fear that I hated him and that I would take revenge. Fantasies came up in which he thought that I was telling his superiors and the police about activities of which he was very much ashamed. I pointed out to him that his fear of attack from me was one reason which prevented him from really considering himself in analysis and that he reassured himself that he was not really a patient by asserting that nothing was going on in the sessions. At that point the patient experienced feelings of admiration toward me because I had not become confused and discouraged by his constant repetition that analysis was a failure. At the next moment, however, he thought that I was very clever, and that I knew how to use "typical analytic tricks" to keep "one up" over patients. He then thought that he himself would try to use a similar technique with people who might try to depreciate him. I then pointed out that as soon as he received a "good" interpretation, and found himself helped, he also felt guilty over his attacks on me, and then again envious of my "goodness." Therefore, he had to "steal" my interpretations for his own use with others, devaluating me in the process, in order to avoid acknowledging that I had anything good left as well as to avoid the obligation of feeling grateful. The patient became quite anxious for a moment and then went completely "blank." He came in the next session with a bland denial of the emotional relevance of what had developed in the session before, and once again the same cycle started all over, with repetitive declarations of his boredom and the ineffectiveness of analysis.

At times it is difficult to imagine how frequent and how repetitive such interactions are, extending as they do over two or three years of analysis; this resistance to treatment illustrates the intensity of the narcissistic patient's need to deny any dependent relationship. It is obvious that consistent examination of the negative transference is even more crucial in these patients than in others undergoing psychoanalysis. These narcissistic patients persistently seek to devaluate the analytic process, to deny the reality of their own emotional life, and to confirm the fantasy that the analyst is not a person independent from themselves. A recent motion picture by Ingmar Bergman, *Persona*, illustrates the breakdown of an immature but basically decent young woman, a nurse, charged with the care of a psychologically severely ill woman presenting what we would describe as a typical narcissistic personality. In the face of the cold, unscrupulous exploitation to which the young nurse is subjected, she gradually breaks down. She cannot face the fact that the other sick woman returns only hatred for love and is completely unable to acknowledge any loving or human feeling expressed toward her. The sick woman seems to be able to live only if and when she can destroy what is valuable in other persons, although in the process she ends up destroying herself as a human being. In a dramatic development, the nurse develops an intense hatred for the sick woman and mistreats her cruelly at one point. It is as if all the hatred within the sick woman had been transferred into the helping one, destroying the helping person from the inside.

This screen play reproduces in essence the transference-countertransference situations that develop in the treatment of severely narcissistic patients. All the patients' efforts seem to go into defeating the analyst, into making analysis a meaningless game, into systematically destroying whatever they experience as good and valuable in the analyst. After many months and years of being treated as an "appendix" of the patient (a process which may be subtle enough to remain unnoticed for a long time) the analyst may begin to feel really "worthless" in his work with such a case. All his comments and interventions seem to dissolve into meaninglessness, and whatever sympathetic feeling he had for the patient is systematically destroyed by the latter. Following an unsuccessful, long treatment, a defensive devaluation of the patient on the analyst's part may occur, reinforcing the patient's feeling that his analyst is becoming one of those dangerous objects from whom he had attempted to escape; or some minor frustration of the patient may grow into a general awareness on the patient's part that he is no longer in control of the analyst. Interruption of treatment may occur at this point; the patient escapes from a hated, frustrating transference object, which he eventually reduces to a "shadow" once more, and the analyst's countertransference may reflect a corresponding feeling of "emptiness," as if the patient had never existed.

There are several technical implications of the above considerations. First, the analyst must continuously focus on the particular quality of the transference in these cases and consistently counteract the patient's efforts toward omnipotent control and devaluation. Then the analyst also has to watch carefully for his long-term countertransference developments. He should bring the countertransference into the analytic process, not by revealing to the patient what his own reaction is, but by consistently recognizing in the countertransference the hidden intention of the patient's behavior. For example, when the patient systematically rejects all the analyst's interpretations over a long period of time, the analyst may recognize his own resultant feelings of impotence and point out to the patient that he is treating the analyst as if he wished to make him feel defeated and impotent. Or, when antisocial behavior in the patient makes the analyst, rather than the patient, worry about the consequences, the analyst may point out that the patient seems to try to let the analyst feel the concern over his behavior because the patient himself cannot tolerate such a feeling. Because these patients treat the analyst as extensions of themselves, or vice versa, the analyst's emotional experience reflects more closely than usual what the patient is struggling with internally, and thus the use of countertransference reactions is particularly revealing in treatment.

One technical problem which is especially difficult for the therapist to handle is the occurrence of sudden "switches" in the emotional attitude of the patient. Especially following moments of understanding or relief, the patient tends to drop an entire subject matter rather than to be obliged either to feel grateful to the analyst for his help, or to be motivated to deepen his understanding of that particular issue. The tendency to devaluate the analyst operates here, together with an effort to rob the analyst of his interpretation; one has to be very attentive to this sudden "disappearance" of what only minutes ago, or a session ago, appeared as an important problem.

One final word about technique. One should probably not treat many of these patients at the same time, because they put a great stress and many demands on the analyst. In addition, it may help to keep in mind that these patients require the longest psychoanalytic treatments in order to break through the pathological character structure activated in the transference.

In the past some clinicians felt that these patients did not develop a transference, and that they always kept a "narcissistic noninvolvement" toward the analyst which prevented analytic work. Actually, these patients develop a very intensive transference that I have described above; what appears as distance and uninvolvement on the surface is underneath an active process of devaluation, depreciation, and spoiling. The undoing of this transference resistance typically brings about intense paranoid developments, suspiciousness, hatred, and envy. Eventually, after many months and sometimes years of treatment, guilt and depression may appear in the patient; awareness of his aggression toward the analyst may develop into guilt over it, and more human concern for the analyst as a person in combination with a heightened tolerance of guilt and depression in general. This is a crucial moment in the treatment of these patients and represents an essential prognostic factor at the same time. Those patients who have at least some tolerance for guilt and depression when the treatment starts do better than those who cannot tolerate these feelings at all. This observation leads us into our next topic: the general issue of prognosis in the psychoanalysis of these patients.

## PROGNOSTIC CONSIDERATIONS

The overall prognosis for narcissistic personalities is guarded. The rigidity and smoothness in functioning of this character structure are great obstacles to analytic progress. From the viewpoint of the patient's pathology, the advantage of a complete characterological "isolation" from any meaningful interpersonal relationship is hard to give up. These patients are able internally to withdraw from social life as effectively as the most severe schizoid character. And yet, they usually seem to be in the center of things, efficiently extracting "narcissistic supplies" while subtly protecting themselves from the painful experience of more meaningful emotional interactions.

I suggested in Chapter 3 that narcissistic personalities, in spite of the fact that their defensive organization is, broadly speaking, similar to that of the borderline personality, benefit very little from expressive, psychoanalytically oriented treatment approaches geared to that category of patients, and that psychoanalysis is the treatment of choice for narcissistic personalities. Some of these patients not only tolerate the analytic situation without excessive regression but are so extremely resistant to any effort to mobilize their rigid pathological character defenses in the transference that they remain untouched by analysis. In patients with narcissistic personalities and overt borderline characteristics (multiple symptomatology, severe nonspecific manifestations of ego weakness, regression to primary process thinking) psychoanalysis is contraindicated. These patients usually cannot tolerate the severe regression and reactivation of very early pathogenic conflicts in the transference, necessary to their analytic treatment, without psychotic decompensation. A more supportive treatment approach seems best for this group. In regard to those narcissistic patients who seem capable of undergoing psychoanalysis, I have found the following prognostic considerations useful in individual cases.

## 1. Tolerance of Depression and Mourning

The prognosis improves for patients who preserve some capacity for depression or mourning, especially when their depressions contain elements of guilt feelings. For example, one narcissistic patient began his treatment by discussing his feelings of remorse over having gotten involved with a woman who had three small children and who was very much in love with him. The children also loved him and he suddenly found himself "surrounded" in an atmosphere of friendliness and love which prevented him from carrying out his usual behavior of "dropping out" after having "made" a woman. (The transference implications of these feelings were taken up only later in his treatment.) This patient was able to improve markedly over a period of several years of analysis.

Two incidents in the treatment of this patient illustrate his gradually increasing tolerance of guilt and depression. After the first year of treatment, and after the exploitative nature of his relationship to women had been explored, the patient impulsively married the same woman and interrupted treatment for several months; he later explained this action as caused by his fear of the analyst's interference with his decision to marry. The marriage represented at this point both a defense against deepening of his guilt feelings and an acting out of his guilt feelings. Two years later we examined an episode which had repeated itself quite frequently. The patient's work led him to other cities where he would briefly become involved with women and then completely forget them the moment he left town. After two years of analysis, he had to visit one town, and he decided not to visit a girl there with whom he had been involved for many years. She still thought that he might eventually marry her, seemed always happy with his visits, and conveyed the impression to the patient that she could not get involved with any other man as long as he was still in her life. In the analysis, we had examined the exploitative nature of his relationship with her and his need to defend against guilt feelings in regard to this girl. After arriving in his hotel at that city, the patient thought with intense pain of the disappointment that she would experience after he left her once more. He also felt an intense sexual excitement pressuring him into seeing her. For hours these two feelings struggled in him and he finally had a crying spell with feelings of sadness and sorrow for both the girl and himself. He felt that to see her would only stir up again false hopes in her, and would be bad for her and for the better part of himself. He also was aware that his sexual excitement represented a wish to gratify her sexually and, thus, to allay his guilt feelings toward her, and was also an attempt to escape from his awareness of the entire problem. He finally decided not to see her, experiencing then an increase in his feelings of love and gratitude toward the girl, together with feelings of sadness and mourning, experiencing her as a good, lost object, and feeling that it was now too late to start a new life with her. I must stress that I at no point interfered with his wishes to see her; his not seeing her did not represent a submission to my will. After this episode the patient became much more tolerant of people who were incapable of action because of their strong feelings, people whom he had always depreciated in the past.

## 2. Secondary Gain of Analytic Treatment

Unfortunately, there are social and professional conditions which give a strong secondary gain to "learning" the method of analysis. The defensive operation of "robbing" the analyst of what he has to give in order to defend oneself against the envy of the analyst and against the need to acknowledge dependency upon him is strongly reinforced under such "learning" conditions. One minister, who had been sent to analysis because of promiscuous sexual behavior, was very happy with the prospect of analytic treatment, which would give him advantages in the professional field of education in which he was involved. This felt advantage presented an insoluble resistance; the gratification of "learning" analysis compensated most effectively for the underlying depreciation of the analyst and for the patient's inability to accept himself as a patient. Candidates for psychoanalytic institutes should not present a narcissistic personality structure (13), but some applicants with such characteristics do manage to be accepted for psychoanalytic training, especially since the intellectually gifted kind of narcissistic personality may have a very promising aura of originality and intellectual curiosity (17). Such candidates remain in analysis in spite of the emotional emptiness that develops in their analyses, and they may even manage to complete their training with no appreciable change in their narcissistic features. What happens is that the ultimate gratification of becoming a psychoanalyst is sufficient to compensate for the envy and hatred of the "giving" analyst, and the candidate's inability to depend on the analyst and to establish a full-fledged transference neurosis on the level of his basic oral-aggressive conflicts remains unnoticed. Eventually, most candidates with narcissistic personality structures stop doing analytic treatment, even if they have graduated from institutes, because their lack of interest in and involvement with patients makes psychoanalysis a boring procedure to them.

## 3. Transference Potential for Guilt versus Transference Potential for Paranoid Rage

Riviere (11) stressed that these patients are incapable of tolerating a dependent relationship with the analyst because of deeply buried but ever-present feelings of unconscious guilt. In contrast, Rosenfeld (12) mentions the underlying paranoid disposition, and the strong oral-sadistic transference, behind these patients' incapacity to tolerate dependency. There are narcissistic patients with each kind of underlying transference potential. Once the typical transference defenses of magical, narcissistic fusion with the analyst and devaluation of him as an independent person, together with the accompanying struggle against real dependency on the analyst, have been resolved, some patients develop intense paranoid reactions in the transference, while other patients seem able to experience at least some guilt and concern over what they are doing to the analyst. Even if their previous history has not given evidence of conscious guilt, this second type of patient (resembling the type described by Riviere) has a better prognosis than the type who experiences a pure paranoid reaction in the transference.

### 4.  The Quality of the Sublimatory Potential

Patients who have been able to achieve some really creative development in a certain area of their life have a better prognosis than those who have no capacity in this regard. Sometimes it is difficult to evaluate this factor, but careful attention to the patient's interests and aspirations will provide this information. For example, one patient had vivid and chronic fantasies of accumulating a collection of antique art, and was very envious of people who possessed ceramics or other objects of this kind. He was, however, completely incapable of differentiating between anything of value and third-rate imitations, and unable or unwilling to inform himself meaningfully about issues of quality. In short, he only wanted to decorate his house the way the people who collected antiques and whom he envied decorated theirs. I must stress that collecting antiques was his main aspiration in regard to personal wealth and yet it was a superficial interest. Another patient was interested in existential philosophy, talked very much about it, and after months of treatment it turned out that he had read only a few books popularizing this particular philosophy. A third patient, although he had reached a high professional level requiring a great deal of reading and formal education, did not read anything other than what was required for his examinations, and, once graduated, was incapable of doing any further reading. In this last case, once the problem of envy of what other people knew and could contribute was analyzed, he was able to read and learn from what he was reading, at the same time being able to learn from his own analysis.

In all the cases just mentioned, the patients had a low sublimatory potential in spite of the fact that superficially they exhibited a special talent or interest. The next few cases present a higher sublimatory potential, and a better prognostic outlook. The patient mentioned above, who impulsively married in the beginning stage of his analysis, was a merchant, interested in history. His interest seemed genuine and was a source of real pleasure for him; he had achieved real depth in that area and yet devaluated his own achievements, because of the unconscious fear that if he were triumphant in anything other people's envy would destroy it. Another patient was an amateur musician, and during the early stages of analysis frequently stated that when he played the piano, the only thing that was good about him came to the surface. Music was like an ideal though mysterious companion; the patient felt that whenever he deeply enjoyed listening or playing, some vaguely experienced trust or confidence in goodness was being reconfirmed.

## 5.  The Degree and Quality of Superego Integration

I have already mentioned that superego integration in narcissistic personalities is poor. Their superegos mainly contain derivatives of primitive, aggressive, distorted parental images without the normal integration of aggressive forerunners with ideal self and ideal object images, and without the later phase of superego depersonification and abstraction. Some of these patients, however, do present a depersonified and abstracted superego in some areas. For example, they may be honest in money matters, in keeping promises, and in emotionally uninvolved daily interactions with others. They may experience shame, if not guilt, when they break minor conventions surrounding interpersonal relationships. These patients have a better prognosis than those in which there is very little of such "minor morality" left. Patients who lie to the analyst over a long period of time, as well as to other people, or present other forms of antisocial behavior, have a bad prognosis. It almost goes without saying that the antisocial personality structure, which represents an extreme form of this lack of superego development, has the worst prognosis of all. There is nothing new in mentioning the absolutely hopeless prognosis for the analytic treatment of antisocial personalities, but I am stressing here the continuum between the narcissistic personality and the antisocial personality which I see as an extreme form of pathological narcissism with, among other features, a complete absence of an integrated superego. In contrast, those narcissistic personalities with obsessive features have a better prognosis. One has to be careful, though, in diagnosing obsessive characteristics in narcissistic patients, because they may convey a false impression of an obsessive person. This is especially true for narcissistic personalities who are highly intellectual and cultivated: the smooth and cold quality of their thinking processes and the absence of emotional reactions may be mistaken for obsessive traits. However, in the truly obsessive personality we find intense and deep emotional reactions at points of anxiety, and at points which represent displacements of their emotional conflicts. For example, obsessive personalities may feel strongly about social, cultural, and political issues, and they may develop a surprising understanding of emotional depth in others while being apparently so "cold" themselves. In contrast, narcissistic personalities show superficial emotions of a quick and transitory kind, against a background of emotional blandness and indifference.

## 6. Presence of Life Circumstances Granting Unusual Narcissistic Gratifications

One element in the patient's life circumstances that leads to a poor prognosis is the opportunity for the patient to act out his needs for power, social importance, and admiration. A power-oriented narcissistic patient may already have achieved such a position in his profession and social life that it may appear to him quite "normal" and, therefore, it is difficult to analyze this form of "chronic acting out." In the same way that the candidate of a psychoanalytic institute may use his analysis as a ladder to professional status, a patient may use a pre-existing outlet for the gratification of his pathological narcissistic needs outside the analytic relationship and thereby compensate for frustration suffered in analysis, resulting in a therapeutic stalemate.

## 7. Impulse Control and Anxiety Tolerance

Narcissistic patients often have relatively good impulse control in all but a few areas which represent a compromise formation permitting the gratification of pathological narcissistic needs. For example, one patient had very good impulse control except for periods of homosexual acting out, in which he would pick up an occasional partner in such an impulsive way that he endangered his social position and risked conflict with the law. This patient used a homosexual experience to escape from the rage that any frustration from his girl friend brought about. If she appeared critical of him, he would leave in his car, pick up a man in a public rest room, have him perform fellatio on him, and then drop that man with a feeling of disgust and return home relieved. It gradually emerged that in the homosexual interaction he had the fantasy that the man who was sucking his penis needed him terribly and that the patient was the owner of all the love and fulfillment that was available in the interaction. He could give this love to the other man, thus proving to himself that he was the wealthy one. Later, after dropping his partner abruptly and depreciating him, he identified himself with the hostile and derogatory mother whom he had envied and hated and with the girl friend who represented his mother. By the whole action, he also took revenge on his girl friend-mother by reassuring himself that he did not need her sexually. In this example, what appeared on the surface to be a lack of impulse control was a specific defensive organization which could be understood and resolved analytically. The prognosis is better for these patients than for those who exhibit poor or nonexistent impulse control, who lose themselves in acting out, such as so-called "chaotic" personalities, or those who combine some form of sexual deviation with an impulse neurosis— alcoholism, drug addiction, etc. Prognosis is also guarded for those patients in whom anxiety immediately brings about generalized acting out or intensification of other symptoms: in short, for those whose anxiety tolerance is very low.

## 8.  Regression toward Primary-Process Thinking

I suggested above that the combination of overt borderline characteristics and narcissistic personality structure usually contraindicates psychoanalytic treatment. Some narcissistic patients may show little symptomatology, good impulse control, and not even too low an anxiety tolerance and, yet, primary process thinking is surprisingly near the surface. For example, one patient functioned quite well in his life, but he had developed over the years the pleasurable fantasy that there was something "Christlike" about him and he enjoyed speculating about the characteristics he shared with Christ. He correctly assessed these fantasies as unrealistic, but at the same time he felt they were very pleasurable. At the beginning of his treatment, the intensity of these fantasies increased to the point that he wondered whether perhaps he was not Christ after all; then he regressed acutely into a schizophrenic reaction, which probably would not have occurred at that point had he not been offered an expressive psychotherapy.

One other point in regard to the regressive potential of the patient; overt borderline features, especially a lack of impulse control, an inability to tolerate anxiety, and a tendency toward primary process thinking, contraindicate psychoanalysis in these cases even if they show the presence of guilt and a potential to experience depression, because in these cases the depression that develops during treatment may regress into a psychotic depression or serious suicidal attempts. Every narcissistic character who is to be successfully treated must undergo periods of severe depression and suicidal fantasies, and if he does not have sufficient ego strength to tolerate this development, his life is in serious danger. In those cases where the ego is weak, supportive psychotherapy is indicated. Among the patients studied in the Psychotherapy Research Project of The Menninger Foundation, those with severe narcissistic character structure combined with overt borderline functioning could be treated quite successfully with a purely supportive approach.

## 9. The Motivation for Treatment

The crucial test of the motivation of these patients comes only after a period of analysis. The usually acceptable motivations for treatment, such as the wish to get rid of symptoms, may prove quite spurious in patients with narcissistic personalities. They may really want to become "perfect," and may enter analysis with such expectations. The question of whether "perfection" will turn out to mean for them freedom from symptoms so that they can be superior to everybody else, or whether it will be exchanged for the wish to get rid of their crippled emotional lives is often difficult to answer at the initiation of treatment. In any case, the more a person wishes to overcome feelings of emptiness, difficulties in empathizing with others, and his internal coldness, the better the prognosis.

## A CRUCIAL PERIOD IN THE TREATMENT

After the patient systematically works through the defensive organization of pathological narcissism, his primitive oral conflicts regularly come to the surface. His intense hatred and fear of the image of a dangerous, aggressive mother are projected onto the analyst as well as onto all other significant beings in his life. At some point, the patient has to become aware that this fear of attack from the mother represents a projection of his own aggression, linked to the rage caused by his frustration by mother. He also has to become aware that his ideal concept of himself is a fantasy construction which protects him from such dreaded relationships with all other people, and that this ideal self concept also contains a hopeless yearning and love for an ideal mother who would come to his rescue. The deep aspiration and love for such an ideal mother and the hatred for the distorted, dangerous mother have to meet at some point, in the transference, and the patient has to become aware that the feared and hated analyst-mother is really one with the admired, longed-for analyst-mother.

At this point, an extremely difficult emotional situation comes about for the patient: he must acknowledge the realistically good aspects of the analyst (mother) which he has previously denied and devaluated and bring upon himself a shattering feeling of guilt because of his previous aggression toward the analyst. The patient may feel despair because he has mistreated the analyst and all the significant persons in his life, and he may feel that he has actually destroyed those whom he could have loved and who might have loved him. Now he may have intense suicidal thoughts and intentions, but if he has been selected for analysis because of his good ego strength, he may work through this conflict without premature reassurance from his analyst. As the narcissistic patient works through this crucial period in the analysis, he comes to acknowledge the analyst as an independent being for whom he can feel love and gratitude. Simultaneously, the patient will begin to acknowledge the independent existence of other significant persons in his life. For the first time he may show an authentic curiosity about, interest in, and satisfaction with what goes on in other human beings. It is as if people were coming alive in the patient's external world as well as in his internal world of objects and self experience, his "representational world" (14). This stage in the analysis contrasts strikingly with the previous emptiness of the fantasy and emotional life of the patient.

Normal regression in the service of the ego involves one special dimension, namely, the reactivation of past internal object relationships as a source of internal support in times of crisis, of loss of external support, or of loneliness. Normally, the emotional wealth derived from past happy relationships with others not only permits the empathic enjoyment of the present happiness of others, but also is a source of internal consolation when reality threatens to bring about loss of self-esteem. Narcissistic patients are not able to resort in this way to their own past. If they are treated successfully, they come to realize a deeper and more meaningful life, and begin to draw from sources of strength and creativity in their newly developing world of internalized object relationships.

The following case history illustrates this crucial period of treatment in one particular patient. At one time, this patient had become aware that he had always treated the analyst as a "mirror" of himself, and had built the analyst up as a kind of powerful slave, totally at the patient's service, something like the genie in the fairy tale of Aladdin's Lamp. He realized that, between the sessions, he had had the feeling that the analyst had disappeared into an only potential existence, as if the analyst were confined in a bottle that the patient could put away. At this point, for the first time after years of analysis, the patient exhibited curiosity about the life of the analyst and envy of the analyst's private life. He became aware of anger and regret at being separated from the analyst over the weekends, and also had feelings of gratitude because the analyst had been willing to "stick with him" in spite of his chronically derogatory behavior. This patient had always depreciated literature, especially poetry, and everything that did not deal with "strong, cold, useful facts."

Then one day he remembered a fairy tale that had impressed him in his early childhood but that he had completely forgotten since. It was the story of "The Nightingale" by Andersen (2) and the patient, an unimaginative person, spontaneously interpreted the story through associations and dreams over a period of several days. He understood that he himself was the Emperor of China in the story, because he was as deprecatory of everybody else as the Emperor. China itself, in that fairy tale, was like the fantasy world of the patient, because everybody was depreciating everybody else in it. The nightingale (the live, real one) was the only warm and loving creature in that world, but the Emperor was not able to love it. Although he enjoyed its song, he dropped it without remorse when the shiny, jewel-covered mechanical substitute was offered to him. The mechanical nightingale covered with jewels and gold represented the Emperor's (patient's) own mechanical lifeless self. When the Emperor became ill and longed for the nightingale's song in order to become well again, the mechanical bird broke down and was no longer available, because the Emperor himself, the patient felt, had destroyed everything surrounding him. One night, when the Emperor was about to die, all the good and bad deeds of his life came back to him and made him suffer. The patient understood this to be an expression of the Emperor's final awareness of the bad sides of himself, and of his despair at ever undoing all the wrongs he had done. The patient felt very moved by the idea that the real-life nightingale came back at last, to sing by the dying Emperor's window and thus saved his life. The patient said, with deep feeling, that he now understood why, as a child, he had been moved to tears by this story and he cried at that point. The survival of the real, good nightingale in the story reaffirmed the patient's faith in the existence of a good being who was still available and had not been killed, in spite of all the Emperor's—and the patient's—greed and destructiveness. The Emperor was saved because he had kept inside of himself such a good and forgiving object. The nightingale also represented the good analyst who had not been killed by the patient's destructiveness.

This example illustrates not only the patient's understanding of a crucial problem in himself, but also his generally deepening awareness of emotional life; for the first time, he could accept a previously depreciated form of literature. To see a patient come alive during treatment, and begin to feel for the first time real concern for and interest in others as well as in an internal life of his own, is a gratifying experience for the analyst. It compensates for the many months and years of emptiness and meaninglessness with which these patients try to drown the analytic situation.

The prognostic considerations examined in this chapter illustrate the limitations and difficulties in the psychoanalytic treatment of patients with narcissistic personality structure. Even if we cannot successfully treat many of these patients, at least they permit us to better understand and resolve narcissistic defenses in patients with less intensive overall character pathology. I believe that careful selection of these cases may bring about more encouraging therapeutic results with those who initially are considered hopeless and are, therefore, not treated, or who are taken into analysis under the erroneous assumption that they fall into the category of the ordinary character neurosis and cause disappointment after many years of analytic work.

# SUMMARY

A general hypothesis regarding the etiology of the narcissistic personality structure is proposed, involving the relationships between pathological narcissism and pathological object relationships. Technical problems in the psychoanalytic treatment of narcissistic personalities are examined—especially their typical transference resistances—and prognostic criteria are outlined.

## BIBLIOGRAPHY

1. Abraham, K. A particular form of neurotic resistance against the psychoanalytic method (1919). *Selected Papers on Psycho-Analysis*. London: Hogarth Press, 1949, pp. 303-311.
2. Andersen, H. C. The nightingale. In: *Tales of Grimm and Andersen*. New York: Modern Library, 1952, pp. 714-721.
3. Fenichel, O. Typology. *The Psychoanalytic Theory of Neurosis*. New York: Norton, 1945, pp. 525-527.
4. Freud, S. On narcissism: an introduction (1914). *Standard Edition*, 14:67-102. London: Hogarth Press, 1957.
5. ———. Libidinal types (1931). *Standard Edition*, 21:215-220. London: Hogarth Press, 1961.
6. Jacobson, E. *The Self and the Object World*. New York: International Universities Press, 1964.
7. Jones, E. The God complex (1913). *Essays in Applied Psycho-Analysis*, 2:244-265. New York: International Universities Press, 1964.
8. Kohut, H. (1968). The psychoanalytic treatment of narcissistic personality disorders. *Psychoanal. Study Child*, 23, 86-113.
9. Reich, A. Narcissistic object choice in women. *J. Am. Psychoanal. Assoc.*, 1:22-44, 1953.
10. ———. Pathologic forms of self-esteem regulation. *Psychoanal. Study Child*, 15:215-232. New York: International Universities Press, 1960.
11. Riviere, J. A contribution to the analysis of the negative therapeutic reaction. *Int. J. Psycho-Anal.*, 17:304-320, 1936.
12. Rosenfeld, H. On the psychopathology of narcissism: a clinical approach. *Int. J. Psycho-Anal.*, 45:332-337, 1964.
13. Sachs, H. Observations of a training analyst. *Psychoanal. Quart.*, 16:157-168, 1947.
14. Sandler, J. & Rosenblatt, B. The concept of the representational world. *Psychoanal. Study Child*, 17:128-145. New York: International Universities Press, 1962.
15. Schafer, R. The loving and beloved superego in Freud's structural theory. *Psychoanal. Study* . . . . 15:163-188. New York: International Universities Press, 1960.
16. Stone, L. The widening scope of indications for psychoanalysis. *J. Am. Psychoanal. Assoc.*, 2:567-594, 1954.
17. Tartakoff, H. H. The normal personality in our culture and the Nobel prize complex. In: *Psychoanalysis—A General Psychology*, ed. R. M. Loewenstein, L. M.

Newman, M. Schur, & A. J. Solnit. New York: International Universities Press, 1966, pp. 222-252.

18. Ticho, E. Selection of patients for psychoanalysis or psychotherapy. Presented at the 20th Anniversary Meeting of the Menninger School of Psychiatry Alumni Association, Topeka, Kansas, May, 1966.

19. Van der Waals, H. G. Problems of narcissism. *Bull. Menninger Clin.*, 29:293-311, 1965.

# Nine

# Clinical Problems of
# the Narcissistic Personality

This chapter continues earlier studies of the diagnosis and psychoanalytic treatment of a specific constellation of character pathology, that of the narcissistic personality (Chapters 1, 4, and 8). In recent years, a consensus has been gradually developing regarding the definition of this pathological character structure and the indication of psychoanalysis as the treatment of choice (3, 7, 8, 9, 10, 13, 15, 16, 17). However, despite the evolving agreement about the descriptive, clinical characteristics of this constellation, divergent views have developed regarding the underlying metapsychological assumptions and the optimal technical approach within a psychoanalytic modality of treatment. In particular, Kohut's approach to the psychoanalytic treatment of narcissistic personality disorders (10) is very different from the approach I outlined earlier (Chapter 8), which is more closely related to the views of Abraham (1), Jacobson (3), Riviere (12), Rosenfeld (13), Tartakoff (15) and van der Waals (17). Therefore, in this chapter I will focus particularly on those aspects of my approach to the understanding and treatment of narcissistic personalities which highlight agreements and disagreements with Kohut's approach.

## CLINICAL CHARACTERISTICS OF THE
## NARCISSISTIC PERSONALITY AS A SPECIFIC TYPE
## OF CHARACTER PATHOLOGY

With respect to clinical characteristics, there is agreement between Kohut's view and that of the other authors whom I have mentioned as representing an alternative view and myself. I describe patients with narcissistic personalities as presenting excessive self-absorption usually coinciding with a superficially smooth and effective social adaptation, but with serious distortions in their internal relationships with other people. They present various combinations of intense ambitiousness, grandiose fantasies, feelings of inferiority, and overdependence on external admiration and acclaim. Along with feelings of boredom and emptiness, and continuous search for gratification of strivings for brilliance, wealth, power and beauty, there are serious deficiencies in their capacity to love and to be concerned about others. This lack of capacity for empathic understanding of others often comes as a surprise considering their superficially appropriate social adjustment. Chronic uncertainty and dissatisfaction about themselves, conscious or unconscious exploitiveness and ruthlessness toward others are also characteristics of these patients. Perhaps one difference in my description from that derived from Kohut's work is my stress on the pathological nature of their internalized object relations, regardless of the superficially adaptive behavior of many of these patients. In addition, I stress the presence of chronic, intense envy, and defenses against such envy, particularly devaluation, omnipotent control, and narcissistic withdrawal, as major characteristics of their emotional life.

## THE RELATIONSHIP OF NARCISSISTIC PERSONALITY TO BORDERLINE CONDITIONS AND THE PSYCHOSES

Regarding this point, important differences exist between my approach and that of Kohut. Kohut differentiates the narcissistic personality disorders from the psychoses and borderline states, but does not make a clear differentiation of "borderline cases" from schizophrenic psychoses (10, p. 18). In my view, however, the defensive organization of narcissistic personalities is both strikingly similar to and different in a specific way from borderline personality organization, which I will outline below. In contrast to Kohut's view, I see important structural differences between borderline personality organization and psychotic structures, and I would not rule out psychoanalysis as the treatment of choice for some borderline conditions.

The similarity of the defensive organization of narcissistic personalities to that of borderline conditions is reflected in the predominance of mechanisms of splitting or primitive dissociation as reflected in the presence of mutually dissociated or split-off ego states. Thus haughty grandiosity, shyness, and feelings of inferiority may coexist without affecting each other. These splitting operations are maintained and reinforced by primitive forms of projection, particularly projective identification, primitive and pathological idealization, omnipotent control, narcissistic withdrawal and devaluation. From a dynamic viewpoint, pathological condensation of genital and pregenital needs under the overriding influence of pregenital (especially oral) aggression characterizes narcissistic personalities as well as borderline personality organization in general.

In this connexion, it is interesting that Kohut acknowledges the presence of "conscious but split-off aspects of the grandiosity" (10, p. 179) and describes in detail "the side-by-side existence of disparate personality attitudes in depth" (p. 183), and the analyst's need to relate the central sector of the personality to the split-off sector. In practice, therefore, Kohut acknowledges a defensive organization which is related to splitting as a predominant mechanism, although he does not relate it to particular vicissitudes of the structural development of the ego.

The difference between narcissistic personality structure and borderline personality organization is that in the narcissistic personality there is an integrated, although highly pathological grandiose self, which, as I have suggested earlier (Chapter 8), reflects a pathological condensation of some aspects of the real self (the "specialness" of the child reinforced by early experience), the ideal self (the fantasies and self images of power, wealth, omniscience, and beauty which compensated the small child for the experience of severe oral frustration, rage and envy) and the ideal object (the fantasy of an ever-giving, ever-loving and accepting parent, in contrast to the child's experience in reality; a replacement of the devalued real parental object). I am adopting here the term "grandiose self," suggested by Kohut, because I think it expresses better the clinical implications of what I referred to earlier as the pathological self structure, or what Rosenfeld (13) called the "omnipotent mad" self. The integration of this pathological, grandiose self compensates for the lack of integration of the normal self-concept which is part of the underlying borderline personality organization: it explains the paradox of relatively good ego functioning and surface adaptation in the presence of a predominance of splitting mechanisms, a related constellation of primitive defenses, and the lack of integration of object representations of these patients. This pathological, grandiose self is reflected in clinical characteristics which, as mentioned before, mostly coincides with the observations of all the authors mentioned. However, a basic disagreement exists between Kohut's views and mine regarding the origin of this grandiose self, and whether it reflects the fixation of an archaic "normal" primitive self (Kohut's view), or whether it reflects a pathological structure, clearly different from normal infantile narcissism (my view).

Before examining this difference in views, a special group of patients needs to be mentioned, who, in my opinion, present the clearest illustration of the intimate relationship between borderline personality organization and the development of the pathological grandiose self. I am referring to those narcissistic personalities who, in spite of a clearly narcissistic personality structure, function on what I have called an overt borderline level, i.e., present the nonspecific manifestations of ego weakness characteristic of borderline personality organization, in addition to the generally similar defensive constellation mentioned. These narcissistic patients present severe lack of anxiety tolerance, generalized lack of impulse control, striking absence of sublimatory channeling, primary process thinking clearly noticeable on psychological tests, and proneness to the development of transference psychosis. In these patients, the pathological narcissistic structure does not provide sufficient integration for effective social functioning, and they usually present a contraindication for analysis (often even for the modified psychoanalytic procedure that I have recommended for most patients with borderline personality organization). These patients characteristically present the repetitive, chronic activation of intense rage reactions linked with ruthless demandingness and depreciatory attacks on the therapist, i.e., "narcissistic rage." One also finds such intense outbursts of rage in borderline patients, usually as part of alternating activation of "all good" and "all bad" internalized object relations in the transference. However, the relentless nature of this rage, the depreciatory quality which seems to contaminate the entire relationship with the therapist, evolves as a complete devaluation and deterioration of all the potentially good aspects of the relationship for extended periods of time so that the continuity of treatment is threatened.

The following case illustrates this development. A patient with a rather typical narcissistic personality, a single woman in her early twenties, came to a psychiatric hospital after gradual breakdown of school performance and social relations, and sexual promiscuity characterized by her tendency to drop any man whom she could not completely control. Both her parents were rather narcissistic and withdrawn, and presented some mild antisocial trends. An older sister was in treatment for antisocial tendencies. Her lack of significant involvement with others started in nursery school, was later smoothed over by the patient's joining mother's efforts to control and manipulate their social environment, and culminated in the chaos of the patient's social life, work, and sexual involvements. After two months of treatment, in which subtle derogation of the therapist and all treatment staff and ongoing manipulation and splitting of staff were predominant features, the therapist absented himself for a week. The patient then changed her controlled derogation into overt anger and rage, and in spite of the efforts of staff managed to convince her parents to take her out of treatment two months later. Throughout this time, the sessions were characterized by ongoing attacks and derogation of the therapist, in short, by narcissistic rage, which could not be treated by an expressive approach.

Narcissistic personalities whose defenses against primitive object relationships related to conflicts around oral aggression have been substantially worked through in analysis may present such rage reaction in the transference at advanced stages of treatment. At times, the transformation of a previously bland, mostly indifferent, apparently well-controlled narcissistic personality into such an openly and chronically raging person may be quite striking. However, it usually can be worked through in more advanced stages of the treatment, and may represent an important move forward. In this connection, careful analysis of the history of such patients often reveals temper tantrums and aggressive outbursts which occurred in the past when they were frustrated, particularly under conditions when they felt they should be securely in control of the situation, and later again in life, when they felt superior to or in control of those against whom their rage was directed.

The situation, therefore, is different in cases where narcissistic rage appears as part of the initial clinical constellation (in narcissistic personalities functioning on an overtly borderline level), as compared to cases where it develops as part of the resolution of pathological narcissism at later stages of the treatment. Early and open expression of narcissistic rage represents a serious risk for the treatment. This is particularly true in narcissistic personalities functioning on a borderline level who present antisocial features or a sexual deviation with strong sadistic components, such as open physical violence toward the objects of their sexual exploits. Also, adolescents with narcissistic personality structure and antisocial behavior frequently show such rage reactions.

For narcissistic personalities functioning on an overt borderline level (particularly the prognostically more guarded cases of narcissistic rage mentioned before), a supportive psychotherapeutic approach may be the treatment of choice. Ideally, the treatment may shift into the general approach for borderline patients that I have recommended, namely, consistent interpretation (not only of the origin of the narcissistic rage, but of the secondary gains derived from its expression in the transference), and limit setting when such secondary gain cannot be avoided by interpretive means alone. When it is possible to structure the external life of the patient in such a way that acting out of narcissistic rage can be controlled and the treatment situation protected so that the analyst can maintain a relatively neutral stance, a systematic interpretation of the defensive functions of the expression of aggression toward the analyst may be possible, with ultimate resolution of the narcissistic rage. In addition to direct expression of primitive aggression, such rage reactions may have the defensive function of protecting the patient against primitive fears of the analyst, or against overwhelming guilt toward him, or against separation anxiety.

In patients with narcissistic personalities in which narcissistic rage develops during later stages of the treatment it is usually less difficult to analyze the origin and functions of rage in the transference. The patient's angry outbursts over minor frustrations, real or fantasied, from the analyst may be an important move forward from the previously subtle devaluations of the analyst so characteristic of narcissistic resistances. To angrily devalue the analyst in an effort to eliminate him as an important object who would otherwise be feared and envied, and on whom the patient so desperately needs to rely, is a characteristic function of the rage reaction. The analyst's internal security and his conviction in what he has to offer realistically to the patient are very important in reassuring the patient against his fantasies of the overwhelming nature of his own aggression.

In summary, then, the pathological grandiose self compensates for the generally "ego weakening" effects of the primitive defensive organization, a common characteristic of narcissistic personalities and patients of a borderline personality organization, and explains the fact that narcissistic personalities may present an overt functioning which ranges from the borderline level to that of better integrated types of character pathology. The differential diagnosis of narcissistic personalities from other types of character pathology can usually be arrived at in a careful analysis of the clinical features; I have examined elsewhere the differential diagnosis of narcissistic personalities with hysterical personalities, infantile personalities, and obsessive compulsive personalities (Chapters 1 and 8; 4). In cases where doubts persist, or the diagnosis cannot be made before the initiation of treatment, the characteristic development of a narcissistic transference differentiates narcissistic personalities from the usual transference neurosis of other cases. On this point, I think, Kohut and I agree.

## THE RELATIONSHIP OF NORMAL TO PATHOLOGICAL NARCISSISM

### 1. Developmental Arrest or Pathological Development?

Kohut (10) thinks that narcissistic personalities remain "fixated on archaic grandiose self-configurations and/or on archaic, overestimated, narcissistically cathected objects" (p. 3). He clearly establishes (p. 9) a continuity of pathological and normal narcissism, in which the grandiose self represents an archaic form of what normally, and in the course of treatment, may become the normal self in a continuous process. His analysis focuses almost exclusively on the vicissitudes of development of libidinal cathexes, so that his analysis of pathological narcissism is essentially unrelated to any examination of the vicissitudes of aggression. Kohut (10) states (p. xv): "Specifically, this study concentrates almost exclusively on the role of the libidinal forces in the analysis of narcissistic personalities; the discussion of the role of aggression will be taken up separately." In addition, Kohut examines narcissism so predominantly from the viewpoint of the quality of the instinctual charge, that he seems to imply the existence of two entirely different, narcissistic and object-oriented, libidinal instincts determined by intrinsic qualities rather than by the target (self or object) of the instinctual investment. In his words (p. 26): "Narcissism, within my general outlook, is defined not by the target of the instinctual investment (i.e. whether it is the subject himself or other people) but by the nature or quality of the instinctual charge." He repeats the essence of this statement later (p. 39, footnote) and considers the development of object love largely independent from that of lower to higher forms of narcissism (pp. 220, 228, 297). Kohut conveys the impression that he analyzes the vicissitudes of normal and pathological narcissism and of normal and pathological object relationships as mostly dependent upon the quality of libidinal cathexes rather than in terms of the vicissitudes of internalized object relations.

I disagree with these viewpoints, and like Jacobson (3), Mahler (11) and van der Waals (17), I think that one cannot divorce the study of normal and pathological narcissism from the vicissitudes of both libidinal and aggressive drive derivatives, and from the development of structural derivatives of internalized object relations (5, 6). In what follows, I will provide clinical material as well as theoretical considerations in support of the following viewpoints:

(a) The specific narcissistic resistances of patients with narcissistic personalities reflect a pathological narcissism which is different from both the ordinary, adult narcissism and from fixation at or regression to normal infantile narcissism. The implication is that narcissistic resistances that develop in the course of interpretation of character defenses in patients other than narcissistic personalities are of a different nature, require a different technique, and have a different prognostic implication than narcissistic resistances of patients presenting pathological narcissism.

(b) Pathological narcissism can only be understood in terms of the combined analysis of the vicissitudes of libidinal and aggressive drive derivatives. Pathological narcissism does not simply reflect libidinal investment in the self in contrast to libidinal investment in objects, but libidinal investment in a pathological self structure. This pathological self has defensive functions against underlying libidinally invested and aggressively invested primitive self and object images which reflect intense, predominantly pregenital conflicts around both love and aggression.

(c) The structural characteristics of narcissistic personalities cannot be understood simply in terms of fixation at an early level of development, or lack of development of certain intrapsychic structures. They are a consequence of the development of pathological (in contrast to normal) differentiation and integration of ego and superego structures, deriving from pathological (in contrast to normal) object relationships.

To summarize these three viewpoints into one overall statement: Narcissistic investment (i.e. investment in the self), and object investment (that is, investment in representations of others and in other human beings), occur simultaneously, and intimately influence each other, so that one cannot study the vicissitudes of narcissism without studying the vicissitudes of object relationships, in the same way one cannot study the vicissitudes of normal and pathological narcissism without relating the development of the respective internalized object relations to both libidinal and aggressive drive derivatives.

## 2. Differential Qualities of Infantile and Pathological Narcissism

What follows are some pertinent clinical observations. The differential diagnosis of narcissistic personalities with obsessive, depressive-masochistic, and hysterical personalities (i.e., of the relatively better functioning narcissistic patients with other types of character pathology) illustrates how narcissistic patients not only seem to love themselves excessively, but do so in a rather poor, often self-demeaning way, so that one concludes that these patients do not treat themselves better than the other people with whom they have relationships (17). Their conviction of being "phony," their deep lack of confidence in anything basically good and worthwhile that could emerge from honest self-exploration, and their occasionally surprising neglect and disregard for their "public image" in terms of honesty, decency and convictions about values, are poor ways of loving oneself.

The following features distinguish pathological narcissism from the normal narcissism of small children: 1) The grandiose fantasies of normal small children, their angry efforts to control mother and to keep themselves in the center of everybody's attention, have by far a more realistic quality than is the case of narcissistic personalities. 2) The small child's overreaction to criticism, failure, and blame, as well as his need to be the center of attention, admiration and love, coexist with simultaneous expression of genuine love and gratitude, and interest in his objects at times when he is not frustrated, and above all, with the capacity to trust and depend upon significant objects. A two and a half year old child's capacity to maintain a libidinal investment in mother during temporary separations is in striking contrast to the narcissistic patients' inability to depend upon other people (including the analyst) beyond immediate need gratification. 3) Normal infantile narcissism is reflected in the child's demandingness related to real needs, while the demandingness of pathological narcissism is excessive, cannot ever be fulfilled, and regularly reveals itself to be secondary to a process of internal destruction of the supplies received. 4) The coldness and aloofness of patients with pathological narcissism at times when their capacity for social charm is not in operation, their tendency to disregard others except when temporarily idealizing them as potential sources of narcissistic supply, and the contempt and devaluation prevalent in most of their relationships are in striking contrast to the warm quality of the small child's self-centeredness. Pursuing this observation into the historical analysis of narcissistic patients, one finds from the age of two to three years a lack of normal warmth and engagement with others, and an easily activated, abnormal destructiveness and ruthlessness.

5) The normal infantile narcissistic fantasies of power and wealth and beauty which stem from the preoedipal period do not imply an exclusive possession of all that is valuable and enviable in the world; the normal child does not need that everybody should admire him for being the exclusive owner of such treasures; but this is a characteristic fantasy of narcissistic personalities. In normal infantile narcissism, fantasies of narcissistic triumph or grandiosity are mingled with wishes that acquisition of these values will make the child lovable, acceptable by those whom he loves and by whom he wants to be loved.

The implication of all this is that pathological narcissism is strikingly different from normal narcissism.

## 3.  Manifestations of Pathological Narcissism in the Analytic Situation

In the transference, one main function of the narcissistic resistances of narcissistic personalities is to deny the existence of the analyst as an independent, autonomous human being, without a simultaneous fusion in the transference such as can be observed with more regressed patients. It is as if the analyst were tolerated in a type of "satellite existence"; over many months and years there are likely to be frequent role reversals in the transference relationship, without any basic change in the total transference constellation. The grandiose self permits the denial of dependency on the analyst. Regularly, however, when it has been possible to work through this defensive constellation, it turns out that this denial of dependency on the analyst does not represent an absence of internalized object relations or of the capacity to invest in objects, but a rigid defense against more primitive, pathological object relations centered around narcissistic rage and envy, fear and guilt because of this rage, and yet a desperate longing for a loving relationship that will not be destroyed by hatred. This defensive constellation is strikingly different from the activation of narcissistic defenses in other types of character pathology.

In patients who do not have the narcissistic personality structure, resentment toward the analyst, disappointment reactions, feelings of shame and humiliation in the process of character analysis are temporary and less intense; and their reactions coexist with a clear capacity for dependence upon the analyst as indicated by separation anxiety or mourning reactions in the transference. In contrast, generalized devaluation and contempt of the analyst are prevalent in the case of narcissistic personalities, often rationalized as "disappointments." There is a persistent absence of separation anxiety or mourning reactions at weekends, vacation, or illness of the analyst, so that even at times of apparent idealization of the analyst the difference between such idealization and that which obtains in other transferences is striking.

Expression of anger and rage in the course of the predominantly negative transference related to the analysis of character defenses in nonnarcissistic patients will not bring about the massive devaluation of the analyst which is typical of narcissistic personalities. The alternation of childlike demands in times of anger with manifestations of love, gratitude, and guilt-activated idealization characteristic of nonnarcissistic patients, gives an entirely different quality to the transference. Narcissistic personalities' curiosity about the analyst's life in areas other than those related to the immediate needs of the patient is often absent for many months or years. The presence of what on the surface seems "normal" (although infantile) idealization simultaneous with almost complete obliviousness toward the analyst alerts us to the difference between normal and pathological idealization. The absence of the capacity to depend upon others on the part of narcissistic personalities, in contrast to the clinging dependency and persistent capacity for a broad spectrum of object relations in borderline patients, contributes fundamentally to the differential diagnosis of narcissistic personalities functioning on an overt borderline level from usual borderline patients. Other elements in this differential diagnosis are the specific characteristics of pathological idealization, the prevalence of omnipotent control and particularly of contempt and devaluation, and the narcissistic withdrawal in the case of narcissistic personalities. Again, the analytic situation provides abundant clinical evidence of a fundamental difference between normal infantile narcissism, fixation at infantile narcissism typical of patients with character pathology other than narcissistic personalities, and the pathological narcissism of narcissistic personalities.

## 4.  Genetic Considerations

This difference becomes even more striking when, in the course of psychoanalytic treatment, the genetic determinants of these patients' narcissistic resistances and related character defenses are analyzed. Such genetic analysis reveals that in contrast to fixation at infantile narcissistic stages of development directly related to frustrations and failures of the mothering figure and other significant childhood objects, narcissistic personalities repeat in the transference early processes of devaluation of significant external objects and of their intrapsychic representations as a secondary elaboration and defense against underlying conflicts around oral rage and envy. They need to destroy the sources of love and gratification in order to eliminate the source of envy and projected rage, while simultaneously withdrawing into the grandiose self which represents a primitive refusion of the idealized images of the parental figures and idealized images of the self, so that they escape from a vicious circle of anger, frustration and aggressive devaluation of the potential source of gratification at the cost of serious damage to internalized object relations. In short, devaluation processes rationalized as "disappointment" reactions in the transference repeat pathological devaluation of parental images, while the defensive structure of the grandiose self actualizes the pathological condensation of components stemming from object relationships reflecting those conflicts.

I mentioned earlier (Chapter 8) that it is an open question to what extent inborn intensity of aggressive drive participates in this picture, and that the predominance of chronically cold, narcissistic and at the same time overprotective mother figures appears to be the main etiological element in the psychogenesis of this pathology. The inclusion of the child in the narcissistic world of mother during certain periods of his early development creates the predisposition for the "specialness" of the child, around which the fantasies of the grandiose self become crystallized. The narcissistic character defenses protect the patient not only against the intensity of his narcissistic rage, but also against his deep convictions of unworthiness, his frightening image of the world as being devoid of food and love, and his self-concept of the hungry wolf out to kill, eat, and survive. All these fears are activated in the transference at the time when the patient begins to be able to depend upon the analyst. The patient now fears his destructive envy of the analyst, and he is uncertain whether his need for love will survive or be stronger than his aggressive onslaughts on the analyst. These developments determine an intensively ambivalent and frightening transference paradigm which needs to be worked through.

## 5. Types of Idealization and the Relationship of Narcissistic Idealization to the Grandiose Self

Regarding the nature of the defensive operations in pathological narcissism, I have already alluded to the fact that these patients' idealization of the analyst is markedly different from the primitive idealization of borderline patients, and from the idealization that occurs in other types of character pathology. Borderline conditions are characterized by what I have called "primitive idealization," namely an unrealistic, "all good" image of the analyst as a primitive good, powerful gratifying object, used as a protection against the "contamination" of the analyst with paranoid projections of an "all bad," sadistic, primitive object. In other words, this primitive level of idealization is related to the predominance of splitting mechanisms. In contrast, in the nonnarcissistic types of character pathology and the symptomatic neuroses, the idealization of the analyst as a good, loving, forgiving parental image is related to the patient's ambivalence, his guilt and concern over the simultaneous presence of both intense love and hatred for the analyst. At this higher level of idealization, the analyst is seen as a parental figure who is all understanding and tolerant and who loves the patient in spite of his "badness." This higher level of idealization is followed by the still more mature type of idealization which includes the projection onto the idealized objects of higher level superego functions dealing with abstract, depersonified value systems: in essence, a normal phenomenon which is characteristic particularly of adolescence and falling in love.

These different types of idealization can be seen as a continuum, from normal primitive to normal adult functioning. All of them, however, are in striking contrast to the idealization of the narcissistic personality, which reflects the projection onto the analyst of the patient's grandiose self. The narcissistic patient extends his own grandiosity to include the analyst, and thus, while apparently free associating in the presence of the analyst, really talks to himself expanded into a grandiose "self-observing" figure to which the patient becomes, temporarily, an attachment or satellite. It needs to be stressed that insofar as the patient "withdraws" that idealization at the end of the hour, and shows a complete absence of real dependency on the analyst, there is no real merger taking place, thus indicating the difference of this reaction from more primitive self-object fusion which characterizes what Jacobson (3) calls psychotic identification and Mahler (11) described as the symbiotic phase of development. Rather than a fusion of self and object image reflecting regression to a very early level of development at which ego boundaries have not yet stabilized, reality testing in a strict sense is maintained in the hours, and transference psychosis does not develop.

Also, insofar as the idealization of the analyst does not alternate with intense projection of a "bad object" onto him (as in the usual borderline conditions), nor involve guilt and reparation (as in normal infantile types of idealization during transference neurosis), narcissistic idealization is a pathological process rather than a normal developmental stage. The genetic origins of this pathology must be located somewhere in between the stage of self-object differentiation (i.e., beyond the level of development characteristic of the psychoses) and the stage of normal integration of self-images into a normal self-structure and of object images into integrated object representations (i.e., the object-relations-derived structures underlying the usual forms of character pathology and symptomatic neuroses). Insofar as a pathological, grandiose self is projected onto the analyst and the patient's "empathy" with that projected self remains, and he attempts to exert maximum control to have the analyst follow exactly what is required in order to maintain the projection and to avoid the emergence of the analyst as an independent, autonomous object, this entire defensive operation reflects what I have described operationally (reformulating Melanie Klein's use of this term) as "projective identification" (Chapter 1), another characteristic mechanism of borderline conditions and narcissistic personalities. The practical consequences of the patient's continuing efforts to force the analyst to behave exactly as the patient needs to see him correspond quite closely to Kohut's descriptions of the mirror transference. What I want to stress again, however, is the specific, peculiar nature of the constellation of pathological narcissism in contrast to narcissistic developments in other types of pathology.

Kohut's thinking about narcissistic idealization is in contrast to the foregoing formulation. He sees narcissistic personalities as suffering from a lack of optimal internalization of the archaic, rudimentary self-object—the idealized parent imago (10, pp. 37-47). He stresses that the small child's idealizations belong genetically and dynamically into a narcissistic context, a proposition which makes sense in the context of Kohut's stress that it is the quality of the libidinal cathexes and not the target of the instinctual investment which determines whether an internalization is basically narcissistic or object oriented. Because of traumatic loss of the idealized object, or a traumatic disappointment in it, optimal internalization does not take place, and, Kohut suggests:

> The intensity of the search for and of dependency on these objects is due to the fact that they are striven for as a substitute for the missing segments of the psychic structure. They are not objects (in the psychological sense of the term) since they are not loved or admired for their attributes, and the actual features of their personalities, and their actions, are only dimly recognized. They are not longed for but are needed in order to replace the functions of a segment of the mental apparatus which had not been established in childhood (pp. 45-6).

In short, he suggests that the idealizing transference of narcissistic personalities corresponds to a fixation at an archaic level of normal development.

In my view, the idealizing transference reflects a pathological type of idealization, and corresponds to the massive activation of the grandiose self in the tranference. Thus, what Kohut calls the mirror transference, and what he calls idealizing transference correspond in my thinking to the alternative activation of components belonging essentially to a condensed, pathological self. This self stems from the fusion of some aspects of the real self, the ideal self, and the ideal object. This condensation is pathological, and does not simply represent fixation at an early stage of development. Kohut himself, in referring to the idealized parent imago, refers to it as an archaic, rudimentary "self-object," and describes "typical regressive swings" during the analysis of narcissistic personality disorders (see 10, diagram 2, p. 97, illustrating how shifts occur from idealizing transference to activation of grandiosity in the patient). I have found the alternative projection of the grandiose self onto one participant of the analytic relationship, while the other one represents the remnants of the real self incorporated as it were in a magical union with the idealized partner, a regular feature of narcissistic resistances.

In my view, the early idealization of the analyst in the

transference does not constitute a paradigm essentially different from the projection of the grandiose self onto him, and frequently contains many elements of the characteristics of the grandiose self. In addition, in the early stages of the analysis, idealization of the analyst serves to re-create the patient's usual incorporative relationships with potential sources of gratification, the idealization of such sources representing the gratifying fantasies that other people, in this case the analyst, still have something valuable that the patient has not yet incorporated and that he needs to make his. The early idealization is also a defense against the danger of emergence of intense envy, and against the processes of devaluation of the analyst. Devaluation of the analyst may protect the patient against envy, but it also destroys his hope of receiving something new and good, and, on a deeper level, reconfirms his fear of not ever being able to establish a mutually loving and gratifying relationship.

Thus, in the early stages of analysis, narcissistic patients typically develop fantasies that their analyst is the best analyst that exists; they do not need to envy any other patients having another analyst; they are the only patient of the analyst, or at least the most interesting patient whom the analyst prefers over all others, etc. Gradually, the idealized features of the analyst, which at first reflect rather conventionally ideal attributes, shift into directions which reveal a particular nature of the patient's grandiose self. Throughout this entire process, switches occur during which the otherwise ideal analyst is supposedly lucky to have such an unusual patient, and the patient can be reassured of the analyst's exclusive interest because no other patient of any other analyst could match such a gratifying analytic experience, etc. This sudden shift from periods in which the analyst is seen as a perfect, God-like creature, into a complete devaluation of the analyst and self-idealization of the patient, only to revert later to the apparent idealization of the analyst while the patient experiences himself as part of the analyst, indicate the intimate connections of the components of the overall condensed structure—the grandiose self—which characterizes narcissistic resistances. The analysis of all these components of this pathological structure reveals defensive functions against the emergence of direct oral rage and envy, against paranoid fears related to projection of sadistic trends on the analyst (representing a primitive, hated, and sadistically perceived mother image), and against basic feelings of terrifying loneliness, hunger for love, and guilt over the aggression directed against the frustrating parental images.

One patient, a fellow professional in treatment with a colleague, felt in the early stages of his treatment that his psychoanalyst had a perfect technique of interpretation. From what he said he had heard and from his own observations about his analyst, he construed the picture of a very thorough, meticulous, somewhat cold and distant but perfectionistic technician, who would see to it that all of the patient's defenses and conflicts would be resolved systematically in the right order. The patient gradually elaborated this vision of his analyst into that of a man who was absolutely certain of himself, incorruptible, rigid but completely stable and reliable, who would not let emotions get in his way, and would interrupt the patient with scientific precision only when and if needed. He felt very reassured by this image of perfection, and one might have thought that this transference constituted an idealization of the analyst as an external object. However, it gradually turned out that the patient had been reading the technical work of a leading psychoanalyst from another city, with the intention of shifting from the present analyst to the other one in case he discovered any shortcoming in his present analyst. In a subtle way, he attempted to force his analyst into conforming with his picture of the perfect analyzing machine, with the qualities of coldness, distance, and olympian untouchability emerging as the main features. This patient presented characterological attitudes very similar to those of the analyst of his fantasies, and had a distant and unfeeling attitude about his own patients while attempting to copy the technique of his analyst. The patient was very proud of his careful, precise, intellectual approach; he also became extremely irritated when anybody invaded what he considered his personal space or time. He presented strong disappointment reactions when the analyst did not conform to the patient's self-image, or when the analyst would give indications of personality characteristics different from those known and particularly understood by the patient, thus threatening him with the presence of an independent, autonomous person. This case illustrates the intimate connection of the idealization of the analyst as representing part of the patient's grandiose self, and the related pathological nature of the idealization process.

## 6. Structural Characteristics and Origins of the Grandiose Self

What are the structural origins and functions of the pathologically condensed grandiose self? In my view, idealized object images which normally would be integrated into the ego ideal and as such, into the superego, are condensed instead with the self-concept. As a result, normal superego integration is lacking, ego-superego boundaries are blurred in certain areas, and unacceptable aspects of the real self are dissociated and/or repressed, in combination with widespread, devastating devaluation of external objects and their representations. Thus, the intrapsychic world of these patients is populated only by their own grandiose self, by devaluated, shadowy images of self and others, and by potential persecutors representing the nonintegrated sadistic superego forerunners, as well as primitive, distorted object images onto whom intense oral sadism has been projected. It needs to be stressed again that these developments occur at a point when self and object images have been sufficiently differentiated from each other to assure stable ego boundaries, so that the pathological condensation occurs after the achievement of the developmental stage which separates psychotic from nonpsychotic structures. Thus created, the pathological grandiose self permits a certain integration of the ego providing a better overall social adaptation than achieved by borderline patients in general. The splitting of the self characteristic of borderline patients is thus compensated for, but at the price of a further deterioration of object relationships, the loss of the capacity to depend, and an ominous capacity for self-protection from emotional conflicts with others by withdrawing into the splendid, grandiose isolation which gives the specific seal to the narcissistic organization.

Another consequence of these developments is that, insofar as superego elements and ego elements are condensed into the grandiose self, certain superego elements will not be available for superego integration, particularly the normal components of the ego ideal. Under these circumstances, the sadistic forerunners of the superego predominate, and superego integration would represent a terrible danger for the ego of pressure from a sadistic, primitive superego. Also, as the normal integration of the ego ideal with other superego structures is missing, the forerunners of later value systems are also missing, and so is the precondition for the internalization of later superego components, mainly the more realistic parental images derived from oedipal conflicts which normally constitute a major cement of superego integration (3). Devaluation of the parents, rationalized as disappointment reactions, is also fostered by this defective development of advanced superego functions, and further interferes with the normal integration of value systems as part of the total personality and the related development of sublimatory potentials.

The final, and most crucial consequence of the establishment of the grandiose self, is the rupture of the normal polarity of self and object images which have been part of the internalized units which fixate and reproduce satisfactory relations with others. The grandiose self permits the denial of dependency on others, protects the individual against narcissistic rage and envy, creates the precondition for ongoing depreciation and devaluation of others, and contributes to distort both the future narcissistic and object investments of the patient.

For all these reasons, pathological narcissism cannot be considered simply a fixation at the level of normal primitive narcissism. Normal narcissism stems from the libidinal investment in an originally undifferentiated self and object image from which later, libidinally invested self and object images will develop. These will eventually determine an integrated self, which incorporates libidinally determined and aggressively determined self-images under the predominance of the libidinally determined ones. This integrated self is surrounded by integrated object representations which in turn reflect the integration of earlier, libidinally invested and aggressively invested object images, the integration also occurring under the predominance of predominantly libidinal object images. In pathological narcissism this normal "representational world" (14) is replaced by a pathological constellation of internalized object relations.

Thus, in contrast to Kohut's view about the nature of the superego pathology in narcissistic personalities, I think these cases do not simply reflect a lack of development of the idealized forerunners of the superego (the components of the ego ideal), but the pathological condensation of such forerunners with ego components. Thus, normal ego and superego boundaries are blurred, and the development of primitive superego structures into an advanced, normal superego is interfered with. There is not merely a "lack" of internalization of certain normal idealized superego forerunners, but an active distortion of them simultaneously with pathological devaluation of the external objects. In more general terms, there is not simply an "absence" of certain structures, but a pathological development of earlier structures so that the later normal ones cannot develop.

## PSYCHOANALYTIC TECHNIQUE AND NARCISSISTIC TRANSFERENCE

If I understand him correctly, Kohut's overall strategy of technique aims at permitting the establishment of a full narcissistic transference, especially the unfolding of the mirror transference reflecting the activation of the grandiose self. He implies that this transference development completes a normal process that has been arrested, namely that of the internalization of the ideal self-object into the superego and the related growth from primitive into mature narcissism. Kohut suggests that "during those phases of the analysis of narcissistic character disturbance when an idealizing transference begins to germinate, there is only one correct analytic attitude: to accept the admiration" (10, p. 264). The analyst, Kohut adds,

> interprets the patient's resistances against the revelation of his grandiosity; and he demonstrates to the patient not only that his grandiosity and exhibitionism once played a phase-appropriate role but that they must now be allowed access to consciousness. For a long period of the analysis, however, it is almost always

deleterious for the analyst to emphasize the irrationality of the patient's grandiose fantasies or to stress that it is realistically necessary that he curb his exhibitionistic demands. The realistic integration of the patient's infantile grandiosity and exhibitionism will in fact take place quietly and spontaneously (though very slowly) if the patient is able, with the aid of the analyst's empathic understanding for the mirror transference, to maintain the mobilization of the grandiose self and to expose his ego to its demands (10, p.272).

Kohut acknowledges, "At first hearing I might seem to be stating that, in instances of this type, the analyst must indulge a transference wish of the analysand; specifically, that the patient had not received the necessary emotional echo or approval from the depressive mother, and that the analyst must now give it to her in order to provide a 'corrective emotional experience'" (p. 290). In objecting to this interpretation, Kohut states, "Although for tactical reasons (e.g., in order to insure the cooperation of the segment of the patient's ego), the analyst might in such instances transitorily have to provide what one might call a reluctant compliance with the childhood wish, the true analytic aim is not indulgence but mastery based on insight, achieved in a setting of tolerable analytic abstinence" (p. 291).

In discussing the results of his approach, he states, "The primary and essential results of the psychoanalytic treatment of narcissistic personalities lie within the narcissistic realm, and the changes achieved, constitute in the majority of cases, the most significant and therapeutically decisive results" (p. 298). He considers the increase and the expansion of the patient's capacity for object love as "the most prominent non-specific change" (p. 296), and says that "the increasing availability of object-instinctual cathexes as the analysis proceeds usually does not indicate that a change of the mobilized narcissism into object love has taken place; it is rather due to a freeing of formerly repressed object libido; i.e., it is the result of therapeutic success in sectors of secondary psychopathology (transference neurosis) in a patient who is primarily suffering from a narcissistic personality disorder" (pp. 296-7).

In my view, Kohut's approach neglects the intimate relationships between narcissistic and object related conflicts, and the crucial nature of conflicts around aggression in the psychopathology of patients with narcissistic personality. While I certainly agree that it is important to permit a full development of the transference rather than prematurely interpreting it, and that the analyst needs to avoid—as in all analytic cases—any moralistic attitude regarding the inappropriate nature of the patient's grandiosity, Kohut's approach may unwillingly foster an interference with the full development of the negative transference aspects, maintain the patient's unconscious fear of his envy and rage, and thus hinder the working through of the pathological, grandiose self. Kohut implies that the mirror transferences which reflect the activation of the grandiose self must be tolerated to permit its full development, because otherwise the narcissistic grandiosity may be driven underground. It seems to me that systematic analysis of the positive and negative aspects of the patient's grandiosity from an essentially neutral position better achieves the goal of full activation of the narcissistic transference.

I agree with Kohut that the psychoanalytic treatment of narcissistic personalities centers on the activation of the grandiose self and the need for helping the patient achieve full awareness of it in a neutral analytic situation, but I think that focusing exclusively on narcissistic resistances from the viewpoint of libidinal conflicts with an almost total disregard of the vicissitudes of aggression in these cases interferes with a systematic interpretation of the defensive functions of the grandiose self. In my view, both the primitive idealization of and the omnipotent control over the analyst need to be interpreted systematically; the patient needs to become aware, obviously in a noncritical atmosphere, of his need to devalue and depreciate the analyst as an independent object, in order to protect himself from the reactivation of underlying oral rage and envy and the related fear of retaliation from the analyst. Fear of retaliation from the analyst (derived from projected sadistic reactions activated by real or fantasied frustrations from him), and fear of guilt (because of the patient's attack on the analyst as a primitive giving object) are prominent motives against which narcissistic resistances have been erected. They need to be explored and interpreted systematically before the transference shifts into the ordinary transference paradigms characteristic of transference neurosis. The patient's efforts to hold on to his grandiose self, and to avoid acknowledging the analyst as an independent, autonomous person, consistently reveal his defense against the intense envy, against the feared relationship with the hated and sadistically perceived mother image, and his dread of a sense of empty loneliness in a world devoid of personal meaning.

In the course of this work, what regularly emerges is that behind the consciously remembered or rediscovered "disappointments" from the parents are the devaluations of the parental images and the real parental figures, carried out in the past in order to avoid the underlying conflicts with them. The patients' disappointments in the analyst reveal not only fantasied—or real—frustrations in the transference: they also reveal dramatically the total devaluation of the transference object for the slightest reason, and thus, the intense, overwhelming nature of the aggression against the object. Direct rage because of frustrations is an infinitely more normal, although an exaggerated type of response. In addition, the implication of "either you are as I want you, or you cease to exist" is also the acting out of unconscious need for omnipotent control of the object, and reflects defenses against aggression. "Disappointment reactions" in these cases reflect conflicts about aggression as well as libidinal strivings and, more immediately, a protection against general activation of oral-aggressive conflicts. The narcissistic transference, in other words, first activates past defenses against deeper relationships with the parents, and only then the real past relationships with them. As is true in so many cases with borderline conditions, the parents did, indeed, disappoint the patient, but in ways and areas which the narcissistic patient usually did not suspect and which only become clear in the later part of the treatment. In short, disappointments in the analyst, unrealistic idealization of him which hides the patient's refusal to acknowledge him as an independent object, and the complex motives for narcissistic withdrawal, need to be carefully scrutinized for underlying contempt and devaluation. This is a striking difference from the technical requirements in the analysis of infantile narcissistic reactions in other types of character pathology.

A crucial technical issue with these patients is the focus on such remnants as the patient possesses of the capacity for love and object investment, and on his realistic appreciation of the analyst's efforts, in order to help the patient avoid misinterpreting the focus on the latent negative transference as the psychoanalyst's conviction that the patient is "all bad." In short, the analyst needs to focus on both the positive and negative transference. In this connection, Kohut quotes me as saying that ego distortions "temporarily require a bit of educational pressure" (10, p. 179), which is a misunderstanding of my views. The analyst certainly needs to avoid educational pressures or a moralistic stance, and I think that the best way to achieve this is by analyzing the motives which determine narcissistic defenses, including the activation of the grandiose self. One prominent reason why these patients cannot tolerate facing their feelings of hatred and envy is because they fear such feelings will destroy the analyst, destroy their hope for a good relationship with him, and crush their hope of being helped. At a deeper level, these patients fear that their aggression will not only destroy the potentially loving and giving object but also their own capacity to give and receive love. Narcissistic patients also attempt, in denying the reality of their emotional relationship with the psychoanalyst, to deny the danger of their destructiveness and to preserve the illusion of being able to "start all over again." This can be observed in some patients with sexually promiscuous narcissistic behavior, in which one function of the promiscuity is to preserve the hope for a better relationship with new objects, and to protect the objects of the patients' sexual impulses from destruction. Often, neglecting to interpret the negative aspects of the transference may heighten the patient's fear over his own aggression and destructiveness, and intensify the need for activation of the narcissistic resistances. In short, the optimal technique for resolution of the narcissistic resistances is the systematic interpretation of both the positive and negative transference aspects rather than focusing exclusively on libidinal elements, or the misunderstanding that interpretation of latent negative resistances means exclusive focus on aggression.

It is important to keep in mind that, except in the most severe cases of narcissistic personality, there are certain normal ego functions which are maintained and certain realistic aspects of the self-concept which continue in existence, side-by-side with the grandiose self. These, of course, constitute the basis for the establishment of a therapeutic alliance, and the related capacity to really listen to the analyst and to identify with him in thinking psychologically about himself. These normal self-aspects can be diagnosed, preserved, and expanded by focusing upon the patient's tendency to split off or devaluate these very functions in himself. The realistic wish to maintain a good relationship with the analyst and to be helped by him is the starting point, one might say, of the recuperation of normal infantile and mature dependency and self-evaluation. Insofar as narcissistic resistances against full awareness of the underlying rage and contempt are also at the service of preserving the good relationship with the analyst, the interpretation of this double function of the narcissistic resistance may greatly help the patient face his split-off contempt and envy. In short, noncritical interpretation of the negative aspects of the transference may help reduce the patient's fear of his own destructiveness and doubts about his goodness.

However, there are cases in which the narcissistic resistances cannot be worked through, and the patient after lengthy periods of stalemate prefers to terminate the treatment, or the analyst feels that he cannot help the patient any further. Under these conditions, a shift into a more supportive approach of the kind which in my opinion is implied (although not intended) in Kohut's approach may be very helpful. This is particularly true for patients with relatively effective social adaptation, who consult because of a symptom which improves in the course of the analysis before working through of their basic narcissistic resistances; and for cases in which secondary gains, particularly important narcissistic gratifications linked to their pathological character structure, militate against the painful nature of analytic work. There are also patients with intense negative therapeutic reactions who can accept certain improvement only at the cost of simultaneously defeating the analyst in his purpose to bring about further change. In many cases of this kind, the treatment may have to shift at some point, into a supportive tolerance of the narcissistic constellation in combination with preparation for termination of the treatment.

There is, however, a dramatic difference between the changes brought about under these circumstances, and the changes brought about when pathological narcissism is systematically worked through. When the pathological narcissism cannot be worked through, and analysis shifts into a supportive approach, the patient's social functioning usually improves noticeably, and his capacity to understand better what goes on in other people and in his interactions with them improves the patient's relationships with others and himself. The patient's ambitions become more realistic, the ways to achieve them more in harmony with his overall life situation and goals, and there is usually an increase of the tolerance of the feelings of boredom and restlessness which are so typical of narcissistic personalities. However, there usually persists a lack of capacity for empathy in depth with others, and a lack of capacity for full development of love relations. Their attitude toward work often reveals the pursuit of some specialized interest or small area of personal investment—whether it is in business, professions, studies, hobbies or collections—where the patient obtains a sense of control and superiority while isolating himself from the broader area of which this particular interest is part.

Paradoxically, narcissistic personalities functioning rather poorly on an overt borderline level, who have undergone supportive psychotherapy, may present a higher level of improvement than patients who originally functioned more effectively and were more intelligent, creative and ambitious. The persistent feelings of emptiness, the "burned out" quality of interests and ambitions that one observes in narcissistic personalities functioning on a borderline level leaves them more willing to settle for rather conventional, often overconventional ways and styles, replacing their old ambitiousness and flamboyance with a gratification of having their life and immediate needs stable and under control. In contrast, the highly gifted, brilliant narcissistic personalities who have undergone psychoanalytic treatment which did not resolve their narcissistic personality structure, tend to experience more dissatisfaction with themselves and with life. They feel that while they can no longer hold on to their old grandiosity, they cannot accept the essentially "mediocre" nature of ordinary life.

The observation of former psychoanalytic candidates (graduated or not) who have undergone psychoanalytic treatment in which the narcissistic resistances were not systematically analyzed and resolved (usually in connection with lack of full exploration of the negative transference dispositions) provide a good illustration of these developments. A composite picture of traits one particularly finds among this group are: a gradual disappointment with intensive psychotherapeutic work with patients, a feeling of boredom when considering the perspective of intensive work with a patient over a period of months or years, and rationalizations of this loss of interest in clinical work in terms of theoretical criticisms of psychoanalytic theory or technique. Frequently these former candidates—or analysts—eagerly explore new treatment methods, particularly those which promise to bring about an immediate activation of emotional reactions or regression. They feel more comfortable with methods which permit "instant intimacy" of a nondifferentiated nature rather than the lengthy, complex building-up of personal relationships in depth. Intelligent and gifted therapists with this character constellation may have a great sensitivity for "small and complex issues" in the treatment, but lose sight of the emotional constellation expressing what is going on between them and the patient. It is interesting to observe how in the postanalytic stage patients with narcissistic personality who have not undergone systematic working through of the narcissistic resistances continue to idealize their analyst for a time, and then gradually shift into a basic indifference. Their retrospective evaluation of analysis is that while it was a very helpful experience, they did not learn anything really new about themselves.

The following case illustrates the patient's pressure for premature termination of the treatment and a consequent shift into a supportive approach. This patient, a businessman in his early 40s with a typical narcissistic personality structure, came because of homosexuality. Over a period of four years of psychoanalysis he improved to the extent that his homosexual impulses and acting out disappeared, and his general adaptation to his family life and work improved markedly. He felt he had achieved the main goal for which he had entered treatment, and was satisfied with his present life in spite of the persisting sensation of boredom, difficulty in empathizing with other people, and an awareness of his limitations in caring for others. His chronic conflicts about envy had decreased, partly because his wishes for wealth and prestige had been gratified. After a lengthy period in which he met my interpretive efforts by insisting that he had achieved all he had expected from psychoanalysis, we finally agreed to consider termination. In the six months before the termination of the analysis, and after a date for termination had been set, his main fear was that I was angry and disappointed because of this decision, and, on a deeper level, he felt that termination represented his escape from a perfectionistic, never-satisfied analyst-mother. At this point, I focused on the patient's fear of rejection by me without persisting in my previous attempts to analyze the underlying conflicts (mainly his paranoid fear of attack and betrayal by me as a sadistic, withholding primitive mother). I did, however, point out to him his fear that I was seeing him as sadistically withholding further analytic work from me, and that he was attributing to me the kind of suspiciousness which he had previously experienced toward me. I also explored with him his fear that I would not accept him as a person in his own right if he did not live up to some kind of perfect standards, which reflected a projection onto me of his own, highly unrealistic aspirations for perfection that we had explored in the past. In the course of this process, the patient's experience of me as an idealized person who could accept him as he was in his own right provided an important source of support to him, helped him tone down his own narcissistic aspirations and achieve further improvement in his relationship with himself as well as with his family. This patient did not experience a full-blown mourning process during the last part of the analysis, nor, as I learned from follow-up information years after the termination of this analysis, did he experience such a period of mourning after the termination. Over the years, his general symptomatic improvement has persisted, and he has gradually accepted the limitation of his internal emotional life. In short, this case illustrates how the protection of narcissistic defenses as part of the process of treatment termination may be helpful when full resolution of the pathological narcissism cannot be achieved.

However, whenever possible, one should attempt to resolve this serious psychopathology in order to achieve a fundamental change in the patient's internal relationship with himself and with others—a shift, in short, from pathological narcissism and object relationships to normal narcissism and object relationships.

The following vignettes illustrate various features of narcissistic transferences.

## Vignette 1

A male patient reacted to the information that I would not be able to see him for one of his appointments later that week with anger, and then, feeling distant and empty in the hour, withdrew into a monotonous recital of disconnected thoughts going through his mind. Exploration of his anger revealed that he felt shocked about the suddenness of the announcement, and about the fact that it did not fit into what he considered to be a predictable pattern (my letting him know weeks ahead when I would not be able to see him, or my secretary letting him know about some unexpected development, i.e., an illness on my part). This patient showed no reactions to weekend separations, and would resume his sessions after vacations as if his last hour had been yesterday. We had explored in some depth his angry reactions to minor frustrations on my part, and his tendency to forget me completely (and his fantasies that, actually, I ceased to exist in between hours) when he felt I had behaved in a stable, completely predictable manner (for example, my comments would confirm his own observations, and I would thus show neither more nor less knowledge about him than he had). During this session, his associations to his anger led into fantasies that one of my children must be ill, and that I was canceling my appointments because I wanted to be with the child. He then expressed fantasies that I had unusually bright or attractive children, and speculated about the ways in which I was spending my free time with my family. In the course of these associations, it became clear that he saw me as a potential source of love and concern for him, and as teasingly withholding that love and concern from him, giving it instead to my children, of whom he felt intensely jealous. At this point he became sad, and commented that it was understandable enough that I should prefer my children rather than a demanding, self-centered person such as he. His reaction then shifted abruptly to a feeling of annoyance with me and of having been trapped by me. At that point, he felt that I was demanding and selfish, asking him to come at hours which were convenient to me, and canceling his hours without any regard to his needs. He felt it was a typical analyst's manipulation to have him think about his motivations when obviously something was wrong with me. His associations then focused on other aspects of my personality which seemed to confirm to him that I had a self-centered, manipulative character, and that I really did not care about him at all. He felt I had simply canceled his hour in order not to have to change my schedule.

What I wish to stress is the suddenness of the shift in the emotional relationship of the patient with me: in contrast to the consistent, many hours of "calm" narcissistic control, he presented a brief period of intense and changing emotional reaction. His reaction illustrates the utilization of the narcissistic defense against his feeling rejected by a hypocritical mother, and the feelings of guilt and unworthiness because of what he considered his excessive demandingness on her. His reaction also illustrates the projection of his demandingness and self-centeredness on her, and the secondary disappointment and devaluation of this maternal image in the transference, thus reestablishing the narcissistic balance.

There was abundant evidence in this case that his mother was, indeed, very self-centered, and had a chronic tendency to manipulate him through guilt feelings; but his feelings of abandonment and unworthiness were intolerable to him, because they were compounded by guilt over his anger toward his mother, and by the projection onto her of his own angry, revengeful feelings.

In this case, the feeling of sadness reflected a temporary awareness of his angry, demanding behavior toward me, and toward his mother in the last resort. However, the sadness also involved his acknowledgment that, in spite of the frustration that he had just experienced from me, I was also the person who could give him love and concern. It was also sadness over his feeling that he could not respond in a loving way to me, that is, to his mother image. I pointed out to the patient that one of the reasons he felt it was so difficult to tolerate his anger and loneliness, and his longing for a good relationship with his analyst (mother) was his despair over his own badness, as if his aggressive fantasies and feelings would eliminate or destroy his right to expect a loving relationship, and his trust in his capacity to give. Again, systematic interpretation of both the positive and negative transference reactions defended against by pathological narcissistic resistances help to integrate love and hatred and, in the last resort, the contradictory self and object images which are split off as part of the primitive ego organization of these patients.

## Vignette 2

A college student in her early 20s was furious because I would be gone for a week, and expressed ragefully her disappointment in what she experienced as my callousness and negligence. She threatened to terminate the treatment, and made me responsible for anything that might happen to her during the time I was away. I interpreted to her the anger over my leaving her, and her projection of that anger onto me so that my going away acquired dangerous, sadistic qualities. I also pointed out to her that because she was so angry with me she was disqualifying me completely not only as a professional, but also, as it were, tearing apart my image inside of her, so that nothing was left but bleak emptiness and my leaving became much worse. In earlier hours, she had expressed the fantasies that I would go away on a professional trip to boastfully let others know about my success with patients, and she had imagined my trip as an ongoing series of feasts which would start out with my proclaiming my greatness and continue with huge, endless dinner parties in which I would greedily devour food ordinarily only available to a select few. These fantasies, expressed in the middle of intense rage, alternated with periods of disdainful calmness in which the patient would act completely indifferent and bored. I now reminded her of these fantasies, and suggested that one of the functions of her intense rage was to erase me as the source of unending envy for her. At this point, still angry but somehow more thoughtful, she exclaimed that what she was really envious of was that I could be satisfied with myself, that I would not crumble under the guilt feelings which she would try to evoke in me, and that I could tolerate feelings of guilt without losing my determination to do what I had decided to. This same patient, at another time when she was again considering termination of her treatment, said that although she knew she really did need to continue in treatment, the idea that she would rob me of the treatment success would go a long way to make life more pleasurable without continuing in treatment.

## Vignette 3

Another patient, after many months of what appeared on the surface to be detachment, gave continuous indication of his need to reassure himself against relentless envy. This was a young college professor who continuously compared the achievements of all other people with his own, and obtained endless gratification from the reassurance that he had achieved much more than anybody else at the same age. He would calculate the relationship between the level of income and the age of friends, the size of houses in relationship to the age of the owner, the number of professional honors and publications of other colleagues in comparison to what he had achieved at the same age, etc. Although he speculated intellectually that perhaps his complete indifference toward me might be related to the fear that he might develop the same reaction with me, and, feeling superior, might evoke my envy and hatred, it took many months until this became an emotional reality. At one point he was able to face the humiliating and painful awareness that to really feel he needed me caused him to envy me because of this very need. If I really had understanding to offer which he lacked, every confirmation of this would create a pang of envy.

## Vignette 4

Still another patient, an industrialist in his middle thirties, came to analysis with the expectation that he was to be "brainwashed" into a state of satisfaction with himself, and to be given a clear system of values and principles for guiding his daily life to replace his chronic sense of uncertainty and futility and his feelings of being "phony." He had become disillusioned with religion, in spite of strenuous efforts in early years to find magic help through a religious commitment, and he was quite aware of his efforts to replace his search for religion with psychoanalysis. In the early stages of his analysis, he saw me as a rigid, dogmatic but deeply convinced high-priest of psychoanalysis, an ambivalent idealization which turned out to be a protective structure against his vision of me as a hypocrite, a man who went through empty rituals because it fitted his pocket—in short, a "phony" as the patient saw himself. It became quite striking to him that there were only three ways in which he could perceive me: either I was a convinced, dogmatic, arbitrary "brainwasher" who would sadistically force him to submit to psychoanalytic dogma; or a cynical manipulator who could exploit him financially; or, even worse, an impotent fool who would believe in a phony method and theory such as psychoanalysis. It took many months for the patient to become aware that in these three alternatives he had excluded the possibility that I, as a psychoanalyst, might have something real and concrete to offer, and that my convictions might reflect my awareness of this fact. This patient insisted on acquiring the "magical" tools of psychoanalysis for achieving happiness, instead of carrying out a realistic work in collaboration with the analyst, partly because he was fearful of his envious impulses.

At one point, he became aware that he used to rapidly scan my office at the beginning of the sessions to make sure everything was exactly as it had been before. It turned out that he was afraid that new objects, books or papers would appear on my desk indicating new acquisitions or tributes that I had received, and it was with a great sense of relief that the patient reassured himself that there was nothing new that would upset him. He also became aware that, at times when he did find new acquisitions in the office, the intrusive thoughts would come to mind that I was Jewish, that Jewish people were extremely grabby and voracious, and that new possessions of mine confirmed my belonging to an empty, hungry, exploitative race. The patient was very much afraid of exploring these fantasies about me, fearing that my self-esteem would crumble under these "poisonous" attacks, and that therefore he would be unable to obtain help and relief in the analysis. Systematic interpretation of the fear over his own aggression, with implicit acknowledgement of the patient's wish to preserve me as an intact, potentially helpful person in the transference as part of his total reaction, permitted the gradual uncovering of the conflicts around contempt, greediness, and hatred against which narcissistic defenses had been erected.

## COUNTERTRANSFERENCE AND THERAPEUTIC MODIFICATION OF THE NARCISSISTIC RESISTANCES

Kohut suggests that unresolved narcissistic disturbances in

the analyst may cause the analyst's uneasiness at being idealized, and bring about a subtle tendency to reject the patient's idealization (10, p. 263). While I agree that unresolved narcissistic conflicts of the analyst may bring about pathological reactions in him to the patient's idealization, I also feel they may foster excessive acceptance as well as rejection of the patient's idealization. Unfortunately, at times analysts treating these patients accept uncritically some aspects of the patient's idealization. To accept the admiration seems to me an abandonment of a neutral position in the same way as does critical "overobjectivity." Narcissistic patients readily react to interpretations as if they were "rejections," and if acceptance of the patient's admiration means to abandon a neutral inter-pretative stance, there exists a danger of the analyst being forced into a situation which the patient can easily interpret, sometimes with justification, as a seduction of the analyst. I have been impressed by how skilfully some narcissistic patients sense those aspects of their idealization of the analyst which fit into the analyst's own narcissistic "weak spots."

The "analyst's uneasiness" regarding the idealization may stem from the peculiar quality of this idealization, namely, the combination of the controlling elements in it, and its particular "switch on-switch off" quality. In other words, the analyst may sense the negative as well as the positive transference im-plications.

In my experience, the main problem regarding the countertransference reactions to narcissistic patients is related to the patient's consistent efforts to deny the existence of the psychoanalyst as an independent person. In this regard, I agree with Kohut's description of the reactions of the analyst to the primitive forms of the mirror transference. Kohut says that, while the analyst "may feel oppressed by the patient's unqualified yet silent demands which, from the point of view of the target of the merger transference, are tantamount to total enslavement—the absence of object-instinctual cathexes often makes it difficult for him to remain reliably attentive during prolonged periods" (p. 275). But I disagree with the implication that the problem is one of the nature of the cathexes, for it seems to me that what is involved is the unconscious tendency to control the analyst, the unconscious mechanisms of devaluation, and the activation of primitive types of projection related to the grandiose self.

A careful study of Kohut's case of Miss F. (10, p. 283-95), illustrating the analyst's reactions to mirror transferences, lends itself to an interpretation along the lines I have suggested in this paper. At one point, the patient was able to "establish connexions between the rage which she experienced against me when I did not understand her demands and the feelings she had experienced in the reaction to the narcissistic frustration which she had suffered as a child" (p. 293). Kohut states: "I was finally able to tell her that her anger at me was based on narcissistic processes, specifically on a transference confusion with a depressed mother who had deflected the child's narcissistic needs on to herself. These interpretations were followed by the recall of clusters of analogous memories concerning her mother's entering a phase of depressive self-preoccupation during later years of the patient's life" (10, p.292). In the light of the overall information given about this case, I would raise the question to what extent, in making this interpretation, was the analyst implicitly blaming the patient's mother for having caused the patient's anger and protecting the patient from full examination of the complex origins of her own rage? In more general terms, I see a danger of a seductive effect given by the combination of the analyst's unquestioning acceptance of the patient's idealization, and by the immediate referral back to the original object of the negative transference without exploring fully the patient's participation in the development of pathological rage within the here and now of the transference.

I have suggested that the patient's subtle, unconscious efforts to deny meaning to the analytic relationship (which may induce in the analyst a chronic sense of frustration, helplessness, boredom, and lack of understanding) are much more difficult for the analyst to tolerate than the unrealistic, primitive idealization, which by its very nature alerts the analyst to the narcissistic functions of this idealization. While it is true that analysts with unresolved conflicts regarding their own narcissism may react with anxiety and rejection, or with uncritical acceptance of the patient's idealization, the main danger is the internal rejection by the analyst of the patient because of the patient's chronic devaluation of the analyst. The analyst may feel, at times, as if the patient were convincing him that there is no such thing as an internal life, that psychological matters are incomprehensible and senseless, and that the patient as well as the total analytic situation has a strange, lifeless, mechanical quality. At other times, the analyst may have a sense of understanding but of complete paralysis, as if he no longer would be able to decide regarding what or when to intervene, or as if the emotional connections among the different aspects of the material were unavailable. At times, there are strong temptations for the analyst to just sit back and let things go, hoping that he will find a way back to an intuitive understanding of the patient later on. If at this point, alerted by this development, the analyst is able to gather the objective evidence in the verbal and nonverbal manifestations of the patient which is related to treating the analyst as nonexistent, immediate changes may occur in the transference making the analytic relationship come alive. The sense of deadening monotony in the analytic situation may derive from very specific aspects of the patient's associations and nonverbal behavior which need to be diagnosed and interpreted.

In one session in the middle of his analysis, I pointed out to a narcissistic patient that I was puzzled by the fact that he seemed to talk about important memories of his past in such a monotonous, subdued tone that it was difficult for me to follow them, and that there seemed to be an obvious discrepancy between what he was saying and the way he was saying it. The patient first had a startled reaction, and after I finished talking, he said that he had not been able to listen attentively to what I was saying, but that he had all of a sudden become aware of my presence. In response to my suggestion to associate to this sudden shock, the patient became aware that he had felt very comfortable exploring his past, feeling that letting his thoughts go into all directions would throw them, as it were, into a big, expectant void—a kind of open, receptive world—which would order and automatically bring back into his mind all that he was expressing, with a clear understanding of what it meant and how it would increase the emotional wealth of his experience.

The patient also felt annoyed about my intrusion, and he had the fantasy that I might feel frustrated and incompetent because he could do his analytical work alone. Later in the session, he said, smilingly, that perhaps he had not been able to pay attention to what I had said, because if I really had something to add which would make a change, this would be a very rude disruption of his feeling that he could do it all alone.

Gradually, in the course of working through of narcissistic resistances, the analyst will experience shifts in the sensation of paralyzing stalemate, such as acute awareness of fleeting emotional states of loneliness, or fears of loss of meaning or of love, or of fears of threatening attacks or of rejection by others, feelings within the analyst which reflect the dissociated, repressed and/or projected self and object images which are coming alive in the transference. These regressive "flashes" of emotional experience, or a gradual shift in the analyst's emotional reaction to the patient's efforts to deny emotional meanings to the hours, is a useful index of the working through of narcissistic resistances. At times, a sudden feeling of becoming "widely awake" to aspects of the material which earlier made no emotional sense, will indicate the shift in the transference-countertransference equilibrium. Insofar as a patient will gladly accept any kind of intellectual explanation which he can "learn" and absorb in his "self-analysis," he will accept the analyst's interpretations; however, the analyst's reflection on such momentary states of mood perceived by him on the basis of what has been conveyed by the patient, or of the analyst's emotional perception of the patient's self-images or object-images activated in the hours will often be arduously resisted by the patient and require much emotional alertness on the analyst's part. It is as if at this stage the analyst would become the depository of the patient's more differentiated self and object images linked with the emotional experiences of abandonment, loneliness, frustration, hopelessness against which the patient was defending himself. It is as if the analyst were now experiencing that part of the normal infantile self of the patient which he had been unable to tolerate and had to dissociate or repress and replace by his pathological grandiose self.

At this stage of development in his analysis, a narcissistic patient drove past a sidewalk on to which a dead cat had been thrown, obviously run over by another car. There was something peculiar in his description of the dead cat, in the way he conveyed the sense of abandonment and total misery expressed in the frozen attitude of the dead animal, but before I had time to explore this matter further, other issues seemed to erase its emotional significance. A few days later, the patient mentioned a hungry cat that had been picked up by his children, and he talked about the desperate way this cat would devour food, always ready to escape from possible blows or attack. When I asked him to associate about this, the patient thought of powerful cats roaming the streets at night and chasing away all rivals while searching for food in garbage cans, with an obvious shift from the hungry, frightened, lonely kitten to the powerful, aggressive, "callous" cat. The subject matter came up again in a brief fantasy of a dark, rainy night and a lonely kitten having difficulty in finding shelter.

What is hard to convey in this brief vignette is the mutual isolation of these rather specific descriptions of a certain state of mind which the patient found very difficult to tolerate in himself. What predominated by far, during that stage, was the patient's haughty self-affirmation, his feeling of powerful superiority as a member of a social group which had inborn stamina and deep roots in the country, in contrast to people he despised, such as foreigners, particularly traumatized refugees. The transference was predominantly narcissistic-grandiose, and we explored consistently his tendency to disregard or forget my comments, to treat me as nonexistent, and to analyze himself on his own. It was now, however, that my own experience shifted from that of meaningless, random listening to material with lack of emotional depth, to the strange experience of occasional moments of strong empathy with the isolated, fleetingly activated descriptions of this image of the hungry little cat, and for the dead cat thrown on the sidewalk. Only then was I able to grasp the connection between the image of the lonely kitten and the traumatized refugee. It was as if the patient was activating whatever deep sources existed in my own past implying a conviction of loneliness and agonizing incapacity to express the need for love and shelter. Again, these were only fleeting experiences in the hours with this patient, and at first it was hard for me to connect these experiences with the material.

However, these experiences and fantasies, and memories of relevant dreams of my own past, would only come up in the hours with this patient, and I gradually discovered their connection with the peculiar cat fantasy material that regularly preceded them. I finally was able to interpret to the patient that he was projecting onto me an image of himself, of his early childhood in which he felt deeply unloved. I reconstructed with him the physical and familiar environment in the context of which he had these experiences on the basis of the different aspects of the "cat material" as well as the general knowledge that we had developed to that point. Retrospectively, the connection of the cat fantasy material with his past was pretty obvious, but I wish to stress how difficult it was to capture this material directly from isolated associations in a stage of the analysis in which the patient was engaged in a defensive deterioration of all meaningful communication, and in which the activation of projected, dissociated remnants of the real infantile self occurred in split-off bits in the counter-transference over periods of many sessions.

Acting out of the countertransference reactions motivated by the patient's ongoing efforts of omnipotent control of the analyst may take the form of "reeducative" efforts on the analyst's part, such as pointing out to the patient how he is "undermining" the analytic process, "paying lip service to free association," etc. The analyst may be tempted, at such times, to become moralistic, or to concern himself excessively with the long-range prognosis of the case, in contrast to evaluating his difficulty in empathizing with the immediate transference development. Psychoanalysts with important unresolved narcissistic conflicts may, during periods of lengthy devaluation on the part of the patient, react by suddenly rejecting narcissistic patients whom they previously considered extremely interesting and "rewarding" (particularly at times when the projection of the grandiose self onto the analyst would feed into the analyst's own narcissistic needs).

The most general point I wish to stress again is that, underlying the narcissistic resistances there exist significant, primitive internalized object relations which are activated in the transference, and may be diagnosed gradually as the narcissistic resistances are worked through. This clinical observation constitutes, it seems to me, a most important documentation of the theoretical assumption that narcissism and object relationships always go hand-in-hand, a point articulately stressed by van der Waals (17).

What follows is the summary of the sequence of transference paradigms representing approximately two years of an advanced stage in the psychoanalytic treatment of a narcissistic personality. The patient was a successful architect in his late 30s, a senior partner of a large architectural firm. This patient's transference remained at a level of a typical narcissistic transference paradigm for over three years. During that time, an early phase of idealization of the analyst, reflecting mainly a reaction formation against pervasive devaluating tendencies, was followed by what might best be called an oscillating situation with alternative activation of the pathological grandiose self and the projection of such a grandiose self onto the analyst. The gradual working through of this paradigm activated intense primitive envy and competitiveness based upon oral envy (rather than oedipal strivings), and eventually, a more direct expression of ambivalence with shifts from oral demandingness and anger to longing for a dependency on a loving, protective father-mother image, and strong guilt feelings for his attacks on the analyst. This transference shifted, in turn, toward a more stable dependency on a loving, protective, father image in the transference, and the patient, after over three years of psychoanalysis, for the first time became really dependent upon the analyst with the development of neurotic mourning reactions to separations from the analyst, and the emergence of material from various levels of childhood conflicts. This stage was followed by a reactivation of emotional withdrawal, and a general emotional emptiness in the hours, which on the surface appeared as a repetition of the earlier stage of narcissistic resistances. However, there was a difference in the patient's reaction, which now had the quality of a suspicious, disgruntled withholding of material, together with what appeared as an unconscious attempt to put the analyst to sleep, or at least to maintain him in a chronic frustration created by monotonous repetitions. The patient, during this time, frequently referred to his mother's sadistic, withholding tendencies, and eventually became aware of his identification with such a mother image, while projecting his own, frustrated, infantile self onto the analyst.

This identification with the aggressor was different from the earlier narcissistic withdrawal in the transference, and the interpretation of this transference pattern brought about an immediate shift, with further deepening of the dependent relationship toward the analyst. The patient now saw him as a protective, loving father toward whom he could turn for the gratification of his dependent childhood needs; and he now felt he could "abandon himself" to the analytic situation. He was struck by this new experience for him, which influenced the relationship with his wife and children, and made him understand the dependent needs of them as well as deepen his own involvement with his family. Now, for the first time, the patient became aware of how his entire attitude toward the analyst had been influenced by his basic conviction that no real relationship would ever occur between him and the psychoanalyst. For example, for a long time he harbored fantasies that a friendly although distant relationship with his psychoanalyst would occur after the termination of the analysis, and that he and the analyst had a secret understanding that in reality the analytic relationship had nothing to do with the descriptions of intense emotional conflicts supposedly occurring during the treatment.

The patient also became aware of the existence of an internal world which was not under his conscious control, and of the excitement and fear in facing this world in the analytic situation.[1] A year later the full development of oedipal conflicts emerged in the transference, and the analysis acquired features of the usual resistances and manifestations of these conflicts.

pathology occurs during the early stages of the treatment.

In general, at times of heightened resistances, earlier, previously abandoned narcissistic resistances may become reactivated, similarly to what occurs with past, abandoned character defenses during stages of shift into new lines of resistance. However, the context in which such reactivation of narcissistic defenses occur, and the differentiated quality of the internalized object relations connected with these resistances, confirm the important structural changes that have taken place in the patient.

## PROGNOSIS OF NARCISSISM, TREATED AND UNTREATED

I have referred to prognostic factors in the psychoanalytic treatment of narcissistic personalities earlier (Chapters 4 and 8), and will limit myself here to briefly enumerating these factors, modifying and adding to my earlier considerations.

Secondary gain of illness, such as life circumstances granting unusual narcissistic gratification to a patient with a socially effective narcissistic personality structure, may be a major obstacle in the resolution of narcissistic resistances. This is also the case when there is secondary gain from analytic treatment itself, such as in the case of candidates with narcissistic personality in psychoanalytic training. The question may be raised whether unusual life gratifications in early adulthood of gifted patients generally militate against treatment in some cases of narcissistic personalities, and whether psychoanalysis during middle and later adulthood might not have better prognosis in some of them.

Another major prognostic factor is the extent to which negative therapeutic reactions develop, typically linked with particularly severe, repressed or dissociated conflicts around envy. This is a type of negative therapeutic reaction not derived from superego factors and more severe than that seen in depressive-masochistic patients with a sadistic although integrated superego. Cases with relatively good quality of superego functioning (reflected in the capacity for real investment in values transcending narcissistic interests) have a good prognostic implication, in contrast to cases in which there are subtle types of manipulative and antisocial behavior, even in the absence of major antisocial features (which would make the prognosis very bad indeed). In simple terms, honesty in their daily life is a favorable prognostic indicator for the analysis of narcissistic personalities. Insofar as a good development of sublimatory channels is intimately linked to the capacity for investment in value systems transcending narcissistic needs, the sublimatory potential of the patient is important too.

In contrast to the outstanding importance of the prognostic factors mentioned so far, tolerance of depression and mourning, and a predominance of transference potential for guilt versus a potential for paranoid rage, are of somewhat less overriding importance. Of even less prognostic importance are the nonspecific manifestations of ego weakness, such as lack of impulse control and of anxiety tolerance, and even the potential for regression to primary process thinking if and when the patient does not function on an overt borderline level. This brings us to the general limitation of a strictly psychoanalytic approach for certain patients with narcissistic personality, namely, the disorganizing effect that psychoanalysis may have for narcissistic patients functioning on an overt borderline level. For such people, I consider this approach generally contraindicated.

A particularly difficult prognostic estimate is involved in the case of potential candidates for psychoanalytic training with narcissistic personality structure. Obviously, the problem only comes up in those relatively well-adjusted narcissistic personalities whose social and professional functioning is satisfactory, who present high intelligence and particular talents, and at times appear unusually promising. In reviewing a number of cases in which, retrospectively, it appeared that mistakes had been made both in accepting and rejecting some candidates, the two major prognostic factors that stand out as prognostically significant are the quality of object relationships and the integrity and depth of the value systems and superego functioning. It needs to be stressed again that I use the concept "quality of object relations" to refer more to the quality of internalized object relations, i.e., the depth of the patient's internal relationships with others, rather than to the extent to which he is involved in social interactions. This clarification may be particularly relevant in discussing Kohut's work, because he tends to use the term "object relations" in its behavioral sense rather than in the sense referred to in this chapter. For instance, he states: "The antithesis to narcissism is not the object relation but object love. An individual's profusion of object relations, in the sense of the observer of the social field, may conceal his narcissistic experience of the object world; and a person's seeming isolation and loneliness may be the setting for a wealth of current object investments" (10, p. 228). Again (p. 283): "The patient established object relations not primarily because she was attracted to people but rather as an attempt to escape from the painful narcissistic tensions." In my view, narcissism (investment in the self), and object relations (investment in significant objects and their representations), go hand-in-hand, and their depth depends not only upon the vicissitudes of the libidinal investment, but, as stressed throughout this chapter, on the aggressive investment as well. For practical purposes, object relations in depth involve the capacity both to love well, and to hate well, and particularly to tolerate varying combinations of loving and hateful feelings, and their toned down mingling in the relationship with the same object and with the self. Normal object relations as well as normal narcissism include an integrative conception in depth of others and oneself. All this is in striking contrast to the frequent blandness and uninvolvement, the lack of commitment to others as well as to any convictions about himself that one sees in narcissistic patients. Paradoxically, such lack of emotional depth and commitment may permit a better social functioning, for example, in certain political and bureaucratic organizations in which lack of commitments means survival and access to the top.

Applying all this to the particular case of prospective psychoanalytic candidates, systematic attempts to evaluate the realness, the aliveness of other people as they come through in the descriptions of the candidate, and the depth of the candidate as he describes himself, are important indicators of the quality of object relations, in addition to more observable aspects of stability, depth, and richness of the relationships with others and himself. The extent to which there is authentic human warmth and depth may be more difficult to evaluate but is even more important than the extent to which there is a commitment to ethical, intellectual, cultural or aesthetic values, the other major prognostic indicator in the special cases under examination. Sometimes the very good outcome in cases of psychoanalytic candidates who at first seemed highly questionable warrants to consider carefully all the elements of individual cases; and with the improvement in our therapeutic techniques there should be an increase in successful outcomes in the future.

While Kohut does not, as far as I can tell, refer specifically to prognostic differences with his approach for narcissistic personalities functioning on various levels of ego and superego integration, he conveys a generally optimistic outlook. Regarding the outcome with this approach he states: "The most prominent nonspecific change is the increase and the expansion of the patient's capacity for object love; the specific changes take place in the realm of narcissism itself" (10, p. 296). Kohut describes, as the result of his treatment approach, the internalization of the idealized parent imago (the archaic aspects of the imago) into the general structure of the ego and the superego (the late preoedipal and oedipal aspects of the imago), leading to an improved functioning of the superego (p. 288-9). Regarding the grandiose self, he states: "The infantile grandiosity becomes gradually built into the ambitions and purposes of the personality and lends not only vigor to a person's mature strivings but also a sustaining positive feeling of the right to success" (p. 299). In my view, and on the basis of Kohut's published writings, his approach leads to a higher level functioning and better adaptation of the grandiose self, in the context of the patient's shift from more primitive to more adaptive levels of mirror transferences, without a basic resolution of what I consider the pathological structure of the grandiose self. This may well be the reason why, in Kohut's findings, there is no direct, specific relationship between the changes in the patient's narcissism and the patient's object relations. It seems to me that the effects of his approach, if not his intentions and technique, have reeducative elements in them which foster a more adaptive use of the patient's grandiosity. A major question, that necessarily must remain open at this point, is what are the long-range effects of such an approach, or, for that matter, of both Kohut's approach and the alternative one I have outlined? A major test of the effectiveness of the treatment of narcissistic personalities is the adaptation of these patients to the stress and crises which the later stages of life unavoidably will bring about. We will need careful follow-up over long periods of time in order to separate the short-range consequences of treatment from the long-term consequences on their personality, intrapsychic and social functioning. This brings me to the last issue of this chapter, namely, the prognosis of untreated narcissism.

I strongly agree with Kohut's conviction that narcissistic personality disorders should be treated by psychoanalysis whenever possible. Even in cases which are functioning quite successfully except for some relatively minor symptoms, and where the combination of intelligence, talents, luck, and success provide sufficient gratifications to compensate for the underlying emptiness and boredom, one should keep in mind the devastating effects that unresolved pathological narcissism often has during the second half of life. In my view, if psychoanalytic treatment can be carried out and is successful, improvement in these cases means a resolution of their pathological narcissism, the development of normal infantile and adult narcissism in the context of normal object relationships in depth, and what often amounts to a dramatic enrichment of life. In contrast, pathological narcissism has ominous long-range prognostic implications, even in cases of relatively young patients with excellent surface adaptation and very little awareness of illness or suffering on the patient's part. If we consider that throughout an ordinary life span most narcissistic gratifications occur in adolescence and early adulthood, and that even though narcissistic triumphs and gratifications are achieved throughout adulthood, the individual must eventually face the basic conflicts around aging, chronic illness, physical and mental limitations, and above all, separations, loss, and loneliness—then we must conclude that the eventual confrontation of the grandiose self with the frail, limited and transitory nature of human life is unavoidable.

It is dramatic how intense the denial of this long-range reality can be in narcissistic personalities, who under the influence of the pathological, grandiose self are unconsciously (and sometimes consciously) convinced of their eternal youth, beauty, power, wealth and the unending availability of supplies of confirmation, admiration, and security. For them, to accept the breakdown of the illusion of grandiosity means to accept the dangerous, lingering awareness of the depreciated self—the hungry, empty, lonely primitive self surrounded by a world of dangerous, sadistically frustrating and revengeful objects. Perhaps the most frightening experience that narcissistic personalities need to ward off and eventually may have to face is that of a surrounding world empty of love and human contact, a world of dehumanized objects within which animate as well as inanimate objects have lost their previous, magically satisfying qualities.

One patient, a nationally known politician, had developed a serious physical illness which brought about the loss of his professional functions. He became depressed and developed deep feelings of defeat and humiliation accompanied by fantasies in which his political opponents were gloating with satisfaction over his defeat. His depression diminished. He went into retirement, but gradually devaluated the areas of political science in which he had been an expert. This was a narcissistic depreciation of that in which he was no longer triumphant, which brought about a general loss of interest in professional, cultural and intellectual matters. His primary areas of professional and intellectual interests no longer seemed exciting and reminded him again and again of his failure. He was resentful of his dependency upon his wife and children, whom he had previously disregarded while dedicating all his energies to his professional life. His fears of being depreciated by his family motivated him toward ever increasing demands for reassurance and respect. Envious of the professional success of his children, and unable to obtain gratification of this success by means of empathic identification with them, he experienced an increasing sense of estrangement which finally evolved into the recurrence of a now severe, chronic depression, with a predominance of impotent rage over mourning processes as such.

The frightening sensation of futility and emptiness, the panic over the disintegration of the personal meaning of one's immediate environment that has been so dramatically evoked in the plays of Samuel Beckett, or in Eugene Ionesco's *The Chairs* and *Exit the King*, illustrate, it seems to me, the devastating effect of the conflicts of old age on persons with narcissistic personality. The normal reaction to loss, abandonment and failure is the reactivation of internalized sources of love and self-esteem intimately linked with internalized object relations, and reflects the protective function of what has been called "good internal objects." Regression in the service of the ego often takes the form of regression to such reactivated internalized object relations of a protective kind, a regression which in turn reactivates, strengthens and broadens the patient's capacity for meaningful relations with others and with humanity and value systems at large. The capacity to work through mourning processes, to be in love, to feel empathy and deep gratification in identifying with loved people and values, a sense of transcendence with nature, of continuation within the historical process, and of oneness with a social or cultural group, are all intimately linked to the normal activation of internalized object relationships at the time of loss, failure, and loneliness.

This is in striking contrast to the vicious circle triggered off by narcissistic loss in the case of narcissistic personalities, where defensive devaluation, primitive envy, and panic because of the reactivated sense of impoverishment further complicate narcissistic loss and failure. This becomes particularly evident in the narcissistic patient's inability to come to terms with old age, to accept the fact that a younger generation now possesses many of the previously cherished gratifications of beauty, wealth, power and, particularly, creativity. To be able to enjoy life in a process involving a growing identification with other people's happiness and achievements is tragically beyond the capacity of narcissistic personalities. Therefore treatment geared to radically changing pathological narcissism may show its ultimate benefits over the entire life span left to the patient.

The clinical study of narcissistic personalities illustrates that the relationships of the individual with himself and with his surrounding human and inanimate world depends upon the development of normal or pathological internalized object relations. The loss of the world of loving and loved internal objects brings about the loss of meaning of the self and of the world. Psychotic depression represents, in many ways, the terrifying stage of awareness of the loss of love and meaning against which narcissistic personalities need to defend themselves, and schizoid emotional dispersal or a paranoid—not necessarily psychotic—reorganization of the world represents an alternative protection for these patients against the bleakness of depression, but at the cost of bringing about further dehumanization and emptiness. Therefore, and in spite of the limited number of patients whom we are able to help and the very extensive analyses required in these cases, it seems worthwhile to invest much effort in the treatment of what so often on the surface, looks deceivingly as if we were dealing with an almost "normal" person.

## BIBLIOGRAPHY

1.   Abraham, K. (1919). A particular form of neurotic resistance against the psychoanalytic method. *Selected Papers*. London: Hogarth Press, 1927.
2.   Jacobson, E. (1954). Contribution to the metapsychology of psychotic identifications. *J. Am. Psychoanal. Ass.* 2, 239–262.
3.   ———, (1964). *The Self and the Object World*. New York: Int. Univ. Press.
4.   Kernberg, O. (1970). A psychoanalytic classification of character pathology. *J. Am. Psychoanal. Ass.* 18, 800–822.
5.   ———, (1971). New developments in psychoanalytic object-relations theory. Parts I and III: Normal and pathological development. (Paper read to the American Psychoanalytic Association.) (Unpublished)
6.   ———, (1972). Early ego integration and object relations. *Ann. N. Y. Acad. Sci.* 193, 233–247.
7.   Kernberg, P. (1971). The course of the analysis of a narcissistic personality with hysterical and compulsive features. *J. Am. Psychoanal. Ass.* 19, 451–471.
8.   Kohut, H. (1966). Forms and transformations of narcissism. *J. Am. Psychoanal. Ass.* 14, 243–272.
9.   ———, (1968). The psychoanalytic treatment of narcissistic personality disorders. *Psychoanal. Study Child* 23, 86–113.
10.  ———, (1971). *The Analysis of the Self*. New York: Int. Univ. Press.
11.  Mahler, M. S. (1968). *On Human Symbiosis and the Vicissitudes of Individuation*, vol. 1: *Infantile Psychosis*. New York: Int. Univ. Press.
12.  Riviere, J. (1936). A contribution to the analysis of the negative therapeutic reaction. *Int. J. Psycho-Anal.* 17, 304–320.

13. Rosenfeld, H. (1964). On the psychopathology of narcissism: a clinical approach. *Int. J. Psycho-Anal.* 45, 332–337.
14. Sandler, J. & Rosenblatt, B. (1962). The concept of the representational world. *Psychoanal. Study Child* 17.
15. Tartakoff, H. H. (1966). The normal personality in our culture and the Nobel Prize complex. In R. M. Loewenstein *et al.* (eds.), *Psychoanalysis: A General Psychology.* New York: Int. Univ. Press.
16. Ticho, E. (1970). Differences between psychoanalysis and psychotherapy. *Bull. Menninger Clin.* 34, 128–138.
17. Van der Waals, H. G. (1965). Problems of narcissism. *Bull. Menninger Clin.* 29, 293–311.

# Ten

# Normal and Pathological Narcissism

In earlier chapters (8 and 9), I have explored the diagnosis and treatment of narcissistic personalities, a specific constellation of character pathology requiring particular modifications of psychoanalytic or psychotherapeutic technique. I have reviewed elsewhere the metapsychological issues underlying the clinical exploration of narcissism (9, 10). I will now outline a summary of the characteristics of normal and pathological narcissism, focus on the underlying structural intrapsychic conditions involved, and spell out their diagnostic and therapeutic implications. Because the term "narcissism" has been used in such a variety of ways over the years, I think it would be helpful to define it first, and then offer a conceptualization of narcissism in terms of intrapsychic structure. Such a structural analysis of narcissism is especially useful in clarifying the distinction between normal and pathological narcissism.

## DEFINITION OF NORMAL NARCISSISM

Following Hartmann (5), I define normal narcissism as the libidinal investment of the self. The self is an intrapsychic structure consisting of multiple self representations and their related affect dispositions. Self representations are affective-cognitive structures reflecting the person's perception of himself in real interactions with significant others and in fantasied interactions with internal representations of significant others, that is, with object representations. The self is part of the ego, which contains, in addition, the object represen-tations mentioned before, and also ideal self-images and ideal object-images at various stages of depersonification, abstrac-tion and integration. The normal self is integrated, in that its component self representations are dynamically organized into a comprehensive whole. The self relates to integrated object representations, that is, to object representations which have incorporated the "good" and "bad" primitive object represen-tations into integrative images of others in depth; by the same token, the self represents an integration of contradictory, "all good" and "all bad" self-images derived from libidinally invested and aggressively invested early self-images.

Therefore, although normal narcissism reflects the libidinal investment of the self, the self actually constitutes a structure that integrates libidinally invested and aggressively invested components; in simple terms, integration of good and bad self-images into a realistic self-concept that incorporates rather than dissociates the various component self represen-tations is a requisite for the libidinal investment of a normal self. This also explains the paradox that integration of love and hatred is a prerequisite for the capacity for normal love.

This definition of the self and of integrated object representations corresponds quite closely to the description of the "representational world" of Sandler and Rosenblatt (16), and to Erikson's definition of ego identity (3). Clinically, an integrated self is characterized by a continuity of the self experience both historically (or throughout time) and cross-sectionally (or throughout simultaneously existing areas of functioning in different psychosocial interactions). Absence of an integrated self is recognized clinically by the existence of contradictory, mutually dissociated or split-off ego states that alternate without ever being integrated. In this case, the individual can "remember" how he felt during experiences opposite to the present one without, however, ever being able to integrate these various experiences. A lack of an integrated self is also characterized by chronic feelings of unreality, puzzlement, emptiness, or general disturbances in the "self feeling"(7) as well as in a marked incapacity to perceive oneself realistically as a total human being. Under these circumstances, the patient may have "insight" in terms of conscious availability of primitive intrapsychic processes, but he can never integrate such primitive cognitive and affective experiences with higher level ones, nor can he integrate subjective experiences at large with the impact of his actual behavior in the interpersonal realm. Insofar as a lack of an integrated self usually coexists with a lack of integration of object representations, these latter are caricatures of superficial, "all good" or "all bad," and the patient has great difficulty integrating the perception of others into a significant whole; therefore, he has no or very little capacity for empathy or for realistic judgment of others in depth, and his behavior is regulated by immediate perceptions rather than by an ongoing, consistent, internalized model of others, which ordinarily would be available to the self.

Returning now to the definition of narcissism as the libidinal investment of the self: It needs to be stressed that such a libidinal investment of the self does not stem simply from an instinctual source of libidinal energy, but from the many relationships between the self and other intrapsychic structures. These include structures within the ego (intrasystemic determinants of narcissism) and structures in other psychic apparatuses, that is, the superego and the id (intersystemic determinants of narcissism).

Jacobson (7) has pointed out that the normal "self feeling" derives from the individual's awareness of an integrated self, while "self esteem" or "self regard" depend upon the libidinal investment of such an integrated self. The level or intensity of self-esteem or self-regard indicates the extent to which there is a narcissistic investment of the self. Self-esteem or self-regard is, however, not simply a reflection of "instinctual cathexes": it always reflects a combination of affective and cognitive components, with the predominance of diffuse affective components at more primitive levels of regulation of self-esteem, and a predominance of cognitive differentiation with "toned-down" affective implications at more advanced levels of regulation of self-esteem. Self-esteem or self-regard represents, therefore, the more differentiated levels of narcissistic investment, while diffuse feelings of well-being, of pleasure with existence, of affective states expressing euphoria or satisfaction, represent the more primitive expressions of narcissism. Thus, as Jacobson has pointed out (7), mood swings are the main indicators of self-regard at primitive levels of superego-determined regulation of self-esteem. At more advanced levels of superego functioning, more precise, delimited cognitive appreciation or criticism of the self replaces the regulation by mood swings.

Because the structures influencing the instinctual investment of the self do so not only in terms of affective and cognitive libidinal investments, but also in terms of aggressively invested interactions, the regulation of normal narcissism can be understood only in terms of the relative predominance of libidinal over aggressive investment by these same intrapsychic structures. Clinically speaking, narcissistic and libidinal investment at large can be understood fully only in the context of a simultaneous analysis of the intrapsychic vicissitudes of libido and aggression.

Which are the intrapsychic structures and the external factors influencing the libidinal investment of the self, that is, normal narcissism?

## 1.  The Ideal Self and Ego Goals

Within the ego itself, the unconscious, preconscious and conscious ego goals (reflecting various stages of development from the primitive ideal self-images to mature goals) represent the level of aspiration, we might say, against which the actuality of the self is measured. As Hartmann (5) pointed out, in addition to the superego-originated self-criticism, there are self-critical functions of the ego, and regulation of self-esteem is achieved by such self-criticism. Bibring (1) described a core predisposition to depression in the ego experience of helplessness and hopelessness when an aspired state of the self is not achieved or is lost. Sandler and Rosenblatt (16) referred to this mechanism in describing the tensions between real and ideal self.

## 2.  Object Representations

An additional structure of the ego involved in regulation of self-esteem, that is, in the provision of narcissistic supplies or libidinal investment of the self, is the world of inner objects or object representations intimately relating to the integrated self. I have earlier referred (9) to the protective functions of object representations at times of life crises or object loss, and have suggested that regression in the service of the ego may be understood in part as a regressive activation of past internalized object relations, in which "good" object representations supply the self with love and reconfirmation in compensation for the disappointments in reality.

## 3.  Superego Factors

Two major structures of the superego regulate self-esteem. The first consists of the various levels of superego structures which carry out a critical assessment of the ego in terms of superego demands and punishment. Jacobson's (7) analysis of levels of superego development and their regulatory effects upon the self by functions ranging from moods to realistic self-criticism is relevant here. The critical or punitive aspects of the superego regulate self-esteem by a predominantly "negative" function of providing criticism of the self. The other superego structure involved in self-esteem regulation is the ego ideal (which results from the integration of ideal object-images and ideal self-images introjected into the superego from infancy and early childhood on) which increases self-esteem when the self lives up to its demands and expectations. Schafer (17) has referred to this protective function of the ego ideal. Clinically, it is dramatic to observe how over-dependent some patients become on external sources of admiration, love, and confirmation when they suffer from an absence or inadequate integration of this particular superego structure.

## 4.  Instinctual and Organic Factors

Turning now to structures related to the id: when basic instinctual needs are met and when the self has been able to satisfactorily negotiate its internal needs with the requirements of the environment, there is an increase in self-esteem. In other words, direct ego-syntonic expression of impulses and, particularly, sublimatory expression of instinctual needs bring about narcissistic gratification. General good health reconfirms both the integrity and the libidinal investment of the self. Because the original self representations are strongly influenced by body images and because the earliest intrapsychic instinctual gratification is closely linked to the re-establishment of physiological equilibria, physical health and illness significantly influence the normal and abnormal equilibrium of narcissistic investment.

## 5.  External Factors

The reality factors influencing the normal regulation of self-esteem may be classified into: 1) libidinal gratifications stemming from external objects; 2) gratification of ego goals and aspirations in social effectiveness or success; and 3) gratification of intellectual or cultural aspirations realized in the environment. These latter gratifications contain value elements and reflect superego and ego demands as well as reality factors. They reflect the importance that cultural, ethical, and esthetic value systems have in regulating self-esteem, in addition to the psychosocial and psychobiological systems mentioned earlier.

In summary, there is an increase of libidinal investment of the self with love or gratification from external objects, success in reality, increase of harmony between the self and superego structures, reconfirmation of love from internal objects, and direct instinctual gratification and physical health.

Normally, an increase of libidinal investment of the self also results in an increase in the libidinal investment in objects: a self with increased libidinal investment, at peace and happy with itself, so to speak, is able to invest more in external objects and their internalized representations. In general, when there is an increase of narcissistic investment, there is a parallel increase in the capacity to love and to give, to experience and express gratitude, to have concern for others, and for an increase in sexual love, sublimation, and creativity. Because normal libidinal investment of external objects and their internal representations is intimately linked to the overcoming of more primitive, mutually dissociated or split expression of love and hate toward objects, an increase of libidinal investment of the self also reassures the self of its "goodness" toward objects and reinforces object ties. Metaphorically speaking, the charging of the battery of the self induces secondarily a recharging of the battery of libidinal investment in objects.

There is a decrease of libidinal investment of the self under such circumstances as loss of external sources of love, failure to obtain ego goals or live up to ego expectations, superego pressures reactive to instinctual urges unacceptable to the superego, inability to live up to the expectations of the ego ideal, general frustration of instinctual needs, or physical illness. Loss or failure in any one of these areas may reverberate in other areas. In pathological mourning, for example, the narcissistic injury resulting from the external loss of an object is reinforced by an increase of superego pressures reflecting unconscious guilt over the loss of the object, and a secondary weakening of the libidinal investment that the self receives from object representations; superego pressure persuades the self that it no longer deserves the love of its internal, as well as of its external objects. Hence, the various intrapsychic structures that regulate the libidinal investment of the self cannot be seen in isolation from each other, but rather, in an overall dynamic equilibrium.

For example, the working-through process of normal mourning involves not only a re-establishment of libidinal cathexes of the self (by identificatory processes by means of which the self acquires characteristics and libidinal investment of the lost object), but also, and very importantly, the restoration or strengthening of the object representations reflecting the lost object and other related "good" internalized objects; in turn, the libidinal investment of internalized objects strengthens the availability of them as potential sources of libidinal gratification for the self.

Normal narcissism depends on the structural integrity of the self and of the other related intrapsychic structures mentioned before. Normal narcissism also depends on the equilibrium between libidinal and aggressive drive derivatives involved in the relations between the self and all these other structures. Aggressive investment of the self stemming from the various structures regulating narcissism mentioned and from external reality all decrease self-esteem. In addition, normal narcissism depends on the developmental level achieved by the self and the related intrapsychic structures in terms of the adult quality and maturity (in contrast to infantile features) of self-expectations, aspirations, models, and ideals. For example, there may be a structural integrity of the self and the superego and the ego ideal, and an integration of internalized object relations, and yet a fixation at infantile narcissistic goals and conflicts. This constellation is typical of most patients with neurotic reactions and character pathology.

## PATHOLOGICAL NARCISSISM

In general, all neurotic conflicts interfere with the optimal relationships of the self with the various instances and structures mentioned. Pathologically severe prohibitions against sexual impulses, for example (because of their unresolved oedipal implications) are reflected in conflictual relationships of the self with external objects, excessive superego pressures on the self, and reduction in the sublimatory potential of the ego, all of which affect the availability of libidinal supplies of the self in various ways. At the same time, the establishment of pathological character patterns as defenses against direct conflictual relations with others and direct confrontation with the forbidden oedipal impulses protect the functioning of the ego and the self; they also protect self-esteem, that is, they have a narcissistic function. Therefore, all patients with neurotic reactions and character pathology have "narcissistic problems": there is a pathological vulnerability of the self, defended against by the pathological character traits, so that when these traits are explored and resolved analytically, narcissistic frustrations and conflicts become activated. It is then that one discovers how the content of ego expectations, goals, and superego demands have remained at an infantile level, in contrast to mature narcissistic aspirations and expectations of the more conflict free areas of the ego.

In general, activation of conflicts around aggression (which reduce the availability or predominance of libidinal investment of the self and of internal and external objects) together with fixation at or regression to neurotic infantile conflicts imbedded in a relatively well-integrated ego and self represent a broad source of frustration and/or distortion of normal narcissism. All these constitute the mildest form of narcissistic disturbance that can be encountered clinically.

A more severe type of narcissistic disturbance can be found in cases where the self has developed pathological identificatory processes to such an extent that it is modeled predominantly on a pathogenic internalized object, while important aspects of the self (as relating to such an object) have been projected onto object representations and external objects. This severer type of narcissistic pathology refers to individuals who (in their intrapsychic life of object relations and in their external life) identify with an object and love an object standing for their (present or past) self. Freud (4) pointed out that the homosexuals' selection of love objects who represented themselves was a major reason which led him to adopt the thesis of narcissism. He considered the love relations of such homosexuals "narcissistic," in contrast to the "anaclitic" or attachment type of love to an object that represents a significant parental image. In order to examine this situation further, let us review once more the libidinal implications of a normal object relation.

The normal relation with an object represents an optimal mixture of "object libidinal" and "narcissistic" ties, in that the investment of objects and the investment of the self in the gratifying relation with such objects go hand in hand (18). Within such a context of a libidinal relation of the self to an object, however, the nature of the object relation may be more or less infantile, so that the self may relate to the object along a spectrum ranging from a purely "anaclitic," child-like search for love—in which dependency, demandingness, and gratitude are mixed—to an adult type of reciprocity, in which a mature, enlightened self-love is condensed with a mature investment of the object in depth. Both adult and infantile narcissism include "self-centeredness," but the self-investment of normal adult narcissism is in terms of mature goals, ideals and expectations, whereas the normal infantile self-investment is in terms of infantile, exhibitionistic, demanding, and power-oriented strivings. And both adult and normal infantile narcissism include object investment, again differing in terms of adult reciprocity versus infantile idealization and dependent orientation. "Anaclitic" relationships, therefore, include regressive features in both self-investment and object-investment, that is, a regression from the adult mixture of narcissistic and object-related investments to the infantile type of mixture of these ties.

The developmental state of the superego (particularly the ego ideal) and the nature of the predominant outcome of the oedipal conflicts (for example, the predominance of fixation and/or regression to pregenital libidinal phases) influence the degree to which any object relation is "anaclitic"; that is, the degree to which there is a regression or fixation to normal infantile characteristics in which the dependent needs color both the self and the object investment in that relationship. In short, normal object relations involve a mixture of narcissistic and object investment, and the nature of narcissistic and object ties varies according to the general level of psychological development. Freud's "anaclitic" type of object love refers to regressive infantile features in both the narcissistic and the object investment of that relationship.

Let us now return to the more severe type of narcissistic disturbance mentioned before. When the libidinal investment of the self is carried out under the condition of an identification of the self with an object, while the self is projected onto an external object that is loved because it stands for the self, the situation is completely different from the normal characteristics of narcissism mentioned before. This type of object relation, which Freud was the first to call "narcissistic," represents a qualitatively different and more severe type of narcissistic pathology than the milder one mentioned before (which simply reflected a regression to and/or fixation at infantile—in contrast to mature—libidinal investment of both self and object). It needs to be stressed, however, that within this more pathological relation of the self identified with an object (for example, in some cases of male homosexuality, with the orally giving and protective mother) to an object identified with the self (the infantile, dependent self in the cases of male homosexuality mentioned), an object relation still exists:

namely, a relation between self and object, both intrapsychically and in external interactions.

A still severer type of narcissistic pathology is characterized by a more profound deterioration of object relations, in which the relation is no longer between self and object but between a primitive, pathological, grandiose self and the temporary projection of that same grandiose self onto objects. ("Grandiose self" is a term suggested by Kohut (11), which I am using in agreement with his clinical description, but in the context of a different metapsychological analysis from the one he proposes). Here the relation is no longer of self to object, nor of object to self, but of self to self. It is really only in this latter case that one may say that a narcissistic relationship has replaced an object relationship.

This is a very different situation from what occurs under some normal circumstances, such as in adolescence, when mutual identifications occur with other objects as representations of the self simultaneously with the consideration of these objects as such, in their own right. Temporary or partial projection of an ideal self in normal friendships of early adolescence (which may include derivatives of homosexual conflicts and infantile libidinal investments) onto an object perceived as similar to the self go hand in hand with object-libidinal ties to such an object, and have a quality entirely different from the projection of a pathological grandiose self onto other objects. I have analyzed these differences in detail in earlier chapters (8 and 9).

The relation of a pathological grandiose self to a temporarily projected pathological grandiose self is characteristic of the narcissistic personality, a specific type of character pathology representing the most severe form of pathological narcissism.

The three levels of pathology of narcissism referred to so far: 1) regression from normal adult to normal infantile narcissism, 2) the relation to an object that represents the self while the self is identified with that object, and 3) the relation of a grandiose self to a temporarily projected grandiose self, all present an integrated structure of the self. Such an integrated self may be a regressed or infantile fixated-self, a distorted self because of predominant identifications with an object, or a pathological grandiose self (characteristic of narcissistic personalities). In contrast to all these conditions, there are other patients who present a lack of an integrated self (generally dissociated or split-off self and object representations): patients presenting borderline personality organization (without the condensation of a pathological, grandiose self structure). In these cases one observes rapid shifts from identifications with a certain self representation, accompanied by projection of a certain object representation onto the external object, to identification with an object representation, accompanied by a projection of a certain self representation onto the external object. In these cases, object relations are shifting and unstable, and chaotic alternation of various types of narcissistic disturbances occurs. It seems preferable not to consider these cases as a particular pathology of narcissism, but rather as representing a general pathology of internalized object relations. Finally, there are cases where lack of differentiation between self and object representations predominates, that is, cases presenting psychotic identifications (6, 7). Here, psychotic conflicts and defenses generally predominate over narcissistic and object-libidinal investments reflecting differentiated relations with others. I do not think that efforts to differentiate object from self investments are relevant under these circumstances; self and object are still (or again) merged.

A general implication of all I have said so far for the clinical theory of narcissism is that economic considerations alone (that is, considerations of intensity or amount of narcissistic investment) do not really say much about the normal or pathological nature of narcissism; they simply reflect the intensity of the general metabolism, so to speak, of internalized object relations. Also, the intensity of libidinal investment of self and objects is intimately related to, and changes in the context of, changing investment of aggression; therefore, economic considerations need to incorporate the combined analysis of aggressive and libidinal ties. Another general implication of this analysis is that efforts to identify narcissistic versus object-related investments of external objects in terms of predominantly interpersonal observations of the nature of the relationship with them would, it seems to me, bring about the loss of the most specific aspects of psychoanalytic thinking regarding normal and pathological narcissism, and would replace them with a simplistic psychosocial model along the lines of "introversion" and "extroversion." The nature of normal and pathological narcissism can be ascertained only by psychoanalytic exploration of intrapsychic, in addition to external object relations, and by a structural analysis of internalized object relations in addition to the examination of economic factors affecting them.

## SOME DIAGNOSTIC APPLICATIONS OF THIS CONCEPTUALIZATION OF NARCISSISTIC PATHOLOGY

One important practical problem is the differentiation of normal from pathological narcissistic developments in adolescence. Deutsch (2) and Jacobson (7) have pointed out that during adolescence there is an increase in manifestations of narcissism. It seems to me that this increase has to be understood not merely in quantitative terms, but also in qualitative terms—that is, in terms of the continuum of various constellations of self and object investment as they emerge in the adolescent's intrapsychic structure.

First, the most normal manifestation of adolescent increase in narcissism is the increase of libidinal investment of the self in the form of self-absorption, increased concern over the self, and grandiose, exhibitionistic, or power-oriented fantasies which reflect both a quantitative shift of libidinal investment from object to self representations, and a qualitative, regressive shift toward more infantile relations between the self and object— for example, the infantile wish to be loved and admired by mother.

A second, more pathological type of adolescent increase in narcissism reflects a pathological identification of the self with infantile objects, and the search for objects that represent the infantile self. As I mentioned before, this is different from the normal increase in early adolescence of object choices presenting features similar to the self while these objects are also invested with authentic interest and love: in this case, narcissistic and object directed investments are amalgamated.

In contrast, in more pathological narcissistic developments, the projection of the self onto the object replaces the object tie, while the self, in the interaction with such an object, represents the object of the reactivated internalized infantile object relation. Some homosexual developments in adolescence are related to this type of narcissistic regression.

Third, and even more pathological, one may find in some adolescents an orientation toward objects that reflect, on psychoanalytic exploration, the projection of a primitive, pathological, grandiose self onto the object, while the patient still maintains this grandiose self, that is, the "self to self" relation referred to before. This is the case of the narcissistic personality structure, and represents the most severe type of narcissistic pathology in adolescence as well as adulthood. Clinically speaking, one finds in these adolescent patients the characteristic grandiosity, contempt, lack of capacity for subtle discrimination of realistic aspects of others, self-righteousness and exploitative or parasitic trends. They also typically present periods of driven investment in activities and relationships that bring about triumph, admiration, or immediate need gratification, alternating with periods of precipitate abandonment of tasks, relationships, and activities that fail to provide sustainment for their grandiosity—they withdraw from and devaluate aspects of social reality to protect themselves against failure.

In general, the more normal the increase of narcissistic investment in adolescence, the more we can describe it in quantitative terms—although a qualitative element is always present. The more pathological the narcissistic shifts, the less they can be understood in quantitative terms alone, and the more we need to clarify the situation structurally, that is, clarify the nature of the pathological object relations involved.

As another application of this structural analysis of narcissism, let us now examine various types of male homosexuality. We may classify male homosexuality along a continuum that differentiates the degree of severity of pathology of internalized object relations. First, there are cases of homosexuality with a predominance of genital, oedipal factors, in which the homosexual relation reflects a sexual submission to the parent of the same sex as a defense against oedipal rivalry. These cases represent the most neurotic and inhibited type of homosexual patients and usually have the best prognosis for psychoanalytic treatment. In these cases, the infantile submissive oedipal self relates to the domineering, prohibitive oedipal father, and this type of male homosexual frequently presents an underlying repression of heterosexual strivings as a consequence of the renunciation of the sexual impulses toward the forbidden oedipal mother.

In a second and more severe type, the male homosexual has a conflictual identification with an image of his mother and treats his homosexual objects as a representation of his own infantile self. In this type of narcissistic investment (the one mentioned by Freud in his 1914 paper on narcissism) the investment of the external homosexual object is indeed, "narcissistic," in the sense that the homosexual object stands for the self. However, although this type of homosexuality is more narcissistic than the one mentioned earlier, it needs to be stressed that there is still an object relation (namely, that between mother and child) enacted in this homosexual tie. The prognosis for this type of homosexuality is more reserved than for the one previously mentioned. Usually, pregenital conflicts predominate over genital ones in these cases, and they present more serious disturbances in their object relations. Various types of severe character pathology are consistent with this type of homosexuality. However, these patients are able to love their objects deeply, if neurotically; and at times their motherly concern for their homosexual partner contains elements of parental identifications which have sublimatory functions and give depth to the relation to the object so that narcissistic and object-related features are both present.

In a third type of homosexual relation, the homosexual partner is "loved" as an extension of the patient's own pathological grandiose self, and hence we find the relation, not from self to object, nor from object to self, but from (pathological grandiose) self to self. This, the most severe type of homosexual involvement, is characteristic of homosexuality in the context of narcissistic personality structure proper, and constitutes the prognostically most severe type of homosexuality. Paradoxically, however, because patients with narcissistic personality structure and a pathological grandiose self often present a better surface functioning than less severe types of character pathology (Chapter 8), some of the socially better functioning homosexuals may actually have the most severe type of homosexual pathology. In these cases, the investment of objects representing the projected grandiose self is usually transitory and superficial; and there is a lack of awareness in depth of or empathy for the object, which corresponds to the lack of integration of both object representations and the real— in contrast to the pathological grandiose—self.

Therefore, the definition of narcissism along the continuum just described, from normal adult to the most severe pathological relation of self to self has eminently practical consequences for diagnosis, prognosis, and treatment. Although most cases of symptomatic neuroses and the less severe or "higher level" types of character pathology (8) present some degree of fixation and/or regression to normal infantile narcissism—with a consequent increase of fantasies and ideals reflecting various types of infantile grandiosity, exhibitionism, and demandingness—this regression does not have particular diagnostic, prognostic, and therapeutic implications. One needs to keep in mind, however, that pathological character traits in all of these cases do have as one function the protection of self-esteem, and therefore, analytic efforts to modify a neurotic character structure always include the implication of a narcissistic lesion (14).

Those cases in which there is a pathological identification of the self with an infantile object and in which the choice of external objects is made in terms of the projection of the self onto such objects usually present more severe types of character pathology and important homosexual conflicts. Although the narcissistic nature of their relation with objects is more predominant, such patients usually do not require specific modifications of psychoanalytic technique. Even when they present manifest or suppressed homosexuality the prognosis for exploratory psychotherapy or psychoanalysis is not unfavorable.

The third, and most severe type of pathological narcissism is that characteristic of narcissistic personalities proper. I have described these elsewhere (Chapters 8 and 9), and will only summarize this syndrome here. These patients present excessive self-absorption hand in hand with a superficially smooth and effective social adaption, but with serious distortions in their internal relations with other people. They present various combinations of intense ambitiousness, grandiose fantasies, feelings of inferiority, and overdependence on external admiration and acclaim; they suffer from chronic feelings of boredom and emptiness, are constantly searching for gratification of strivings for brilliance, wealth, power, and beauty, and have serious deficiencies in their capacity to love and to be concerned about others. Other predominant characteristics include a lack of capacity for empathetic understanding of others, chronic uncertainty and dissatisfaction with their life, conscious or unconscious exploitiveness and ruthlessness towards others and, particularly, the presence of chronic, intense envy and defenses against such envy.

The prognosis for psychoanalysis and all kinds of psychotherapeutic treatment is more guarded in these cases than in all the earlier ones mentioned, although it has improved as a result of recent progress in psychoanalytic technique; sexual deviations presenting in patients with this type of character pathology are often quite resistant to treatment.

## THE TREATMENT OF
## NARCISSISTIC PERSONALITIES

There has been some confusion in the literature over the relationship between the narcissistic personality and borderline conditions in general. Summarizing what I have said elsewhere on this issue (Chapters 8 and 9) the structural characteristics of the ego and the defensive organization of narcissistic personalities are both strikingly similar to and specifically different from borderline personality organization.

The similarity with borderline conditions resides in the predominance of mechanisms of splitting or primitive dissociation as reflected in the presence of mutually dissociated or split-off ego states. Thus, haughty grandiosity, shyness, and feelings of inferiority may co-exist in narcissistic personalities without affecting each other. Splitting mechanisms are reinforced by primitive types of projection and idealization, by omnipotent control, narcissistic withdrawal, and devaluation: all these defenses are characteristic of both borderline personality organization and narcissistic personalities.

The difference between narcissistic personality structure and borderline conditions is that, in the former there is an integrated although highly pathological "grandiose self," a term suggested by Kohut (11). In my thinking, this grandiose self is a pathological condensation of rudiments of the real self, the ideal self, and the ideal objects of infancy and early childhood, and thus incorporates some components that would otherwise become integrated into the superego. As a result, superego integration is defective, ego and superego boundaries are blurred in certain areas, and the entire intrapsychic world of object relations deteriorates; it is replaced by the grandiose self and by devalued, shadowy representations of self and others and potentially persecutory images representing the non-integrated sadistic superego-forerunners. The pathological grandiose self compensates for the primitive dissociation or splitting of the self, but at the price of a deterioration of object relations much more severe than that of nonnarcissistic borderline patients.

The pathological grandiose self explains the narcissistic patients' paradox of relatively good surface functioning and social adaptation in the presence of a predominance of splitting mechanisms and severe ego pathology. However, there are some narcissistic personalities who function on what I have called an overt borderline level, that is, they present the nonspecific manifestations of ego weakness characteristic of borderline personality organization, including severe lack of anxiety tolerance, generalized lack of impulse control, striking absence of subliminatory channeling, and primary-process thinking—evident on psychological testing.

In practice, one can differentiate three levels of functioning of narcissistic personalities. First, there are narcissistic personalities whose surface adaptation is more effective, and who present talents, skills, and/or high intelligence which grant them outstanding success in their social life and provide them with unusual availability of gratification from external sources in the form of success and admiration. These patients would not come for treatment unless they presented some serious neurotic symptoms, sexual disturbances, or chronic difficulties in intimate relations with others—in their marriage, for instance. One might say that their gains from their illness often compensate for the disturbances that stem from the pathology of their object relations. Because of the devastating effects of pathological narcissism on the adjustment to later stages of life, these patients, in spite of their good surface functioning, should be treated.

However, insofar as the treatment of choice in these cases is psychoanalysis, and psychoanalytic treatment requires a certain initial motivation to help withstand the serious increase of anxiety and awareness of conflicts unavoidable during analytic treatment, the decision of whether to treat or not sometimes becomes quite difficult. At times it may be preferable to provide the patient with immediate, short-term psychotherapeutic support in an acute crisis and wait for further increase in self-awareness or frustrations in real life—to which these patients are particularly prone—and start psychoanalytic treatment later. I have recently become more optimistic about the treatment of some of these patients who start their analysis in their late thirties and forties, even though lengthy psychoanalytic treatment may be involved.

A second group of patients, representing the majority of narcissistic personalities who come for treatment, are those with severe disturbances in object relations along the lines mentioned in the clinical definition of this syndrome. They frequently present complicating neurotic symptoms and sexual difficulties, and are disturbed by the serious defects in their capacity for establishing lasting emotional and sexual relationships and by their chronic feelings of emptiness. The treatment of choice for these cases is psychoanalysis, and recent developments in the psychoanalytic technique geared to these patients have made the prognosis much better (Chapter 9). Although a controversy exists at present regarding the technical theories and approaches to the psychoanalytic treatment of these patients between Kohut (11, 12) on the one hand, and other authors, including myself, on the other (7, 15, 18), I wish to stress the basic agreement, as I see it, between Kohut and myself regarding the clinical description of the syndrome of the narcissistic personality on this middle spectrum of cases, and regarding the definite indication of psychoanalysis for them.

The third group of narcissistic personalities is represented by patients who function overtly on a borderline level and, as mentioned before, present nonspecific manifestations of ego weakness. I have elsewhere (Chapters 8 and 9) recommended a mostly supportive psychotherapeutic approach to this group. More recently, however, I have become impressed with the possibility of treating them with a supportive-expressive psychotherapy. This technical approach requires that the more blatant defensive operations in the transference that are producing a devaluation of the therapist (and unconscious destruction of the knowlege and help received from him) be interpreted, while other aspects of the grandiose self are respected, and a gradual re-educative effort is made to render the patients' narcissism more adaptive and "toned down."

Some narcissistic patients with overt borderline functioning, particularly those who present intense rage reactions or "narcissistic rage," may require an expressive psychotherapeutic approach; I have recently attempted to carry out in some of these cases the general expressive psychotherapeutic approach that I have recommended for the treatment of borderline personality organization in general (Chapter 3). Unfortunately, their tendency to develop severe types of negative therapeutic reaction often brings treatment to a premature interruption. In general, the prognosis for this subgroup of narcissistic patients with chronic rage who function on a borderline level is guarded.

Finally, patients with narcissistic personality and overt borderline functioning who also present strong antisocial features have a very poor prognosis. This, of course, is maximally true for antisocial personalities proper who, in addition to generally extreme distortions and deterioration of superego functions and object relations, present typical narcissistic defensive structures.

I have outlined the psychoanalytic treatment of narcissistic personalities elsewhere (Chapters 8 and 9) and will not repeat myself here. The general strategy described in the discussion of the initial phase of treatment of borderline patients (Chapter 6), applies specifically to the therapeutic work with narcissistic patients functioning on an overt borderline level. There are some particular technical problems that narcissistic patients present, and I will limit myself here to mentioning some of these predominant technical problems of psychotherapy (in contrast to psychoanalysis) with these patients.

One major problem in many cases is the need to focus on what appears as pathological or contradictory dependency on the therapist. The patient seems to be asking the therapist to do something for him all the time, to give him "more," to come up with "new formulations," while at the same time, the patient is unconsciously depreciating the psychotherapeutic work, that which he is actually receiving from the therapist. Psychotherapy takes on the aspect of a search for "magic food," in contrast to the patient's acceptance of the real contributions by the therapist. Underlying this problem one regularly finds unconscious envy of the therapist's capacity and skills, of his knowledge, understanding, and convictions, and the need to spoil or destroy these skills in the actual psychotherapeutic relationship. These patients attempt to replace real contributions from the therapist with "magic" ones, which, by definition, can be magically incorporated by the patient without having to acknowledge any gratitude to the therapist or having to experience envy for what the therapist realistically has and the patient does not have. As the "magic" wears off or is, in turn, destroyed by the patient's sense that no really significant relation or work is building up in the hours, increasing demands on the therapist, an uncanny sensation of emptiness and rage because of the frustrations in the treatment develop, further intensify the envy of the therapist, and create vicious circles threatening the very continuation of the treatment.

Another major technical problem with these patients is their very low frustration tolerance; they combine nonspecific aspects of ego weakness and specific narcissistic vulnerability, and feel easily hurt or rejected because of minor frustrations from or shortcomings of the therapist. The therapist's awareness of their vulnerabilities to narcissistic frustrations and their reactive rage reactions and/or protective withdrawal in their extratherapeutic interactions may help him to point out not only how and why they avoid getting involved in work, in social relationships, in marriage, but also how the need to escape from feared frustrations and rage about them operates in the transference, in the patient's hypersensitivity to the therapist and his narcissistic withdrawal from or rage with the therapist. A related issue is these patients' hypersensitivity to any "failure"; to them "failures" often mean not being able to be the first, the only one, or the preferred one in a competitive situation. Inhibition of their competitiveness may be interpreted erroneously as an inhibition of oedipal rivalry, rather than stemming from the narcissistic vulnerability of the grandiose self. It is often possible to help them become aware of the fact that they have to be the winners of any competition or they will be unable to participate at all; this is a frequent mechanism in school failures of borderline narcissistic adolescent patients.

Another frequent problem, particularly of narcissistic men in their relations with women, is the presence of intense, paranoid fears of sexual involvement, derived from their unconscious projection of their own hostility (toward primitive mother images) onto the women with whom they get involved. These fears may determine chronic social and sexual isolation, and contribute to the development of stalemates in the transference. The transference relationship is safe because it is "asexual," and may represent the only available object relation in the patient's life, actually replacing the patient's efforts to improve his social functioning. It is frequently possible to reduce these paranoid reactions and improve the nature of these patient's sexual relationships without full exploration or resolution of the underlying conflicts: the excessive demandingness, the arrogant, parasitic, and exploitive relationships these patients develop with women as well as in other interpersonal interactions, may be tactfully explored and modified by supportive, reeducative means.

The therapist's direct encouragement of adaptive usage of the patient's narcissistic needs, and the therapist's support of better solutions that the patient finds in conflictual areas of his life may at times be very effective, because this direct support reinforces the patient's unconscious tendency to incorporate what he sees as significant aspects of the psychotherapist. In other words, the patient "learns" from the therapist in an unconscious effort to "take away" from him and make "his own" what he would otherwise envy in him.

In general terms, a narcissistic identification with an idealized and envied image of the therapist, an image that has become more realistic and toned down as a result of the therapist's partial acceptance and partial interpretation of this idealization, may occur as a consequence of introjection by the patient of this ideal image into his grandiose self, thus producing a more adaptive utilization of this pathological structure in his daily life. This mechanism (of projection and modified reintrojection of a primitive idealization related to the grandiose self) may be helpful both in the most severe types of narcissistic personality functioning on an overt borderline level, and in the most effectively functioning ones who consult a psychiatrist for an immediate traumatic situation but are unwilling or unable to explore their underlying personality difficulties in depth. Sometimes a brief crisis intervention of a supportive kind can be highly effective with a generally well-functioning narcissistic personality. However, I think that we owe it to our patients to consider in every case of narcissistic personality whether psychoanalytic treatment is indicated and whether there are particular contraindications to it. I have seen narcissistic patients who have refused the recommendation of psychoanalytic treatment for their pathological character structure, but who have eventually come back to treatment, months or even many years later, and obtained significant psychoanalytic help in modifying their subtle and yet devastating character pathology. Sometimes the best treatment for a patient with narcissistic personality and highly effective social functioning, who consults for an acute crisis situation, is to provide him with short-term, supportive psychotherapy, and to suggest the possibility of psychoanalytic treatment as a long-range plan for later on.

Returning once more to the treatment of narcissistic

personalities who function on an overt borderline level, one final technical problem is that of severe acting out, particularly of narcissistic rage. Acting out needs to be controlled, first by means of interpretive efforts, and then, if these are not effective, by a sufficient degree of structuring of the patient's life outside the treatment hours. Under these latter circumstances, aggressive behavior needs to be brought under control in the hours as well, and then interpreted—including the interpretation of the patient's perception of the therapist's intervention. The general strategy and technique for dealing with uncontrollable acting out in borderline cases applies here (Chapter 6).

In conclusion, psychoanalytic psychotherapy with patients presenting a narcissistic personality with overt borderline features should include supportive and expressive elements, and combine the general strategy of treatment of borderline patients with the specific technical approaches derived from recently developed knowledge regarding the optimal psychoanalytic technique with less regressed narcissistic patients. Although we do not yet possess as systematic an approach in this psychotherapy as we do for a standard psychoanalytic procedure with narcissistic patients, rapid developments of our understanding of them should increase significantly the effectiveness of clinical work with the entire range of narcissistic pathology.

## SOME PROBLEMS REGARDING TERMINOLOGY AND THE METAPSYCHOLOGICAL IMPLICATIONS OF NARCISSISM

I have then implied that the term narcissism should be reserved for the normal and pathological vicissitudes of the libidinal investment of the self, and that, therefore, one cannot analyze narcissism as if it were a drive independent of internalized object relations. The question of the ultimate nature of narcissism leads into the questions of the ultimate nature of libido as a drive and of the normal or pathological nature of the self and its component elements; in turn, the nature of the self is intimately related to the normal or pathological structures derived from internalized object relations.

I have not here touched upon the question of the ultimate nature of libido as a drive, except in stating that self-esteem or self-regard is not simply a reflection of "instinctual cathexes," but always reflects a combination of affective and cognitive components. Implicit in these formulations has been a general metapsychological formulation of the relation between libido as a drive and affect dispositions as the crucial expressions of instinctual urges within the psychic apparatus.

I have developed this analysis elsewhere (10) and I will limit myself here to briefly summarizing my proposals: 1) affects represent inborn dispositions to a subjective experience along the dimensions of pleasure and unpleasure; 2) affects are fixated by means of memory traces into a primitive, "affective memory" constellation or unit incorporating self components, object components, and the affect state itself; and 3) differentiation of affect occurs in the context of the differentiation of internalized object relations.

I have proposed that pleasurable and painful affects are the major organizers of the series of "good" and "bad" internalized object relations, and that they constitute the major motivational or drive system that organizes intrapsychic experience. Libido and aggression are not external givens to this development, but represent the overall organization of drive systems in terms of the general polarity of "good" and "bad." Affect states first determine the integration of both internalized object relations and the overall drive systems and, later, signal the activation of the drive and represent that drive in the context of the activation of specific internalized object relations.

In short, libido and aggression differentiate out of the undifferentiated matrix common to the ego and the id. The organization of these two drives occurs under the influence of the developing internalized object relationships, which, in turn, are integrated under the organizing influence of affects.

My formulations imply that "cathexes" are, first of all, "affective cathexes," that is, the quantitative element or economic factor involved in the intensity of primitive affect dispositions, which are activated in the context of primitive units of internalized object relations; affects actually are the organizers of such primitive units. Gradually, affects differentiate, and their quantitative or economic aspects become intimately linked with the organization of motivational systems, or drives, into the "libido" series and the "aggression" series. Later, affects have a crucial function in signaling the predominant quality of libidinal, aggressive, or combined libidinal-aggressive motivational systems. Their quantitative elements or "cathexes" originally reflected the subjective, intrapsychic impact of gratification or frustration of physiological needs, but gradually they depend more and more on the subject's total interpretation of the immediate affective arousal in terms of its meaning for self and object, in terms of ego values and superego pressures, etc. Therefore, it seems to me most practical to use the term "cathexis" to refer to the function of affects as indicators of predominant motivational systems. This assumes that, originally, cathexes were "almost" pure affective cathexes, while eventually, the affect has more of a signal function, indicating the quantitative intensity of the motivational system (rather than indicating the intensity of a drive unrelated to internalized object relations or to higher cognitive functions).

So that one might say that "cathexes" are at first "affect cathexes" and have a crucial function in organizing overall "instincts" as intrapsychic drive systems; eventually "cathexes" become "instinctual or drive cathexes," indicating by means of a predominant affective state the intensity and the type of the motivational system that predominates in a certain situation. Affects are the elements of psychic experience that remain closest to the biological sources of psychic functioning. The biologically determined intensity of affects can be channeled into ever more complex intrapsychic motivational systems; but—except under extreme circumstances—there is no direct mechanical relationship between biological pressures and psychic functioning.

Therefore, the ultimate nature of narcissism—the expression of self-directed libido—as a drive, or even as a reflection of the equilibrium between libido and aggression as they invest the self—is dependent upon the development of affect dispositions of the libidinal and aggressive series as they relate to the development of internalized object relations and their structuring into the ego, superego, and id. This conceptualization underlies the structural and clinical analysis of normal and pathological narcissism presented in the first three sections of this chapter.

I have also applied this conceptualization of the vicissitudes of drives, affects, and internalized object relations to the problem of primary and secondary narcissism elsewhere (9, 10) and will only summarize my viewpoints here. As I have implied in the first section of this chapter, an intimate connection exists between the investment in the self and investment in objects. The work of Jacobson (7), Mahler (13), and van der Waals (18), as well as my own earlier studies all point to our present understanding that self and object representations stem from a primary undifferentiated self-object representation out of which narcissistic and object investment develop simultaneously. Therefore, in contrast to the traditional psychoanalytic viewpoint according to which there first exists a narcissistic investment of libido and later an object investment of libido, and in contrast to Kohut's (11, 12) view that narcissistic investment and object investment start out together and then evolve independently, and that aggression in narcissistic personalities is in large part secondary to their narcissistic lesions, it is my belief that the development of normal and pathological narcissism always involves the relationship of the self to object representations and external objects, as well as instinctual conflicts involving both libido and aggression. The general implication is that the concept of "primary narcissism" no longer seems warranted because, metapsychologically, "primary narcissism" and "primary object investment" are in effect coincidental; the libidinal investment of a primary "all good" self-object representation, the aggressive investment of a primary "all bad" self-object representation, and the vicissitudes of the development and interrelationships of these two primary structures precedes the development of the libidinal investment of a differentiated self.

There is also another use of the term narcissism which seems to be going slowly out of existence. This is the concept of "narcissistic neuroses" as applied to the functional psychoses, particularly to schizophrenia and other related syndromes. The psychoanalytic study of psychotic conditions in the last thirty years has revealed the presence of primitive, pathological internalized object relations in these patients which are activated in their transferences. These patients' capacity to develop intense psychotic, in contrast to neurotic, transferences has made the term "narcissistic neuroses"—which implied that they could not develop a transference—rather obsolete.

In summary, if my formulations are valid, it would seem that the study of narcissism cannot be divorced from the study of the vicissitudes of both libido and aggression and from the study of the vicissitudes of internalized object relations. Clinically speaking, whenever we talk about "narcissistic conflicts," we are talking about the normal and pathological relations between the self and the other intrapsychic structures and environmental factors mentioned (in the first part of this chapter) as influencing the libidinal (and aggressive) investment of the self. As we organize the various manifestations of normal and pathological narcissism into an integrated spectrum, it should be possible to become more specific about what type and/or degree of narcissistic pathology we are referring to in concrete instances. By the same token, the term "narcissistic resistances" may become more meaningful in referring to a spectrum of defensive operations protecting self-esteem and the integrity of the self in the transference, a spectrum ranging from the nonspecific narcissistic functions of pathological character traits in general (all character defenses have a function of protecting self-esteem), to the specific defensive operations of narcissistic personalities in particular.

As our clinical and theoretical understanding of narcissism progresses, some of the confusing terminological issues and discrepancies between metapsychological formulations and clinical observations may be resolved into a more sharpened, circumscribed, and clinically relevant usage of the term narcissism.

## BIBLIOGRAPHY

1.  Bibring, Edward: The Mechanism of Depression. In *Affective Disorders*, edited by Greenacre, Phyllis. New York: International Universities Press, 1953.

2.  Deutsch, Helene: *Psychology of Women*. Volume 1: Girlhood. New York: Grune and Stratton, 1944, pp. 94–98.

3.  Erikson, E. H.: The Problem of Ego Identity. *J. Amer. Psychoanal. Assn.*, 4:56–121, 1956.

4.  Freud, S.: On narcissism: an introduction (1914). *Standard Edition*, 14:67–102, London: Hogarth Press, 1957.

5.  Hartmann, Heinz: (1950) Comments on the Psychoanalytic Theory of the Ego. In *Essays on Ego Psychology*. New York: International Universities Press, 1964, pp. 113–141.

6.  Jacobson, Edith: Contribution to the Metapsychology of Psychotic Identifications. *J. Amer. Psychoanal. Assoc.*, 2:239–262, 1954.

7.  Jacobson, Edith: *The Self and the Object World*. New York: International Universities Press, 1964.

8.  Kernberg, Otto F.: A Psychoanalytic Classification of Character Pathology. *Journal of the American Psychoanalytic Association*, 18:800–822, 1970.

9.  ———: New Developments in Psychoanalytic Object Relations Theory. Parts I and III: Normal and Pathological Development. Presented to the American Psychoanalytic Association, Washington, D. C., 1971 (Unpublished).

10. ———,: New Developments in Psychoanalytic Object-Relations Theory. Part II: Instincts, Affects, and Object Relations. Presented at the Royden Astley Memorial Symposium on Narcissism, Pittsburgh, Pa., September, 1973 (unpublished).

11. Kohut, H.: *The Analysis of the Self*. New York: International Universities Press, 1971.

12. ———,: Thoughts on Narcissism and Narcissistic Rage. *The Psychoanalytic Study of the Child*, 27:360–400, 1972.

13. Mahler, Margaret, S.: *On Human Symbiosis and the Vicissitudes of Individuation. Volume I. Infantile Psychosis*. New York: International Universities Press, Inc. 1968.

14. Reich, Wilhelm: *Character Analysis*. New York: Noonday Press, 1949.

15. Rosenfeld, H.: On the Psychopathology of Narcissism: A Clinical Approach. *Int. J. Psycho-Anal.*, 45:332–337, 1964.

16. Sandler, J. and Rosenblatt, B. The Concept of the Representational World. *Psychoanal. Study of the Child*, 17:128–145, 1962.

17. Schafer, Roy: The Loving and Beloved Superego in Freud's Structural Theory. *The Psychoanalytic Study of the Child*, 15:163–188, 1960.

18. Van der Waals, H. G.: Problems of Narcissism. *Bull. Menninger Clin.*, 29:293–311, 1965.

# CREDITS

**Chapter 1**

Reprinted from *Journal of the American Psychoanalytic Association*, Vol. XV, No. 3 (July, 1967). Presented at the fall meeting of the American Psychoanalytic Association, New York, December, 1966. From the work of the Psychotherapy Research Project of The Menninger Foundation, Topeka, Kansas. The investigation was supported by Public Health Research Grant MH 8308 from the National Institute of Mental Health, and previously supported by the Foundation's Fund for Research in Psychiatry and the Ford Foundation.

**Chapter 2**

Reprinted from *Journal of the American Psychoanalytic Association*, Vol. XIII, No. 1 (January, 1965). Presented at the fall meeting of the American Psychoanalytic Association, New York, December 1963. The Menninger Foundation, Topeka, Kansas.

**Chapter 3**

Reprinted from *The International Journal of Psycho-Analysis*, Vol. XLIX, Pt. 4 (1968). From the work of the Psychotherapy Research Project of the Menninger Foundation and presented at the fifty-fourth annual meeting of the American Psychoanalytic Association, Detroit, May, 1967. For the project's support, see credit for Chapter 1.

**Chapter 4**

Reprinted from *Journal of the American Psychoanalytic Association*, Vol. XIX, No. 4 (October, 1971). Presented at the fifty-seventh annual meeting of the American Psychoanalytic Association, San Francisco, May, 1970. For the project's support, see credit for Chapter 1.

**Chapter 5**

Published here for the first time.

**Chapter 6**

This chapter also appears in *Parameters in Psychoanalytic Psychotherapy*, edited by G. D. Goldman and D. S. Millman. Charles C Thomas, Springfield, Illinois in press.

**Chapter 7**

Presented at the Symposium on Emptiness, thirteenth conference of the Council of Psychoanalytic Psychotherapists, New York, March, 1974.

**Chapter 8**

Reprinted from *Journal of the American Psychoanalytic Association*, Vol. XVIII, No. 1 (January, 1970). From the work of the Psychotherapy Research Project of the Menninger Foundation and presented at the fifty-fifth annual meeting of the American Psychoanalytic Association, Boston, May, 1968. For the project's support, see credit for Chapter 1.

**Chapter 9**

Reprinted from *The International Journal of Psycho-Analysis*, Vol. LV, Pt. 2 (1974). Presented in a shorter version at the twenty-eighth International Psycho-Analytical Congress, Paris, July, 1973.

**Chapter 10**

Published here for the first time.

# BIBLIOGRAPHY

Abraham, K., (1919). A particular form of neurotic resistance against the psychoanalytic method. *Selected Papers on Psycho-Analysis.* London: Hogarth Press, 1949, pp. 303-311.

Adler, G. (1973). Hospital Treatment of Borderline Patients. *American Journal of Psychiatry.* 130: 32-35.

Andersen, H. C. (1952). The Nightingale. *Tales of Grimm and Andersen.* New York: Modern Library, pp. 714-721.

Bellak, L. & Hurvich, M. (1969). A Systematic Study of Ego Functions. *Journal of Nervous and Mental Disease,* 148: 569-585.

Benedek, T. (1954). Countertransference in the Training Analyst. *Bull. Menninger Clin.,* 18: 12-16.

Bergeret, J. (1970). Les Etats Limites. *Revue Francaise de Psychoanalyse,* 34:605-633.

————, (1972). *Abrege De Psychologie Pathologique.* Masson & Cie Paris.

Bibring, Edward. (1953). The Mechanism of Depression. In *Affective Disorders.* ed. Phyllis Greenacre. New York: Int. Univ. Press, pp. 13-48.

————, (1954). Psychoanalysis and the Dynamic Psychotherapies. *J. Amer. Psychoanal. Assoc.* 2:745-770.

Bion, W. R. (1957). Differentiation of the Psychotic from the Non-psychotic Personalities. *Int. J. Psycho-Anal.,* 38:266-275.

————. (1967). *Second Thoughts:* Selected Papers on Psychoanalysis. London: Heinemann, pp. 86-109.

Boyer, L. B. (1971). Psychoanalytic Technique in the Treatment of Certain Characterological and Schizophrenic Disorders. *Int. J. Psycho-Anal.,* 52: 67-85.

———— and Giovacchini, P. (1967). *Psychoanalytic Treatment of Characterological and Schizophrenic Disorders.* Jason Aronson, Inc., New York.

Burstein, E., Coyne, L., Kernberg, O. & Voth, H. (1969) The Quantitative Study of the Psychotherapy Research Project. In: "Psychotherapy and psychoanalysis: Final report of the Menninger Foundation's Psychotherapy Research Project," by O. Kernberg, E. Burnstein, L. Coyne, A. Appelbaum, L. Horowitz, and H. Voth. *Bull. Menninger Clinic,* 1972, pp. 1-85.

Chessick, R. (1971) Use of the Couch in the Psychotherapy of Borderline Patients. *Archives of General Psychiatry*, 25: 306-313.

Cohen, M. B. (1952) Countertransference and Anxiety. *Psychiatry*. 15: 231-243.

Collum, J. (1972) Identity Diffusion and the Borderline Maneuver. *Comprehensive Psychiatry*. 13:179-184.

Cooperman, M. (1970) Defeating Processes in Psychotherapy. Reported in Transactions of the Topeka Psychoanalytic Society, *Bull. Menninger Clinic*, 34:36-38.

Deutsch, Helene. (1942) Some New Forms of Emotional Disturbance and Their Relationship to Schizophrenia. *Psychoanal. Quart.*, 11:301-321.

——. (1944) *Psychology of Women. Volume 1: Girlhood;* New York: Grune and Stratton, pp. 94-98.

Duvocelle, A. (1971) L'Etat Limite ou Borderline Personality Organization. These Pour Le Doctorat En Medecine, Lille.

Easser, B. R. & Lesser, S. R. (1965) Hysterical Personality: A Re-evaluation. *Psychoanal. Quart.*, 34:390-405.

Eissler, K. R. (1953) The Effect of the Structure of the Ego on Psychoanalytic Technique. *J. Amer. Psychoanal. Assoc.*, 1:104-143.

Ekstein, R. & Wallerstein, J. (1956) Observations on the Psychotherapy of Borderline and Psychotic Children. *The Psychoanalytic Study of the Child*, 11:303-311. New York: Int. Univ. Press.

Erikson, E. H. (1956) The Problem of Ego Identity. *J. Amer. Psychoanal. Assn.*, 4:56-121.

——. (1959) Growth and Crises of the Healthy Personality. In: *Identity and the Life Cycle, Psychological Issues*, New York: Int. Univ. Press. 1:50-100.

Fairbairn, W. R. D. (1940) Schizoid factors in the personality *An Object-Relations Theory of the Personality*. New York: Basic Books, 1952, pp. 3-27.

——. (1944) Endopsychic Structure Considered in Terms of Object-Relationships. *An Object-Relations Theory of the Personality*. New York: Basic Books, 1952, pp. 82-136.

——. (1951) A Synopsis of the Development of the Author's Views Regarding the Structure of the Personality. *An Object-Relations Theory of the Personality*. New York: Basic Books, 1952, pp. 162-179.

Fenichel, O. (1945) Typology. In: *The Psychoanalytic Theory of Neurosis*. New York: Norton, pp. 525-527.

Fliess, R. (1942) The Metapsychology of the Analyst. *Psychoanal. Quart.*, 11:211-227.

——. (1953) Countertransferences and Counteridentification. *J. Am. Psychoanal. Assoc.*, 1:268-284.

Frank, J. D. et. al. (1952) Two Behavior Patterns in Therapeutic Groups and Their Apparent Motivation. *Hum. Rel.*, 5:289-317.

——. (1959). The Dynamics of the Psychotherapeutic Relationship. *Psychiatry*. 22:17-39.

Freud, A. (1936) The Ego and the Mechanisms of Defense. New York: Int. Univ. Press, 1946, pp. 45-57, 117-131.

Freud, S. (1910) The Future Prospects of Psycho-Analytic Therapy. Standard Edition. London: Hogarth Press, 1957, 11:139-151.

——. (1912) Recommendations for Physicians on the Psycho-Analytic Method of Treatment. Standard Edition. London: Hogarth Press, 1958, 12:109-120.

——. (1914) On Narcissism: An Introduction. Standard Edition. London: Hogarth Press, 1957, 14:67-102.

——. (1923) The Ego and the Id. Standard Edition. London: The Hogarth Press, 1961, 19:13-66.

——. (1925) Negation. Standard Edition. London: Hogarth Press, 1961, 19:235-239.

——. (1927) Fetishism. Standard Edition. London: Hogarth Press, 1961, 21:149-157.

——. (1931) Libidinal Types. Standard Edition. London: Hogarth Press, 1961, 21:215-220.

——. (1937) Analysis Terminable and Interminable. Standard Edition. London: The Hogarth Press, 1961, 23:216-253.

——. (1938) Splitting of the Ego in the Process of Defence. Standard Edition. London: Hogarth Press, 1964, 23:275-278.

Fromm-Reichmann, F. (1950) *Principles of Intensive Psychotherapy.* Chicago: University of Chicago Press.

——. (1952) Some Aspects of Psychoanalytic Psychotherapy with Schizophrenics. In: *Psychotherapy with Schizophrenics,* ed. Ed. B. Brody & F. C. Redlich. New York: Int. Univ. Press, pp. 89-111.

——. (1958) Basic Problems in the Psychotherapy of Schizophrenia. *Psychiatry.* 21:1-6.

Frosch, J. (1964) The Psychotic Character: Clinical Psychiatric Consideration. *Psychiatric Quarterly,* 38:81-96.

——. (1970) Psychoanalytic Considerations of the Psychotic Character. *J. Amer. Psychoanal. Assoc.,* 18:24-50.

——. (1971) Technique in Regard to Some Specific Ego Defects in the Treatment of Borderline Patients. *Psychoanal. Quart.,* 45:216-220.

Gary, G. (1972) The Borderline Condition: A Structural-Dynamic Viewpoint. *The Psychoanalytic Review,* 59:33-54.

Geleerd, E. R. (1958). Borderline States in Childhood and Adolescence. *The Psychoanalytic Study of the Child,* 13:279-295. New York: Int. Univ. Press.

Gill, M. M. (1951) Ego psychology and psychotherapy. *Psychoanal. Quart.,* 20:62-71.

——. (1954) Psychoanalysis and Exploratory Psychotherapy. *J. Amer. Psychoanal. Assoc.,* 2:771-797.

Giovacchini, P. L. (ed). (1972) *Tactics and Techniques in Psychoanalytic Therapy.* Jason Aronson, Inc.

Gitelson, M. (1952) The Emotional Position of the Analyst in the Psycho-analytic Situation. *Int. J. Psychoanal.,* 33:1-10.

——. (1958) On Ego Distortion. *Int. J. Psycho-Anal.,* 39:245-257.

Glover, E. (1955) *The Technique of Psycho-Analysis.* New York: Int. Univ. Press.

——. (1955) The Analyst's Case-List (2). *The Technique of Psycho-Analysis.* London: Bailliare; New York: Int. Univ. Press, pp. 185-258.

Greenson, R. R. (1954) The Struggle Against Identification. *J. Am. Psychoanal. Assoc.,* 2:200-217.

——. (1958) On Screen Defenses, Screen Hunger, and Screen Identity. *J. Am. Psychoanal. Assoc.,* 6:242-262.

——. (1967) *The Technique and Practice of Psychoanalysis.* New York: Int. Univ. Press.

——. (1970) The Unique Patient-Therapist Relationship in Borderline Patients, Presented at the Annual Meeting of the American Psychiatric Association. (Unpublished)

Grinker, R., Sr., Werble, B. & Drye, R. (1968) *The Borderline Syndrome.* New York: Basic Books, Inc.

Guntrip, H. (1968) *Schizoid Phenomena, Object Relations and the Self.* New York: Int. Univ. Press, pp. 275-309.

Hartmann, H. (1950) Comments on the Psychoanalytic Theory of the Ego. In: *Essays on Ego Psychology.* New York: Int. Univ. Press, 1964, pp. 113-141.

——. (1953) Contribution to the metapsychology of schizophrenia. In: *Essays on Ego Psychology.* New York: Int. Univ. Press, 1964, pp. 182-206.

——, Kris, E., & Loewenstein, R. M. (1946) Comments on the Formation of Psychic Structure. In: *The Psychoanalytic Study of the Child.* New York: Int. Univ. Press, 2:11-38.

——, & Loewenstein, R. M. Notes on the Superego. In: *The Psychoanalytic Study of the Child,* New York: Int. Univ. Press, 1962, 17:42-81.

Heimann, P. (1950) On Counter-Transference. *Int. J. Psychoanal.,* 31:81-84.

——. (1955) A Combination of Defence Mechanisms in Paranoid States. In: *New*

*Directions in Psycho-Analysis,* ed. M. Klein, P. Heimann, & R. E. Money-Kyrle. London: Tavistock Publications. pp. 240-265.

——. (1955) A Contribution to the Re-evaluation of the Oedipus Complex: The Early Stages. In: *New Directions in Psycho-Analysis,* ed. M. Klein, P. Heimann, & R. E. Money-Kyrle, New York: Basic Books, pp. 23-38.

——. (1960) Countertransference. *Brit. J. Med. Psychol.,* 33:9-15.

Hoch, P. H. & Polatin. P (1949) Pseudoneurotic Forms of Schizophrenia. *Psychiat. Quart.,* 23:248-276.

——. Cattell, J. P. (1959) The Diagnosis of Pseudoneurotic Schizophrenia. *Psychiat. Quart.,* 33:17-43.

Holzman, P. S. & Ekstein, R. (1959) Repetition-Functions of Transitory Regressive Thinking. *Psychoanal. Quart.,* 28:228-235.

Hurvich, M. (1970) On the Concept of Reality Testing. *International Journal of Psycho-Analysis,* 51:299-312.

Jacobson, E. (1953) Contribution to the Metapsychology of Cyclothmic Depression. In: *Affective Disorders,* ed. P. Greenacre. New York: Int. Univ. Press, pp. 49-83.

——. (1954) Contribution to the Metapsychology of Psychotic Identifications. *J. Amer. Psychoanal. Assoc.,* 2:239-262.

——. (1954) Psychotic Identifications. In: *Depression.* New York: Int. Univ. Press, 1971, pp. 242-263.

——. (1957) Denial and Repression. *J. Am. Psychoanal. Assoc.,* 5:61-92.

——. (1964) *The Self and the Object World.* New York: Int. Univ. Press.

Jones, E. (1913) The God Complex *Essays in Applied Psycho-Analysis,* New York: International Universities Press, 1964, 2:244-265.

Keniston, K. (1968) *Young Radicals.* New York: Harcourt, Brace and World, Inc.

——. (1970) Student Activism, Moral Development and Morality. *Amer. J. Orthopsychiat.,* 40:577-592.

Kernberg, O. (1960) Manejo de la Contra-Transferencia en la Escuela Analitica de Washington. Presented to the Chilean Society of Psychoanalysis, (unpublished).

——. (1966) Structural Derivatives of Object Relationships. *Int. J. Psycho-Anal.,* 47:236-253.

——. (1970) A Psychoanalytic Classification of Character Pathology. *Journal of the American Psychoanalytic Association,* 18; 800-802.

——. (1971) New Developments in Psychoanalytic Object Relations Theory. Parts I and III: Normal and Pathological Development. Presented to the American Psychoanalytic Association, Washington, D. C., (Unpublished).

——. (1972) Early Ego Integration and Object Relations. *Ann. N. Y. Acad. Sci.* 193, 233-247.

——. (1973) New Developments in Psychoanalytic Object-Relations Theory. Part II: Instincts, Affects, and Object Relations. Presented at the Royden Astley Memorial Symposium on Narcissism, Pittsburgh, Pa., (Unpublished).

——; Burnstein, E.; Coyne, L.; Appelbaum, A.; Horwitz. L., and Voth, H. (1972) Psychotherapy and Psychoanalysis: Final Report of the Menninger Foundation's Psychotherapy Research Project. *Bull. of the Menninger Clinic,* 36:1-275.

Kernberg, P. (1971) The Course of the Analysis of a Narcissistic Personality with Hysterical and Compulsive Features. *J. Am. Psychoanal. Ass.* 19; 451-471.

Khan, M. M. R. (1960) Clinical Aspects of the Schizoid Personality: Affects and Technique. *Int. J. Psycho-Anal.,* 41:430-437.

——. (1964) Ego Distortion, Cumulative Trauma, and the Role of Reconstruction in the Analytic Situation. *Int. Psycho-Anal.* 45:272-279.

——. (1969) On Symbiotic Omnipotence. In *The Psychoanalytic Forum.* John A. Lindon (ed.) New York, Jason Aronson, Inc.

Klein, M. (1934) A Contribution to the Psychogenesis of Manic-Depressive States. *Contributions to Psycho-Analysis 1921-1945.* London: Hogarth Press, 1948, pp. 282-310.

————. (1940) Mourning and Its Relation to Manic-Depressive States. *Contributions to Psycho-Analysis 1921-1945.* London: Hogarth Press, 1948, pp. 311-338.
————. (1945) The Oedipus Complex in the Light of Early Anxieties: General Theoretical Summary. *Contributions to Psycho-Analysis 1921-1945.* London: Hogarth Press, 1948, pp. 377-390.
————. (1946) Notes on Some Schizoid Mechanisms. *Int. J. Psychoanal.* 27:99-110.
————. (1952) The Origins of Transference. *Int. J. Psychoanal.,* 33:433-438.
Knight, R. P. (1953) Borderline States. In: *Psychoanalytic Psychiatry and Psychology,* ed. R. P. Knight & C. R. Friedman. New York: Int. Univ. Press, 1954, pp. 97-109.
————. (1953) Management and Psychotherapy of the Borderline Schizophrenic Patient. In *Psychoanalytic Psychiatry and Psychology,* ed. R. P. Knight & C. R. Friedman. New York: Int. Univ. Press, 1954, pp. 110-122.
Kohut, H. (1966) Forms and Transformations of Narcissism. *J. Am. Psychoanal. Ass.* 14; 243-272.
————. (1968) The Psychoanalytic Treatment of Narcissitic Personality Disorders. *Psychoanal. Study Child.* 23; 86-113.
————. (1971) *The Analysis of the Self.* New York: Int. Univ. Press.
————. (1972) Thoughts on Narcissism and Narcissistic Rage. *The Psychoanalytic Study of the Child,* 27:360-400.
Laughlin, H. P. (1956) The Neuroses in Clinical Practice, Philadelphia: Saunders. pp. 394-406.
Lidz, R. W. & Lidz, T. (1952) Therapeutic Considerations Arising From the Intense Symbiotic Needs of Schizophrenic Patients. In: *Psychotherapy with Schizophrenics,* ed. E. B. Brody & F. C. Redlich. New York: Int. Univ. Press, pp. 168-178.
Little, M. (1951) Countertransference and the Patient's Response to It. *Int. J. Psychoanal.,* 32: 32-40.
————. (1958) On Delusional Transference (Transference Psychosis) *Int. J. Psycho-Anal.,* 39:134-138.
————. Countertransference (1960) *Brit. J. Med. Psychol.,* 33:29-31.
————. (1960) On Basic Unity. *Internat. J. Psychoanal.,* 41:377-384; 637.
Luborsky, L. (1962) The Patient's Personality and Psychotherapeutic Change. In: *Research in Psychotherapy, vol. II.* H. H. Strupp & L. Luborsky, eds. Washington, D. C., Amer. Psycholog. Assn., pp. 115-133.
Macalpine, I. (1950) The Development of the Transference. *Psychoanal. Quart.,* Vol. 1, 19:501-539.
Mahler, M. S. (1968) *On Human Symbiosis and the Vicissitudes of Individuation, Infantile Psychosis.* New York: Int. Univ. Press.
————. (1971) A Study of the Separation-Individuation Process and Its Possible Application to Borderline Phenomena in the Psychoanalytic Situation. *Psychoanalytic Study of the Child,* 26:403-424. New York/Chicago: Quadrangle Books.
Main, T. F. (1960) The Ailment. *Brit. J. Med. Psychol.,* 33:29-31.
Masterson, J. (1967) The Psychiatric Dilemma of Adolescence. Boston: Little, Brown, pp. 119-134.
————. (1972) *Treatment of the Borderline Adolescent: A Developmental Approach.* New York: Wiley-Interscience.
Menninger, K. A. (1958) *Hope Theory of Psychoanalytic Technique* New York: Basic Books.
————. (1959) *Amer. J. Psychiat.* 116:481-491.
————, Mayman, M., & Pruyser, P. (1963) *The Vital Balance.* New York: Viking Press, pp. 213-249.
Meza, C. (1970) El Colerico (Borderline). Editorial Joaquin Mortiz, Mexico.
Money-Kyrle, R. E. (1956) Normal Countertransference and Some of its Deviations. *Int. J. Psychoanal.,* 37:360-366.

Orr, D. W. (1954) Transference and Countertransference: A Historical Survey. *J. Am. Psychoanal. Assoc.*, 2:621-67.

Paz, C. (1969) Reflexiones Tecnicas Sobre El Proceso Analitico en los Psicoticos Fronterizos. *Revista de Psicoanalisis*, 26:571-630.

Racker, H. (1953) A Contribution to the Problem of Countertransference. *Int. J. Psychoanal.*, 34:313-324.

———. (1957) The Meanings and Uses of Countertransference. *Psychoanal. Quart.*, 26:303-357.

Rangell, I., (1955) Panel Report: The Borderline Case. *J. Am. Psychoanal. Assoc.*, 3:285-298.

Rapaport, D. (1957) Cognitive Structures. In: *Contemporary Approaches to Cognition*. Cambridge: Harvard Univ. Press, pp. 157-200.

———. & Gill, M. M. (1959). The Points of View and Assumptions of Metapsychology, *Int. J. Psychoanal.*, 40:153-162.

———. & Gill, M. M. & Schafer, R. (1945-1946), *Diagnostic Psychological Testing*, 2 vols. Chicago: Year Book Publishers, 1:16-28; 2:24-31, 329-366.

Reich, A. (1951) On Countertransference. *Int. J. Psychoanal.*, 32:25-31.

———. (1953) Narcissistic Object Choice in Women. *J. Am. Psychoanal.* Assoc., 1:22-44.

———. (1960) Further Remarks on Countertransference. *Int. J. Psychoanal.*, 41:389-395.

———. (1960) Pathological Forms of Self-Esteem Regulation. *The Psychoanalytic Study of the Child*, New York: Int. Univ. Press, 15:215-232.

Reich, Wilhelm. (1949) *Character Analysis*. New York: Noonday Press.

Reider, N. (1957) Transference Psychosis. *J. Hillside Hosp.*, 6:131-149.

Riviere, J. (1936) A Contribution to the Analysis of the Negative Therapeutic Reaction. *Int. J. Psycho-Anal.* 17; 304-320.

Robbins, L. L. (1956) Panel Report: The Borderline Case. *J. Am. Psychoanal. Assoc.*, 4:550-562.

———. & Wallerstein, R. S. (1959) The Research Strategy and Tactics of the Psychotherapy Research Project of the Menninger Foundation and the Problem of Controls. In: *Research in Psychotherapy*, ed. E. A. Rubinstein & M. B. Parloff. Washington, D.C.: Amer. Psycholog. Assn., pp. 27-43.

Robins, L. N. (1966) Deviant Children Grown Up. Baltimore: Williams & Wilkins, pp. 287-309.

Romm, M. (1957) Transient Psychotic Episodes during Psychoanalysis, *J. Amer. Psychoanal. Assoc.*, 5:325-341.

Rosenfeld, H. (1949) Remarks on the Relation of Male Homosexuality to Paranoia, Paranoid Anxiety and Narcissism. *Int. J. Psychoanal.*, 30:36-47.

———. (1952) Transference-Phenomena and Transference-Analysis in an Acute Catatonic Schizophrenic Patient. *Int. J. Psychoanal.*, 33:457-464.

———. (1955) Notes on the Psychoanalysis of the Super-ego Conflict in an Acute Schizophrenic Patient. In: *Psychotherapy of Schizophrenia and Manic-Depressive* States, ed. Azima and Glueck, Jr. Washington: Amer. Psychiat. Assoc.

———. (1958) Contribution to the Discussion on "Variations in Classical Technique." *Int. Jour. Psychoanal.*, 39:238-239.

———. (1963) Notes on Psychopathology and Psychoanalytic Treatment of Schizophrenia. In *Psychotherapy of Schizophrenia and Manic-Depressive* States, ed. H. Azima & B. C. Glueck, Jr. [Psychiatric Research Report #17] Washington, D. C.: American Psychiatric Association, pp. 61-72.

———. (1964) On the Psychopathology of Narcissism: A Clinical Approach. *Int. J. Psychoanal.*, 45:332-337.

———. (1970) Negative Therapeutic Reaction. Reported in Transactions of the Topeka Psychoanalytic Society, *Bull. of the Menninger Clinic*, 34:189-192.

Sachs, H. (1947) Observations of a Training Analyst. *Psychoanal. Quart.*, 16:157-168.

Sandler, J. & Rosenblatt, B. (1962) The Concept of the Representational World. *Psychoanal. Study of the Child*, 17:128-145.

Savage, C. (1961) Countertransference in the Therapy of Schizophrenics. *Psychiatry*. 24:53-60.

Schafer, R. (1960) The loving and beloved superego in Freud's structural theory. *The Psychoanalytic Study of the Child*, 15: 163-188. New York: International Universities Press.

Schlesinger, H. (1966). In Defense of Denial. Presented to the Topeka Psychoanalytic Society, June 1966. (Unpublished).

Schmideberg, M. (1947) The Treatment of Psychopaths and Borderline Patients. *Amer. J. Psychother.*, 1:45-70.

Segal, H. (1964) *Introduction to the Work of Melanie Klein*. New York: Basic Books.

Sharpe, E. F. (1931) Anxiety, Outbreak and Resolution. In: *Collected Papers on Psycho-Analysis*. London: Hogarth, 1950, pp. 67-80.

Spitz, R. A. (1956) Countertransference: Comments on its Varying Role in the Analytic Situation. *J. Am. Psychoanal. Assoc.*, 4:256-265.

Sterba, R. (1934) The Fate of the Ego in Analytic Therapy. *Int. J. Psycho-Anal.*, 15:117-126.

Stern, A. (1938) Psychoanalytic Investigation of and Therapy in the Borderline Group of Neuroses. *Psychoanal. Quart.*, 7:467-489.

———. (1945) Psychoanalytic Therapy in the Borderline Neuroses. *Psychoanal. Quart.*, 14:190-198.

Stone, L. (1951) Psychoanalysis and Brief Psychotherapy. *Psychoanal. Quart.*, 20:215-236.

———. (1954) The Widening Scope of Indications for Psychoanalysis *J. Amer. Psychoanal. Assoc.*, 2:567-594.

Strachey, J. (1934) The Nature of the Therapeutic Action of Psycho-analysis. *Int. J. Psycho-Anal.*, 15:127-159.

Sullivan, H. S. (1953) *Conceptions of Modern Psychiatry*. New York: Norton.

———. (1953) *The Interpersonal Theory of Psychiatry*. New York: Norton.

Tartakoff, H. H. (1966) The Normal Personality in Our Culture and the Nobel Prize Complex. In: *Psychoanalysis-A General Psychology*, ed. R. M. Loewenstein, L. M. Newman, M. Schur, & A. J. Solnit. New York: Int. Univ. Press, pp. 222-252.

Thompson, C. M. (1952) Countertransference. *Samiksa*, 6:205-211.

Ticho, E. (1966) Selection of Patients for Psychoanalysis or Psychotherapy. Presented at the 20th Anniversary Meeting of the Menninger School of Psychiatry Alumni Association. Topeka, Kansas. (Unpublished.)

———. (1972) The Development of Superego Autonomy. *Psychoanal. Rev.* 59:218-233

———. (1970) Differences Between Psychoanalysis and Psychotherapy. *Bull. Menninger Clin.* 34, 128-138.

———. (1972) The Effects of the Psychoanalyst's Personality on the Treatment. In Vol. 4 ed. John A. Lindon pp. 137-151. *Psychoanalytic Forum*. New York: Int. Univ. Press.

Tower, L. E. (1956) Countertransference. *J. Am. Psychoanal. Assoc.*, 4:224-255.

Van der Waals, H. G. (1965) Problems of Narcissism. *Bull. Menninger Clin.*, 29:293-311.

Werble, B. (1970) Second Follow-Up Study of Borderline Patients. *Archives of General Psychiatry*, 23:3-7.

Waelder, R. *et al.* (1958) Ego distortion (Panel Discussion). *Int. J. Psycho-Anal.*, 39:243-275.

Wallerstein, R. S. (1967) Reconstruction and Mastery in the Transference Psychosis. *J. Amer. Psychoanal. Assoc.*, 15:551-583.

———. & Luborsky, L., Robbins, L. L. & Sargent, H. D. (1956) The Psycho-Therapy Research Project of The Menninger Foundation: Rationale, Method and Sample Use: First Report. *Bull. Menninger Clinic*, 20:221-278.

———. & Robbins, L. L. (1956) The Psychotherapy Research Project of the Menninger Foundation (Part IV: Concepts). *Bull. Menninger Clin.*, 20:239-262.

Weigert, E. (1952) Contribution to the Problem of Terminating Psychoanalyses. *Psychoanal. Quart.*, 21:465-480.

Will, O. A. (1959) Human Relatedness and the Schizophrenic Reaction. *Psychiatry.* 22:205-223.

Weisfogel, J., Dickes, R. & Simons, R. (1969) Diagnostic Concepts Concerning Patients Demonstrating Both Psychotic and Neurotic Symptoms. *The Psychiatric Quarterly,* 43:85-122.

Winnicott, D. W. (1949) Hate in the Counter-transference. *Int. J. Psychoanal.*, 30:69-75.

———. (1955) The Depressive Position in Normal Emotional Development. *Brit. J. Med. Psychol.*, 28:89-100.

———. (1960) Countertransference. *Brit. J. Med. Psychol.*, 33:17-21.

———. (1963) The Development of the Capacity for Concern. *Bull. Menninger Clin.*, 27:167-176.

Wolberg, A. (1973) *The Borderline Patient.* Intercontinental Medical Book Corporation, New York.

Zetzel, E. R. (1956) Current Concepts of Transference. *Int. J. Psychoanal.*, 37:369-376.

———. (1966) The Analytic Situation. In: *Psychoanalysis in the Americas,* ed. Litman. New York: Int. Univ. Press, 1966, pp. 86-106.

———. (1971) A Developmental Approach to the Borderline Patient. *American Journal of Psychiatry,* 127:867-871.

Zilboorg, G. (1941) Ambulatory Schizophrenias. *Psychiatry.* 4:149-155.

———. (1957) Further Observations on Ambulatory Schizophrenia. *Amer. J. Orthopsychiat.* 27:677-682.

# INDEX

221014